The Future of Interfaith Dialogue

A Common Word Between You and Us (*ACW*) is an open letter, dated 13 October 2007, from leaders of the Islamic religion to those of the Christian religion. It calls for peace between Muslims and Christians and seeks common ground and understanding between both religions. This volume examines the document from a number of perspectives. Exploring the events that led to *ACW*, it provides an overview of responses to the document and its use of scripture. It also relates the reception of *ACW* to several specific and contrasting contexts, and recommends new avenues for *ACW*-inspired discussion. Advancing debate and dialogue between Jews, Muslims and Christians, this volume promotes a distinctive methodology for interreligious studies, and serves as an invaluable resource for students and scholars of theology and religious studies.

Yazid Said is Lecturer in Islam at Liverpool Hope University and an Anglican priest. A scholar of medieval Muslim political and legal thought, he is the author of *Ghazali's Politics in Context* (2013).

Lejla Demiri is Professor of Islamic Doctrine at the Centre for Islamic Theology, University of Tübingen. Her research explores Muslim–Christian theological encounters. She is the author of *Muslim Exegesis of the Bible in Medieval Cairo* (2013).

The Future of Interfaith Dialogue

Muslim–Christian Encounters through
A Common Word

Edited by

YAZID SAID

Liverpool Hope University

LEJLA DEMIRI

University of Tübingen

CAMBRIDGE
UNIVERSITY PRESS

CAMBRIDGE
UNIVERSITY PRESS

University Printing House, Cambridge CB2 8BS, United Kingdom

One Liberty Plaza, 20th Floor, New York, NY 10006, USA

477 Williamstown Road, Port Melbourne, VIC 3207, Australia

314–321, 3rd Floor, Plot 3, Splendor Forum, Jasola District Centre,
New Delhi – 110025, India

79 Anson Road, #06-04/06, Singapore 079906

Cambridge University Press is part of the University of Cambridge.

It furthers the University's mission by disseminating knowledge in the pursuit of
education, learning, and research at the highest international levels of excellence.

www.cambridge.org
Information on this title: www.cambridge.org/9781107134348
DOI: 10.1017/9781316466834

© Cambridge University Press 2018

First published 2018

Printed in the United States of America by Sheridan Books, Inc.

A catalogue record for this publication is available from the British Library.

ISBN 978-1-107-13434-8 Hardback

Contents

Contributors

Mustafa Abu Sway is the first holder of the Integral Chair for the Study of Imam Ghazali's Work at Al-Aqsa Mosque and al-Quds University. He has been Professor of Philosophy and Islamic Studies at al-Quds University in Jerusalem since 1996. Professor Abu Sway earned his PhD from Boston College (1993) on 'The development of Al-Ghazali's genetic epistemology'. He taught at the International Islamic University in Malaysia (1993–6), and was a visiting Fulbright Scholar-in-Residence at the Wilkes Honors College at Florida Atlantic University (2003–4) and a Visiting Professor of Islamic Studies at Bard College, New York (Fall 2008 and 2010–11). Among his published works are two books: *Studies in Islamic Epistemology: The Case of Al-Ghazzali* (1995) and *Fatawa Al-Ghazzali* (1996).

Peter Admirand is a lecturer in the School of Theology, Philosophy, and Music at Dublin City University and the coordinator of the Centre for Interreligious Dialogue (CIRD). He is also a co-chair of the Irish Council of Christians and Jews and an academic staff member of DCU's Institute for International Conflict Resolution and Reconstruction. He is the author of *Amidst Mass Atrocity and the Rubble of Theology: Searching for a Viable Theodicy* (2012) and the editor of *Loss and Hope: Global, Inter-religious, and Interdisciplinary Perspectives* (2014, 2015). He has recently completed a book manuscript titled *Humbling Faith: Brokenness, Doubt, Dialogue – What Can Unite Atheists, Theists, and Non-Theists*.

Asma Afsaruddin is Professor of Near Eastern Languages and Cultures in the School of Global and International Studies at Indiana University,

Bloomington. She received her PhD from Johns Hopkins University in 1993 and previously taught at Harvard and Notre Dame Universities. Her research focuses on pre-modern and modern Islamic thought and intellectual history, Qur'an and Hadith studies, and interfaith relations. Afsaruddin is the author and/or editor of seven books, including the recently published *Contemporary Issues in Islam* (2015), the award-winning *Striving in the Path of God: Jihad and Martyrdom in Islamic Thought* (2013) and *The First Muslims: History and Memory* (2008). She has received grants from the Mellon and Guggenheim Foundations and was named a Carnegie Scholar in 2005.

Clare Amos was, until her retirement in December 2017, Programme Coordinator for Interreligious Dialogue and Cooperation at the World Council of Churches in Geneva. Previously until September 2011 she was Director of Theological Studies in the Anglican Communion Office, with responsibility for both theological education and interfaith concerns. She is a Biblical scholar by background and has taught this subject inter alia in Jerusalem, Beirut, Cambridge, South London and Kent. She has a particular interest in how Biblical studies interfaces with a number of contested issues in the Middle East or in interreligious relations. In October 2012 she was awarded a Lambeth Doctorate of Divinity by the Archbishop of Canterbury to mark her contribution to the dissemination of Biblical studies.

Matthias Böhm trained in economics and studied Catholic theology and philosophy at St Georgen, a Jesuit graduate school for theology (Diploma 2009). Since 2010, he has worked as a scientific referee at Christlich-islamische Begegnungs- und Dokumentationsstelle (CIBEDO; the Institute for Christian–Islamic Encounter and Documentation). He is interested in pastoral care and is completing his PhD dissertation on 'similarities and differences between Islamic finance and Catholic social teaching' at the Faculty of Catholic Theology, Johannes Gutenberg University, in Mainz.

Amir Dastmalchian has held research fellowships at the Islamic College (London) and the University of Geneva and has taught at King's College London and Canterbury Christ Church University. He is a member of the editorial board of the *Journal of Shi'a Islamic Studies*, having previously served as an Assistant Editor. His research interests cover the philosophy of religion, interreligious dialogue and Islamic studies.

Lejla Demiri is Professor of Islamic Doctrine at the Centre for Islamic Theology, University of Tübingen. She studied Islamic theology in Istanbul (BA and MA at Marmara University) and Christian theology in Rome (Post-Graduate Diploma and Licentiate at the Pontifical University of Gregoriana). After her PhD (2008) studies at the University of Cambridge, she worked as a Junior Research Fellow at Trinity Hall, Cambridge (2007–10). She then held a post-doctoral fellowship at the Berlin-based research programme Europe in the Middle East – the Middle East in Europe (2010/2011) and a Zukunftsphilologie fellowship (2011/12) at the Free University of Berlin. Her research explores Muslim–Christian theological encounters, and she is the author of *Muslim Exegesis of the Bible in Medieval Cairo* (2013). She also serves as Team Leader (Middle East and North Africa) and Section Editor (Turkish world) for the Christian–Muslim Relations 1500–1900 (CMR1900) project, which is producing *Christian–Muslim Relations: A Bibliographical History (1500–1900)* (2012–).

Marianne Farina is a religious sister of the Congregation of the Sisters of the Holy Cross, Notre Dame, Indiana. She is Professor of Philosophy and Theology at the Dominican School of Philosophy and Theology in Berkeley, California. She is a member of the core doctoral faculty, and a faculty member for the Center for Islamic Studies, at the Graduate Theological Union. Sister Marianne teaches courses that focus on subjects such as social ethics, virtue, sexual ethics, philosophical ethics, Islamic philosophy, human rights, peace-building, and interreligious dialogue. She received a master of arts in pastoral theology from Santa Clara University and a PhD in theological ethics from Boston College. Sister Marianne worked for eleven years in Bangladesh as a teacher, pastoral assistant and school supervisor. While in Bangladesh, she ministered with Muslim, Christian, Hindu, Buddhist and Tribal families and communities. Her recent writings have focused on such topics as the virtue theories of Thomas Aquinas and Abū Ḥāmid al-Ghazālī, the challenges of Muslim–Christian dialogue, comparative theology and faith in human rights. Marianne also organises a number of workshops on social justice, cross-cultural communication and interfaith dialogue in Africa, Asia and the United States.

Reuven Firestone is Regenstein Professor of Medieval Judaism and Islam at Hebrew Union College–Jewish Institute of Religion (HUC–JIR) in Los Angeles and a senior fellow at the University of Southern

California Center for Religion and Civic Culture. An ordained rabbi (HUC 1982), he received his PhD in Arabic and Islamic Studies from New York University in 1988. From 1987 to 1992, he taught Hebrew literature and directed the Hebrew and Arabic language programmes at Boston University and has taught at HUC–JIR since 1993. Firestone is the author of a number of books, including *Journeys in Holy Lands: The Evolution of the Abraham–Ishmael Legends in Islamic Exegesis* (1990), *Jihad: The Origin of Holy War in Islam* (1999) and *Who Are the* Real *Chosen People? The Meaning of Chosenness in Judaism, Christianity and Islam* (2008).

Michael Louis Fitzgerald is a member of the Society of Missionaries of Africa and has been involved in Christian–Muslim relations in different capacities: as director of the Pontifical Institute of Arabic and Islamic Studies in Rome, and as secretary and then president of the Pontifical Council for Interreligious Dialogue at the Vatican. For a little more than six years he was Apostolic Nuncio to Egypt. On retiring, he took up residence in Jerusalem.

Jonathan Kearney has lectured in Islamic Studies and Jewish Studies at Dublin City University since 2015. Before that he lectured in Religious Studies at St Patrick's College, Drumcondra (2012–15). He has also lectured in Islamic Studies, Jewish Studies, Biblical Hebrew and Classical Arabic at University College Dublin, Trinity College Dublin and St Patrick's College, Maynooth. His main scholarly interests are the textual bases of Judaism and Islam, mediaeval Jewish Biblical interpretation, religions and language, religious minorities in Muslim-majority countries and authority and liminality in religions.

Daniel A. Madigan is an Australian Jesuit priest who in 2008 joined Georgetown University's Department of Theology, where he is currently Director of Graduate Studies. He is also a senior fellow of the Al-Waleed Centre for Muslim–Christian Understanding, and an Honorary Professorial Fellow of the Australian Catholic University. Before moving to Georgetown he taught in Rome (2000–7), where he was the founder and director (2002–7) of the Institute for the Study of Religions and Cultures at the Pontifical Gregorian University. His main fields of teaching and research are Qur'anic studies, interreligious dialogue (particularly Muslim–Christian relations) and comparative theology.

Rusmir Mahmutćehajić is a Bosnian academic, author and former government minister. He has been Professor of both the Theory and Mathematical Modelling of Electromagnetic Waves and of Islamic Phenomenology. As a politician, he served his country as Deputy Prime Minister and as Energy Minister of Bosnia through the process of independence and four of the five years of war (1991–5). For the past twenty years, he has been President of International Forum Bosnia, a prominent civil society organisation dedicated to the development of critical intelligence and a plural society in Bosnia. He is the author of more than twenty-five books in Bosnian, some fifteen of which have been published in English, French, Italian, Bulgarian, Albanian and Turkish translations. He is also the author of several hundred academic articles and essays on the social and political issues affecting his country, political philosophy, philosophy of religion more generally, religious phenomenology, the critique of ideology, the religious traditions and the potential for interfaith dialogue viewed from a Muslim perspective, literary criticism and the history of his country. He is the editor of the *Forum Bosnae* journal and a member of the editorial board of the Philosophy of Religion – World Religions book series (Brill).

Ingrid Mattson holds the London and Windsor Community Chair in Islamic Studies at Huron University College at the University of Western Ontario in London, Canada. Formerly, she was Professor of Islamic Studies, founder of the Islamic Chaplaincy Program and Director of the Macdonald Center for Islamic Studies and Christian–Muslim Relations at Hartford Seminary in the USA. She is the author of *The Story of the Qur'an: Its History and Place in Muslim Life* (2013) and other works focusing on Qur'anic studies, theological ethics and interfaith engagement. Between 2006 and 2010 Mattson served as President of the Islamic Society of North America (ISNA); she previously served two terms as vice president.

Yazid Said is Lecturer in Islam at Liverpool Hope University. He studied English Literature and Classical Arabic at the Hebrew University in Jerusalem and Christian Theology at the University of Cambridge. After being ordained an Anglican priest, he completed his PhD at the University of Cambridge (2010) on the medieval Muslim theologian Abū Ḥāmid al-Ghazālī. He subsequently held a post-doctoral fellowship at McGill University in Canada (2010–11) and the Woods–Gumbel Fellowship at the Tantur Ecumenical Institute in Jerusalem (2011–12). From February 2013 until December 2014, he was Lecturer in Islamic Studies at Mater

Dei Institute of Education in Dublin. He then became a Research Fellow at the Centre for Islamic Theology in the University of Tübingen, Germany (2015–16). His research is focused on medieval Muslim political and legal thought and on Christian–Muslim theological encounters. He is the author of *Ghazali's Politics in Context* (2012).

Sarah Snyder is the Archbishop of Canterbury's Adviser for Reconciliation, and a theologian at the Divinity Faculty, University of Cambridge. She has worked with the Cambridge Interfaith Programme for many years, directing the International Summer Schools for faith leaders from conflict zones and co-ordinating Scriptural Reasoning. She was formerly Director of Partnerships at Religions for Peace, the world's largest coalition of religious leaders across the religious spectrum. She is Founding Director of the Rose Castle Foundation for Peace and Reconciliation, and works as a mediator among faith communities in conflict. She trained initially as an anthropologist, living and working among communities in northern Mali, Kenya, Bangladesh and Peru.

Pim Valkenberg was born in the Netherlands, where he studied theology and religious studies. In 1990 he defended his PhD on Thomas Aquinas and his use of Scripture at the Catholic Theological University of Utrecht. He worked for twenty years at the Catholic University (now Radboud University) of Nijmegen, where he also studied Arabic and was involved in several Abrahamic dialogue initiatives. In 2006 he became an Associate Professor of Theology at Loyola University Maryland in Baltimore. At present he is Professor of Religion and Culture in the School of Theology and Religious Studies at the Catholic University of America in Washington, DC. His field of specialisation is Christian–Muslim dialogue both in the medieval period and in the present. He has published several books in English, most recently *Sharing Lights on the Way to God: Muslim–Christian Dialogue and Theology in the Context of Abrahamic Partnership* (2006), *World Religions in Dialogue: A Comparative Theological Approach* (2013), *Renewing Islam by Service: A Christian View of Fethullah Gülen and the Hizmet Movement* (2015) and *Nostra Aetate: Celebrating 50 Years of the Church's Dialogue with Jews and Muslims* (2016).

Rowan Williams became Master of Magdalene College, Cambridge, in 2013 after ten years as Archbishop of Canterbury. He was the Lady Margaret Professor of Divinity at Oxford before becoming Bishop of

Monmouth in 1992. He is internationally well known as a theologian, poet and commentator on current affairs.

Tim Winter is the Shaykh Zayed Lecturer in Islamic Studies at the Faculty of Divinity, University of Cambridge; Director of Studies in Theology at Wolfson College and Dean and Founder of the Cambridge Muslim College. He was educated at the universities of Cambridge, Al-Azhar, London and Oxford and received his PhD from the Free University of Amsterdam. He has published and contributed to numerous academic works on Islamic theology and Christian–Muslim relations. He is the editor of the *Cambridge Companion to Classical Islamic Theology* (2008). He has translated a number of books from Arabic, including several sections of al-Ghazālī's *Iḥyā' 'ulūm al-dīn*. His most recent book is *Commentary on the Eleventh Contentions* (2012). He is a leading Muslim figure in interfaith dialogue, and one of the major signatories of *A Common Word*.

Acknowledgements

The editors of this volume would like to express their gratitude to the Mater Dei Trust in Dublin, who funded the conference 'A *Common Word* and the Future of Muslim–Christian dialogue' held at Mater Dei Institute of Education in Dublin (6–7 December 2013), which paved the way to this project. Special thanks go to Dermot Lane, the Chair of the Mater Dei Trust, and Ethna Regan, the Head of the School of Theology, Philosophy and Music at Dublin City University, and all the members of the Theology School at Mater Dei Institute at the time before its full incorporation into Dublin City University, for their help and generous support in hosting the conference, which brought leading Muslim, Christian and Jewish scholars together to examine the unique contribution of *ACW* to the history of Muslim–Christian relations. Although the conference was instrumental in planting the first seeds of this volume, we include a number of additional papers which did not feature on the conference programme. On this occasion we would also like to remember Kieran Flynn, who attended the conference and whose paper was well received, but who sadly died before he was able to submit his chapter for publication.

Introduction

Lejla Demiri

A decade has passed since the promulgation of *A Common Word Between Us and You*. One of the major interfaith initiatives of our time, this open letter from Muslim leaders comprised an ambitious call for a better understanding between Muslims and Christians worldwide and an invitation to work for the common good in the interests of a wider humanity. Since its launch on 13 October 2007 the *ACW* document has prompted a remarkably fecund response in the form of joint statements, gatherings of religious scholars, academic events, conferences, workshops, seminars and grassroots community activities. It has inspired the publication of a great number of papers, books, dissertations and other academic and non-academic writings. Of strikingly broad interest and appeal, *ACW* has been discussed both in university settings and in interfaith gatherings locally and internationally. The official *ACW* website offers an exhaustive account of these dialogical 'fruits of *A Common Word*'.[1]

What is it that made this initiative so cathartic? By no means has every response been fully approving of its tone, language or content. Plenty of critics have interrogated its choice of scriptural passages, its theology, its style and its vocabulary, as evidenced by some of the contributions to the present volume. Some respondents have taken issue with Muslim doctrinal or contextual presuppositions which they find to be present and problematic in the *ACW* document. Yet virtually all respondents acknowledged the genuineness of its call for dialogue, receiving it as an

---

[1] www.acommonword.com. See also Sarah Markiewicz, *World Peace through Christian–Muslim Understanding: The Genesis and Fruits of the Open Letter 'A Common Word Between Us and You'* (Göttingen: V&R Unipress, 2016), pp. 203–64.

honest and gracious invitation to promote peace and social justice in a time of international mistrust and turmoil. Further, it has been generally recognised that much of the success of *ACW*'s impact lies in its global character and remit. This was not the call of a few Muslim individuals working in a regional context. Instead, for the first time in the history of Muslim–Christian relations, Muslims of different theological schools from around the globe addressed a peaceable invitation to dialogue towards all Christians worldwide. This international and cross-denominational character lent enormous weight to the document. Rooted in global Islam, the impact of *ACW* has also been global.

Since the earliest days of the Islamic religion, and despite political realities which were often difficult and competitive, Muslims and Christians found ways to consider each other and to discuss their distinctive theologies. These encounters generated a vast and many-genred literature on both sides. The modern *Christian–Muslim Relations: A Bibliographical History* project[2] bears witness to this: the mere identification and mapping of all the writings of Christians and Muslims about each other's religion, in a wide diversity of languages, from the emergence of Islam until 1700, has filled the pages of eleven large volumes, and more documents and books continue to come to light.[3] Despite their sometimes distressing limitations and failings, these historical writings are an important heritage for modern-day Muslim–Christian relations and remain relevant to interfaith discussions and theological conversations today, especially for thinkers able to consider history not as 'a burden on the memory, but an illumination of the soul'.[4]

Against the background of this long narrative of engagement, *ACW* is hardly unique in its desire to enable interfaith conversation. But what makes it quite exceptionally refreshing, for all its imperfections and the criticisms which it has attracted, are the striking graciousness of its language in addressing the 'Other' and its openness to a balanced and fair hearing of the Other's sacred scriptures. Readers note quickly that the text is not written in a polemical spirit. Nor does it have an apologetic purpose or engage in any kind of one-upmanship. The aim is evidently to direct our attention to what it finds to be common ground, namely, the

---

[2] For more on the project, see www.birmingham.ac.uk/schools/ptr/departments/theology andreligion/research/projects/CMR1900/index.aspx.

[3] For details of the series, see www.brill.com/publications/christian-muslim-relations-bibliographical-history.

[4] John Edward Emerich Acton, *Lectures on Modern History* (London: Macmillan, 1906), p. 317.

two shared principles of love of God and love of neighbour, on the basis of which we may venture a theological engagement shaped by mutual trust and friendship. Yet *ACW* does not look for a lowest common denominator, nor does it reach any shallow and concordist verdict which sets aside the weighty theological differences that exist between the Muslim and Christian worlds of thought.

The present volume, which continues this exegetic and discursive process, is dedicated to a close reading and study of the text, context and reception of *A Common Word*, and has been divided into five parts.

Part I, which seeks to shed light on the document's genesis, opens with Tim Winter's chapter, which tries to understand the text in a context of political trauma shaped by 'the West's military and economic interventions in the Muslim world'. It was these which ultimately galvanised the birth of the *ACW* document, 'one of our era's most significant initiatives in the field of interreligious engagement', as the author suggests. The chapter reflects on *ACW*'s purpose, language and approach to scripture, and its theological repercussions for Muslims and Christians living in today's context of globalisation and rapid change. Islam and Christianity, Winter concludes, though 'plurivocal traditions with evolving and conflicting theologies' which offer different understandings of the Divine nature and the love of God, witness to the fact that, through the *Common Word*, 'some words at least are recognisably held in common'.

Winter's essay is followed by Jonathan Kearney's chapter, which offers a critical analysis of *ACW* in relation to the earlier *Amman Message (AM)*. The chapter looks at *AM* not only as 'a necessary precursor and vital companion to *ACW*', but also as a significant tool for non-Muslims in their understanding of, and engagement with, Islam and Muslims today. After a brief outline of *AM* and its context, some observations on its genetic relationship to *ACW* are proposed. The chapter concludes with a critical analysis of the document and its methodology, at the same time acknowledging 'the motivating spirit behind both the *AM* and *ACW* – one of mutual respect, tolerance and, above all, the need to always talk to and listen to one another', hoping that this effort 'will positively transform and enrich the lives of people everywhere'.

Chapter 3 is by Michael L.ouis Fitzgerald, who considers some formal dialogue meetings held between Christians and Muslims from the time of the Second Vatican Council until the *ACW* initiative, demonstrating that the latter was not a creation *ex nihilo*. A brief account is given of the events leading up to *ACW*, and then attention is turned to the Muslim–Catholic meetings that have followed this initiative. The chapter further underlines the 'spirit of openness' of *ACW*, while also highlighting certain weaknesses. Here the author summarises the analysis made by Maurice Borrmans, who has been highly critical of *ACW* and yet welcomes it as 'the dawn of a new stage in Muslim–Christian dialogue'. In conclusion, Fitzgerald acknowledges the *ACW* document as 'a stimulus to engage' in theological dialogue through which 'we can help one another to understand the logic of our respective belief systems'. But he suggests that *ACW* has had a disappointingly limited impact, particularly in the Arabic-speaking world.

Part II of our collection showcases some responses and reactions to *ACW*. It opens with '*A Common Word* for the Common Good', the official response of Rowan Williams, the Archbishop of Canterbury when *A Common Word* was issued, whose text, although it appears on his website, has never before appeared in print. Many see it as the most substantial Christian response to *ACW*, reflecting a consultation with 'church representatives and Christian scholars' from around the world. Williams welcomes *ACW* as a 'recognition that the ways in which we as Christians and Muslims speak about God and humanity are not simply mutually unintelligible systems'. He celebrates key points of convergence, but does not hesitate to raise sensitive issues such as love in relation to Christian understandings of God as Trinity, the problems of human failure, defeat and suffering and the relation of religion to violence. The chapter concludes by proposing a range of ways and principles for dialogue that should help Christians and Muslims to seek together 'the common good in the way of God'.

The following chapter, by Ingrid Mattson, takes the form of a Muslim reflection on Williams' chapter, reflecting on ways in which *ACW* has empowered communities to engage in interfaith dialogue. Mattson finds Williams' response to be generous, hospitable and affable, albeit from her perspective 'unduly focused on religiously justified violence by Muslims, with little interrogation of violence perpetrated and justified by Christians'. However, she does acknowledge that 'Williams has elsewhere written and spoken about the history and ongoing existence of violence, including economic violence, in his own society', thus suggesting that Williams' response to *ACW* should not be considered 'the sum total of his views on the matter'. Commenting on Williams' recommendations in the section entitled 'Seeking together in the way of God', she highlights the value of *ACW* as 'primarily pastoral'. She calls it a 'permission slip for ordinary Christians and Muslims' in their aim 'to be good neighbours'. As Mattson concludes, '*ACW* liberates good-hearted Christians and

Muslims to be mutually hospitable and to collaborate in good works.' Thus the value of *ACW* and the positive Christian responses to it lies in the fact that they 'simply cleared the path of hate and suspicion that had seeped into their religious communities'.

The subsequent chapter, by Reuven Firestone, consists of a response to *ACW* coming from his Jewish tradition, which, as has often been observed, is not directly addressed by the open letter. Firestone problematises the assumption of loving one's neighbour by analysing the birth pangs of religion and the resulting complexity of historical relationships between 'the established religion' and 'the newly emerging religion'. Judaism, Christianity and Islam, the author argues, experienced both their own religious birth and the birth of religious competitors, and the trauma of both experiences has become deeply embedded in their religious worldviews. Most religious believers are unaware of the profound influence these narratives have on their perspective towards the religious 'Other'. Greater awareness of this phenomenology of religious parturition can be of significant service in realising the goals of *ACW*. Firestone offers some suggestions for addressing this problem: to work within our communities and with those outside our own spiritual circles, to promote 'a more compassionate perspective towards the religious "Other"' and 'to transcend our ingrown fear, born of the trauma of religious parturition, so that we can recognise the dignity and love of the religious "Other"'.

Sarah Snyder's chapter presents a descriptive analysis of the official responses to *ACW* from different church leaders and communities, and the controversies that sometimes followed them concerning 'the nature of God', 'love of God and neighbour', the definition of 'neighbour' and the 'relevance of *ACW* to today's context'. The chapter provides a comprehensive analysis of the leading Christian responses (from churches and church institutions throughout Europe and the United States as well as from individuals in Nairobi, Jakarta, Kuala Lumpur, Beirut, Tripoli, Cambridge, Frankfurt, Melbourne, Yale and elsewhere) and notes certain patterns of internal difference. It concludes with a reflection on canons of dialogue whose objective, according to the author, should be about 'discovering a *better quality of disagreement*, rather than seeking common ground'.

In the last chapter of Part II, Peter Admirand highlights 'the need of self-critique and humility within interfaith dialogue', using *ACW* as a case study. He examines *ACW* 'through a Christological lens to gauge whether the positive call of inviting Christians to dialogue was thwarted or hampered by an insufficiently developed and nuanced

Christology within that invitation'. The chapter takes the Gospel parable of the Pharisee and the tax collector as a guide for humility and self-critique. Taking the author's 'Catholic tradition into account, it examines the historical tenor and current state of Catholicism's openness to self-critique and change'. Finally, the chapter seeks similar space for humility and self-critique in *ACW*, as it argues for the relevance of Christian belief in Christ to be expressed more clearly within the document. While praising *ACW* for having 'drawn Christians and Muslims together', the chapter's critical reading is meant to challenge both sides in the conversation.

Part III is given over to some critical readings of the use of scripture in the *ACW* document. In Chapter 9, Asma Afsaruddin scrutinises the reading of Qur'anic texts in the interfaith dialogue environment. Warning that 'interfaith dialogue can be both a richly rewarding learning experience and a minefield', the author raises two questions. First, how is one to establish a general protocol for a respectful and candid dialogue that is mutually beneficial and illuminating? Second, what sources can be invoked to establish an authentic dialogue and define its guiding principles? Focusing on the Muslim scripture, the chapter discusses the exegeses of three sets of Qur'anic verses that specifically deal with the mechanics of interfaith dialogue and commend respect for religious sensibilities. The chapter consults a number of major exegetical works from pre-modern and modern periods that have allowed diverse and historically contingent perspectives to emerge that nevertheless continue to exercise considerable pressure in the modern context. Her piece concludes with 'a reflection upon the further implications of these exegeses for fostering better interfaith understanding between Muslims and their dialogue partners in today's globalising world, implications that could not have been evident to our pre-modern predecessors, who inhabited a very different world'.

In the following chapter, Daniel A. Madigan, taking seriously the double commandment of love that constitutes the kernel of *ACW*'s call for dialogue, argues that the heart of the Gospel lies not in the commandments, but rather in a recognition of the graciousness of God towards us in spite of our signal failure to live the ideals that those commandments represent. He asserts that the Gospel ought to elicit from us first of all an acknowledgement of failure – a *mea culpa*. He further proposes that dialogue matures when it is based on a mutual acknowledgement of failure rather than an exchange about shared ideals, allowing him to conclude that real and fertile dialogue happens when we 'acknowledge our need for forgiveness – from God and each other' and 'recognise our common reliance on nothing else but God's mercy at work in us and through us'.

In Chapter 11, Pim Valkenberg draws attention to a problem which, he thinks, has sometimes hindered *ACW* from being an effective dialogical instrument. This relates to the translation of the words *kalima sawā'* in Q 3:64 as 'a common word', which seems to suggest the possibility of a common ground between Christians and Muslims as a prerequisite or goal of their dialogue. The chapter scrutinises, first, the historical context of this verse and the history of its interpretation. Second, it proposes an alternative interfaith hermeneutic which would avoid the notion of a common ground. Third, it refers to the Netherlands as a case that shows why *ACW* might fail to work in certain contexts unless it is interpreted differently. An alternative rendering of *kalima sawā'* as 'a word of justice' or 'an equitable word', according to Valkenberg, 'may open up new possibilities for a dialogue between Muslims and Christians that centres on matters of peace and justice rather than on dogmatic statements', and might help to broaden the Christian reception of *ACW*.

The section concludes with a chapter by Clare Amos, whose primary concern is to assess the Biblical texts used in *ACW*, the criteria which might have guided their selection and the rules by which they are interpreted. It also looks at the terminology used to describe Christian scripture in both the English and Arabic versions of the document, and asks what this might suggest about the intended difference in the readership of the two versions. Some attention is also given to ways in which the treatment of Muslim and Christian scripture differs in the document. The conclusion reached is that though Biblical texts are treated respectfully by the Muslim authors of *ACW*, the selection of passages and the interpretative principles employed underline the Muslim provenance of the document. Some comparison is also made with the treatment of scripture in the process known as 'Scriptural Reasoning' (SR), although differences with SR are also noted, notably the fact that SR's method of dialogical conversation is not recognisably present in *ACW*.

Part IV considers the reception of *ACW*. The chapter by Rusmir Mahmutćehajić opens with a theoretical reflection on the definition of the 'Other'. The author argues that the concept of another human being exists only as reflected in the concrete self that bears it; every 'self' has the right to its own representation; there is no independent, objectively existing concept determining the existence of particular individuals. With respect to the *ACW* document, the chapter holds, Christian and Muslim individuals need to be seen as microcosms of individuality without reducing them to instances of opposed global entities in inter-action. The chapter examines a number of questions as to how *ACW* should be viewed, given Muslim cultural and political diversity and the all-too-widespread conflict in the so-called Muslim world. How can one's representations of the 'Other' be liberated from framings intended to benefit political power? After sketching Bosnian pluralism in history, the chapter concentrates on the reception and interpretation of *ACW* within the social, cultural and political milieu of Bosnia. The author then concludes that initiatives like *ACW* can help us to reach for the 'ethically based recognition of our common essence', though 'they can equally be abused by those who view dialogue as a tool for managing division'.

In Chapter 14, Mustafa Abu Sway addresses the Biblical and Qur'anic principle of 'love of neighbour' in the *ACW* document and the conditions that render the implementation of this sublime virtue unattainable under certain circumstances. After reviewing the Islamic theological and juridical roots of the status of the 'People of the Book' qua neighbours and the nature of normative relationships, he investigates the details of life in the Middle East, and most especially the Holy Land. *A Common Word*, according to Abu Sway, shows the clear need for 'a new practical pact between the major religions, a pact to end all forms of injustice'. Emphasising the importance of upholding justice, the author further argues that 'the inability to administer justice by loving the neighbour is detrimental to a wholesome rela-tionship with God, even if you pay lip service and profess faith in His Oneness'.

In his own chapter, Matthias Böhm reflects on the reception history of *ACW* in Germany. Despite growing scholarly interest in *ACW* in German academia, the author states that 'on the ground, in parishes and mosques, *ACW* remains no more than a marginal document'. The chapter reflects on this low level of *ACW* awareness in Germany, exploring the factors that ensure that the document is still 'an unknown word' there. In doing this, the chapter also discusses the history of the Muslim presence in Germany with its figures, diverse institutions and official representatives. It also examines the wider lack of knowledge of Islam in German society, concluding with some suggestions for creating a greater awareness of *ACW* among the country's Christian and Muslim populations. For although in parishes and mosques *ACW* has remained mostly 'a marginal note', the author strongly believes that 'its implications for more practical and pastoral questions are important in trying to foster neighbourly and peaceful relations.'

Considering *ACW* 'a call to action and its lengthy theological content a mere preamble', Amir Dastmalchian's chapter is focused on the implications of *ACW* for musical interaction between Muslims and Christians. The chapter explores the potential for using music in Christian–Muslim engagements, since 'in some contexts, non-discursive dialogue can be more effective than discursive dialogue', and because 'music is a particularly powerful means of expression'. While acknowledging Muslim reservations surrounding the term 'music', the author argues that three genres of aural art – the recitation of the Qur'an, the call to prayer and the recitation of liturgy – offer scope for all Muslims to participate in interreligious dialogue by means of music. Similarly, he contends that Gregorian, Ambrosian, Mozarabic and other forms of Christian liturgical chant offer scope for Christians to share in this form of dialogue. Musical dialogue initiatives offer, the chapter concludes, 'the opportunity for the spirit of dialogue to touch the lives of those whom it may otherwise never reach'.

Part V, comprising two chapters, discusses the future of Christian–Muslim dialogue in relation to *ACW*. Marianne Farina's chapter offers 'suggestions for developing a new phase of *ACW* discussions'. The author proposes a contextual theological model as a crucial tool for future *ACW* deliberations. Contextual theology, recognising three critical sources for theological study – scripture, tradition and socio-political context – would draw participants from local communities and the academy together in the discussion of sacred texts. The author argues that a contextual model for *ACW* would foster full engagement in four critical dialogues: life, social justice projects, spiritual experiences and theological study. Further, it would offer a forum that goes beyond formal gatherings and academic settings into Christian and Muslim faith communities. The author also proposes that *ACW* discussions should encourage intra-religious exchanges, for dialogue with co-religionists is crucial for an honest exchange with people of other faiths. Finally the chapter recommends 'an inductive, inclusive and evaluative process for the study of, and dialogue about, "our common word" that, like God's word itself, is ongoing'.

The volume concludes with a chapter by Yazid Said which reflects on two major themes which have arisen throughout the book. First, we are to acknowledge the importance of our doctrinal differences by not taking a reductionist view of *ACW*. Second, we should recognise common goals and common marks of faith as we seek the good of our world. The chapter then turns to explore ways in which *ACW* connects with classical sources of Islam and Christianity, focusing on the works of Imām Abū Ḥāmid al-Ghazālī and St Augustine of Hippo. Emphasising that these medieval sources are 'more than just a museum piece', the chapter examines how their reflections on the subject of love may enrich our current debate and our engagement for the future, providing us with the tools for an honest and profound dialogic groundwork. Rather than simply converging on love of God and neighbour as a neutral and dry abstraction, the chapter aptly concludes that we should confess in heartfelt human terms that 'humility is the much-needed common word for our world today'.

The importance of this volume lies in the fact that its contributors evince a commitment to a rigorous academic engagement while keeping in view the broader framework of the significance of theology, religious studies and *ACW* for the common good. This team of experienced academics builds on a variety of perspectives, a vast wealth of critical scholarship and years of practical experience with communities. The chapters thus examine appropriate ways of understanding and addressing the call of *ACW* in its contextual evolution, interrogate past methods of dialogue and open up the prospect of shaping a future rooted in the best of the tradition of Muslim–Christian engagement down the centuries. Our book is thus intended for academics as well as practitioners in pastoral and religious callings who are involved or concerned with conversations across the religious divide. It also aims to offer a set of resources and readings for theology students engaged in interreligious studies and the history of this dialogue, which is probably the most important inter-cultural conversation taking place in our troubled, but not hopeless, times.

PART I

THE CONTEXT OF *A COMMON WORD*

Past and Present

The Inception of *A Common Word*

Tim Winter

A Common Word, a document which may be considered one of our era's most significant initiatives in the field of interreligious engagement, continues and repristinates a long and complex heritage stretching back to the earliest times of the Islamic religion. The Muslim historians report that following his initial encounter with the angel Gabriel and his reception of the first verses of the Qur'an, the Prophet Muhammad visited a Christian relative in order to seek some clarity about what had happened to him. The Christian, 'who used to read the Gospel', heard the Prophet out, and after listening to verses from the new Qur'anic scripture replied, 'That was the Angel of Revelation whom God sent down upon Moses. If thy day of need witnesseth me alive, I shall help thee.'[1] A constructive engagement with Christians through the medium of scripture and in the assurance of a certain common heritage, feeling and mutual benefit thus appears as a naturally Islamic practice embedded in the earliest moments of the religion.

Subsequent Qur'anic deliverances evolved a nuanced continuation of this scriptural focus, addressing Christians as 'people of the book' (*ahl al-kitāb*). Although the Qur'an was evidently announcing the beginning of a new horizon in salvation history, it also understood itself to be in significant continuity with earlier Abrahamic religion, at least to the extent that this had been faithfully preserved from the time of its revelation. The Prophet experienced his mission as the retrieval of a primordial *ur-monotheismus,* a belief in One God native to the human soul, evident

---

[1] Bukhārī, *Ṣaḥīḥ*, 'Bad' al-waḥy', 3; translation in Muhammad Asad, *Ṣaḥīḥ al-Bukhârî: The Early Years of Islam* (Gibraltar: Dar al-Andalus, 1981), p. 8.

through the natural world and affirmed by prophecy through the ages. Abraham, Moses, Jesus and a series of others were presented as restorers of the same message, the essence of which is the honouring of one's duties to the One God and to His human creatures. Latter-day representatives of earlier chapters in this Abrahamic saga, despite having fallen into strife with one another (Q 5:17) and having accumulated several critical errors, are still to be respected, even honoured; and the Qur'an is able to speak appreciatively of Christian leaders (Q 57:27). This respect, however, coexists with the Qur'an's allusive but unmistakeable rejection of the three most difficult and contested convictions of Christian theology (Trinity, Incarnation and Atonement) as these had taken shape during the previous centuries of controversy, and which, in ways reminiscent of some radical forms of Protestantism, it saw itself as correcting or abolishing in the name of a return to the original beliefs held by Jesus the Messiah and by the earlier prophets. Through its simultaneous affirmation and critique of Christians and Christianity, the Qur'an is in essence attempting to resolve the ancient dogmatic disputes which had divided the Christian world. In the words of a historian,

> In the seventh-century context [...] Islam was not so much an innovation, nor merely an imposture; rather it was a response to a conjuncture in the history of the Church at which Christianity's inherent intellectual implausibility had become impossible to hide or mend.[2]

This Qur'anic reformation moment in the *historia monotheistica* was immediately followed by the early Muslim conquests and the establishment of an imperium which brought Muslims and Christians together in a range of ways, some amicable and others adversarial. Over centuries, the populations of the majority of Christian lands opted to convert to Islam, so that the Middle Eastern and North African Muslims with whom Christians dialogue today are overwhelmingly descendants of those who came to accept the Qur'an's distinctive understanding of Christianity. Christians who did not enter the newly repaired Abrahamic faith were allowed to maintain their religious observances and familial and economic lives in exchange for accepting Muslim overlordship and a set of legal disadvantages. In this environment of 'protection' (*dhimma*), Muslims and Christians coexisted in ways that were typically stable and at times convivial, although the leaders of both traditions tended to

---

[2] Garth Fowden, 'Gibbon on Islam', *English Historical Review*, 131/549 (April 2016), 261–92, at p. 280, commending and paraphrasing the position of Edward Gibbon.

maintain a staunch polemical stance in their writings. On the side of the 'superseded' religion this began with St John Damascene (d. 749), who set the tone by considering Muhammad a false prophet and a harbinger of Antichrist.[3] His loyalties to the Umayyad caliphate, under which he held the office of minister of finance, ironically also began the history of Christian animus against fellow Christians who chose to dialogue and engage with Islam: some called him a 'cursed favourer of Saracens'. On the Muslim side, theological responses to Christianity, a religion which despite continued conversions remained vibrant across the Muslim world, ranged from the polite curiosity of the Abbasid caliph al-Mahdī (r. 775–85) in his dialogue with an equally courteous Nestorian patriarch,[4] to a more rebarbative genre in the later medieval period, exemplified by the works of Shihāb al-Dīn al-Qarāfī (d. 1285)[5] and Ibn Taymiyya (d. 1328),[6] which probably reflected Muslim anxieties over the Crusades and the threat of Christian cooperation with the Mongols.

The demise of the medieval paradigms was symbolised by Napoleon's invasion of Egypt in 1798. Although Napoleon opportunistically claimed to be a Muslim for the purposes of that campaign, and some of his senior officers did formally enter Islam, it was increasingly clear to Muslims that the West's erstwhile religious identity was being challenged by a new and secular paradigm rooted in national pride and scientific and technical prowess. When the captured Algerian resistance leader Emir Abdel Kader (d.1883) wrote his *Letter to the French* he was aware that his readers were caught up in a complex process of change that was sweeping them far from established Muslim assumptions about the 'people of the book'.[7] From that time onward Muslim assessments of what was once Christendom tended to assume that the dominant mode of address should be pragmatic rather than theological. The polemic shifted into a new register of discourse which took aim at Western materialism, imperialism and global dominance as seen from the novel and uncongenial perspective of Muslim weakness. This ethos of Third World *ressentiment*

---

[3] Jean Damascène, *Écrits sur l'Islam: présentation, commentaires et traduction par Raymond Le Coz* (Paris: Éditions du Cerf, 1992).

[4] Hans Putman, *L'Église et l'islam sous Timothée I (780–823): étude sur l'église nestorienne au temps des premiers 'Abbasides: avec nouvelle édition et traduction du Dialogue entre Timothée et al-Mahdi* (Beirut: Dar el-Machreq, 1975).

[5] Diego R. Sarrió Cucarella, *Muslim-Christian Polemics across the Mediterranean: The Splendid Replies of Shihāb al-Dīn al-Qarāfī (d. 684/1285)* (Leiden: Brill, 2015).

[6] Taqi al-Din ibn Taymiyya, *Réponse raisonnable aux chrétiens*, ed. and trans. Laurent Basanese (Damascus and Beirut: Institut Français du Proche-Orient, 2012).

[7] Abd el-Kader, *Lettre aux Français*, trans. René Khawam (Paris: Phébus, 1977).

was summed up in the claim by Sudanese politician Ṣādiq al-Mahdī that 'today we face an economic and military giant with the moral scruples of a flea. It is not a pleasant encounter'.[8]

Muslim political impotence contributed to several very conspicuous sources of humiliation. The loss of Palestine in 1948 and the reluctance of Western governments to promote the refugees' right of return have been the most neuralgic. The Muslim world's inability to succour the Bosnian Muslims during the 1992–5 conflict with Serb and Croat irredentists, which culminated in the Srebrenica massacre, added to the sense of helplessness in the face of Western strategic choices. The American-led invasion of Iraq in 2003 and the disorder which followed added still more humiliation and anguish. In this resentful atmosphere many Muslims came to view the West as a demonic and profane principle, entrenched in hedonism and a determination to achieve global dominance and the propagation of its own values wherever it could.

Some, however, were conscious that the West was still at important junctures susceptible to its older religious moods and motivations. There had been a strong element of Christian rhetoric in Western support for the Zionist movement[9] and in the Serbian campaign in Bosnia.[10] But the Iraq invasion brought this religious modality of modern Westernness to Muslim eyes and ears in a new and intensified way. President George W. Bush's use of the word 'crusade' and his frequent echoing of religious and Biblical themes in his public speeches served to strengthen an already ongoing shift in the Muslim perception of Western intention, and this was further reinforced by the sense that his ally Tony Blair was one of the most noticeably religious politicians the United Kingdom had known for decades.[11] After the Iraq invasion, the Muslim image of the godless but technically adept West was partially reversed in favour of much older perceptions of a malignant and deceitful crusading enemy, a 'Dark Other' with explicitly Christian intentions.[12]

---

[8] Cited in Altaf Gauhar, *The Challenge of Islam* (London: Islamic Council of Europe, 1978), p. 119.

[9] Donald M. Lewis, *The Origins of Christian Zionism* (Cambridge: Cambridge University Press, 2014).

[10] Michael A. Sells, *The Bridge Betrayed: Religion and Genocide in Bosnia* (Berkeley: University of California Press, 1998).

[11] Anthony Seldon, *Blair* (London: Free Press, 2004), pp. 515–32; see also Seldon's 'Tony Blair was driven by God and George W. Bush' in the *Daily Mirror* (London), 6 July 2016.

[12] For some surveys of American political Christianity, see Benjamin Lynerd, *Republican Theology: The Civil Religion of American Evangelicals* (New York: Oxford University Press, 2014); David Domke, *God Willing? Political Fundamentalism in the White House, the 'War on Terror' and the Echoing Press* (London: Pluto Press, 2004). For a

In the aftermath of the Iraq invasion, Muslim religious and secular intellectuals had struggled at first to find a secular and utilitarian gloss on the event. However, the official Anglo-Saxon *casus belli*, grounded in claims that the Iraqi authorities possessed weapons of mass destruction and had been implicated in the 2001 terrorist attacks on the United States, was credited only by a very few in the region, and a hunt for an alternative account seemed necessary. A more attractive explanation proposed that the catalyst for American 'shock and awe' lay in the Bible-believing worldview of President Bush and key members of his staff and the US military establishment.

Despite the fact that most mainline church leaders declined to support the war, the evidence for a fundamentalist Christian motivation for the Iraq invasion seemed extensive. President Bush himself was clearly a religious man with a strong belief in his own chosenness, having claimed explicitly that 'God wants me to be President'.[13] Historian Arthur Schlesinger was calling him 'the most aggressively religious president in American history'.[14] Palestinian leader Mahmoud Abbas described how Bush had told him that he was 'driven by a mission from God. God would tell me: "George, go and fight those terrorists in Afghanistan." And I did.'[15] Many pointed in alarm to Bush's dedication to the sermons of Oswald Chambers (d. 1917), an evangelical chaplain who had accompanied British troops during the Gallipoli and Gaza campaigns of the First World War, and who held pungent views about the need for a militant confrontation with Islam. Bush's appointee in the search for Osama Bin Laden, General William Boykin, was also articulating a staunchly anti-Islam message and a strong conviction that the 'War on Terror' was a crusade.[16] America would only be victorious against its Muslim enemies 'if we come against them in the name of Jesus', he stated.[17] Attorney-General John Ashcroft startled more secular Washington insiders by having himself anointed with holy oil when he took office,[18] and provoked protests

---

more polemical commentary on how 'Bush has Christianised the war in Iraq', see Paul Vallely, 'The fifth crusade: George Bush and the Christianisation of the war in Iraq', *Borderlands: A Journal of Theology and Education*, 4 (Summer 2005), 7–11.

[13] Kevin Philips, *American Theocracy: The Peril and Politics of Radical Religion, Oil, and Borrowed Money in the 21st Century* (London: Penguin, 2006), p. xxiv.

[14] Ibid.

[15] Ibid., p. xxxviii.

[16] For more on Boykin as Christian warrior, see Jan G. Linn, *What's Wrong with the Christian Right* (Boca Raton, FL: BrownWalker Press, 2004), pp. 61–3.

[17] Chris Hedges, *American Fascists: The Christian Right and the War on America* (London: Jonathan Cape, 2007), p. 29.

[18] Philips, *American Theocracy*, p. 118.

from a large number of Muslim organisations when he aired similarly negative views about Islam.[19]

A further catalyst of this shift in Muslim perceptions of the United States was the conspicuous drama of American interrogation methods.[20] While Western journalists reported the use of physical torture against terrorism suspects at Guantánamo, Abu Ghraib and elsewhere, Muslim attention was also focused on the prominence of religious themes. At Guantánamo, interrogators believed religious humiliation to be an effective means of weakening detainees' resistance. After attending prayer meetings with the camp director, interrogators would subject detainees to loud Arabic evangelical music, pretend to baptise inmates forcibly, engage in forms of 'Qur'an abuse', and make remarks such as 'A holy war is occurring between the Cross and the Star of David on one side, and the Crescent on the other.'[21] At Abu Ghraib, the soldiers eventually found guilty of abuse had also boasted of their 'Christian' credentials.[22]

American interrogation techniques rooted in cultural awareness training about Arab values and vulnerabilities were naturally experienced as provocative by Arab public opinion. Methods designed to maximise Arab shame unintentionally produced a public relations disaster in a region which already felt itself humiliated and despised. A Kuwaiti businessman paid for a full-page newspaper feature denouncing Qur'an abuse as part of an American crusading policy, while an article in the same newspaper reflected on the American president's alleged sympathy for end-time dispensationalist theologies which hoped to provoke the final battle which would enable the Second Coming of Christ.[23] Another newspaper similarly explained to its readers that American violence could only be understood in terms of the Bush administration's belief that 'occupying Iraq confirms the predictions of the Bible; it is one incident in a series of events before the return of Christ'. The article then discussed the militant dispensationalist views of several key members of Bush's team.[24]

---

[19] *Los Angeles Times*, 6 February 2002; Jocelyn Cesari, *When Islam and Democracy Meet: Muslims in Europe and the United States* (Basingstoke: Palgrave Macmillan, 2004), p. 41.

[20] For these, see the first-hand account of Tony Lagouranis, *Fear Up Harsh: An Army Interrogator's Dark Journey through Iraq* (New York: NAL Caliber, 2007).

[21] Andy Worthington, *The Guantanamo Files: The Stories of the 774 Detainees in America's Illegal Prison* (London: Pluto, 2007), pp. 195, 198, 260.

[22] Philip Gourevitch, *Standard Operating Procedure: A War Story* (London: Picador, 2008), pp. 64, 83, 127, 214.

[23] *Al-Watan*, 9 August 2005, 9 October 2006.

[24] *Al-Hayat*, 24 October 2003.

Particularly salient in the regional debate were Arab Christian journalists and academics, who felt themselves in a position to explain the 'theocon' agenda to their compatriots: Ghassan Rubeiz, former secretary for the Middle East of the World Council of Churches, wrote influential articles explaining to regional readers the growth of radical Protestant politics in the United States,[25] while the Coptic sociologist Samīr Murqus published a series of books with titles like 'American Imperialism: The Triad of Wealth, Faith and Power', in which he assessed the roots and contemporary political expression of what he believed to be America's faith-based foreign policy.[26] This was reinforced by the translation into Arabic of English-language surveys of the American religious right and its influence in Washington.[27] Across the Muslim world the same change in perception was rampant. The Egyptian journalist Majdī Kāmil published his 'Christian Zionism, Islamic Extremism, and the Doomsday Scenario', pointing to some parallels between Islamist and hard-line Christian political ideologies.[28] Pakistani public opinion was influenced by books such as Abid Jan's *Afghanistan: The Genesis of the Final Crusade*.[29] The same shift was assisted in Turkey by authors such as Şule Akbulut Albayrak.[30]

It was this widespread sense that a fundamentalist Christian agenda was driving American violence in the Middle East and threatening the region's complex sectarian balance which provided the crucible for *A Common Word*. The specific trigger, however, was the controversial lecture given at Regensburg University by Pope Benedict XVI five years and one day after the September 11 terrorist attacks.[31] Benedict XVI, in a complex academic disquisition on what he saw as the natural synergy

[25] E.g., *Daily News* (Egypt), 6 April 2007.

[26] Samīr Murqus, *al-Imbarāṭūriyya al-Amrīkiyya: thulāthiyyat al-tharwa, al-dīn, al-quwwa, min al-ḥarb al-ahliyya ilā mā baʿda 11 Sabtambar* (Cairo: Maktabat al-Shurūq al-Dawliyya, 2003).

[27] These included Jeremy Scahill, *Blackwater: The Rise of the World's Most Powerful Mercenary Army* (London: Serpent's Tail, 2007), and Kimberly Blaker, *The Fundamentals of Extremism: The Christian Right in America* (New Boston, MI: New Boston Books, 2003).

[28] Majdī Kāmil, *al-Masīḥiyya al-Ṣihyūniyya, al-taṭarruf al-Islāmī, wa-l-sīnāriyū l-kārithī* (Damascus and Cairo: Dar al-Kitāb al-ʿArabī, 2007).

[29] Abid Jan, *Afghanistan: The Genesis of the Final Crusade* (Lahore: Pragmatic Publishers, 2006). For a more recent example of the genre, see Masood Ashraf Raja, *The Religious Right and the Talibanization of America* (Basingstoke: Macmillan, 2016).

[30] Şule Akbulut Albayrak, *Hıristiyan Fundamentalizmi* (Istanbul: Etkileşim, 2007).

[31] 'Faith, reason and the university: memories and reflections', 12 September 2006. https://w2.vatican.va/content/benedict-xvi/en/speeches/2006/september/documents/hf_ben-xvi_spe_20060912_university-regensburg.html. Accessed 28 September 2016. See Sarah Markiewicz, *World Peace through Christian-Muslim Understanding: The Genesis and*

of Europe, Christianity, morality and reason, had cited a Byzantine emperor's jeremiad against Islam without being at all clear about what he himself made of the emperor's remarks. He went on to cite the orientalist Roger Arnaldez (d. 2006) to imply that Islamic thought supports a simple-minded command ethic and denies the moral reasonableness of God. Again it was unclear whether the pope was commending this view or whether he was aware that Arnaldez was writing about a minoritarian and contested Muslim position. Given these ambiguities it was not difficult to draw the conclusion that the pope viewed Islam as the barbarian antithesis of a Europe which rationally worshipped a reasonable and moral God. Some commentators did indeed read the lecture in that way, and that reading proved popular among some leaders of Europe's far-right movements.[32] One American Catholic writer hailed the pope's speech as timely because 'the West is once again under siege. [...] there is a new form of conquest: immigration coupled with high fertility'.[33] However, other commentators, including Hans Küng, accused Benedict XVI of 'serious errors of fact and judgement'.[34]

The wave of Muslim outrage triggered by the pope's delphic words, which spilled over into violence against Christians in several countries, was riding on the wider Muslim fear that the West's military and economic interventions in the Muslim world were being eased by a theologically grounded hatred of Islam. Muslim communities, frustrated by poor government at home and the spectacle of Israeli and American entrenchment in Islam's heartlands, seemed willing to be drawn into a reactive spiral of fundamentalist identity-seeking which appeared to mirror Israeli and American fundamentalism and its tendency to political and violent expression.

Among Muslim elites it was clear that some form of initiative was urgently necessary in order to obstruct this slide into mutual demonization and anathema. The secular classes in the region, taken aback by the religionising of American politics and preoccupied with the domestic

---

Fruits of the Open Letter 'A Common Word between Us and You' (Göttingen: V&R Unipress, 2016), pp. 151–92.

[32] Thierry Bordet, *The Significance of Borders: Why Representative Government and the Rule of Law Require Nation States* (Leiden: E. J. Brill, 2012), p. 4.

[33] Joseph Fessio, SJ, 'On Pope Benedict XVI's address at the University of Regensburg', *The Wanderer*, 28 September 2006.

[34] 'Serious errors of both fact and judgement: an interview with Hans Küng', *The Times*, 16 September 2006. For a Muslim refutation, see Muhammad Silvio Gualini, *Muslims and Christians Divided under the Same God?* (Bloomington, IN: Author House, 2011).

suppression of Islamism, proved unable to generate such an interruption. It was clear in any case that the initiative should emanate not from the rulers but from the religious establishment. That establishment, however, seemed in many ways gravely inadequate to the task. Following the abolition of the Ottoman caliphate and its supreme religious office, the position of the Shaykh al-Islām, in 1924, Sunni Islam, the faith of almost 90 per cent of Muslim believers, had lacked a central institution which might voice or coordinate a reaction to local Muslim or foreign Christian extremism. In the volatile post-Srebrenica environment this incapacity was crucially damaging Sunnism's ability to unite in the face of such threats and to articulate clearly the Muslim majority's rejection of fundamentalism and confrontation. On the national level, Muslim countries usually maintained Ministries of Religious Affairs, Grand Muftis and rectors of venerable seminaries, but these were poorly networked, and were also under increasing threat from the Wahhabism exported by Saudi Arabia, which dismissed the traditional Sunni leadership as unduly conciliatory and tainted by heretical innovations. Underfunded, and frequently frustrated by claustrophobic governmental control, the Sunni religious elites appeared impotent and divided in the face of the new challenges, and unlikely to correct Western perceptions of the Islamic religion as unloving, irrational, anti-Christian and generally complicit in fundamentalism and xenophobia.

It fell to a hybrid group mainly composed of Western-educated Middle Eastern intellectuals, led by Prince Ghazi bin Muhammad of Jordan (b. 1966), to identify a means by which the Sunni mainstream might articulate a credible and audible voice to counteract the negative images promoted by those whom Ghazi identified as the 'neocons and theocons'.[35] Shocked by the sectarian violence into which Iraq had collapsed following the United States–led invasion, members of this circle had already composed a document known as the *Amman Message*, which was promulgated in 2004 with the endorsement of Jordanian king Abdullah II.[36] This declaration affirmed that the major sects of the Islamic world should cooperate in a spirit of mutual acceptance and respect. In itself this was not particularly novel. However, the form the statement took, of a collective platform signed by a wide range of Muslim political and religious leaders, including many heads of state, deans of religious universities and most

[35] Interview with Prince Ghazi cited in Markiewicz, *World Peace through Christian-Muslim Understanding*, p. 104.
[36] Ibid., pp. 127–50.

of Islam's leading scholars from all the major denominations, made it something radically new in Islamic history, drawing very loosely on the ancient ideal of scholarly consensus (*ijmāʿ*) but in a new format which by virtue of modern communications and media techniques could quickly assemble hundreds of endorsements and reach a potentially unlimited number of recipients.

Three years later, against the backdrop of a further growth in Christian and Muslim fundamentalism and an escalating security crisis in Iraq, the concept underlying this intra-faith initiative was applied again, this time on a more ambitious interfaith level. Already, one month after the Regensburg address, Prince Ghazi and thirty-six other signatories had despatched an open letter to the Vatican to draw the pope's attention to the errors implied by his speech, and to the shared emphasis on love in Islam and Christianity.[37] The Vatican's reply was dilatory enough to provoke Prince Ghazi into crafting a much longer open letter. He shared a draft with a core group of scholars, including Yemeni Sufi authorities Habib Ali al-Jifri and Habib Umar bin Hafiz, Mauritanian jurist Abdullah bin Bayyah, Egyptian Grand Mufti Ali Gomaa and Iranian-American scholar Seyyed Hossein Nasr, who suggested a few minor emendations. The core group and Prince Ghazi's secretariat then circulated the final text, now entitled *A Common Word between Us and You*, to a list of Muslim leaders, including many who had signed the *Amman Message* three years previously. Almost all signed the document, which was then launched publicly on 13 October 2007.

The document is unusual not only in its format, but also in existing primarily as a phenomenon of cyberspace, a medium which has become pivotal in the Islamic world as it has in the West. The website www .acommonword.com was registered immediately before the launch and has served as the authoritative home and point of information about the document, which remains without an original and authorised printed edition, even though Muslim publishers have reissued the text for mass circulation.[38] Thanks in part to its online availability and promotion, responses were rapid. In the Islamic world the initiative was received with sympathy, and the number of signatories slowly grew from 138 until it

---

[37] 'Open letter to Pope Benedict XVI.' http://theislamicmonthly.com/open-letter-to-pope-benedict-xvi/. Accessed 28 September 2016.

[38] For instance, Lejla Demiri (ed.), *A Common Word: Text and Reflections: A Resource for Parishes and Mosques* (Cambridge: Muslim Academic Trust, 2011). This has been reprinted in Malaysia, and translated into several languages, including Albanian, Bulgarian and Spanish.

reached more than three hundred two years later. More detailed Muslim theological and scholarly reactions were fairly infrequent, however, perhaps because the document contained little that, from a Muslim perspective, seemed new or controversial.

The addressees themselves, by contrast, were very quickly galvanised by the document, whose global potential for promoting peace and defusing tensions seemed so evident and timely. Most of the major Christian addressees soon responded, including the Patriarch of Russia, the Archbishop of Canterbury, the World Council of Churches, the Baptist World Alliance and the president of the Lutheran World Federation. Later in 2007 an open letter occupying a full page of the *New York Times* presented a Protestant response, entitled *The Yale Response*, signed by more than three hundred significant evangelical and reformed pastors and theologians.[39] Some of these also attended a major *ACW* conference held at Yale University in July 2008, an event of great significance given the Muslim perception that the Bush team was being driven by a certain type of evangelical worldview.[40] Conscious that it was being left behind, the Vatican itself began to respond, and Pope Benedict XVI accepted an invitation jointly to establish a regular Catholic–Muslim Forum to be held every two years in Rome or in a Muslim country. In November 2008, he attended the first of these himself and offered a presentation in which he endorsed the core themes of the initiative, recognised the need to overcome prejudice and misinformation and affirmed that both Islam and Christianity hinge on the principles of love of God and love of neighbour.[41] In the subsequent years a remarkable effusion of writing, preaching and seminar work continued to appear, taking the form of several major books and dozens of articles and essays.

In part this enthusiasm reveals that Christians share *ACW*'s anxieties about the state of the world in the aftermath of the Iraq invasion. The authors typically seek to clarify their own religious positions

---

[39] *New York Times*, 18 November 2007; *A Common Word Between Us and You: 5-Year Anniversary Edition* (Amman: Royal Aal Al-Bayt Institute for Islamic Thought, 2012), pp. 143–62. www.acommonword.com/a-common-word-between-us-and-you-5-year-anniversary-edition/. Accessed 28 September 2016.

[40] Some of the proceedings were published in Miroslav Volf, Ghazi bin Muhammad and Melissa Yarrington (eds.), *A Common Word: Muslims and Christians on Loving God and Neighbor* (Grand Rapids, MI: Eerdmans, 2010).

[41] 'Address of His Holiness Benedict XVI to participants in the seminar organized by the "Catholic–Muslim Forum"', 6 November 2008. www.vatican.va/holy_father/benedict_xvi/speeches/2008/november/documents/hf_ben-xvi_spe_20081106_cath-islamic-leaders_en.html. Accessed 28 September 2016.

for the benefit of Muslim readers, including a statement of their commitment to peace, and emphasising in particular their assurance that the Trinity is a monotheistic doctrine and ought to be regarded as such by Muslims. They also express their gratitude for the letter's affirmation of the principle of religious freedom, an Enlightenment ideal which is often curtailed by Muslim governments anxious about the intrusions of missionaries among volatile populations. The writing is sometimes orotund and sometimes guarded and tentative; but most of the Christian responses evince a distinct excitement at having heard, perhaps for the first time, a Muslim voice that was clearly a mainstream one endorsed by the religion's major figures, which created a discursive environment which they could comfortably inhabit and to which they could respond.

Ostensibly *ACW* is a commentary on a Qur'anic invitation:

Say: O people of the Book! Come to a common word (*kalima sawā'*) between us and you; that we shall worship none save God, and that we shall ascribe no partner unto Him, and that none of us shall take others for lords beside God. And if they turn away, then say: Bear witness that we are they who have surrendered [unto Him].

(Q 3:64)

The dialogical context is evident from the outset: the Prophet is being summoned to summon Christians to a 'word' held in common, or what might today be designated a 'joint platform'. Apart from those who thought they detected in this verse an implicit criticism of Trinitarian belief, the Christian recipients were hardly very challenged by these demands. The 'word' was experienced not only as a discursive position about interreligious love and conviviality, but implicitly as the nature of the discourse itself, which seemed to create an important new *habitus* for Muslim–Christian dialogue. Many readers commented on the energetic, resonant and hospitable language of *ACW*, and in fact this constituted a major part of its appeal. The letter seemed to fall as a surprising music upon these Christian ears.

After citing the Qur'anic invitation to 'a common word', the document proceeds to summon Christians and Muslims to unite around what it considers to be the 'Two Greatest Commandments': love of God and love of neighbour. In the subsequent discussions both of these loves turned out to require considerable exegesis. *ACW* provides only a bare outline for this, presumably out of a due caution concerning internal Christian and Muslim diversity and the inherent difficulty of the subject. Love is scarcely the easiest principle to define, being a very deep function of the soul, 'of which you have been given only a little knowledge' (Q 17:85). *ACW*, while insisting that these commands unite us, declines to define love, God or neighbour, and the reception of the document has largely homed in on these areas of potential misunderstanding or difference.

That Muslims and Christians worship the same God is insisted on by *ACW*, being already an axiom for Muslims (Q 29:46). However, Christians have often demurred. General Boykin was far from alone in calling the Muslim God 'not a real God'.[42] One important outcome of *ACW* was to bring out an explicit acceptance (in most cases very readily forthcoming) that the God of Islam is also the God of Christianity, in spite of different theological definitions and assumptions about God's inner life and salvific agency. For Catholics, this had already been accepted by a key declaration of the Second Vatican Council.[43] Among Protestants the situation was much less clear, but the *Yale Response* clearly accepted it. A little later Miroslav Volf's book affirming the claim provided one of *ACW*'s most significant and serious theological fruits.[44]

The basic method of *ACW* is to juxtapose scriptural passages from the two religions in order to demonstrate a substantive, while not precise, convergence of values and purposes. Scripturality thus lies at the document's heart. The Qur'an itself appears to supply the warrant for this procedure, holding that 'We have sent you revelation as We sent it to Noah and those who came after him' (Q 4:163). The scriptures – scholarly questions of interpolation aside – share the same divine source, and for Muslims at least, juxtaposition is therefore quite natural. From a Christian perspective, although some have argued that the Qur'an is also in some sense divinely inspired,[45] this method has sometimes seemed more counter-intuitive and problematic. In its emphatic focus on scripture rather than on a later magisterium it might also seem more Protestant than Catholic

---

[42] Hedges, *American Fascists*, p. 29. See also Karl Barth, *Church Dogmatics* II/1 (Edinburgh: T&T Clark, 1957), pp. 448–9, who sees Islam as a supreme form of paganism.

[43] *Nostra Aetate* (1965). Before Vatican II the Catholic position had been similar to that of Barth; official teaching then underwent a 'titanic' rupture: see Christian S. Krokus, 'Louis Massignon's influence on the teaching of Vatican II on Muslims and Islam', *Islam and Christian-Muslim Relations*, 23 (2012), 329–45, at p. 331. The watershed seemed to have been Paul VI's visit to Palestine, where he encountered Muslim faith at first hand, generating the encyclical *Spiritus paracliti*.

[44] Miroslav Volf, *Allah: A Christian Response* (New York: HarperOne, 2011); see also Miroslav Volf (ed.), *Do We Worship the Same God? Jews, Christians and Muslims in Dialogue* (Grand Rapids, MI: Eerdmans, 2012).

[45] Significant figures here include Louis Massignon, W. Montgomery Watt and Hans Küng.

or Orthodox, and this again seems to underline the analogy between Islam and the Reformation.[46] Yet the reception of *ACW* has relied less on the participants' formal theologies of revelation than on the unmistakeable beauty and religious power of the scriptural texts, which shine through the veils imposed by translation and unfamiliarity. Again the Qur'an is clearly aware of this possibility of a non-discursive elation and an aesthetic-spiritual impact, when it speaks of certain monks: 'When they hear what is revealed to the Messenger, you see their eyes fill with tears because of the truth they have recognised' (Q 5:83). *ACW* seems to call forth an element of deep although indefinable recognition. Rowan Williams intuited this when he wrote that *ACW* reminded him of the Psalms.[47] The Prophet himself had said, with reference to Qur'anic revelation, 'I have been given one of the flutes of David.'[48]

Still, some pointed out an important asymmetry. While for Christians scripture is most usually seen as a witness or pointer to the true revelation, which is God in Christ, in Islam revelation is not the Prophet so much as the book itself. The scripturality of *ACW* is born not of contemporary interreligious techniques such as Scriptural Reasoning (in fact, the document is indifferent to all contemporary theory) but of a foundational and very Muslim assurance that the word of God is not only the necessary point of departure and ground of all human initiatives that seek to please Him, but is itself a theophany. The centrality of scripture confers a kind of real presence upon *ACW*, as the Qur'an is taken by almost all Muslims to be God's 'uncreated speech' (*kalām Allāh al-qadīm*), which suffuses its hearers with blessings and whose reading is itself a sacramental and mysterious participation in the eternal divine nature. For Seyyed Hossein Nasr, engaging with the Qur'an produces 'an echo in the minds and world of the men who read it, and returns them to a state in which they participate in its paradisal joy and beauty. Herein lies its alchemical effect'.[49]

Whether or not Islam's idiom of scripturality imposes an asymmetry and bias in *ACW*'s summons, this alchemical power of scripture may help to explain the distinctive texture and power of the whole document,

[46] For an exploration of this similarity, see Ralf K. Wüstenberg, *Islam ist Hingabe: Eine Entdeckungsreise in das Innere einer Religion* (Gütersloh: Gütersloher Verlagshaus, 2016).

[47] Rowan Williams, Chapter 4 in this volume.

[48] Bukhārī, *Ṣaḥīḥ*, 'Faḍā'il al-Qur'ān', 31; Muslim, *Ṣaḥīḥ*, 'Musāfirīn', 235.

[49] Seyyed Hossein Nasr, *Islamic Art and Spirituality* (Ipswich, UK: Golgonooza, 1986), p. 77; for the phenomenon of the Qur'an as a kind of Real Presence, see John Herlihy, *Holy Qur'an: An Intimate Portrait* (Miami: Ansar Books, 2014).

which is manifest even in its English version. Written originally in English and only later translated into Arabic, *ACW* adventurously seeks to use the sacred possibilities of a somewhat archaic English as the vehicle for a formal Muslim letter to Christians. The Authorised Version of the Bible is matched to Marmaduke Pickthall's Jacobean English translation of the Qur'an, an exercise which brings to the surface Pickthall's project of echoing the Authorised Version's semiticisms in order to allow the Qur'an a rather literal but unmistakeably quasi-Biblical voice. Pickthall, an Arabist whose father had been an Anglican rector, is in a sense one of the wordsmiths who have allowed *ACW* to reach across the Muslim–Christian boundary with such surprising ease and effect. The result is rather successfully to de-exoticise Muslim God-talk. Just as Islam over the centuries transcended its original Arabic matrix and found a voice in other languages, so that its highest poetic works are probably in Persian and Turkish rather than in the Arabic of the original Qur'anic recital, so too the mobility of its monotheism and its convergences with Biblical themes and moods have here allowed a deep and convincing inhabiting of the English language.[50] Conversely, the letter's semiticised syntax and rhetoric allowed a very smooth and natural translation of *ACW* into Arabic, which met with the approval of theologically meticulous but monoglot Arab signatories.

Likewise psalm-like is the document's incantatory or mantic adversions to the divine presence, in the context of a strong emphasis on the principle of love, presented as a very personal and passional interaction between God and His creatures. It is here that many Christians unfamiliar with Muslim doctrine professed themselves taken aback by *ACW*, feeling that love is a quintessentially Christian manner of describing the human–divine relation (the fact that the Psalms were written by Jews and not Christians does not seem to have deterred these critics!). Patriarch Alexy II of Moscow, however, noted what he took to be the distinctively Christian idiom of God's love for His human children,[51] an image apparently foreign to Islam, with its well-known mistrust of anthropomorphism. Again, as with the choice of a Jacobean English idiom, questions were being

---

[50] Some of the document's critics thought its language intrinsically un-Muslim, as though a Muslim document to Christians must always use the conventional idioms of Muslim homiletics, however difficult these might prove for Christian leaders unfamiliar with them. For a discussion see Markiewicz, *World Peace through Christian-Muslim Understanding*, p. 174.

[51] Alexy II, 'Response to the Open Letter of 138 Muslim theologians', in *ACW: 5-Year Anniversary Edition*, pp. 181–6, at p.182.

raised about the Islamic authenticity of *ACW*. The document presents the world's Muslim leadership speaking in a language familiar to Christians. But does the emphasis on love as the basis of its 'Two Commandments' make this a Christianised, unnatural recasting of Muslim priorities and categories?[52]

Prince Ghazi's writings after the publication of *ACW* tended to focus mainly on this question. Aware that the extreme evangelicals who gave their blessing to US foreign policy in Israel and Iraq (thereby straddling the weak Jordanian state) typically portrayed Islam as a religion of unbending law rather than of love, the prince published a very lengthy monograph entitled *Love in the Holy Qur'an*,[53] written with *ACW's* characteristic diction. He also sought to endow university chairs for the study of love in Christianity and Islam. The theological exercise proved quite straightforward: *al-Wadūd*, the Loving, is one of God's names in the Qur'an itself (Q 11:90; 85:14), and two even more abundantly present and salient divine names, *al-Raḥmān* and *al-Raḥīm*,[54] turn out to transcend their conventional English translations of 'Compassionate' and 'Merciful', thanks to an etymology rooted in the Arabic word *raḥim*, signifying a mother's womb. The idea of the divine regard for humanity as analogous to parental love is therefore entirely native to Islam, although the Hadith seem to prefer maternal resonances, rather than the Biblical idea of God's fatherhood.[55]

The debate over this point on occasion deteriorated into an unseemly competition over whether Christian conceptions of *agape* were in some sense superior (or inferior) to Muslim ideas about God's *raḥma*. It was clear, however, that both religions taught the prior nature of God's love,

---

[52] For the doubters, see Markiewicz, *World Peace through Christian-Muslim Understanding*, p. 174. Markiewicz indicates that chief among them on the Catholic side was the Jesuit Samir Khalil, who in order to make this case committed a number of errors: for Khalil, the concept of the neighbour is alien to the Qur'an, the principle of love is not one of the Qur'anic divine names, for Muslims to speak of the love of God is a 'novelty', etc.

[53] Ghazi bin Muhammad, *Love in the Holy Qur'an* (Chicago: Kazi, 2010).

[54] See Eric Ormsby, *Al-Ghazālī: Love, Longing, Intimacy and Contentment: Kitāb al-maḥabba wa'l-shawq wa'l-uns wa'l-riḍā: Book XXXVI of The Revival of the Religious Sciences, Iḥyā' 'ulūm al-dīn* (Cambridge: Islamic Texts Society, 2011), p. xii, for the observation that the root *r-ḥ-m* incorporates the conventional and personal sense of the English word 'love', while *w-d-d* denotes a principle which is 'sovereign and disinterested; it does not presuppose a recipient in need of mercy nor is it the result of any "empathy" on God's part'.

[55] For instance, the famous Hadith in which the Prophet says, 'God shall be more merciful (*arḥam*) to His servants than is this woman to her child'. Bukhārī, *Ṣaḥīḥ*, 'Adab', 18; Muslim, *Ṣaḥīḥ*, 'Tawba', 26.

with human love for God and others being consequent upon it; it was clear, also, that Islam, like Christianity, considered love to be the motive force of the cosmos and the defining and irreplaceable catalyst of virtue and the approach to God. The greatest medieval Muslim theologian, Abū Ḥāmid al-Ghazālī (d. 1111), had explored all this with great subtlety.[56] But so powerful and yet so elusive and affective a principle could hardly furnish the basis for an exact theological grading of the religions of the kind that some participants on both sides seemed to desire. For instance, how might one decide whether God's love is best expressed through the Son's sacrifice to the Father on the Cross on behalf of a humanity caught in the grip of original sin, or by a Divine strategy of forgiveness which is so grounded in love and compassion that it is able to forgive human beings directly, without any need for a cosmic sacrifice? Relatedly, does the principle of loving one's enemies mean that one should love them entirely, including their vices, which God does not love? Does one love even pharaoh and the devil?[57] Implicitly or explicitly such questions coloured much of the debate, notably at the 2008 Yale conference. The questions are also implicit in Prince Ghazi's post-*ACW* book on love, and in a monograph on Christian and Muslim understandings of love published by an influential *ACW* signatory, former Bosnian vice president Rusmir Mahmutćehajić.[58]

On such rocks the discussion often seems to have grounded. Christians and Muslims affirm that they love the same God, but is it the same love? How do their different understandings of the Divine nature shape their understanding of God's love for us, and our love for God and each other? In what way are the loves different, and what might this tell us about the respective faiths, or their ethical and social vision, or about how God is at

---

[56] Ghazālī, cited in Ormsby, *Al-Ghazālī, Love, Longing, Intimacy and Contentment*, p. 2; see Ormsby's summary: 'the love of God in its all-consuming ardour which he expounds and defends as the ultimate goal of every human endeavour' (pp. xii–xiii). This is echoed in Ghazi, *Love in the Holy Qur'an*, in the chapter entitled 'Love is the root of Creation' (pp. 21–30). For a comparative Muslim consideration of the issues, see for example Mahnaz Heydarpoor, *Love in Christianity and Islam: A Contribution to Religious Ethics* (London: New City, 2002), which demonstrates key similarities, including the two religions' belief that God's love for man is prior to and not conditional upon man's response to God.

[57] Ghazi, *Love in the Holy Qur'an*, pp. 37–53, provides a scriptural discussion of this, reaching the usual Muslim conclusion that although God's love is gratuitous and prior, some humans are loved more than others; this can be readily substantiated from Biblical texts also.

[58] Rusmir Mahmutćehajić, *On Love: In the Muslim Tradition* (Ashland, OH: Fordham University Press, 2007).

work in each? Moreover, as both are plurivocal traditions with evolving and conflicting theologies, can there in any case be a reification of either which allows any resolution of these comparative questions? This is perhaps one reason why the *ACW*'s dialogical entailments have seemed to falter whenever the discussion becomes competitive rather than respectfully inquisitive. The religions' positions are neither easily vulnerable nor uncontroversially epitomised. Is there, for instance, a single Christian doctrine of the Trinity, the Incarnation or the Atonement, to which Muslims might react? Nevertheless, Islam's ongoing challenge to *ACW*'s addressees represents a brave and uncommonly fruitful attempt to reify the two religions sufficiently to allow a believable conjunction of themes, demonstrating, at least to the satisfaction of most participants, that some words at least are recognisably held in common.

2

From Intra-Religious to Interreligious Dialogue

The Amman Message *as a Precursor and Companion to the* A Common Word *Initiative*

Jonathan Kearney

INTRODUCTION

Anybody who studies and writes about the contemporary Middle East will be aware that the rapidly changing situation there makes much of what we produce as scholars highly tentative and provisional – something true of all academic endeavours to some degree.[1] Particularly relevant to our present purpose are the increased propaganda, visibility and activity of the self-styled 'Islamic State' in Syria and Iraq and its declaration of a caliphate (29 June 2014) under the rule of the so-called Caliph Ibrahim (Abu Bakr al-Baghdadi, born 1971). One is keenly aware, of course, that this represents far more than an inconvenience for academics who may need to revise their theories and their work. Far more important are the very real suffering of the people of these beautiful lands and horribly unnecessary loss of life on a massive scale. However, while there may be a temptation to allow these tragic events to dishearten us and discourage us from our work, if anything, the reality of the horrific and chaotic situation makes endeavours such as the *Amman Message* and the *A Common Word* declaration all the more important, if not absolutely

---

[1] The official website of the *Amman Message* has itself changed since its first appearance. The changes to the website are not insignificant, and will be referred to within the text of this chapter. Those wishing to access the text of the *AM* used as the basis of this chapter can do so using the Internet Archive 'Wayback Machine': https://archive.org/web/. The official website of the *AM* as it was on 31 December 2015 can be found at https://web.archive.org/web/20151231202232/http://ammanmessage.com/. Importantly for this chapter, this version of the website shows how visitors can use links to access the texts of the 'Fatwas of the 'Ulama' discussed below.

imperative. This chapter is dedicated in all humility to the memory of all those innocents – of every religion and none – who have lost their lives in the present conflict.

In one of their responses to some 'frequently asked questions' about the *ACW* initiative, Prince Ghazi bin Muhammad of Jordan and Aref Nayed mention how 'the momentum for [*ACW*] started with the Amman Message'.[2] Another question in the same place asks – somewhat disingenuously, one suspects – 'Should you [that is, Muslims] not fix your own problems first and stop your infighting before you address others?' Again, the respondents cite the *Amman Message* as constituting such a 'basis of inner healing and reconciliation', and quite rightly point out that the two processes (speaking among ourselves and speaking to others – *intra-religious* and *interreligious* dialogue) are by no means mutually exclusive.[3] In both of these answers, Prince Ghazi and Professor Nayed clearly acknowledge that fruitful *interreligious* dialogue is contingent on an active and coherent *intra-religious* dialogue. The *Amman Message* (*AM*) is an extremely significant example of an attempt to engender and foster such an *intra-religious* dialogue.[4]

This chapter offers a brief introduction to the *AM* not just as a necessary precursor and companion to *ACW*, but also as a valuable tool for non-Muslim engagement with and understanding of Islam and Muslims. In this latter regard, the *AM* shares *ACW*'s goals of fostering interreligious understanding and dialogue. More specifically, the *AM* offers non-Muslim readers an insight into the workings of Islam as a religious *system*; the opportunity to experience the very real diversity of contemporary Islam through encounter with authentic Muslim voices, thereby countering the monolithic orientalist constructions of Islam (unfortunately still present in a range of sources, popular and otherwise); and a window onto one of the most central questions in contemporary Islam, that of religious authority. Following a brief outline of the *AM* and its contexts, some tentative evaluations of the *AM* and its impact – both actual and potential – are offered, as well as some observations on its vital importance to *ACW*.

---

[2] Ghazi bin Muhammad and Aref Nayed, 'Frequently asked questions that Muslims have been asked about "A Common Word"', in Miroslav Volf, Ghazi bin Muhammad and Melissa Yarrington (eds.), *A Common Word: Muslims and Christians on Loving God and Neighbor* (Grand Rapids, MI: Eerdmans, 2010), p. 173.

[3] Ibid., p. 175.

[4] All references to the *AM* are based on *The Amman Message* (Amman: Royal Aal Al-Bayt Institute for Islamic Thought, 2008).

THE *AMMAN MESSAGE* AND ITS EVOLUTION

The public proclamation of the *AM* began with the reading of a statement on *Laylat al-Qadr* (27 Ramaḍān 1425/9 November 2004) in the Hashemite Mosque in Amman in the presence of King Abdullah II, the main force behind the initiative. This statement – which will be referred to as the *original Amman Message* – in its own words, 'sought to declare what Islam is and what it is not, and what actions represent it and what actions do not. Its goal was to clarify to the modern world the true nature of Islam and the nature of true Islam',[5] itself later summarised as 'a message of devotion to God, love of the neighbor, goodwill, moderation and peace'.[6] The text stressed 'equanimity, balance, moderation, and facilitation' as foundational values of Islam.[7] The *AM* is firmly rooted in the Islamic scripture: some twenty-one explicit quotations from the Qur'an are given in support of its assertions. Prince Ghazi bin Muhammad (cousin of King Abdullah, who has played a major role in the formation and dissemination of the *AM*) summarises its content in the following way: 'It thus constitutes a definitive demarcation of true Islam in all its forms, and an authoritative identification – if not a definition – of orthodoxy in Islam.'[8]

Since that first proclamation in November 2004, the *AM* has expanded to become a composite, evolving and virtual text based on three core statements – the so-called 'Three Points of the Amman Message'. The *AM* is supported by an extensive and lavish publishing operation and web presence, and in 2007 a research body, the Royal Islamic Strategic Studies Centre, was established to promote it. The first point of the centre's charter usefully defines its function, using a designation for the vision of Islam which the *AM* seeks to articulate: 'The primary goal of The Royal Islamic Strategic Studies Centre [...] is to protect, preserve and propagate traditional, orthodox, "moderate" Islam as defined by the international Islamic Consensus on the "Three Points of the Amman Message" arrived at over the years 2005–2006.'[9]

The expansion of the *original AM* began when King Abdullah sent three questions to twenty-four leading *'ulamā'* (religious scholars) 'in

---

[5] *AM*, p. v.

[6] Ibid., p. 84.

[7] Ibid., p. 9.

[8] Ghazi bin Muhammad, 'Introduction', in Ghazi bin Muhammad (ed.), *True Islam and the Islamic Consensus on the Amman Message* (Amman: Royal Aal Al-Bayt Institute for Islamic Thought, 2006), p. 1.

[9] http://rissc.jo/about-rissc/. Accessed 18 July 2016.

order to give this statement [that is, the *original AM*] more religious authority'.[10] The answers to these three questions, which, with one exception, are presented as fatwas (juridical opinions issued by muftis in response to a question posed by a Muslim), were originally accessible through the *AM* website; however, subsequently, this section of the website has been removed.[11] This recourse to the traditional scholarly religious authorities of Islam – the *'ulamā'* – is in keeping with the words of the *original AM*: 'Hope lies in the scholars of our nation.'[12] The choice of the original twenty-four scholars aimed to be both inclusive and influential: ten fatwas from Sunni scholars; ten from Twelver (or Ja'farī) Shī'ī scholars; two from Zaydī Shī'ī scholars; one from an 'Ibāḍī scholar; and a letter (clearly presented as not constituting a fatwa) from the Agha Khan, imam of the Ismā'īlī Shī'a. The questions posed were the following: (1) Who is a Muslim? (2) Is *takfīr* permitted? That is, is it permissible for one Muslim to declare another Muslim an unbeliever (*kāfir*)? and (3) Who has the right to issue a fatwa?

King Abdullah then convened a conference in July 2005 in Amman, where, the so-called 'Three Points of the Amman Message' based on the fatwas of the *'ulamā'*, were formulated and then endorsed by some 201 scholars and political leaders.[13] These 'Three Points' were further endorsed at a number of subsequent conferences.[14] The website of the *AM* also invited (and continues to invite) the visitor personally to endorse it, thereby offering virtual readers a level of agency in the construction of an Islamic consensus (*ijmā'* – on which term and its implications, more later) on these key issues. In summary, then, the *AM*, in its most readily accessible form, consists of four key elements: (1) the *original AM* – the

---

[10] *AM*, p. v.

[11] At the time of writing, the *AM* website informs those who access it of the existence of fatwas in the section 'Grand List of Endorsements' by writing the word *fatwa* in italics after the name of the endorsing scholar: links to the fatwas themselves are no longer provided. See http://ammanmessage.com/grand-list-of-endorsements-of-the-amman-message-and-its-three-points/. Accessed 18 July 2016. According to the website of the *AM*, the fatwas (up to 2007) have been summarised and described in Ghazi bin Muhammad (ed.), *True Islam*. See http://ammanmessage.com/true-islam-and-the-islamic-consensus-on-the-amman-message/. Accessed 18 July 2016.

[12] *AM*, p. 14.

[13] 'True Islam and its role in modern society', Amman, Jordan, 27–9 Jumāda I 1426/4–6 July 2005.

[14] For a list of the eight conferences held between July 2005 and July 2006, and the 501 signatories to the 'Three Points of the *Amman Message*', see *AM*, pp. 23–4. The Three Points exist in two versions: Version 1, also known as the official version (*AM*, pp. 16–18), and Version 2 (*AM*, pp. 18–21).

statement from November 2004; (2) the so-called 'Three Points of the Amman Message' in two versions (there are minimal differences between the two);[15] (3) the 'Grand List' of 552 signatories; and (4) the fatwas of the *'ulamā'*.

THE 'THREE POINTS' OF THE *AMMAN MESSAGE*

The first of the 'Three Points' addresses the first two (very closely related) questions that were circulated to the *'ulamā'*, namely, (1) *Who is a Muslim?* and (2) *Is takfīr permitted?* The First Point declares that a Muslim is an adherent of any one of eight listed *madhāhib* (singular: *madhhab*; schools of Islamic jurisprudence) of Sunni, Shī'a and 'Ibāḍī Islam, of those who subscribe to the Ash'arī Creed, those who practise what the text describes as 'real' Sufism, or those who subscribe to – again in the words of the text itself – 'real' Salafī thought. The First Point continues by stating that it is both 'impossible and impermissible' to declare such a Muslim as a *kāfir*. The first point then moves from the individual to the collective level by declaring that the *takfīr* of any group of Muslims which 'does not deny any necessarily self-evident tenet of religion' is likewise 'impossible and impermissible'.[16]

The Second Point addresses the issue of diversity within Islam, noting that the *'ulamā'* of the various *madhāhib* are unanimous in their agreement on the fundamentals of Islam (the *uṣūl*), here expressed in terms of the *Five Pillars of Islam* and the *Six Articles of Īmān* as described in the *Ḥadīth of Jibrīl*.[17] Where differences among the *madhāhib* do exist, these are to be found in what are identified as the 'ancillary branches of religion' (the *furū'*). The unity of all Muslims is also stressed: 'There exists more in common between the various schools of Islamic jurisprudence than there is difference between them.'[18] Diversity of opinion among the scholars in these matters (within a larger, commonly agreed fundamental framework) is to be viewed positively, not as something inherently negative; indeed it is described as 'a mercy'.[19]

---

[15] The two versions of the 'Three Points' can be readily compared: Version 1 (*AM*, pp. 16–18), Version 2 (*AM*, pp. 19–21).

[16] *AM*, pp. 16–17.

[17] For a translation of this key text, see Sachiko Murata and William C. Chittick, *The Vision of Islam* (London: I. B. Tauris, 2006), pp. 8–27.

[18] *AM*, p. 17.

[19] Ibid., pp. 17–18. The text of Version 1 of the Three Points adds: 'Long ago it was said that variance in opinion among the *'ulamā'* (scholars) "is a good affair"' (*AM*, p. 18),

The Third Point addresses the third question circulated to the *'ulamā'*: (3) *Who has the right to issue fatwas?* Perhaps unsurprisingly, given its provenance, it affirms that only those scholars who are deemed qualified according to the traditional requirements and norms of the established legal schools may issue a fatwa. Also, the fatwa must be issued in accordance with the established methodologies of the *madhhab*.

THE GRAND LIST (AM, PP. 23–81)

The 'Three Points' are followed by what is described as the 'Grand List', which presents the names of the 'religious and political leaders who have endorsed the Amman Message and its Three Points'.[20] The fifty-eight-page list contains a total of 552 names and organisational affiliations (or political functions) of those Muslims from eighty-four countries who signed the 'Three Points'. This list of names is keyed to a list of the eight conferences where the *AM* was endorsed.

THE FATWAS OF THE 'ULAMĀ'

The fatwas of the *'ulamā'* are presented by the *AM* website as both an endorsement of the *original AM* and an integral part of the evolving *AM*. We might refer to them as the 'empowering instruments' of the evolving document. The fatwas (and one letter) were listed in five groups: Sunnī, Ja'farī Shī'ī, Zaydī Shī'ī, 'Ibāḍī and Ismā'īlī Shī'ī.[21] Visitors to the *AM* website could click on the name of the issuing mufti, which was linked to the text of his fatwa. The fatwas varied in length from one page to twenty-six, the average length being five pages. The fatwas were reproduced in their original languages: twenty-one in Arabic alone, two in both Arabic and Persian, and one in English. Unfortunately, no translations of these into English (the main language of the initiative) were provided on the website. This deprived the non-Arabic- and non-Persian-speaking reader of the opportunity to explore the subtlety and sophistication of these texts, and – as we will mention later – leaves room for potentially damaging ambiguities and misunderstandings. The fact that even the texts

---

while Version 2 states: 'Long ago it was said that variance in opinion among the *'ulamā'* (scholars) "is a mercy"' (*AM*, p. 21).

[20] *AM*, p. 23.

[21] As previously noted, the letter of endorsement from Shāh Karīm al-Ḥusaynī, Āghā Khān IV, Imam of the Ismā'īlī Shī'a, was not presented as a fatwa.

of fatwas (in *any* language) are no longer accessible via the website is a cause of further concern.[22]

ENDORSEMENT OF THE READER

Finally, the *AM* website invites visitors themselves to 'fully endorse the Amman Message and its "Three Points"'. In so doing, they can actively participate in and consolidate the consensus that the *AM* seeks to articulate and engender. On 31 December 2015, some 69,585 people had 'endorsed' the *AM* online since 1 March 2007, an average of 150 people per week. However, data on the numbers of those who have endorsed the *AM* no longer appear on the website.[23]

CONTEXTS OF THE *AMMAN MESSAGE*

In order to appreciate the *AM* and its goals fully, it is necessary to address briefly the context in which it emerged. Although the years that have passed since its first proclamation do not constitute an especially long period, the many momentous events have since taken place in the Muslim-majority countries of South-West Asia and North Africa have transformed the region dramatically. As noted previously, anybody writing about this region knows how quickly what one writes may become out-of-date. The *AM* – just like *ACW* – if it wishes to succeed needs to adjust to these new, and indeed ever-changing, circumstances. In this regard the web presence is especially helpful as it allows the documents to evolve in accordance with changing circumstances.

But to return to the original context: the *AM* identifies its immediate temporal context as 'this difficult juncture' in the history of the Umma.[24] The causes of these difficult circumstances are identified as being both external and internal in origin: 'Today the magnanimous message of Islam faces a vicious attack from those who through distortion and fabrication

---

[22] As noted in footnote 1, the official website of the *AM* has changed and no longer includes links to the fatwas of the twenty-four leading scholars. At the time of writing (18 July 2016), the *AM* website informs those who access it of the existence of a fatwa from a particular scholar in the section 'Grand List of Endorsements' by writing the word *fatwa* in italics after the name of the endorsing scholar; links to the fatwas themselves are no longer provided. See http://ammanmessage.com/grand-list-of-endorsements-of-the-amman-message-and-its-three-points/. Accessed 18 July 2016.

[23] See Internet Archive: https://web.archive.org/web/20151231202232/http://ammanmessage.com/. Accessed 5 July 2016.

[24] *AM*, p. 3.

try to portray Islam as an enemy to them. It is also under attack from some who claim affiliation with Islam and commit irresponsible acts in its name.'[25] The central issue here is the representation – or rather the *misrepresentation* – of Islam, from whatever quarter: hostile outsiders or self-styled insiders. In the eyes of the framers of the *AM*, this two-fold misrepresentation requires correction. Writing in 2006, Prince Ghazi noted that 'unfortunately Islam is today the most misunderstood, most misrepresented and consequently most vilified religion in the world'.[26]

The Third Point of the *AM* – the attempt to regulate the issuing of fatwas – could in some sense be seen as speaking to the heart of the matter: the question of the locus of religious authority in Islam. While the traditional religious authorities of Islam have always faced challenges from dissenting voices, the information technology revolution that has swept (and continues to sweep) the world has provided once-marginal voices (with limited local traction) with a potentially global audience. The World Wide Web has, like the printing press before it, radically democratised access to information. A cheap handheld computer enables anybody who so wishes easily to access the authoritative texts of Islam: the Qur'an and the Hadith in addition to a wide range of translations of and commentaries on these texts. Access to and engagement with these texts are now virtually unlimited and no longer need to take place in the trad-itional context of a formal Islamic education, with its long-established systems of self-regulation and licensing: one can now discuss questions of *Fiqh* (Islamic jurisprudence) and *'Aqīda* (creed) in open and largely unregulated virtual spaces. It is also possible for those with no formal training in the Islamic sciences or affiliation with established institutions to set themselves up as 'cyber muftis', issuing fatwas of the kind that the *AM* describes as 'ignorant and illegitimate'.[27]

Closely related to the issue of religious authority is the question of *takfīr* – the activity that the First Point of the *AM* sought effectively to prohibit. *Takfīr* is one of the chief juridical/theological tools employed by a range of groups that claim the legitimate right to use violence in the furtherance of their particular interpretations of Islam. Once *takfīr* is pronounced on an individual or group, that individual or group loses the inviolability due to their blood, honour and property as Muslims, to use the terminology of the Sunna echoed in the *AM*. Historically *takfīr* has

[25] Ibid., p. 4.
[26] Ghazi bin Muhammad, 'Introduction', in *True Islam*, p. 1.
[27] *AM*, p. vi.

been very rarely used, the Khawārij of the early Islamic centuries being among its best-known early proponents.[28] Pronouncing *takfīr* was something that engendered *fitna* (or schism) in the Umma, something to be avoided at all costs. King Abdullah makes reference to such groups when he summarises the aims of the *AM* thus: 'The ultimate goal is to take back our religion from the vocal, violent, and ignorant extremists who have tried to hijack Islam over the last hundred years.'[29]

The *AM* could be seen as an attempt by the magisterial, traditional scholarly elite of Islam to reassert its religious authority at a time when this authority is being questioned in an unprecedented manner and in some cases completely rejected. The reasons behind the need for such a reassertion of authority are complex, contested and ultimately beyond the scope of this chapter. However, one could point to a *perception* that some members of this traditional scholarly elite appear to have allied themselves with a political order that has not spoken to the wishes, needs and aspirations of most Muslims, particularly in Muslim-majority countries. The so-called Arab Spring, the civil war in Syria and their continuing repercussions only serve to highlight further the complexity of these issues.

Although no direct mention is made of the 11 September 2001 attacks on the United States of America, these events and the reactions to them – including the United States–led invasions of Afghanistan and Iraq and the various forms of resistance they engendered – form an immediate background to the *AM*. Those who carried out the 11 September attacks claimed their actions were a direct result of their 'authentic' interpretation of or adherence to Islam. Many non-Muslims took this claim at face value and came to believe that there was something inherently hostile, violent or threatening about Islam. Of course, for the majority of the world's more than 1.5 billion Muslims these particular acts of terror represented a perversion of *their* Islam, a supremely damaging act of *misrepresentation*. Is there a possible danger – however small – that if the *AM* is seen as any kind of response to the attacks of 11 September that it is seen to be endowing those attacks with a signification they neither have nor deserve? Namely, that the attacks and their perpetrators in some way represent Islam and Muslims – thus inadvertently feeding into the

---

[28] For a short introduction to the Khārijites and their ideas, see Giorgio Levi Della Vida, 'Khāridjites' in E. van Donzel et al. (eds.), *Encyclopedia of Islam II* (Leiden: Brill, 1997), vol. 4, pp. 1074–7.

[29] King Abdullah II, 'Traditional Islam: The path to peace', address delivered to the Catholic University of America, Columbus School of Law, on 13 September 2005.

pernicious misconception that Muslims are collectively responsible for these or any other violent acts carried out by those claiming to be acting in the name of Islam?

The Hashemite context of the *AM* is not without significance. The document itself speaks of the 'inherited spiritual and historical responsibility carried by the Hashemite monarchy, honoured as direct descendants of the Prophet [Muḥammad], the Messenger of God – peace and blessings upon him – who carried the message'.[30] King Abdullah's ancestors held the office of Sharīf of Mecca for more than a thousand years. His great-great-grandfather, Sharīf Hussein bin Ali, declared himself King of the Arab Lands in 1916 and led the Arab Revolt against Ottoman rule. Sharīf Hussein also briefly claimed the title of Khalīfa (caliph) in 1924 following the abolition of the office by the Turkish Republic. Both the sharifate and Hussein's claim to the caliphate ended after the expulsion of the Hashemites from the Hijaz by the conquering Saʿūd family in 1925.[31] King Abdullah's father, King Hussein II bin Talal (1935–99), ruled the Hashemite Kingdom of Jordan for forty-seven years (1952–99), a remarkable period in any context, but especially so when one considers the turbulence of those years in the region. King Abdullah succeeded his father in 1999 aged thirty-seven. Issued just five years into the young king's reign, the *AM* could be seen as an ambitious attempt to establish (or re-establish) both local and global authority and influence for the Hashemites.

ANALYSIS

At the beginning of this chapter we noted that engaging with the *AM* can be an enriching experience for non-Muslims. Non-Muslim readers can learn much about Islam from a range of diverse, authentic and

[30] *AM*, p. 4.

[31] The Saʿūd family have their origins in the Najd region in the centre of the Arabian Peninsula. Their rise to political ascendancy in Arabia was accompanied by their alliance with the revivalist scholar and preacher Muḥammad ibn ʿAbd al-Wahhāb (1703–92). Ibn ʿAbd al-Wahhāb's interpretation of Islam has come to be the de facto official form of Islam in the Kingdom of Saudi Arabia. The term 'Wahhābī', though commonly used by outsiders, is not favoured by insiders, who prefer to refer to themselves as Muwaḥḥidūn (proponents of unity, '*tawḥīd*'). For a brief discussion of the rise of the Saʿūd family, see Madawi Al-Rasheed, *A History of Saudi Arabia* (Cambridge: Cambridge University Press, 2002), pp. 14–38. For an anthropological discussion of the contrast between Ḥijāzī and Najdī culture, see Mai Yamani, *The Cradle of Islam: The Hijaz and the Quest for an Arabian Identity* (London: I. B. Tauris, 2004).

authoritative Muslim voices represented in the *AM*. Indeed, the *AM* could be seen as an ideal introduction to Islam. Anybody wishing to engage with *ACW* (and dialogue with Muslims) needs some knowledge of what Islam actually is: the *AM* offers an ideal entry point for such a journey. Encountering the diversity of Muslim voices in the *AM* will also help counter the (unfortunately) still-widespread orientalist (and, all too frequently, plainly Islamophobic) constructions and misrepresentations of Muslims as an undifferentiated mass and Islam as a stagnant and stultified monolith. The *AM*, with its attempt to formulate and articulate a universal consensus among Muslims on the key issues described earlier, also shows how Islam has traditionally operated as a religious system: that is, with *ijmā'* (consensus) as a central theme. The fatwas (if made readily available in translation) will also allow non-Muslim readers to see the highly sophisticated nature of the traditional Islamic sciences in action. We have also mentioned how the *AM* offers non-Muslim readers a window onto one of the most central questions among contemporary Muslims: the location and nature of religious authority and the related issue of the use of *takfīr* as a tool to justify the violent pursuit of political acts in the name of Islam. But the utility of the *AM* in this regard should not cause us to neglect its principal aim – to defend Islam and Muslims from misrepresentation, hostile attacks and disunity – or *fitna*. This is, without doubt, a noble aim and a service to all people, as the continuous tradition of Islamic learning is one of the great intellectual achievements of humanity.

However, before concluding, it is important to point to a few potentially problematic issues with the *AM* – issues that may also be problematic in terms of *ACW*. As mentioned in the introduction to this chapter, *ACW* presents itself as a document that builds upon the consensus created by the *AM*. The two initiatives and the resulting documents are inextricably linked. For instance, the most recent edition of *ACW* makes a total of ten references to the *AM*, most of them in connection with its vital role as a precursor to *ACW* in terms of both content and methodology.[32] A good example is provided by Lumbard:

To understand the genesis of ACW, it is thus important that one take into account the accomplishments of the Amman Message [...]. On the one hand, the lead-up

---

[32] *A Common Word Between Us and You: 5-Year Anniversary Edition* (Amman: Royal Aal Al-Bayt Institute for Islamic Thought, 2012), p. 17 (three times), p. 18 (twice), p. 19 (twice), pp. 254, 256 and 257. (Unless otherwise indicated, throughout this chapter all references to *ACW* are taken from this edition.)

to the Amman Message established the mechanisms by which consensus could be reached among Muslim scholars of all branches. And on the other hand, the final declaration of the Amman Message answers one of the main objections that many have had to ACW, those who claim that Muslims need to denounce extremism before there can be true dialogue.[33]

First there is the question of the fatwas of the scholars, which are presented as being both an endorsement and an integral part of the *AM*. However, the reality is somewhat more complex and nuanced. Of the twenty-four scholars from whom fatwas were sought, ten of these did not attend any of the conferences or meetings listed in the 'Grand List' – they only provided fatwas.[34] While their fatwas may certainly have formed the basis for the formulation of the Three Points, and while physical attendance at a conference should not be a prerequisite of full endorsement, it could be seen as a little misleading to list them as 'fully endorsing' the *AM*, particularly in light of the contested nature of the 'endorsement' of Mufti Muhammad Taqi Usmani, on which see later discussion.

In the same way, the figure of a little less than seventy thousand online endorsers mentioned previously could be critiqued. What exactly does such an endorsement mean? Anybody familiar with the World Wide Web will know the ease with which people can present themselves and their opinions online in a way that may not reflect their opinions beyond the virtual world of the Internet. If endorsement of the *AM* simply entails clicking a mouse, is such an endorsement particularly valuable? One must ask what exactly such an endorsement *means*, what its implications are on the ground. In terms of bare statistics, 70,000 represents less than 0.005 per cent (0.004458 per cent) of the world's approximately 1.57 billion Muslims. This does not constitute – thus far – a particularly broad reach of the *AM*.

As noted previously, the fatwas, which varied greatly in both their length and their content, though once accessible in their original Arabic (and Persian) on the website, are not made available in translation. For those unable to read Arabic (or Persian), their content, which is often very subtle and nuanced, is, unfortunately, inaccessible. One small illustrative example is the fatwa of Shaykh Mufti Muhammad Taqi Usmani (of Darul Uloom in Karachi, an institution associated with the Deobandi

---

[33] Joseph Lumbard, 'The uncommonality of "A Common Word"', in *ACW: 5-Year Anniversary Edition*, pp. 11–50, at p. 17.

[34] Notable *marāji'* of the Iraqi and Iranian Shi'a (Grand Ayatollahs Sistani, al-Fayad, al-Hakim, al-Bashir and Sadr, Khamene'i and Lankarani) are among these.

revivalist tendency). The *AM* website notes that the shaykh both provided a fatwa, and attended two conferences at which he endorsed the *AM*. In his response to the first question, 'Who is a Muslim?', having offered a definition of Islam drawn from the fourteenth-century Persian scholar Sa'd al-Dīn al-Taftāzānī (d. 1390), Shaykh Usmani notes that there are three types of *madhāhib* that claim to be part of Islam. The first of these, in which he explicitly mentions two groups, 'Qādiyānīs' (members of the Ahmadiya Muslim Community) and the 'Alawites, he describes as non-Muslims, and declares that pronouncing *takfīr* upon them is necessary.[35] However, a number of today's 'Alawites (known formerly as Nuṣayrīs, and best known these days as the group to which the ruling Asad family of Syria belong) consider themselves to be Shī'ī Muslims and claim adherence to the Ja'farī *madhhab*; indeed, they have fatwas from the Shī'ī *'ulamā'* in support of that position.[36] Clearly there is a tension here between such claims and the position of Shaykh Usmani.[37] Where such tensions exist, how are they to be resolved? Can the *AM* claim to constitute a universal consensus in such circumstances? Are the fatwas too broad to cohere?

Regarding the involvement of Shaykh Usmani, one should also note that a number of Sunni websites contain discussions as to whether he has actually endorsed the *AM*, as the website and book claim he has.[38] Indeed Shaykh Usmani himself claims not to have endorsed the *AM*: 'I am not a signatory of the Amman message.'[39] While Shaykh Usmani is but one

[35] The 'Alawites discussed here are not to be confused with the Kurdish and Turkish Alevis, a distinct group despite the similarity of their names. On the Alevis, see Markus Dressler, 'Alevis' in G. Krämer et al. (eds.), *Encyclopedia of Islam III* (Leiden: Brill, 2009), vol. 1, pp. 93–121.

[36] Probably one of the best known of these fatwas is that issued by the leading Shī'ī Lebanese scholar and leader Musa al-Sadr (1928–78?), on which see Fouad Ajami, *The Vanished Imam: Musa al-Sadr and the Shia of Lebanon* (Ithaca, NY: Cornell University Press, 1986), p. 174. Meir M. Bar-Asher identifies 'two distinct trends' among the contemporary 'Alawites of Syria, one rural and conservative in terms of its distinct identity, the other urban, assimilationist and Shia-identifying; 'Nusayris' in Josef M. Meri (ed.), *Medieval Islamic Civilization: An Encyclopedia* (Abingdon: Routledge, 2006), vol. 2, p. 570. The issue of the relationship between the 'Alawites and Twelver Shi'ism is also addressed by Aron Friedman in one of the most recent, most comprehensive surveys of the group: *The Nuṣayrī-'Alawīs: An Introduction to the Religion, History and Identity of the Leading Minority in Syria* (Leiden: Brill, 2010), pp. 235–8.

[37] https://web.archive.org/web/20131203004020/http://ammanmessage.com/index.php?option=com_content&task=view&id=72&Itemid=42. Accessed 24 October 2016.

[38] See for example: https://insideismailism.wordpress.com/2016/09/25/decoding-the-amman-message/ (specifically section 3.4). Accessed 24 October 2016.

[39] www.askimam.org/public/question_detail/15072. Accessed 3 November 2016. See also www.askimam.org/public/question_detail/15064.

voice, his is an extremely important and influential one.[40] And though this issue as to whether Shaykh Usmani 'fully endorses' the *AM* might be seen as a minor one, the possible ambiguity is a cause for concern in that it has the potential to weaken the allegedly 'unanimous religious and political consensus' that the *AM* aimed to achieve.[41]

Another issue is that of the term *consensus*, one of the most frequently used terms in the *AM* and its associated literature. However, in the context of Islam the word *consensus* has a far greater force than the rather overused, fuzzy and somewhat anodyne English-language term. In *Fiqh* (or Islamic jurisprudence), consensus (in Arabic: *ijmāʿ*) is a technical term, denoting one of the two secondary sources of Islamic law, the two primary sources being the Qur'an and the Hadith. However, the exact nature of what constitutes *ijmāʿ* is not universally understood or agreed upon. The *AM* speaks of itself as amounting to 'a historical, universal and unanimous religious and political consensus (*ijmāʿ*) of the *Ummah* (nation) of Islam in our day, and a consolidation of traditional, orthodox Islam'.[42] Although the *AM* is certainly momentous, this last point might be seen by some as wishful thinking rather than a reflection of reality.

One might also point to the use of the adjective *real* to modify both Sufism and Salafism in the First Point as potentially problematic. Again, the question of authority arises: who is to decide what constitutes 'real' Sufism or 'real' Salafism? Clearly, these are highly subjective and malleable terms the use of which implies interpretative judgements. While the framers of the *AM* may have had particular criteria in mind for distinguishing between the 'real' and the inauthentic (such as those of Ghazzālian Sufism), these criteria are nowhere articulated in the *AM*. Even if clear criteria for determining the 'real' were explicitly mentioned, the highly contested nature of what constitutes the 'real' form of anything would remain problematic.[43]

Another (and quite possibly the most serious) problem with the *AM* is a methodological one. Those who are disenchanted with and alienated

---

[40] Shaykh Usmani is listed as the world's nineteenth most influential Muslim in the *Muslim 500*, another supporting document of both the *AM* and *ACW*, and is referred to as 'the intellectual leader of the Deobandi movement'. See S. Abdallah Schleifer (ed.), *The Muslim 500: The World's 500 Most Influential Muslims, 2014–2015* (Amman: Royal Islamic Strategic Studies Centre, 2014), pp. 70–1.

[41] *AM*, p. vii.

[42] Ibid.

[43] That said, the polyvalent and open nature of the word 'real' might be seen by some as a strength of the document.

from the traditional, magisterial scholarly elite of Islam (the *'ulamā'*) – for whatever reasons – are unlikely to pay much heed when that same traditional scholarly elite seeks to reassert its claims to exclusive religious authority. In this sense, the *AM* may be said to be preaching to the converted, those already *within*; but if those alienated from tradition, the *madhāhib* and the *'ulamā'* are to be reached and convinced, other, less traditional means need to be sought. Other, non-religious factors need also to be addressed. People embrace *takfīrī* ideologies for a wide range of complex reasons (many of them social, political and economic), not necessarily religious ones – if indeed it is ever possible to isolate the purely *religious*. While the problems presented by *takfīrī* ideologies most certainly require sophisticated Islamic theological and jurisprudential responses, especially given that the *takfīrīs* use religious texts to justify their beliefs and actions, it is vital that social and political responses accompany the religious responses.

A final point is the association of the initiative with vested political interests. Despite the Hashemites' claim to historical and spiritual responsibility (they are part of the political establishment of the Muslim-majority Arabic-speaking Middle East – the old order, despite their new young king), they are also regarded by the United States as 'key allies' in the region, not something that will endear them to many of those to whom the document aims to speak. In this regard, there may be a danger that some would cynically perceive the *AM* as an attempt to foster a more Western-friendly Islam and an Umma more compliant to neo-liberal or neo-colonial Western ambitions in the region. We might also note in this regard that the *AM* speaks of itself as having been unanimously endorsed by 'over 500 leading Muslim scholars worldwide'.[44] However, a number of these figures are politicians and diplomats rather than scholars. Former President Hosni Mubarak of Egypt is one such politician. Overthrown by a popular revolution in 2011, Mubarak, who had ruled since 1981, came to represent the undemocratic, unelected dinosaur dictators of the Middle East. Given his widespread unpopularity and subsequent overthrow, Mubarak's endorsement of the *AM* may be seen as a liability rather than a benefit. In a similar vein, the 2013/2014 edition of *The Muslim 500: The 500 Most Influential Muslims in the World* contains an introduction by Professor S. Abdallah Schleifer that surveys developments in the Muslim world in 2013.[45] This introduction is characterised by a

[44] *AM*, p. vii.
[45] S. Abdallah Schleifer (ed.), *The Muslim 500: The World's 500 Most Influential Muslims, 2013/2014* (Amman: Royal Islamic Strategic Studies Centre, 2013), pp. 8–17.

strong anti–Muslim Brotherhood tone, and appears in places to be an apology for the military coup in Egypt.[46] One might also mention the fact that the *Muslim 500* lists King Abdullah II of Jordan as the world's fourth most influential Muslim.[47]

A final point to be made is the reliance of the *AM* (and much of its later associated literature) on the enigmatic Vincenzo Oliveti's analysis of what he identifies as 'Jihadi-Takfiri-Salafism' in his rather sensationally titled work *Terror's Source: The Ideology of Wahhabi-Salafism and Its Consequences.*[48] Oliveti is described thus in the book: 'Professor Vincenzo Oliveti is considered one of Europe's leading experts on the Arabic language and on Islamic Studies.'[49] However, Oliveti has so far escaped closer identification. He does not appear to be associated with any university or research institute. In *Terror's Source*, Oliveti presents a step-by-step explanation of the source of 'Islamic terrorism' – namely,

---

[46] For a particularly powerful example of this anti–Muslim Brotherhood tone, see Schleifer, *The Muslim 500, 2013/2014*, p. 14: 'What the [Muslim Brotherhood] spokesmen said fit into one of the journalists['] own narratives; that whoever is elected in a free and fair democratic election is a democrat – as if a free and fair election could turn the member of a religious authoritarian movement into a democrat – and whoever staged a coup d'etat against the winner of a democratic election was by definition an enemy of democracy. Of course, if anyone could have persuaded the armed forces in Germany to stage a coup d'etat after Hitler and his National Socialist Party (Nazi) won the 1933 free and democratic elections, the world would have been spared many million dead. As was the case, it took Hitler less than six months in power to destroy democracy.' Schleifer's argument here, while not devoid of validity, is expressed in a rather heavy-handed fashion. The implicit comparison of the Muslim Brotherhood to the Nazis is unlikely to do anything but alienate those even vaguely sympathetic to that organisation. The partisan tone of Schleifer's introduction is not, one fears, something that will aid the building of bridges and the formulation of a consensus. One should also note that Dr Mohamed Morsi, Egypt's first democratically elected head of state, having been deposed by a coup d'état, has been sentenced to death by an Egyptian court, allegedly for his 2011 escape from the Wadi el-Natroun prison. The death sentence, which was handed down on 16 May 2015, was endorsed by Egypt's Grand Mufti, Shawqī Ibrāhīm 'Allām (appointed 2013).

[47] Schleifer, *The Muslim 500, 2013–2014*, pp. 40–1.

[48] Vincenzo Oliveti, *Terror's Source: The Ideology of Wahhabi-Salafism and Its Consequences* (Birmingham: Amadeus, 2001). Oliveti offers a succinct presentation of his book and its purpose: 'This book *identifies* the ideological source of terrorism emanating from the Islamic World; *differentiates* between it and traditional "orthodox" Islam; *examines* in detail all its tenets and doctrines; *explains* how it has spread and how it is gaining ground; *warns* of the dangers of its continued growth; and finally, *prescribes* how to combat and defeat this ideology and thereby stop terrorism at its source' (ibid., p. iii; italics in original). For a very favourable review of *Terror's Source*, see the long review article by Terry Eagleton, 'Roots of Terror', *The Guardian*, 6 September 2003. A more sober view of Oliveti's work is presented by Malcolm Yapp in his review article 'Islam and Islamism', *Middle Eastern Studies*, 40 (2004), pp. 161–82, at pp. 173–4.

[49] Oliveti, *Terror's Source*, p. 113.

the theological tendency which he identifies as *Takfirism*. While Oliveti's work is undoubtedly interesting and highly nuanced (and indeed persuasive) in places, the work as a whole gives the impression of an almost-mathematical accumulation of 'proofs' leading to an inexorable result (with the implication of an equally simple solution). The influence of Oliveti's analysis is clearly visible in the language of the *AM*, with its frequent references to what it refers to as 'traditional' and 'moderate' Islam – again, highly subjective and interpretative terms. This influence has become even clearer: pages 20–9 of the *Muslim 500* (entitled 'The House of Islam' and which attempts to offer a clear picture of Islam) is taken directly from Oliveti's *Terror's Source*.[50]

CONCLUSION

In conclusion, despite these criticisms, which I hope have been understood as constructive rather than gratuitous, it is imperative to end by praising the intentions behind the *AM* and wishing the initiative every possible success. It is also important to acknowledge the excellent opportunity that it offers non-Muslims to engage with Islam and Muslims in an authentic and sophisticated fashion. This is a useful benefit of the *AM*. However, our focus here has been on the vital importance of the *AM* as a necessary precursor and vital companion to *ACW*. As previously noted, *ACW* is very explicit in acknowledging its debt to the *AM*; indeed, the many references to the latter in the former suggest that the *AM* is a sine qua non of *ACW*:

While the Regensburg address may have been an unintended efficient or proximate cause for [*ACW*], it did not serve as its source. [...] Many [...] would put the starting point in July 2005 with the Amman Conference entitled 'The International Islamic Conference: True Islam and its Role in Modern Society' [...]. In this way, an intra-Islamic initiative laid the groundwork for this interfaith initiative.[51]

One sincerely hopes that the motivating spirit behind both the *AM* and *ACW* – one of mutual respect, tolerance and, above all, the need always to talk to and listen to one another – will positively transform and enrich the lives of people everywhere.

---

[50] Schleifer, *The Muslim 500, 2013–2014*, pp. 20–9.
[51] Lumbard, 'The Uncommonality of "A Common Word"', p. 17.

3

A *Common* *Word* Leading to Uncommon Dialogue

Michael Louis Fitzgerald

INTRODUCTION: DIFFERENT FORMS
OF DIALOGUE

What does dialogue between religions imply? The convenient fourfold typology of dialogue first proposed in the document known as 'Dialogue and Mission'[1] points to different types of dialogue: the 'dialogue of life', 'where people strive to live in an open and neighbourly spirit, sharing their joys and sorrows, their human problems and preoccupations';[2] the 'dialogue of action', where people of different religions work together to promote justice, reconciliation and peace; and the 'dialogue of religious experience', 'where persons, rooted in their own religious traditions, share their spiritual riches, for instance with regard to prayer and contemplation, faith and ways of searching for God or the Absolute'.[3] In the light of the *A Common Word* (*ACW*) initiative, this chapter will be concerned mainly with the fourth type, of 'dialogue of discourse'. That may sound

---

[1] Secretariat for Non-Christians, 'The attitude of the Church towards the followers of other religions: reflections and orientations on dialogue and mission', 1984, §§ 28–35. www.pcinterreligious.org/uploads/pdfs/Dialogue_and_Mission_ENG.pdf. Accessed 1 October 2016. See Francesco Gioia (ed.), *Interreligious Dialogue: The Official Teaching of the Catholic Church from the Second Vatican Council to John Paul II (1963–2005)* (Boston: Pauline Books & Media, 2006), pp. 1125–6.

[2] Congregation for the Evangelization of Peoples and Pontifical Council for Inter-Religious Dialogue, 'Dialogue and proclamation: reflections and orientations on interreligious dialogue and the proclamation of the Gospel of Jesus Christ', Vatican City, 19 May 1991, § 42. www.vatican.va/roman_curia/pontifical_councils/interelg/documents/rc_pc_interelg_doc_19051991_dialogue-and-proclamatio_en.html. Accessed 1 October 2016. See Gioia, *Interreligious Dialogue*, p. 1171.

[3] Ibid.

like a tautology, but it refers to exchanges of a formal nature, whatever their content may be. It would be helpful first to give a rapid survey of Roman Catholic participation in formal dialogue with Muslims, both before and after the *ACW* initiative, and then to give a brief assessment of the impact of this initiative.

DIALOGUE BETWEEN MUSLIMS AND CATHOLICS BEFORE *A COMMON WORD*

The discussion here will not refer to pre-modern engagement like that of the oriental Christian leaders with Muslims during the Abbasid period, such as the meeting of Catholicos Timothy I with Caliph al-Mahdī, nor to the later efforts of Western missionaries, such as the Jesuits at the court of the Moghul emperor Akbar, in Fatehpur Sikri.[4] Attention will be confined to Roman Catholic involvement in dialogue with Muslims after the Second Vatican Council.[5]

The foundational document of Vatican II on interreligious relations, *Nostra Aetate,* was approved in October 1965, but already in May of the previous year a special office for monitoring these relations had been created in the Vatican by Pope Paul VI (1963–78). From 1967 onwards the president of this office extended a gesture of friendship to Muslims through an annual message on the occasion of Eid al-Fitr, the feast to mark the end of Ramadan. Yet it was not until the next decade that official dialogue with Muslims really began.

Here, it is good to mention some of these reciprocal visits. In December 1970, a delegation from the Supreme Council for Islamic Affairs in Cairo visited the Secretariat for Non-Christians, and in September 1974 Cardinal Pignedoli, the president of this office, together with the secretary and the desk officer for Islam, reciprocated the visit. In April 1974, Cardinal Pignedoli journeyed to Saudi Arabia for an audience with King Faysal. In November of that year, a delegation of experts in Islamic law from Saudi Arabia held discussions in the Vatican on the question of human rights.[6] In June 1976, Cardinal Pignedoli, again accompanied

---

[4] On these dialogues one could consult Jean-Marie Gaudeul, *Encounters and Clashes: Islam and Christianity in History.* Volume I: *A Survey* (Rome: Pontificio Istituto di Studi Arabi e d'Islamistica, 2000), pp. 36–8, 240–5.

[5] For the texts of the teaching authority of the Catholic Church which provide the foundation for engagement in dialogue, see Maurice Borrmans, 'The Roman Catholic Church and the letter of the 138 Muslim religious leaders', *Current Dialogue,* 54 (July 2013), 54–8.

[6] See Michael L. Fitzgerald, 'The Secretariat for Non-Christians is ten years old', *Islamochristiana,* 1 (1975), 87–95.

by the secretary and the desk officer for Islam, paid a visit to Iran. This brought about a visit by an Iranian delegation to the Vatican the following year. That year also saw exchanges taking place with a delegation of Muslims from Indonesia.

The 1970s also witnessed an important number of international meetings of Christians and Muslims. Perhaps the first was that convoked by the World Council of Churches in Broumana, Lebanon, in 1972. There were two gatherings in Cordoba, Spain, in 1974 and 1977; two meetings were organised by the Centre d'Études et de Recherches Économiques et Sociales (CERES) in Tunisia, the second of which discussed a truly theological topic, 'The Meaning and Levels of Revelation'; a dialogue seminar took place in Tripoli, Libya, in February 1976, between a Vatican delegation and a team of Muslim experts selected by the Arab Socialist Party of Libya, a meeting to which Colonel Gaddafi invited several hundred spectators; and in April 1978 there was an exchange in Cairo between al-Azhar and the Vatican Secretariat for Non-Christians.

In the following decade new partners invited the Vatican office to engage in dialogue. The first of these was the Aal al-Bayt Foundation, set up by Prince Hassan bin Talal, who was at the time crown prince of Jordan. The Aal al-Bayt opened up dialogue first with the Anglicans and then with the Greek Orthodox, but Prince Hassan wished for an official dialogue with the Catholic Church, and this was started. The World Islamic Call Society, based in Tripoli, Libya, also established relations with the Pontifical Council for Interreligious Dialogue (PCID, the new name given to the Secretariat for Non-Christians). Finally dialogue was initiated with Shi'i Muslims through the Iranian Islamic Culture and Relations Organisation, based in Tehran. It could be noted that the topics examined in the exchanges with these organisations have more often been of an ethical or social nature than of a theological one. Themes such as the rights of children, the role of women in society, religious education, justice in international trade relations, business ethics; questions concerning migration, media and religion; respect for the environment and questions of bioethics have all been discussed. In most of these meetings the same pattern has been followed: first the position of each religion regarding the question under discussion is outlined, then a description of the actual situation is given, and finally some suggestions for joint action are formulated.

To offset the danger of being over-extended through bilateral dialogues with Muslims in different countries, in 1995 the PCID took the step of setting up the Islamic–Catholic Liaison Committee with international Islamic organisations of a religious nature. The committee has been meeting yearly since this date. Al-Azhar, being considered a national rather than an international body, was not included as a member of this committee, to its great disappointment. This led, in 1998, to the formation of a separate joint committee with al-Azhar, which, in the meantime, had established its own Permanent Committee for Dialogue with Monotheistic Religions.

Despite the mention of all these engagements, it should not be thought that among Catholics only the Holy See was engaging in dialogue with Muslims. Following the encouragement given by the Second Vatican Council in *Nostra Aetate*, different local churches were developing relations with Muslims. To give but one example, a Catholic institution in Austria, the Religionstheologisches Institut St Gabriel in Mödling, sometimes alone, sometimes with the assistance of the Austrian Ministry of Foreign Affairs, arranged a series of high-powered meetings from 1975 onwards, but particularly between 1992 and 2008. The meeting held in 1977, on 'The God of Christianity and of Islam', aimed at promoting a deeper theological understanding of God for improved mutual knowledge and cooperation.[7]

There were some Muslim and Christian scholars in the French-speaking world who were dissatisfied with these official meetings. They felt that through such meetings not much progress was being made in dialogue, since participants tended to remain set in their own positions. This led them to form, in 1977, a joint working group, Groupe de Recherches Islamo-Chrétien (GRIC). This is an organisation whose members speak in their private capacity, not as official representatives. It has branches in Tunisia, Morocco, France, Lebanon and Spain. A common topic is chosen and each branch tackles a particular aspect of the topic. At an annual general meeting the results are pooled and discussed until there is an agreement on what can be published. The first topic chosen was 'revelation', and other theological topics have not been neglected.[8]

---

[7] See Andreas Bsteh, *Geschichte eines Dialoges: Dialoginitiativen St. Gabriel an der Jahrtausendwende* (Mödling: Verlag St Gabriel, 2013).

[8] See GRIC, *The Challenge of the Scriptures, the Bible and the Qur'an* (Maryknoll, NY: Orbis Books, 1989); 'État et religion', *Islamochristiana*, 12 (1986), 49–72; *Foi et justice. Un défi pour le christianisme et pour l'islam* (Paris: Centurion, 1993); *Péché et responsabilité éthique dans le monde contemporain* (Paris: Bayard, 2000).

EVENTS LEADING TO THE *A COMMON WORD*
INITIATIVE

It is generally thought that the *ACW* initiative developed from a response to quotations and remarks about Islam made by Pope Benedict XVI (2005–13) in the introduction to his talk 'Faith, Reason and the University' delivered in Regensburg on 12 September 2006. There were incidents of violent reaction around the world, as some Muslims were led to believe that Pope Benedict XVI had deliberately denigrated Islam.[9] The first response from Muslim scholars, however, took the form of an open letter dated 15 October 2006. The letter, based on a close examination of what Pope Benedict XVI actually said, was signed by thirty-eight scholars, and was facilitated by HRH Prince Ghazi bin Muhammad bin Talal, chairman of the board of the Royal Aal al-Albayt Institute for Islamic Thought, based in Amman, Jordan.[10]

This institution has been mentioned previously in connection with the dialogue in which the PCID has been engaged. It is interesting to note that when King Abdullah II succeeded to the throne of Jordan following the death of his father, King Hussein, he appointed his cousin, Prince Ghazi, as head of the Aal al-Bayt Institute in place of his uncle, Prince Hassan. When the PCID made contact with Prince Ghazi to enquire whether the dialogue would continue, the answer was negative. The institute wished to turn its attention to fostering unity among Muslims. This concentration of might be termed 'Islamic ecumenism' may help to explain why the signatories to the open letter represent a wide variety of countries and also of tendencies within Islam, Sunni, Shi'a and Zaydi.

Almost a year later, on 13 October 2007, a further letter, signed this time initially by 138 scholars, was sent to Christian religious leaders of many different denominations.[11] This letter, entitled *A Common Word between Us and You*, presents love of God and love of neighbour as the

---

9 See for instance the report by Anthony Shadid, 'Remarks by Pope prompt Muslim outrage, protests', *Washington Post*, 16 September 2006. www.washingtonpost.com/wp-dyn/content/article/2006/09/15/AR2006091500800.html. Accessed 28 September 2016.

10 The text of the letter, in both Arabic and English, is reproduced in the dossier published in *Islamochristiana*, 32 (2006), 273–97. The dossier also contains the published version of Pope Benedict XVI's speech, in the original German, including the added footnote in which Pope Benedict XVI explains that the quotation from Manuel II Paleologus in no way represented his own opinion, and that he had no intention of offending Muslims (p. 275, note 3).

11 The text of this letter is reproduced in the special dossier published in *Islamochristiana*, 33 (2007), in English, 241–61 and in Arabic, 262–80.

common ground of Christianity and Islam. It ends with an appeal: 'Finally, as Muslims, and in obedience to the Holy Qur'an, we ask Christians to come together with us on the common essentials of our two religions. [...] Let this common ground be the basis for all future interfaith dialogue between us.'[12]

DIALOGUE BETWEEN CATHOLICS AND MUSLIMS AFTER A COMMON WORD

As mentioned already, the *ACW* invitation to dialogue was sent to a large number of Christian religious leaders. Dr Rowan Williams, the then-Archbishop of Canterbury, had probably hoped that a response could be given ecumenically. Later in the same month of October he met Pope Benedict XVI in Naples during the meeting of 'People and Religions' organised by the St Egidio community and must have broached the question then. The Holy See decided, however, to respond on its own to the invitation. Rowan Williams, nonetheless, made his response after consulting a wide range of Christian leaders, as he explains in Chapter 4 of this volume. An exchange of correspondence ensued between Cardinal Bertone, the secretary of state, on behalf of Pope Benedict XVI, and Prince Ghazi, on behalf of the signatories of *ACW*.[13] After a preliminary meeting of a few experts from both sides, the decision was taken to set up the Catholic–Muslim Forum.

The first seminar under the auspices of this new Forum was held in the Vatican between 4 and 6 November 2008. The overall theme discussed by the twenty-five Christian and twenty-four Muslim participants, 'Love of God, Love of Neighbour', reflected the contents of the *ACW* document. The discussion took place in two stages: first on the theological and spiritual foundations of love of God and love of neighbour, and then on the dignity of the human person and mutual respect. On the third day, a long final declaration, listing fifteen points, was approved. The participants were then received in audience by Pope Benedict XVI. Dr Seyyed Hossein Nasr and Dr Mustafa Cerić, the former Grand Mufti of Bosnia-Herzegovina, gave short addresses, to which the pope replied.[14]

---

[12] *Islamochristiana*, 33 (2007), 254.
[13] For the texts of the letters, see *Islamochristiana*, 33 (2007), 286–88.
[14] For a short report on the seminar by one of the participants, the addresses during the papal audience, the text of the final declaration (in both English and Arabic) and the list of participants, see *Islamochristiana*, 34 (2008), 261–72. Further information, including the texts of all the papers read, can be found at www.acommonword.com.

The last article in the final declaration of this seminar reads: 'We look forward to the second Seminar of the Catholic–Muslim Forum to be convened in approximately two years in a Muslim-majority country yet to be determined.'[15] This second seminar was in fact held a little more than three years later at the Baptism Site of Jesus Christ in Jordan (21–3 November 2011). This time the overall theme chosen was 'Reason, Faith and the Human Person'. According to Cardinal Jean-Louis Tauran, the head of the Catholic delegation, this gave an opportunity to deepen the topic of the first seminar, but perhaps it reflected more closely the content of the speech of Pope Benedict XVI in Regensburg, which had been the occasion of the *ACW* initiative.[16] There were twenty-four participants on each side. On the second day, they were all received by King Abdullah II, who expressed the wish that such meetings should continue. The final declaration, which mentions the 'respectful and friendly atmosphere' of the meeting, is short and expressed in general terms. It ends by stating that 'Catholics and Muslims look forward to continuing their dialogue as a way of furthering mutual understanding, and advancing the common good of all humanity, especially its yearning for peace, justice and solidarity'.[17] Though this statement gave no indication as to when a further seminar might be held, the third meeting of the Catholic–Muslim Forum took place in Rome between 11 and 13 November 2014. The theme addressed on this occasion was 'Working Together to Serve Others'.[18]

It can be observed that the establishment of this new Catholic–Muslim Forum did not monopolise the relations of the Vatican with Muslims. The PCID continued its regular meetings, as a partner in the Islamic–Catholic Liaison Committee, with the World Islamic Call Society, the Islamic Culture and Relations Organisation, Al-Azhar (at least until 2011) and the Royal Aal al-Bayt Institute for Interfaith Studies, Jordan. Dialogue under other auspices continued also in different places and at different levels. Mention could be made of the regular meetings promoted by the Capuchins in Istanbul, which in recent years have discussed the topics 'Sacred Books', 'Believers Confronted with Modernity' and 'Reason and Faith'. The GRIC has continued its work, and celebrated in Rabat and

---

[15] See *Islamochristiana*, 34 (2008), 267.

[16] The dossier published in *Islamochristiana*, 37 (2011), 264–85 contains a short report by the editor of *Islamochristiana*, who participated in the seminar; the word of welcome from Prince Ghazi; the introductory remarks of Cardinal Tauran; two of the papers presented; the final declaration in both English and Arabic and the list of participants.

[17] *Islamochristiana*, 37 (2011), 283.

[18] See *Islamochristiana*, 40 (2014), 311–12.

Casablanca its thirtieth anniversary. Regional meetings of Muslims and Catholics have continued in the United States, examining such themes as 'Interreligious Education', 'Religious Freedom', the 'Concept of Mission' and 'Stories of Abraham'. A meeting of priests and imams was held in Lyon (21 November 2009), and Catholic and Muslim women met in Rome (18 February 2009). Common pilgrimages have taken place, such as the annual pilgrimage to the church of the Seven Sleepers in Vieux-Marché, France, and a Marian pilgrimage in Lourdes. This list could be completed by reference to countless encounters between Catholics and Muslims that have been organised in Africa and Asia. Reports on these meetings are not always readily available, but they may be found in local church bulletins and newsletters.

AN EVALUATION OF THE *A COMMON WORD* INITIATIVE

Before sharing my own concluding reflections, I would like to summarise the analysis made by Fr Maurice Borrmans of *The Letter of the 138*, as he always calls it.[19] Borrmans considers the first letter, *The Letter of the 38*, 'unfortunately polemical',[20] though it could be said that the authors of the letter were merely pointing out where they felt Pope Benedict XVI was mistaken. Much more time was given to the composition of the second letter, to which the increase in signatures from 38 to 138 is seen as a sign of an enlarged consensus (*ijmāʿ*).[21] According to Borrmans, this second document is traditional in that it presents an accumulation of quotations from the Qur'an and from the Hadith, though isolating them from their contexts to allow for a wider interpretation.[22] He further considers it to be innovative, since it offers a redefinition of monotheism. The document focuses on the first part of the *shahāda*: 'There is no god but God';[23] it states that 'Muslims, Jews and Christians have at their heart the same confession of the one and unique living God, (set) in the framework of the two-fold commandment to love God and one's neighbour'.[24] The authors, says Borrmans, 'seek to define monotheism by this double love

---

[19] See Maurice Borrmans, 'The Roman Catholic Church and the letter of the 138 Muslim religious leaders', *Current Dialogue*, 54 (2013), 54–72.
[20] Ibid., p. 72; see also p. 62.
[21] Ibid., p. 58.
[22] Ibid., p. 62.
[23] Ibid., p. 60.
[24] Ibid., p. 58.

of God and of the neighbour, thus giving to the reading of the Qur'an this note of "spiritual internalisation", which the letter of the 38 had already revealed. [...] The conventional attitudes of obedience, submission and adoration are replaced by a vocabulary which seems common to Muslims, Jews and Christians.'[25] A 'spirit of openness' is displayed, notes Borrmans, deserving of a positive response. For instance, Biblical texts are quoted without any reference to falsification (*taḥrīf*). In the Arabic text, Christians are referred to as *masīḥiyyūn*, not as *naṣārā* (a Qur'anic term to which they generally object), and *muslim* is always translated as 'one who surrenders to God', not as 'Muslim', i.e., one who belongs to a specific religion.[26]

Borrmans nevertheless expresses some regrets with regard to this document. The Qur'anic texts quoted are well known, but the document passes over in silence 'certain Qur'anic verses which are still problematic for Christians'.[27] There are texts with more warlike accents that are 'still waiting for a re-reading to contextualise their content'. Peter Admirand touches on this concern in Chapter 8 of this volume. Borrmans further finds it regrettable that 'the letter nowhere denounces [...] the acts of violence or terrorism that certain groups of Muslims are committing today "in the name of God"'. Yet the letter is welcomed by Borrmans as 'the dawn of a new stage in Muslim–Christian dialogue'. It must provide Christians and Muslims with 'an opportunity for sharing and exchanging their spiritual experiences and theological renewal'.[28] Indeed, it could be said that the invitation goes beyond dialogue, being 'ultimately an appeal to unite the witness of believers [...] confronted with the dangers of the present, because the three monotheistic religions have to guarantee peace to humankind today', Borrmans concludes.[29]

It would seem useful also to summarise the appreciation of the *ACW* document published by staff members of the Pontifical Institute of Arabic and Islamic Studies.[30] They remark on the broad scope of this text, not only on account of the variety of personalities who have appended their signature to it and of those to whom it is addressed, but also because the authors are not engaged in a plea *pro domo* but rather situate themselves as partners within humanity. The basis for their proposal is seen to be

[25] Ibid., p. 61.
[26] Ibid., p. 62.
[27] Ibid., p. 58.
[28] Ibid., p. 63.
[29] Ibid., p. 61.
[30] See *Islamochristiana*, 33 (2007), 280–82.

both ample and solid, calling attention to the urgency of respecting the rights of God as also the rights of human beings, taking into account the present conditions of our world but opening up the perspective of the future. Particularly appreciated is the willingness to acknowledge the 'Other' in what that 'Other' holds most dear, something which is seen to be the sole guarantee of a fruitful relationship between culturally and religiously differing communities. Note is taken of the respectful way in which Biblical texts are quoted and interpreted, and of a new and creative approach to the Qur'anic text and to the prophetic tradition. This document is seen as a real encouragement to persevere in dialogue, and as a sign for those who have knowledge, a gift from the Merciful God.

For my own part, I find the text of the *ACW* document refreshing. In giving examples of the ongoing dialogue with Muslims, I noted some occasions when theological questions were on the agenda, but very often such questions were avoided. I have often heard, and had it said to me, that theological dialogue between Christians and Muslims is impossible. If what is meant by 'impossible' is that it is not possible for Christians and Muslims to reach full agreement about their respective beliefs, then I obviously agree. But if by theology we mean 'faith seeking understanding',[31] then surely we can speak theologically to one another. We can help one another to understand the logic of our respective belief systems. We can come to a less dismissive and more respectful attitude to one another. The *ACW* document is a stimulus to engage in this type of theological dialogue, which is still somewhat *uncommon*.

On the other hand, I do not think that too much importance should be attributed to this document. It has not revolutionised Christian–Muslim dialogue. This has continued and continues to be practised according to its different forms all around the world. In fact, it could be said that the impact of the *ACW* has been somewhat limited. It would seem to me that this impact has been felt more within the English-speaking world than elsewhere. Although the document was published in both Arabic and English, and many of its signatories are Arabic-speaking Muslims, it would seem to have had little echo in the Arabic-speaking world. This was at least my impression over the years that I recently spent in Egypt (2006–12), although I must admit that I was not monitoring the whole of the Arab press. The feeling I had was that the *ACW* initiative was really designed for the Western world, and could even be considered an

---

[31] See Anselm of Canterbury, *Proslogion, proemium*, in J. P. Migne (ed.), *Patrologia Latina* (Paris, 1841–55), Vol. 153, p. 225A.

instrument of *da'wa*, an attempt to show that Islam is a religion truly worthy to be embraced. I would be very happy if it turned out to be an important document for the formation of imams who would then be able to help their communities to grow in a spirit of respectful dialogue not only with Christians, but with all people, whatever their religious beliefs.

PART II

RESPONSES TO *A COMMON WORD*

4

A *Common* *Word* for the Common Good

Rowan Williams

INTRODUCTION

The publication in 2007 of the *A Common Word* declaration was undoubtedly a watershed moment in Muslim–Christian dialogue. For the first time, a significantly broad-based group of Muslim scholars had developed together a sophisticated and imaginative statement of where Islamic and Christian reflection on revelation might converge for the good of the whole human family. Utilising the tools of scholarly exegesis and motivated by a manifestly genuine desire to offer resources for conversation and co-operation, the text did not set out to resolve areas of deep dispute, nor did it simply advocate a generalised goodwill, but it provided an intellectually and spiritually serious statement of the kinship between what the two faiths take for granted about God and about humanity. In this regard, it represented a genuinely fresh approach – or, perhaps better, an approach that looked back to the era when Jews, Christians and Muslims were able to recognise in each other a common understanding of what might be called the grammar of the divine. The great mediaeval philosophers of all these traditions assumed that at least there was some sense in which they were not confronted in each other's discourses by outright idolatry and unrelieved error. Convergence on a shared confession of divine freedom, divine faithfulness and divine compassion was still to be recognised, even in the context of conflicts as intractably severe as our current agonies and tragedies.

It did not prove easy to put together a co-ordinated Christian response, though there were some excellent theological commentaries, notably from North American theologians, especially at Yale. But Lambeth Palace eventually assembled a large and diverse Christian group to discuss the issues that were arising and to think about how best to reply to the invitation to candid and reflective exchange. The group of leaders and scholars was not minded to attempt a joint statement, but warmly encouraged the Archbishop of Canterbury to prepare a commentary in the light of the views and perspectives expressed in the meeting, and this was what was to become the document 'A Common Word for the Common Good'. Drafted with the skilled support of the archbishop's staff, who deserve the warmest thanks and praise for their work, it set out to do – essentially – two things. First, it sketched out some areas where the differences between Muslim and Christian language were perhaps more deep-rooted than a first glance might suggest, especially in regard to the fact that Christians would want to see divine love as *constitutive* of divine identity, not just *characteristic* of it. This was not designed to reintroduce a tension that the Muslim document had overcome; it was a further invitation to examine how far we could go together in exploring convergence and divergence. And, second, it looked to what dialogue could and should make possible in our wider social context, arguing that religious diversity was a source of potential strength in society and that a strong and joyful commitment to the truth of a revealed faith ought to deliver us from the fearfulness that breeds violence: only if you do not really believe in the eternal liberty and majesty of God will you imagine that God needs to be defended by human power or supported by coercion and terror. Islam and Christianity have at times been guilty of this aberration, there is no doubt; but a fuller grasp of what faith claims to be true about God, a grasp of just that 'grammar' of discourse about the God beyond idols and human projections, can liberate us from the anxious feeling that God needs us to keep him safe, or even that God's honour requires to be upheld by violence of word and act.

So the reply was an attempt to echo what the original document had done, an attempt to do some primary theological reflection directly *in the presence of* another religious tradition, without compromise but without defensiveness, in the hope of finding a way together of serving the needs of a divided, fearful world. Time will tell whether this exchange in 2007–8 will bear lasting fruit; but there can scarcely be any doubt that the need for such reflection is even more urgent ten years on. If these documents opened up some new doors for conversation and some new horizons for hopefulness, they will have done their work. And this retrospective look at the exchange will, I hope, stir up another round of work together.

In the decade intervening, the sky has apparently become darker than ever: the spread of brutal, coercive and uncompromising forms of Islamic practice has brought grief and anger to many devout Muslims across the world who long for a humane and loving relationship with all their neighbours; Western military adventures and interventions, combined with religious and racial bigotry, have brought similar grief and anger to most Christians, and have assisted the recruiting efforts of the most intransigent and violent elements in other communities. The death toll continues to rise, and the Middle East has become less and less of a diverse, plural pattern of ethnicities and faiths, more of a battlefield both for local sectarianism and for dubious international agendas. All that the 2007–8 exchange meant seems to be under threat. But the energy and vision of the *A Common Word* text are still alive, and it is important to honour what the text produced and to carry on the task of discerning response and practical furtherance. I hope these pages will serve that end.

A Common Word *for the Common Good*

To
the Muslim Religious Leaders and Scholars
who have signed
A Common Word Between Us and You
and to Muslim brothers and sisters everywhere

Grace, Mercy and Peace be with you

Preface

Dear Friends:

We are deeply appreciative of the initiative you have taken and welcome *A Common Word Between Us and You* as a significant development in relations between Christians and Muslims. In your letter you have addressed 27 Christian leaders and "leaders of Christian Churches everywhere" and many of those addressed have already responded or set in motion processes through which responses will in due course be made. Having listened carefully to Christian colleagues from the widest possible range of backgrounds, most significantly at a Consultation of Church representatives and Christian scholars in June 2008, I am pleased to offer this response to your letter, with their support and encouragement.

We recognise that your letter brings together Muslim leaders from many traditions of Islam to address Christian leaders representative of the diverse traditions within Christianity. We find in it a hospitable and friendly spirit, expressed in its focus on love of God and love of neighbour – a focus which draws together the languages of Christianity and Islam, and of Judaism also. Your letter could hardly be more timely, given the growing awareness that peace throughout the world is deeply entwined with the ability of all people of faith everywhere to live in peace, justice, mutual respect and love. Our belief is that only through a commitment to that transcendent perspective to which your letter points, and to which we also look, shall we find the resources for radical, transforming, non-violent engagement with the deepest needs of our world and our common humanity.

In your invitation to "come to a common word" we find a helpful generosity of intention. Some have read the invitation as an insistence that we should be able immediately to affirm an agreed and shared understanding of God. But such an affirmation would not be honest to either of our traditions. It would fail to acknowledge the reality of the differences that exist and that have been the cause of deep and – at times in the past – even violent division. We read your letter as expressing a more modest but ultimately a more realistically hopeful recognition that the ways in which we as Christians and Muslims speak about God and humanity are not simply mutually unintelligible systems. We interpret your invitation as saying 'let us find a way of recognising that on some matters we are speaking enough of a common language for us to be able to pursue both exploratory dialogue and peaceful co-operation with integrity and without compromising fundamental beliefs.'

We find this recognition in what is, for us, one of the key paragraphs of your letter:

"In the light of what we have seen to be necessarily implied and evoked by the Prophet Muhammad's (pbuh) blessed saying: *'The best that I have said – myself, and the prophets that came before me – is: "there is no god but God, He Alone, He hath no associate, His is the sovereignty and His is the praise and He hath power over all things"'*, we can now perhaps understand the words *'The best that I have said – myself, and the prophets that came before me'* as equating the blessed formula *'there is no god but God, He Alone, He hath no associate, His is the sovereignty and His is the praise and He hath power over all things'* precisely with the 'First and Greatest Commandment' to love God, with all one's heart and soul, as found in various places in the Bible. That is to say, in other words, that the Prophet Muhammad (pbuh) was perhaps, through inspiration, restating and alluding to the Bible's First Commandment. God knows best, but certainly we have seen their effective similarity in meaning. Moreover, we also do know (as can be seen in the endnotes), that both formulas have another remarkable parallel: the way they arise in a number of slightly differing versions and forms in different contexts, all of which, nevertheless, emphasize the primacy of total love and devotion to God."

The double use of 'perhaps' in that passage allows for openness, exploration and debate – made possible because certain aspects of the ways in which we structure our talk about God in our respective traditions are intelligible one to the other. We read it as an invitation to further discussion within the Christian family and within the Muslim family as well as between Muslims and Christians, since it invites all of us to think afresh about the foundations of our convictions. There are many things between us that offer the promise of deeper insight through future discussion. Thus for us your letter makes a highly significant contribution to the divinely initiated journey into which we are called, the journey in which Christians and Muslims alike are taken further into mutual understanding and appreciation. The confession that "God knows best" reminds us of the limits of our understanding and knowledge.

In the light of this letter, what are the next steps for us? We draw from *A Common Word Between Us and You* five areas which might be fruitfully followed through.

First, its focus on the love and praise of God, stressing how we must trust absolutely in God and give him the devotion of our whole being – heart, mind and will – underlines a shared commitment: the fixed intention to relate all reality and all behaviour intelligently, faithfully and practically to the God who deals with us in love, compassion, justice and peace. One of the areas we can usefully discuss together is the diverse ways in which we understand the love of God as an absolutely free gift to his creation. There are bound to be differences as well as similarities in the ways we understand and express God's love for us and how we seek to practise love for God and neighbour in return, and in what follows we consider how these might be explored in a spirit of honest and co-operative attention.

Second, its commitment to a love of neighbour that is rooted in the love of God (and which, for Christians, is part of our response to the love of God for us) suggests that we share a clear passion for the common good of all humanity and all creation. In what follows we shall seek to identify some practical implications for our future relations both with each other and with the rest of the world.

Third, the concern to ground what we say in the Scriptures of our traditions shows a desire to meet each other not 'at the margins' of our historic identities but speaking from what is central and authoritative for us Here, however, it is especially important to acknowledge that the Qur'an's role in Islam is not the same as that of the Bible in Christianity; Christians understand the primary location of God's revealing Word to be the history of God's people and above all the history of Jesus Christ, whom we acknowledge as the Word made flesh, to which the Bible is the authoritative and irreplaceable witness. For the Muslim, as we understand it, the Word is supremely communicated in what Mohammed is commanded to recite. But for both faiths, scripture provides the basic tools for speaking of God and it is in attending to how we use our holy texts that we often discover most truly the nature of each other's faith.[1] In what follows we shall suggest how studying our scriptures together might continue to provide a fruitful element of our engagements with each other in the process of "building a home together", to pick up an image popularised by Rabbi Jonathan Sacks in a recent book.[2]

---

[1] As the staff of the Pontifical Institute for Arabic and Islamic Studies wrote in their appreciation of your letter: "We are pleased to see that the biblical and Gospel quotations used in this document come from the sources and that explanations given are on occasion based on the original languages: Hebrew, Aramaic and Greek. This is evidence of deep respect and genuine attentiveness to others, while at the same time of a true scientific spirit."(issued by Pontificio Istituto di Studi Arabi e d'Islamistica [PISAI], Rome, 25th October 2007).

[2] Jonathan Sacks, *The Home We Build Together: Recreating Society* (London: Continuum, 2007).

Fourth, and growing out of this last point, the letter encourages us to relate to each other from the heart of our lives of faith before God. However much or little 'common ground' we initially sense between us, it is possible to engage with each other without anxiety if we truly begin from the heart of what we believe we have received from God; possible to speak together, respecting and discussing differences rather than imprisoning ourselves in mutual fear and suspicion.

Finally, we acknowledge gratefully your recognition that the differences between Christians and Muslims are real and serious and that you do not claim to address all the issues. Yet in offering this focus on love of God and neighbour, you identify what could be the centre of a sense of shared calling and shared responsibility – an awareness of what God calls for from all his human creatures to whom he has given special responsibility in creation. In our response, it is this search for a common awareness of responsibility before God that we shall seek to hold before us as a vision worthy of our best efforts.

This response therefore looks in several directions. It seeks to encourage more reflection within the Christian community, as well as to promote honest encounter between Christian and Muslim believers; and it asks about the possible foundations for shared work in the world and a shared challenge to all those things which obscure God's purpose for humanity.

THE ONE GOD WHO IS LOVE

At the origins of the history of God's people, as Jewish and Christian Scripture record it, is the command given to Moses to communicate to the people – the *Shema,* as it has long been known, from its opening word in Hebrew:

Hear, O Israel: The LORD our God, the LORD is one!
You shall love the LORD your God with all your heart, and with all your soul, and with all your strength.[3]

(Deuteronomy 6:4–5)[4]

---

[3] Taken from the *English Standard Version* of the Bible.
[4] Unless otherwise stated, quotations from the Bible are taken from the *New Revised Standard Version* (copyright 1989 by the Division of Christian Education of the National Council of Churches of Christ in the USA).

Such an imperative, as your letter makes clear, is of central authority for Muslims too.

Hear, O Israel: The LORD our God, the LORD is one!: The *tawhid* principle[5] is held out in your letter as one of the bases for agreement. In addition to the passages you quote to demonstrate *tawhid*, we read in the Qur'an:

God: there is no god but Him, the Ever Living, the Ever Watchful.[6]

(al-Baqara 2:255)[7]

He is God the One, God the eternal. He fathered no one nor was he fathered. No one is comparable to Him.

(al-'Ikhlas 112:1–4)

This last text reminds the Christian that this great affirmation of the uniqueness of God is what has often caused Muslims to look with suspicion at the Christian doctrines of God. Christian belief about the Trinity – God as Father, Son and Holy Spirit – appears at once to compromise the belief that God has no other being associated with him. How can we call God *al-Qayyum*, the Self-sufficient, if he is not alone? So we read in the Qur'an

The East and the West belong to God: wherever you turn, there is His Face. God is all pervading and all knowing. They have asserted, "God has a child." May He be exalted! No! Everything in the heavens and earth belongs to Him, everything devoutly obeys His will. He is the Originator of the heavens and the earth, and when He decrees something, He says only "Be," and it is.

(al-Baqara 2:115–117)

Muslims see the belief that God could have a son as suggesting that God is somehow limited as we are limited, bound to physical processes and needing the co-operation of others. How can such a God be truly free and sovereign – qualities both Christianity and Islam claim to affirm, for we know that God is able to bring the world into being by his word alone?

Here it is important to state unequivocally that the association of any other being with God is expressly rejected by the Christian theological tradition. Since the earliest Councils of the Church, Christian

---

[5] *tawhid:* that God is one, monotheism. *shirk:* the association of God with other beings who are not divine, whether other 'gods', saints, mediators of various kinds.

[6] *al Qayyum* can also be translated as "Self-subsistent" and "Self-sufficient".

[7] Unless otherwise stated all quotations from the Qur'an are taken from *A New Translation* by M. A. S. Abdel Haleem (Oxford: Oxford University Press, 2005).

thinkers sought to clarify how, when we speak of the Father 'begetting' the Son, we must put out of our minds any suggestion that this is a physical thing, a process or event like the processes and events that happen in the world. They insisted that the name 'God' is not the name of a person like a human person, a limited being with a father and mother and a place that they inhabit within the world. 'God' is the name of a kind of life, a 'nature' or essence – eternal and self-sufficient life, always active, needing nothing. But that life is lived, so Christians have always held, eternally and simultaneously as three interrelated agencies are made known to us in the history of God's revelation to the Hebrew people and in the life of Jesus and what flows from it. God is at once the source of divine life, the expression of that life and the active power that communicates that life. This takes us at once into consideration of the Trinitarian language used by Christians to speak of God. We recognise that this is difficult, sometimes offensive, to Muslims; but it is all the more important for the sake of open and careful dialogue that we try to clarify what we do and do not mean by it, and so trust that what follows will be read in this spirit.

In human language, in the light of what our Scripture says, we speak of "Father, Son and Holy Spirit", but we do not mean one God with two beings alongside him, or three gods of limited power. So there is indeed one God, the Living and Self-subsistent, associated with no other; but what God is and does is not different from the life which is eternally and simultaneously the threefold pattern of life: source and expression and sharing. Since God's life is always an intelligent, purposeful and loving life, it is possible to think of each of these dimensions of divine life as, in important ways, like a centre of mind and love, a person; but this does not mean that God 'contains' three different individuals, separate from each other as human individuals are.

Christians believe that in a mysterious manner we have a limited share in the characteristics of divine life.[8] Through the death and rising to life of Jesus, God takes away our evildoing and our guilt, he forgives us and sets us free. And our Scriptures go on to say[9] that he breathes

---

[8] God is love. Whoever lives in love lives in God and God in him (1 John 4:16); see also 2 Peter 1.4: Thus [God] has given us, through these things, his precious and very great promises, so that through them you may escape from the corruption that is in the world because of lust, and may become participants in the divine nature.

[9] As in Paul's First Letter to the Corinthians, 15:45–49 and the Letter to the Galatians, 4:6, for example.

new life into us, as he breathed life into Adam at the first, so that God's spirit is alive in us. The presence and action of the Holy Spirit is thus God in his action of sharing life with us.[10] As we become mature in our new life, our lives become closer and closer (so we pray and hope) to the central and perfect expression of divine life, the Word whom we encounter in Jesus – though we never become simply equal to him. And because Jesus prayed to the source of his life as 'Father',[11] we call the eternal and perfect expression of God's life not only the Word but also the 'Son'. We pray to the source of divine life in the way that Jesus taught us, and we say 'Father' to this divine reality. And in calling the eternal word the 'Son' of God, we remind ourselves that he is in no way different in nature from the Father: there is only one divine nature and reality.

Because God exists in this threefold pattern of interdependent action, the relationship between Father, Son and Holy Spirit is one in which there is always a 'giving place' to each other, each standing back so that the other may act. The only human language we have for this is <u>love</u>: the three dimensions of divine life relate to each other in self-sacrifice or self-giving. The doctrine of the Trinity is a way of explaining why we say that God <u>is</u> love, not only that he shows love.

When God acts towards us in compassion to liberate us from evil, to deal with the consequences of our rebellion against him and to make us able to call upon him with confidence, it is a natural (but not automatic) flowing outwards of his own everlasting action. The mutual self-giving love that is the very life of God is made real for our sake in the self-giving love of Jesus. And it is because of God's prior love for us that we are enabled and enjoined to love God.[12] Through our loving response, we can begin to comprehend something of God's nature and God's will for humankind:

[10] God's love has been poured into our hearts through the Holy Spirit that has been given to us (Romans 5:5)

[11] In Matthew 6:9–15 Jesus says: "Pray then in this way: Our Father in heaven, hallowed be your name. Your kingdom come. Your will be done, on earth as it is in heaven. Give us this day our daily bread. And forgive us our debts, as we also have forgiven our debtors. And do not bring us to the time of trial, but rescue us from the evil one. For if you forgive others their trespasses, your heavenly Father will also forgive you; but if you do not forgive others, neither will your Father forgive your trespasses."

[12] Something similar seems to be implied by the ordering of the loves in the Qur'anic verse 5:54 in which it is said that "*God will bring a new people: He will love them, and they will love Him.*"

"Whoever does not love does not know God, because God is love"
(1 John 4:8).

So Christians go further than simply saying that God is a loving God or that love is one of his attributes among others. We say that God does not love simply because he <u>decides</u> to love. God is always, eternally, loving – the very nature and definition of God is love, and the full understanding of his unity is for Christians bound up with this.

Understanding the **"breadth and length and height and depth"** of the love of God[13] is a lifetime's journey; so it is not remotely possible to consider it with satisfactory thoroughness within the confines of this letter. However, it is necessary at this point to stress two qualities of God's love that are crucially important for the Christian: it is unconditional,[14] given gratuitously and without cause; and it is self-sacrificial.[15]

In the birth, life, death, resurrection and ascension of Jesus Christ, the loving nature of God is revealed. We see how Jesus, both in his ministry and in his acceptance of a sacrificial death at the hands of his enemies, offers a love that is given in advance of any human response; it is not a reward for goodness – rather it is what makes human goodness possible, as we change our lives in gratitude to God for his free gift. In the words of a well-known English hymn, it is "Love to the loveless shown, that they might lovely be."[16] And because of this, it is also a love that is vulnerable. God does not convert us and transform us by exercising his divine power alone. So infinite is that power, and so inseparable from love, that no defeat or suffering, even the terrible suffering of Jesus on the cross, can overcome God's purpose.

So, when we seek to live our lives in love of God and neighbour, we as Christians pray that we may be given strength to love God even when God does not seem to give us what we think we want or seems far off (a major theme in the writings of many Christian mystics, who often speak of those moments of our experience when God does not seem to love us as we should want to be loved); and we pray too for the strength to love

---

[13] I pray that you may have the power to comprehend, with all the saints, what is the breadth and length and height and depth, and to know the love of Christ that surpasses knowledge, so that you may be filled with all the fullness of God. (Ephesians 3:18–19)

[14] One of the most influential and beloved New Testament texts illuminating the love of God is the parable of the Prodigal Son – sometimes called the parable of the Loving Father (Luke 15:11–32)

[15] "For God so loved the world that he gave his one and only begotten Son, that whoever believes in him shall not perish but have eternal life" (John 3:16)

[16] In "My song is love unknown" by Samuel Crossman (1664)

those who do not seem to deserve our love, to love those who reject our love, to love those who have not yet made any move in love towards us.

We seek to show in our lives some of the characteristics of God's own love. We know that this may mean putting ourselves at risk; to love where we can see no possibility of love being returned is to be vulnerable, and we can only dare to do this in the power of God's Holy Spirit, creating in us some echo, some share, of Christ's own love. And in the light of all this, one area where dialogue between Christians and Muslims will surely be fruitful is in clarifying how far Muslims can in good conscience go in seeing the love of God powerfully at work in circumstances where the world sees only failure or suffering – but also, to anticipate the challenge that some Muslims might make in answer, how far the Christian tradition of accepting suffering on this basis may sometimes lead to a passive attitude to suffering and a failure to try and transform situations in the name of God's justice.

Thus, as Christians, we would say that our worship of God as threefold has never compromised the unity of God, which we affirm as wholeheartedly as Jews and Muslims. Indeed, by understanding God as a unity of love we see ourselves intensifying and enriching our belief in the unity of God. This indivisible unity is again expressed in the ancient theological formula, which we can trace back to the North African theologian Saint Augustine, *opera Trinitatis ad extra indivisa sunt* – all the actions of the Trinity outside itself are indivisible. So, although the Trinity has been a point of dispute with Jews and Muslims, and will no doubt continue to be so, we are encouraged that *A Common Word Between Us and You* does not simply assume that Christians believe in more than one god.[17] We are, therefore,

[17] We understand that this is the reading given to the Qur'anic verse al-Zumar 29:46 (*"our God and your God are one [and the same]"*) and al-'Imran, 3:113–115, quoted in your letter. It is also our interpretation of the passage in your letter that reads: 'Clearly, the blessed words: *we shall ascribe no partner unto Him* relate to the Unity of God. Clearly also, worshipping *none but God*, relates to being totally devoted to God and hence to the *First and Greatest Commandment*. According to one of the oldest and most authoritative commentaries (*tafsir*) on the Holy Qur'an – the *Jami' Al-Bayan fi Ta'wil Al-Qur'an* of Abu Ja'far Muhammad bin Jarir Al-Tabari (d. 310 A.H. / 923 C.E.) – *that none of us shall take others for lords beside God*, means "that none of us should obey in disobedience to what God has commanded, nor glorify them by prostrating to them in the same way as they prostrate to God". In other words, that Muslims, Christians and Jews should be free to each follow what God commanded them, and not have "to prostrate before kings and the like"; for God says elsewhere in the Holy Qur'an: *Let there be no compulsion in religion....* (*Al-Baqarah*, 2:256). This clearly relates to the Second Commandment and to love of the neighbour of which justice and freedom of religion are a crucial part.'

encouraged in the belief that what both our faiths say concerning the nature of God is not totally diverse – there are points of communication and overlap in the way we think about the divine nature that make our continued exploration of these issues worthwhile, despite the important issues around whether we can say that God is love in his very nature.

It was, therefore, appropriate that Cardinal Bertone, in his letter to Prince Ghazi bin Muhammad bin Talal welcoming *A Common Word Between Us and You* on behalf of Pope Benedict XVI, wrote:

> Without ignoring or downplaying our differences as Christians and Muslims, we can and therefore should look to what unites us, namely, belief in the one God, the provident Creator and universal Judge who at the end of time will deal with each person according to his or her actions. We are all called to commit ourselves totally to him and to obey his sacred will.[18]

To what extent do the Christian conviction of God as Love and the all-important Islamic conviction that God is "the Compassionate, the Merciful" (*ar-rahman ar-rahim*) represent common ground, and to what extent do differences need to be spelled out further? This is a very significant area for further work. But your letter – and many of the Christian responses to it – do make it clear that we have a basis on which we can explore such matters together in a spirit of genuine – and truly neighbourly! – love.

Responding to the Gift of Love

Beloved, let us love one another, because love is from God; everyone who loves is born of God and knows God.[8] Whoever does not love does not know God, for God is love.[9] God's love was revealed among us in this way: God sent his only Son into the world so that we might live through him.[10] In this is love, not that we loved God but that he loved us and sent his Son to be the atoning sacrifice for our sins.[11] Beloved, since God loved us so much, we also ought to love one another.[12] No one has ever seen God; if we love one another, God lives in us, and his love is perfected in us.

(1 John 4:7–12)

God will bring a new people: He will love them, and they will love Him.

(al-Ma'ida 5:54)

What has been said so far is intended to highlight the way in which we as Christians see love as first and foremost a gift from God to us which makes possible for us a new level of relation with God and one

---

[18] Letter dated 19 November 2007.

another. By God's outpouring of love, we come to share in the kind of life that is characteristic of God's own eternal life. Our love of God appears as a response to God's prior love for us in its absolute gratuity and causelessness.

Thus to speak of our love for God is before all else to speak in words of praise and gratitude. And for both Jews and Christians, that language of praise has been shaped by and centred upon the Psalms of David:

[1] I will extol you, my God and King, and bless your name forever and ever.

[2] Every day I will bless you, and praise your name forever and ever.

[3] Great is the LORD, and greatly to be praised; his greatness is unsearchable.
...

[15] The eyes of all look to you, and you give them their food in due season.

[16] You open your hand, satisfying the desire of every living thing.
...

[21] My mouth will speak the praise of the LORD, and all flesh will bless his holy name forever and ever.

(Psalm 145)

In words like these, we hear many resonances with the language of your letter, suggesting a similar kind of devotion expressed in words of love, praise and thanks. The language of the Psalms, like the language you have used, looks to a God of ultimate creative power who is loving and compassionate, generous, faithful and merciful, and upholds justice. In the Psalms, generation after generation has found inspiration and encouragement in the heights, depths and ordinariness of human life. Countless Christians and Jews use them daily. They show, in the words of your letter, how worshippers "must be grateful to God and trust Him with all their sentiments and emotions", and that "the call to be totally devoted and attached to God heart and soul, far from being a call for a mere emotion or for a mood, is in fact an injunction requiring all-embracing, constant and active love of God. It demands a love in which the innermost spiritual heart and the whole of the soul – with its intelligence, will and feeling – participate through devotion."

The Psalms are the songs of a worshipping community, not only of individuals, a community taken up into love and adoration of God, yet acknowledging all the unwelcome and unpalatable aspects of the world we live in – individual suffering and corporate disaster, betrayal, injustice and sin. They are cries of pain as well as of joy, of bewilderment as well as trust, laments for God's apparent absence as well as celebrations of his presence. They are a challenge to find words to praise God in all circumstances. Your letter, in opening up for us some of the riches of the devotion of the Qur'an helps us appreciate afresh the riches of the Psalms. Perhaps in future the statement in the Qur'an, *"to David We gave the Psalms"* (4:163), might encourage us to explore further together our traditions and practices of praise and how in our diverse ways we seek to bring to God the whole of our human imagination and sensitivity in a unified act of praise.

The Psalms teach us that the name of God, God's full, personal, mysterious and unsearchable reality, is to be continually celebrated and the life of faith is to be filled with praise of God.[19] We love God first not for what he has done for us but 'for his name's sake' – because of who God *is*. Even in the midst of terrible suffering or doubt it is possible, with Job, to say: **"Blessed be the name of the Lord"** (Job 1:21). In the prayer which Jesus taught to his disciples the leading petition is: **"Hallowed be your name"** (Matthew 6:9). This means not only that honouring and blessing God is the first and most comprehensive activity of those who follow Jesus; it also encourages Christians to give thanks for all the ways in which God's name is proclaimed as holy and to be held in honour – by Christians, by people of other faiths and indeed by the whole order of creation which proclaims the glory of God.[20]

9 Mountains and all hills, fruit trees and all cedars!

10 Wildw animals and all cattle, creeping things and flying birds!

11 Kings of the earth and all peoples, princes and all rulers of the earth!

12 Young men and women alike, old and young together!

13 Let them praise the name of the LORD, for his name alone is exalted; his glory is above earth and heaven.

(Psalm 148)

---

19 Psalm 145:1 quoted above and, e.g., Psalm 113:1–6:

1Praise the LORD! Praise, O servants of the LORD; praise the name of the LORD.

2Blessed be the name of the LORD from this time on and for evermore.

3From the rising of the sun to its setting the name of the LORD is to be praised.

4The LORD is high above all nations, and his glory above the heavens.

5Who is like the LORD our God, who is seated on high,

6who looks far down on the heavens and the earth?

20 Amongst many examples see Psalm 148:9–13 quoted above and

1The heavens are telling the glory of God; and the firmament proclaims his handiwork.

2Day to day pours forth speech, and night to night declares knowledge. (Psalm 19:1-2)

So, with all creation, we join together in this chorus of universal praise – echoed so vividly in some of the phrases quoted in your letter.[21.]

Jesus said "I came that they [we] **may have life, and have it abundantly**" (John 10:10), and offering such praise and honour to God is in many ways the heart of the new life. The conviction that the love of God lives in us through his Holy Spirit, that to God we owe the very breath of life within us, is the motivation for our response to God's love – both in loving God and loving neighbour. We know from personal experience that true love can not be commanded or conditioned; it is freely given and received. Our love of God, as already indicated, is first and foremost a response of gratitude enabling us to grow in holiness – to become closer and closer in our actions and thoughts to the complete self-giving that always exists perfectly in God's life and is shown in the life and death of Jesus.

Towards this fullness we are all called to travel and grow and we shall want to learn from you more about the understandings of love of God in Islam as we continue this journey, exploring the implications of this love in our lives and our relationships with each other. Jesus, on the night before he died, said, **"I give you a new commandment, that you love one another. Just as I have loved you, you also should love one another"** (John 13:34). Responding to this new commandment to dwell in the love he bears us means allowing it to transform us and, so transformed, to love others – irrespective of their response.

Love of Our Neighbour

[Jesus said:] 'You have heard that it was said, "You shall love your neighbour and hate your enemy."[44] But I say to you, Love your enemies and pray for those who persecute you,[45] so that you may be children of your Father in heaven; for he makes his sun rise on the evil and on the good, and sends rain on the righteous and on the unrighteous.[46] For if you love those who love you, what reward do you have? Do not even the tax-collectors do the same?[47] And if you greet only your brothers and sisters, what more are you doing than others? Do not even the Gentiles do the same?[48] Be perfect, therefore, as your heavenly Father is perfect'

(Matthew 5:43–8).

[21] "The words: *His is the sovereignty and His is the praise and He hath power over all things,* when taken all together, remind Muslims that just as everything in creation glorifies God, everything that is in their souls must be devoted to God: *All that is in the heavens and all that is in the earth glorifieth God…*(al-Taghabun, 64:1)" "God says in one of the very first revelations in the Holy Qur'an: *So invoke the Name of thy Lord and devote thyself to Him with a complete devotion* (al-Muzzammil, 73:8)"

We support the clear affirmation in your letter, through texts from the Qur'an and the Bible, of the importance of love for the neighbour. Indeed, your letter can be considered an encouraging example of this love. We endorse the emphasis on generosity and self-sacrifice, and trust that these might be mutual marks of our continuing relationship with each other. The section in your letter on love for the neighbour is relatively brief, so we look forward to developing further the ways in which the theme is worked out within our traditions. We believe we have much to learn from each other in this matter, drawing on resources of wisdom, law, prophecy, poetry and narrative, both within and beyond our canonical scriptures[22] to help each other come to a richer vision of being loving neighbours today.

For Christians, our love for God is always a response to God's prior free love of humankind (and all creation). Enabled by this gift of love, our love becomes by grace something that mirrors the character of God's love and so can be offered to the stranger and the other. A full exploration of the significance of this will only be possible as we grow in our encounters together but, within the confines of this letter, we would want to draw attention to two aspects of the love of neighbour that are important for Christians.

The first is illustrated in St Luke's gospel when Jesus, having given the Dual Commandment of love as the response to the question "what must I do to inherit eternal life?", goes on to tell the parable of the Good Samaritan when asked to explain "who is my neighbour?"[23] Commentary on this parable frequently points to the way

---

[22] The stories of saints and other exemplary people can often be of special value in conveying the quality of love.

[23] Just then a lawyer stood up to test Jesus. 'Teacher,' he said, 'what must I do to inherit eternal life?' [26]He said to him, 'What is written in the law? What do you read there?' [27]He answered, 'You shall love the Lord your God with all your heart, and with all your soul, and with all your strength, and with all your mind; and your neighbour as yourself.' [28]And he said to him, 'You have given the right answer; do this, and you will live.' [29] But wanting to justify himself, he asked Jesus, 'And who is my neighbour?' [30]Jesus replied, 'A man was going down from Jerusalem to Jericho, and fell into the hands of robbers, who stripped him, beat him, and went away, leaving him half dead. [31]Now by chance a priest was going down that road; and when he saw him, he passed by on the other side. [32]So likewise a Levite, when he came to the place and saw him, passed by on the other side. [33]But a Samaritan while travelling came near him; and when he saw him, he was moved with pity. [34]He went to him and bandaged his wounds, having poured oil and wine on them. Then he put him on his own animal, brought him to an inn, and took care of him. [35]The next day he took out two denarii, gave them to the innkeeper, and said, "Take care of him; and when I come back, I will repay you whatever more you spend." [36]Which of these three, do you think, was a neighbour to

in which Jesus challenges the assumptions of the question; instead of defining a necessarily limited group of people who might fit the category of 'neighbours' to whom love should be shown, he speaks of the need to prove ourselves neighbours by compassion to whoever is before us in need or pain, whether or not they are akin to us, approved by us, safe for us to be with or whatever else. Such neighbourliness will mean crossing religious and ethnic divisions and transcending ancient enmities. So the 'neighbour' of the original Torah is defined by Jesus as whoever the 'other' is who specifically and concretely requires self-forgetful attention and care in any moment. Thus to be a neighbour is a challenge that continually comes at us in new ways. We cannot define its demands securely in advance; it demands that we be ready to go beyond the boundaries of our familiar structures of kinship and obligation, whether these are local, racial or religious. For that reason – developing a helpful symbolic reading of this parable – Christian thinkers have often said that Jesus himself is our first 'neighbour', the one who comes alongside every human being in need.[24] We look forward to the opportunity to explore with you how this teaching about being a neighbour relates to the Qur'anic imperative to care for neighbour and stranger (an imperative that seems to be derived here from the worship of God).[25]

The second aspect, already mentioned above, is Jesus' teaching about the love of those who do not necessarily love you. We have quoted above the version attributed to St Matthew, but the Gospel according to Luke contains a similar passage:

If anyone strikes you on the cheek, offer the other also; and from anyone who takes away your coat do not withhold even your shirt.[30] Give to everyone who begs from you; and if anyone takes away your goods, do not ask for them again.[31] Do to others as you would have them do to you …[35] But love your enemies, do good, and lend, expecting nothing in return. Your reward

---

the man who fell into the hands of the robbers?' [37]He said, 'The one who showed him mercy.' Jesus said to him, 'Go and do likewise.' (Luke 10:25–37)

[24] Cf. Karl Barth's similarly reversing reading of this parable: 'The primary and true form of the neighbour is that he faces us as the bearer and representative of the divine compassion,' *Church Dogmatics*, volume I/2, eds. G. W. Bromiley and T. F. Torrance (Edinburgh: T&T Clark, 1956), p. 416.

[25] "*Worship God; join nothing with Him. Be good to your parents, to relatives, to orphans, to the needy, to neighbours near and far, to travellers in need, and to your slaves.*" (4:36)

will be great, and you will be children of the Most High; for he is kind to the ungrateful and the wicked.[36] Be merciful, just as your Father is merciful
(Luke 6:29-31,35-36).

This radical teaching, which Jesus presents precisely as a higher inter- pretation of what it means to love the neighbour, is grounded, as we have seen, in the way in which God loves. It teaches us to recognise as neighbour even those who set themselves against us. This is partly required by humility before the design of God in history and the limited nature of our perspective, for we do not know, as Christians have often said, who among those who confront us in hostility today will turn out to be our friends on the last day, when we stand before our Judge. It is partly, too, 'that we may be children of our Father in heaven,'[26] learning to share the perspective of God, who reaches out and seeks to win all his creatures to his love, even those who turn away from it. This resonates with what is said in the Qur'an: *"God may still bring about affection between you and your present enemies – God is all powerful, God is most forgiving and merciful"* (Al-Mumtahana 60:7). Where love replaces enmity we can recognise the work and way of God.

SEEKING THE COMMON GOOD
IN THE WAY OF GOD

THE COMMON GOOD

"Love works no ill to his neighbour"
(Romans 13:10)

"Let brotherly love continue. Be not forgetful to entertain strangers"
(Hebrews 13:1–2)

There are many practical implications that flow from our understandings of love of God and love of neighbour, including those mentioned in your letter regarding peacemaking, religious freedom and the avoidance of violence.[27] In response we should like to offer a vision, grounded in absolute faithfulness to our respective religious convictions, that

---

[26] Cf. Matthew 5:45.
[27] Among the many items for this agenda one respondent, Colin Chapman, suggests:
  - **Our histories:** we need to recognise the legacy of 1400 years of sometimes difficult relationships between Christians and Muslims. Both faiths have at different times and in different places been associated with conquest and empire. And while there have been times of peaceful co-existence, conflicts between Muslims and Christians

we believe we can share in offering to our fellow believers and our neighbours (in the widest sense).

To believe in an absolute religious truth is to believe that the object of our belief is not vulnerable to the contingencies of human history: God's mind and character cannot be changed by what happens here in the world. Thus an apparent defeat in the world for our belief cannot be definitive; God does not fail just because we fail to persuade others or because our communities fail to win some kind of power. If we were to believe that our failure is a failure or defeat for God, then the temptation will be to seek for any means possible to avoid such an outcome. But that way lies terrorism and religious war and persecution. The idea that any action, however extreme or disruptive or even murderous, is justified if it averts failure or defeat for a particular belief or a particular religious group is not really consistent with the conviction that our failure does not mean God's failure. Indeed, it

in the past (and present) have left their mark on the collective memory of both communities.

- The wide variety of reasons for tensions in different situations today: while there are some common factors in all situations where Muslims and Christians live side by side, in each situation there is also likely to be a unique set of factors – political, economic, cultural or social – which contribute to these tensions.
- Christians and Muslims as minorities: we recognise that 25% of Muslims worldwide are living in minority situations, and Christians also in many parts of the world find themselves as minorities. In contexts like these both Christians and Muslims face similar dilemmas and may have more in common with each other than with their secular neighbours.
- The Israeli-Palestinian conflict is at or near the top of the list of issues that concern both Christians and Muslims all over the world. This conflict is quite unique in the way that religion and politics are so thoroughly intertwined. Christian and Muslim leaders therefore have a special responsibility both to educate their own communities about 'the things that make for peace' and to appeal to their political leaders to work for a just resolution of the conflict.

Love of the neighbour, as *A Common Word Suggests*, provides a firm basis on which to address many of these immediate issues that affect Christian – Muslim relations all over the world. When Muslims point to the saying of Muhammad "None of you has faith until you love for your brother (or neighbour) what you love for yourself", Christians point to the Golden Rule as taught by Jesus: 'In everything do to others as you would have them do to you; for this is the law and the prophets' (Matthew 7:12). This must mean in practice, for example, that when western Christians try to put themselves in the shoes of the Christians in Egypt and reflect on how they would like to be treated in that minority situation, this should affect the way that they think about Muslim minorities in the West. The principle of reciprocity seems to many to be a natural expression of love of the neighbour, since it means wanting for our neighbours what we want for ourselves. Its acceptance by both Christians and Muslims would help to resolve many of the tensions experienced by both Christian and Muslim minorities.

reveals a fundamental lack of conviction in the eternity and sufficiency of the object of faith.

Religious violence suggests an underlying religious insecurity. When different communities have the same sort of conviction of the absolute truth of their perspective, there is certainly an intellectual and spiritual challenge to be met; but the logic of this belief ought to make it plain that there can be no justification for the sort of violent contest in which any means, however inhuman, can be justified by appeal to the need to 'protect God's interests'. Even to express it in those terms is to show how absurd it is. The eternal God cannot need 'protection' by the tactics of human violence. This point is captured in the words of Jesus before the Roman governor: **"My kingdom is not of this world. If it were, my servants would fight"** (John 19:36).

So we can conclude that the more we as people of genuine faith are serious about the truth of our convictions, the more likely we will be to turn away from violence in the name of faith; to trust that God, the truly real, will remain true, divine and unchanging, whatever the failures and successes of human society and history. And we will be aware that to try and compel religious allegiance through violence is really a way of seeking to replace divine power with human; hence the Qur'anic insistence that there can be no compulsion in matters of religious faith (al-Baqarah, 2:256)[28] and the endorsement in your letter of "freedom of religion". It is crucial to faith in a really existing and absolute transcendent agency that we should understand it as being what it is quite independently of any lesser power: the most disturbing form of secularisation is when this is forgotten or misunderstood.

This has, indeed, been forgotten or misunderstood in so many contexts over the millennia. Religious identity has often been confused with cultural or national integrity, with structures of social control, with class and regional identities, with empire; and it has been imposed in the interest of all these and other forms of power. Despite Jesus' words in John's gospel, Christianity has been promoted at the point of the sword and legally supported by extreme sanctions;[29] despite

---

[28] *There is no compulsion in religion.*

[29] There has been, and continues to be, a tradition within Christianity that has argued the moral rightness of using force in certain carefully defined circumstances, most notably through the application of the "just war" criteria formulated by St Augustine of Hippo and developed by St Thomas Aquinas.

the Qur'anic axiom, Islam has been supported in the same way, with extreme penalties for abandoning it, and civil disabilities for those outside the faith. There is no religious tradition whose history is exempt from such temptation and such failure.

What we need as a vision for our dialogue is to break the current cycles of violence, to show the world that faith and faith alone can truly ground a commitment to peace which definitively abandons the tempting but lethal cycle of retaliation in which we simply imitate each other's violence.[30] Building on our understanding of God's love for us and, in response, our love for God and neighbour we can speak of a particular quality to the Christian approach to peace and peace-making: the moment of <u>unconditioned</u> positive response, the risk of offering something to one whom you have no absolutely secure reason to trust.

Many Christians have said that your letter represents such an offering – a gift with no certainty of what might be the response. We want to acknowledge the courage of such a move, and respond in kind. Let us explore together how this dimension of Christian language, born of the unconditional and self-sacrificial love of neighbour, can be correlated with the language of the Qur'an.

Such an approach can take us beyond a bland affirmation that we are at peace with those who are at peace with us to a place where our religious convictions can be a vehicle for creating peace where it is absent.

Such a commitment to seek together the common good can, we are convinced, sit alongside a fundamental recognition that, even with

---

[30] And here we must recognise, in the words of the initial reflections on *A Common Word* offered by Daniel Madigan SJ "... an honest examination of conscience will not permit us to forget that our future is not threatened only by conflict between us. Over the centuries of undeniable conflict and contestation between members of our two traditions, each group has had its own internal conflicts that have claimed and continue to claim many more lives than interconfessional strife. More Muslims are killed daily by other Muslims than by Christians or anyone else. The huge numbers who went to their deaths in the Iran-Iraq war of the 1980's were virtually all Muslims. Scarcely any of the tens of millions of Christians who have died in European wars over the centuries were killed by Muslims. The greatest shame of the last century was the killing of millions of Jews by Christians conditioned by their own long tradition of anti-Semitism and seduced by a virulently nationalist and racist new ideology. The last 15 years in Africa have seen millions of Christians slaughtered in horrendous civil wars by their fellow believers... So let us not be misled into thinking either that Muslim-Christian conflict is the world's greatest conflict, or even that war is the most serious threat to the human future."

our commitments to love God and neighbour, we cannot expect to find some 'neutral' positions beyond the traditions of our faith that would allow us to broker some sort of union between our diverse convictions. Far from being a cause for concern, holding fast to our truth claims whilst rejecting violence does two very positive things at once. First it affirms the transcendent source of faith: it says that our views are not just human constructions which we can abandon when they are inconvenient. Second, by insisting that no other values, no secular values, are absolute, it denies to all other systems of values any justification for uncontrolled violence. Transcendent values can be defended through violence only by those who do not fully understand their transcendent character; and if no other value is absolute, no other value can claim the right to unconditional defence by any means and at all costs.

So, even if we accept that our systems of religious belief cannot be reconciled by 'rational' argument because they depend on the gift of revelation, we rule out, by that very notion, any assumption that coercive human power is the ultimate authority and arbiter in our world. Given, as we have acknowledged, that Christian history contains too many examples of Christians betraying that initial turning away from the cycle of retaliation, we can only put forward such a vision in the form of a challenge to Christians as much as Muslims: how did we ever come to think that the truly transcendent can ever be imagined or proclaimed in a pattern of endless and sterile repetition of force?

And here we can together suggest a way in which religious plurality can be seen as serving the cause of social unity and acting as a force for the common good. As people of faith, we can never claim that social harmony can be established by uncontrolled coercive power. This means that we are not obliged to defend and argue for the legitimacy and righteousness of any social order. As the world now is, diverse religious traditions very frequently inhabit one territory, one nation, one social unit (and that may be a relatively small unit like a school, or a housing co-operative or even a business). In such a setting, we cannot avoid the pragmatic and secular question of 'common security': what is needed for our convictions to flourish is bound up with what is needed for the convictions of other groups to flourish. We learn that we can best defend ourselves by defending others. In a plural society, Christians secure their religious liberty by advocacy for the liberty of people of other faiths to have the same right to be heard in the continuing conversation about the direction and ethos of society.

And we can extend this still further. If we are in the habit of defending each other, we ought to be able to learn to defend other groups and communities as well. We can together speak for those who have no voice or leverage in society – for the poorest, the most despised, the least powerful, for women and children, for migrants and minorities; and even to speak together for that great encompassing reality which has no 'voice' or power of its own – our injured and abused material environment, which both our traditions of faith tell us we should honour and care for.

Our voice in the conversation of society will be the stronger for being a joint one. If we are to be true to the dual commandment of love, we need to find ways of being far more effective in influencing our societies to follow the way of God in promoting that which leads to human flourishing – honesty and faithfulness in public and private relationships, in business as in marriage and family life; the recognition that a person's value is not an economic matter; the clear recognition that neither material wealth nor entertainment can secure a true and deep-rooted human fulfilment.

SEEKING TOGETHER IN THE WAY OF GOD

A Common Word Between Us and You issues a powerful call to dialogue and collaboration between Christians and Muslims. A great deal is already happening in this sphere on many levels, but the very wide geographical (43 countries) and theological diversity represented among the signatories of your letter provides a unique impetus to deepen and extend the encounters. As part of the common shape and structure of our language about God we can acknowledge a shared commitment to truth and a desire to discern how our lives may come to be lived in accordance with eternal truth. As we have noted above, the Christian understanding of love, coupled with our common acknowledgement of the absolute transcendence of the divine, encourages us towards a vision of radical and transformative non-violence. We are committed to reflecting and working together, with you and all our human neighbours, with a view both to practical action and service and to a long term dedication to all that will lead to a true common good for human beings before God.

This is a good moment to attempt to coordinate a way forward for our dialogue. We suggest an approach drawing on *Dialogue and Proclamation*, a 1991 Vatican document whose four categories of inter-religious dialogue have been found widely helpful. They are:

a *the dialogue of life*, "where people strive to live in an open and neighbourly spirit";
b *the dialogue of action*, "in which Christians and others collaborate for the integral development and liberation of people";
c *the dialogue of theological exchange*, "where specialists seek to deepen their understanding of their respective religious heritages"; and
d *the dialogue of religious experience*, "where persons rooted in their own religious traditions share their spiritual riches".

This typology can be applied more generally to the whole pattern of encounter between Christians and Muslims, even where this is not directly described as 'dialogue'.

Three imperatives are suggested by this:

a to strengthen grass-roots partnerships and programmes between our communities that will work for justice, peace and the common good of human society the world over;
b to intensify the shared theological discussions and researches of religious leaders and scholars who are seeking clearer insight into divine truth, and to realise this through building and sustaining of groups marked by a sense of collegiality, mutual esteem, and trust;[31]
c to deepen the appreciation of Christian and Muslim believers for each other's religious practice and experience, as they come to recognise one another as people whose lives are oriented towards God in love.[32]

---

[31] While such colloquia should be characterised by a high degree of academic rigour, they should also draw on and express the personal commitment of religious leaders and scholars to their respective faiths.
[32] This will require spending time in each other's presence, exploring the depth of each other's spirituality, and acknowledging both the variety and the depth of prayer, remembrance and celebration in both faiths.

These different kinds of encounter need to be held together to ensure a balanced and effective pattern of encounter. The approach of your letter shows the importance of shared and attentive study of Biblical and Qur'anic texts as a way of ensuring both that all dimensions of encounter are present and also that Christians and Muslims are held accountable to, and draw on the riches of, their respective traditions of faith whilst recognising the limitations – at least initially – in our ability to comment authoritatively on the others' scriptures.[33]

As we noted earlier, the role of the Qu'ran in Islam is not really parallel to the role of the Bible in Christianity. For Christians, God's Word was made flesh in Jesus Christ. Our understanding of the Scriptures is that they witness to and draw their authority from Christ, describing the witness of prophets and apostles to his saving work. They are the voice of his living Spirit who, Christians believe, dwells among us and within us. Nevertheless, for us as for you, reading the Scriptures is a constant source of inspiration, nurture and correction, and this makes it very appropriate for Christians and Muslims to listen to one another, and question one another, in the course of reading and interpreting the texts from which we have learned of God's will and purposes. And for Christians and Muslims together addressing our scriptures in this way, it is essential also to take account of the place of the Jewish people and of the Hebrew scriptures in our encounter, since we both look to our origins in that history of divine revelation and action.

The use of scriptures in inter-religious dialogue has considerable potential, but there are also risks in this approach when we think we know or understand another's sacred texts but in fact are reading them exclusively through our own spectacles. We hope that one early outcome of studying and discussing together will be to work out wise

---

[33] The Christian Bible, Old and New Testaments together, forms a large narrative (with, admittedly, many subordinate parts some of which do not well fit the 'narrative' model) from creation to new creation, from the Garden of Eden to the New Jerusalem which comes down from heaven to earth. Within this narrative, Jesus Christ is presented as the climax of the story of the world's creation on the one hand and of the call of Abraham on the other: the stories of Jesus are not *just* 'stories of Jesus' but 'stories of Jesus seen as the fulfilment of covenant and creation'. The multiple teachings which are found variously throughout the Bible – doctrine about God, rules for behaviour, religious practices etc. – are set, and best understood, within that overall story. It would be worth exploring in some detail how Muslims see these aspects of Christian scripture and whether there are ways in which such a perception would create new kinds of possibilities for dialogue.

guidelines, practices and educational resources for this element of our engagement.

Given the variety of forms of encounter which are to be held together as we deepen our engagement with each other, we can identify three main outcomes which we might seek together. They will depend on the establishment and maintenance of credible and durable structures of collegiality, trust and respect between key individuals and communities in our two faiths. The three outcomes are:

a   Maintaining and strengthening the momentum of what is already happening in Christian-Muslim encounter. An important stream flowing into this will be the continuing conversations around your letter and the Christian responses to it. Reaching back before that also, there has been a growing corpus of action and reflection in this area at least from *Nostra Aetate* (1965) onwards. The recent gathering of Muslim religious leaders and scholars in Mecca and the subsequent convening of a conference in Madrid, for example, is another promising development. It is important that any new initiatives acknowledge this wider picture of Christian-Muslim encounter, and position themselves in relation to it, learning from both its achievements and set-backs.

b   Finding safe spaces within which the differences – as well as the convergences – between Christians and Muslims can be honestly and creatively articulated and explored. Our two faiths have differed deeply on points of central importance to both of us, points of belief as well as points of practice. It is essential for the health of our encounter that we should find ways of talking freely yet courteously about those differences; indeed, honesty of this kind has been described as the most certain sign of maturity in dialogue.

c   Ensuring that our encounters are not for the sake of participants alone, but are capable of having an influence which affects people more widely – Christians and Muslims at the level of all our local communities, and also those engaged in the wider realities of our societies and our world. Seeking the common good is a purpose around which Christians and Muslims can unite, and in leads us into all kinds of complex territory as we seek to find ways of acting effectively in the world of modern global and democratic politics.

Within the wide diversity of patterns of encounter and participation, it will be desirable to establish some broad priorities in order to keep Christian-Muslim relations focused and effective around a number of core themes. Again, three steps seem worth establishing here:

a First, there is an urgent need in both our traditions for education about one another. We are all influenced by prejudices and misunderstandings inherited from the past – and often renewed in the present through the power of media stereotyping. Teaching and learning about the reality and diversity of Islam as Muslims practise their faith should be a priority as important to Christians as understanding of actual Christianity should be to Muslims. In concrete terms, such educational programmes might be initially be focused on those preparing clergy and imams respectively for public inter-faith roles and on those providing religious education to young people.

b Second, opportunities for lived encounter with people of different faiths, both within and across national boundaries, need to be multiplied and developed in an atmosphere of trust and respect. These should take place on many different levels and in many different settings. Such opportunities might usefully be focused on educational projects, efforts towards the attainment of the Millennium Development Goals and shared work for reconciliation in situations of conflict and historic enmities.

c Finally, for encounters to be sustainable over a long period of time, there needs to be commitment to the process and to one another on the part of all participants. Such a commitment, growing into affection, respect, collegiality and friendship, will be an expression of love of neighbour; it will also be done in love for God and in response to God's will.

We believe that *A Common Word Between Us and You* opens the way for these steps to be approached in a new spirit. The limitations of making further statements or sending further letters in advance of meeting together are obvious, however good and friendly the intentions. We greatly look forward therefore to discussing face to face some of the questions arising from these exchanges of letters, exploring – as was said earlier – both the concepts that have been sketched and the new possibilities for creative work together for the good of our world.

So to your invitation to enter more deeply into dialogue and collaboration as a part of our faithful response to the revelation of God's purpose for humankind, we say: Yes! Amen.

In the love of God,

+ Rowan Cantuar:

14 July 2008

5

The World in Which We Respond to God's Word

Ingrid Mattson

Dealings with other people, when there is oneness of purpose, may lead to mutual affection, and when purposes differ, they may lead to strife and altercation. Thus, mutual dislike and mutual affection, friendship and hostility, originate. This leads to war and peace among nations and tribes.

(Ibn Khaldūn, *al-Muqaddima*)[1]

It is this basic truth, articulated by Ibn Khaldūn (d. 1406), one of the most original pre-modern analysts of human civilisations, which is the raison d'être of *A Common Word*. Unless a common purpose is found among people who consider themselves different – that is, 'other people' – when these people have to 'deal' with each other, conflict will result. This may be a stark conclusion, but it is one proven by history.

ACW opens with the following statement:

Muslims and Christians together make up well over half of the world's population. Without peace and justice between these two religious communities, there can be no meaningful peace in the world. The future of the world depends on peace between Muslims and Christians.[2]

Thus, according to *ACW*, it is a necessary condition for peace in the world that Muslims and Christians do not make their religious differences a reason for hostility. One simply cannot dispute the maths. Islam and Christianity are global religions, which is to say that Muslims and Christians are found all over the world. If our religions are essentially

---

[1] Ibn Khaldun, *The Muqaddimah: An Introduction to History*, trans. Franz Rosenthal, abridged and ed. N. J. Dawood (Princeton, NJ: Princeton University Press, 1967), p. 336.
[2] *A Common Word* (English version), p. 2. www.acommonword.com/downloads-and-translations/.

hostile towards each other, if our orthodox theologies teach us to hate each other, then anger, intolerance and violence, justified by religious discourse and motivated by religious sentiment, will be endemic to societies across the world.

ACW was a response to a characterisation of Christianity and Islam which suggested an essential incompatibility, hostility and absence of the necessary conditions for dialogue and reconciliation between the two. Most devastating was the characterisation, cited by Pope Benedict in his Regensburg address, of Islam as essentially irrational. Given that reason is, in most philosophical and theological systems, a defining feature of the human being, there is little besides denying that Muslims have a soul that would have felt more dehumanising than denying the rationality of our religion. The insult to and mischaracterisation of Islam were felt keenly by Muslim theologians and interfaith activists as a betrayal by a church with whom they had been engaged in friendly and open dialogue in recent decades. The revival of the mediaeval European polemic that Islam is irrational seemed to be a misguided, essentialising search for Christian and Islamic identities which would make the former uniquely, and inexorably, part of Europe.[3] Muslims did not feel that the statements were any less harmful when they were reassured by some Catholic friends that Islam was not the main concern of the address, but was only being 'used' to make an argument in support of a Christian Europe.

In this context, what made so many Muslims excited and encouraged to sign on to ACW, and to be part of its propagation, was the fact that, rather than responding to the insult in kind, rather than continuing the centuries-old cycle of polemic and apologetics, ACW was an attempt at a fresh start. In an environment where terrorists were using Islam to rationalise violence and oppression, no responsible Muslim leader wanted to respond to Regensburg in a hostile, argumentative tone. We were alarmed at the violent extremists' tactical leveraging of Islamic discourse

---

[3] 'This inner rapprochement between Biblical faith and Greek philosophical inquiry was an event of decisive importance not only from the standpoint of the history of religions, but also from that of world history – it is an event which concerns us even today. Given this convergence, it is not surprising that Christianity, despite its origins and some significant developments in the East, finally took on its historically decisive character in Europe. We can also express this the other way around: this convergence, with the subsequent addition of the Roman heritage, created Europe and remains the foundation of what can rightly be called Europe' (Pope Benedict XVI, 'Faith, reason and the university: memories and reflections', 12 September 2006. https://w2.vatican.va/content/benedict-xvi/en/speeches/2006/september/documents/hf_ben-xvi_spe_20060912_university-regensburg .html. Accessed 19 October 2016.

and sentiments and understood that our Christian friends would naturally be alarmed as well. We had to give our friends, including the Catholic Church and its leader, the benefit of the doubt. We were determined to leave the insult behind and propose a new foundation for a positive, harmonious relationship between Christians and Muslims.

While *ACW* tried to reframe the relationship between Christians and Muslims, it is subject to interpretation by a wide diversity of Christian and Muslim communities and movements. Not everyone wants to reframe the relationship. Some are ideologically committed to polemics, believing it is their religious duty to attack what they consider to be falsehood through any means available. Others are more strategic, understanding that attacking people seldom succeeds in opening their hearts and minds, yet they are still convinced they have a full understanding of the other's beliefs, and that those beliefs are wrong. Thus, their goal is to continue to attack those beliefs, rather than to try to have a better understanding of the 'Other' and to find common ground by doing so. For militant ideologues, peace is not a goal; rather, peace creates an existential void, and they find their deepest personal meaning and identity by engaging in violence, sanctified by religion or nationalism.[4] On the other side of the ideological spectrum are religious scholars and activists who believe that God does not want religious diversity wiped out by any means necessary, and that peaceful relations among Christians and Muslims are a divinely sanctioned goal. Thus, *ACW* was not sent into a vacuum, but into communities of theologians, ethicists and religious leaders who had been theorising and practising interfaith engagement – or actively rejecting it – for many decades.

Given this history and context, it is not surprising that 'A Common Word for the Common Good',[5] the response to *ACW* from Rowan Williams, written in 2008 when he was Archbishop of Canterbury and head of the global Anglican Communion,[6] was largely thoughtful and friendly. Williams is an outstanding theologian with a keen interest in social justice who gives the impression of being a person who has savoured

---

[4] 'The enduring attraction of war is this: Even with its destruction and carnage it can give us what we long for in life. It can give us purpose, meaning, a reason for living.' Chris Hedges, *War Is a Force That Gives Us Meaning* (New York: Anchor Books, 2002), p. 3.

[5] Chapter 4 in this volume.

[6] Rowan Williams was Archbishop of Canterbury from 2002 to 2012, when he stepped down to become Master of Magdalene College, Cambridge. His current official title is 'The Right Reverend and Right Honourable The Lord Williams of Oystermouth.' For the sake of simplicity and consistency, in this chapter I will refer to him as Williams.

the fruits of a rich spiritual life. Williams says that he finds in the invitation of *ACW* a 'helpful generosity of intention', and the same can be said about Williams' response. While some other Christians have read *ACW* with a hermeneutic of suspicion, Williams says he finds in it 'a hospitable and friendly spirit', and he reciprocates in the same spirit, addressing his response to 'Muslim brothers and sisters everywhere' and with the salutation 'Dear friends'.[7] Attributing good faith to the Muslims who issued the invitation to *ACW* is an important choice made by Williams. No dialogue, no discussion and certainly no sense of common purpose, can exist between Christians and Muslims if one side is seen as untrustworthy, devious and deceitful.

As head of the Church of England, Williams was responsible for a church deeply entwined, historically, constitutionally and ceremonially, with the state. At the same time, since the late twentieth century, the United Kingdom has legislatively committed itself to freedom of religion for all its citizens. Around the time Williams took leadership of the Church of England, Muslims constituted approximately 5 per cent of the population. The acceptance of Muslims, most of them non-white and immigrants from lands formerly colonised by the British Empire, has not been universally enthusiastic, to say the least.[8] Racism, Islamophobia and discrimination are regular issues of concern in modern Britain. For its part, the Church of England has necessarily been involved in decisions to extend institutional religious accommodation to Muslims, such as having Muslims serve as chaplains in the military and in prisons, and establishing spaces for Islamic prayers in schools. The practical implementation of religious accommodation for the minority Muslim community has entailed, no doubt, a measure of awkwardness, mistakes and hurt feelings.[9] The British Muslim community is still in the early stages of establishing its own religious and educational institutions, organisational frameworks, scholars and strategic vision. Until relatively recently, academic theologians such as Williams would have found few intellectual peers among the Muslim community in Britain, although the country can boast as its own one of the most

---

[7] Williams, Chapter 4.

[8] See, for example, the 1997 Runnymede Trust report entitled 'Islamophobia: A Challenge for Us All'. www.runnymedetrust.org/uploads/publications/pdfs/islamophobia.pdf. Accessed 4 September 2016.

[9] For an analysis of these challenges, see Ingrid Mattson, 'Of fences and neighbors: an Islamic perspective on interfaith engagement for peace', October 2013. http://ingridmattson.org/article/of-fences-and-neighbors/. Accessed 4 September 2016.

eminent living Muslim theologians, Tim Winter, dean and founder of the Cambridge Muslim College.

As head of the Anglican Communion, Williams was a shepherd to diverse communities scattered across the globe, some of them living in Muslim-majority countries. There is no naïve encounter between our communities, and trust is not easily found among Christians and Muslims across the world. Globally, many Muslims still view the Anglican Church primarily through the experience of British colonialism, seeing the church as complicit in subjugating Muslim lands and having leveraged British imperial power for evangelism. Suspicion that the spirit of 'missions' lies behind any interfaith initiative disquiets many ordinary Muslims. For Anglicans in Muslim-majority lands, where religious freedom is too rarely protected by law, it is Muslim officials who hold the reins of power, and some have abused that power to intimidate or subjugate Christians, while others do not do enough to protect Christian minorities from extremist groups. Williams says that his response to *ACW* was crafted after a formal consultation of church representatives and Christian scholars in 2008 where he 'listened carefully to Christian colleagues from the widest possible range of backgrounds'.[10] No doubt Williams heard heart-breaking and repulsive stories about the abuse of Christians in places such as Pakistan and Nigeria.

To craft an honest and meaningful response to *ACW* that would be interpreted as such by global Anglicans as well as British Christians and Muslims and academic colleagues was undoubtedly a challenge. We must take this real-world background into consideration in reading Williams' response to *ACW*. As we shall discuss further later, the response nevertheless seems, from our perspective, unduly focused on religiously justified violence by Muslims, with little interrogation of violence perpetrated and justified by Christians. However, Williams has elsewhere written and spoken about the history and ongoing existence of violence, including economic violence, in his own society,[11] so we should not consider his response to *ACW* the sum total of his views on the matter. Indeed, during the closing press conference, where I spoke alongside Ali Gomaa and Rowan Williams, the latter called Christians to pay more heed to the deep structures of economic violence that put and keep people in poverty.[12]

---

[10] Williams, Chapter 4.

[11] Such as his book co-edited with Larry Elliott, *Crisis and Recovery: Ethics, Economics and Justice* (New York: Palgrave Macmillan, 2010).

[12] Steve Doughty, 'Archbishop calls for financiers to set "just and reasonable" interest rates', *Daily Mail*, 15 October 2008.

It should also be noted that Williams' response to *ACW* was primarily intended to offer topics for discussion at the *A Common Word* meeting of Anglicans and Muslims in Cambridge in 2008. As he says, 'The limitations of making further statements or sending further letters in advance of meeting together are obvious, however good and friendly the intentions', and 'face to face' discussions are greatly anticipated. The events of the Cambridge conference are listed in the 'Communiqué' issued on the final day of the conference and included lectures, group discussions and shared meals.[13] What happened between Williams' initial response to *ACW* and the final 'Communiqué' for the Cambridge conference is not documented, but these moments of human connection were surely as important as any texts issued.

Time does not heal all wounds, but spending time together, with full attention and empathy, is surely a balm that contributes to healing. Yet even those who sincerely wish to listen, to open their hearts and to seek common ground might find it difficult to do so. As every counsellor knows, even when a person wishes to leave behind old patterns of thinking and acting, it might not be possible, at least without much exertion over an extended period. Behavioural scientists say what many of the spiritual counsellors of our religious communities have long known, which is that negative thoughts and actions contribute to ingrained habits, changing the very structure of our hearts and minds. Some of these changes leave a permanent mark, so that even if we try to think differently, we are constantly exerting our will to reject our now-instinctive negative impulses.

At the Cambridge conference, and at other meetings of *ACW*, it has been my observation that most of the participants struggle to overcome ingrained habits of suspicion and defensiveness. The times when Christians and Muslims are mixed in together with each other, at mealtimes, at refreshment breaks, in hallways when we are stretching our legs waiting for a meeting to begin, are those when we are most open to each other as human beings, when we are the most present to each other. We are most guarded when we are in a formal setting, representing 'our side', deeply aware that we will be held accountable by our communities for what we say on their behalf, sometimes fearful that we will lose their allegiance if we veer too far, too quickly, from familiar positions.

---

[13] Rowan Williams and Ali Gomaa, 'Communiqué from A Common Word Conference', issued on 15 October 2008 at *A Common Word* Conference at the University of Cambridge. www.acommonword.com/communique-from-a-common-word-conference/. Accessed 4 September 2016.

In his recommendations in the section entitled 'Seeking Together in the Way of God', Williams says that we have to ensure that 'our encounters are not for the sake of participants alone' but can affect 'all our local communities'.[14] It is precisely at this intersection of authority and power that we – religious scholars, authorities and leaders – have to recognise humbly that we have been the problem as often as we have been the solution. In our desire to fortify the walls of our distinct religious identities, we have frequently impeded the 'dialogue of life', where 'people strive to live in an open and neighbourly spirit'. Historical accounts of Muslim and Christian clergy scolding their communities for mingling, celebrating each other's festivals and falling in love, are not in short supply.[15]

To this end, it is my observation that the value of *ACW* is primarily pastoral. The *ACW* is not anything close to a systematic theological document; rather, it is a 'permission slip' for ordinary Christians and Muslims to do what they want to do, that is, to be good neighbours. Like many theological documents, *ACW* is a corrective response to bad theology and destructive ideology. In my travels across much of North America and Europe, I have heard the same concern from ordinary Christians and Muslims trying to work together for peace and harmony: they have been told by people from their own faiths that they should not trust the 'Other', that they are disloyal to their community by working with the 'Other', that the 'Other' is not a brother or sister in any sense of the word, but an enemy to God and to their people. The value of *ACW* is that it is a simple, straightforward refutation of those claims. *ACW* liberates good-hearted Christians and Muslims to be mutually hospitable and to collaborate in good works. What else explains the enthusiasm with which *ACW* has been received across so many communities, and which we have all observed? Without any input from me, for example, shortly after *ACW* was issued, a small Franciscan congregation partnered with Muslims in my local community to create a 'welcoming ceremony' for the statement. There were songs, cakes and prayers joyfully shared among Christians and Muslims in Hartford, Connecticut. Why the enthusiasm? *ACW* and its positive responses from Christian leaders did not teach this community something new; these documents simply cleared the path of hate and suspicion that had seeped into their religious communities.

---

[14] Williams, Chapter 4.

[15] Some examples can be found in the following works: Alexandra Cuffel, 'From practice to polemic: shared saints and festivals as "women's religion" in the medieval Mediterranean', *Bulletin of the School of Oriental and African Studies, University of London*, 68/3 (2005), 401–19; Janina M. Safran, 'Identity and differentiation in ninth-century Al-Andalus', *Speculum*, 76/3 (2001), 573–98.

In his response to *ACW*, Williams addresses a number of topics subsumed under the broad banner of love of God and love of neighbour. In addition, Williams highlights three issues which are roughly summarised here. First, authenticity in dialogue, in particular the role that scripture should or should not play in establishing common theological ground for our dialogue; second, the conditions, including an ideological commitment to pluralism and political freedom, which allow us to explore our common concerns; third, practical suggestions for how we might move forward with our shared calling and responsibility before God and humanity. In the years that followed the Cambridge conference, many other conferences, symposia and publications, undertaken under the banner of *ACW*, engaged with many of Williams' concerns and suggestions, as well as those of other respondents. What follows is not a point-by-point response to Williams' response, although many of his points will be addressed in some way. It should also be noted that I have no comprehensive knowledge of Williams' writings and thought. I have consulted a number of his works to give some context and nuance to his comments; nevertheless, it is possible that I have misunderstood the implications of some of his statements, and I welcome clarification and correction in the future. My primary goal in this analysis is to respond to some of Williams' key questions as raised in his response to *ACW*, to bring to the surface some implications which I see as potentially problematic and to address some of the practical issues and urgent needs that Christians and Muslims must face in the decade after the publication of *ACW* if we truly wish the world to be at peace.

SCRIPTURE AS COMMON OR FALLOW GROUND IN *ACW*

Tim Winter writes:

Strait indeed is the gate through which the theologian walks, when seeking to represent the Other, particularly his or her own world's most significant Other, on its own terms, rather than on the terms of a theology of religions or a map of salvation history which he or she finds comfortable. Yet courtesy to strangers, as an Abrahamic virtue, must ultimately be about allowing them to bear witness to themselves, while remaining, without compromise, in commitment to one's own absolute covenant with God.[16]

---

[16] Tim Winter, 'Jesus and Muhammad: new convergences', *Muslim World*, 99/1 (2009), 21–38, at p. 21.

It is, therefore, eminently appropriate that Williams begins his response to ACW with an exposition on the Christian view of God in the light of its call to love 'the One God'. Williams is well aware that the doctrine of the Trinity has featured prominently in Muslim polemic against Christians for centuries, and that the majority of traditional Muslim scholars have considered all forms of Trinitarian doctrine to be condemned by the Qur'an. At the same time, Williams adopts a non-suspicious reading of ACW's call and welcomes what is apparently implied therein, which is that the Christians to whom the call is made believe in the same God as Muslims.

Yet Williams, like many other Christian respondents to ACW, is concerned that the scriptural evidence chosen to support the statement that Christians believe in 'the One God' leaves out the definitive Christian belief that Jesus is God. Indeed, in ACW, Jesus' teachings on the *Shema* are cited, but no Gospel passages which Christians cite to claim the divinity of Jesus are referenced. This leads us back to the perennial question, revisited in the wake of ACW by Miroslav Volf[17] and others, of whether Muslims accept that they and Christians worship the same God, whether that God is believed to be incarnate in Jesus and whether Christians can accept that Muslims worship the same God, if the divinity of Jesus is denied. Unlike some other Christian respondents, Williams never implies any bad faith on the part of the writers of ACW, suggesting that they were trying to trick Christians into affirming Islam's understanding of monotheism by their selection of Biblical passages. Rather, he points out that this is, to some extent, a consequence of trying to find common ground through scripture alone, a point that is taken further by Daniel A. Madigan in the present volume.[18] Williams says:

the role of the Qur'an in Islam is not really parallel to the role of the Bible in Christianity. For Christians, God's Word was made flesh in Jesus Christ. Our understanding of the Scriptures is that they witness to and draw their authority from Christ, describing the witness of prophets and apostles to his saving work. They are the voice of his living Spirit who, Christians believe, dwells among us and within us. Nevertheless, for us as for you, reading the Scriptures is a constant source of inspiration, nurture and correction, and this makes it very appropriate for Christians and Muslims to listen to one another, and question one another, in

---

17 Miroslav Volf, *Allah: A Christian Response* (New York: HarperCollins, 2011).
18 See Chapter 10 in this volume.

the course of reading and interpreting the texts from which we have learned of God's will and purposes.[19]

Here, Williams articulates a common understanding of a fundamental difference between the understanding of God's word in Islam and Christianity, wherein the Qur'an is God's word in the former, while Jesus is God's word in the latter, with Scripture, according to Williams, serving as a 'witness'. This ontological distinction between the Qur'an and the Bible, and implied functional equivalency between the Qur'an and Jesus, while commonplace, is misleading. One of the weaknesses of *ACW* and its responses is that each document makes claims about the 'Islamic' or the 'Christian' position, with little or no acknowledgement that there are significant theological differences within each group. For many Evangelical Christians, for example, the authority of the Bible as God's word is certainly stronger than in other denominations. Nevertheless, given that Williams' position is at least a mainstream or dominant Christian understanding of authority, and, especially, that he consulted a wide range of Christian leaders for his response, one could conclude that Williams sees major weakness in the way in which *ACW* seeks common ground, forcing Christians into a typically Islamic scriptural hermeneutic. But there is diversity in Islamic thought as well, critically, over the issue of what it means for the Qur'an to be 'God's word'. While the majority see the Qur'an as the only infallible source of God's guidance because it is the word of the living God, some other schools of thought see the Qur'an as the created word of God, unique, but not alone, as a source of guidance.[20] Even the majority school, however, does not believe that God's word is limited to the Qur'an. The Qur'an says:

If all the trees on earth were pens, and the sea – then seven more seas – were ink, the words of God would not be exhausted. Indeed, God is Mighty; Wise.

(Q 31:27)

Further, for the vast majority of Muslims (and once more we must acknowledge the internal diversity of Islamic thought), the Qur'an cannot be understood without the interpretation provided by the teachings and the life of the Prophet Muhammad. Even more, for the majority of Muslims, the denial that Muhammad is God's messenger is an act of disbelief. His

---

[19] Williams, Chapter 4.

[20] For an introduction to the different Islamic schools of thought regarding the ontological status of the Qur'an and related authority, see Ingrid Mattson, *The Story of the Qur'an: Its History and Place in Muslim Life*, 2nd edition (Malden, MA: Wiley-Blackwell, 2013), pp. 250–6.

normative example is a source of knowledge about the Divine will, and hence must be studied and implemented in a conscientious fashion.[21] But while *ACW* cites the Prophet Muhammad in places, it nowhere asserts that Christians must accept Muhammad as God's messenger in order to be considered people who worship the One God. Did Muslims also, then, leave too great a portion of their beliefs at the door in order to find common ground with Christians in *ACW*? Is *ACW* no more than a reductionist and selective call, which leaves each community a shadow or fragment of itself?

I would return to my assertion that *ACW* was never intended to be a comprehensive statement of Islamic or Christian doctrine. What is asserted is not *all* of what we believe, but some of what we believe. These are not marginal beliefs, but fundamental beliefs as affirmed by the mainstream theologians of each community. But we also share the belief that God is greater than our understandings, and that God's word is unending, and this, indeed, allows for fruitful discussions which start in scriptures and expand to explore the implications of the lives of Jesus and Muhammad.

LOVE AND MERCY

Going beyond what we have in common to what we believe in particular is important in understanding even our basic shared affirmation that we must 'love God'. Williams asks:

To what extent do the Christian conviction of God as Love and the all-important Islamic conviction that God is 'the Compassionate, the Merciful' (*ar-rahman ar-rahim*) represent common ground, and to what extent do differences need to be spelled out further?[22]

Since the publication of *ACW*, there have been some helpful explications in English of the significance of God's love in Islam, most notably Ghazi bin Muhammad's monograph, *Love in the Holy Qur'an*. He notes that in Islamic theology

God's love is not merely one of God's acts or actions, but one of God's very Own Divine Qualities or Names. This can be seen by the many Divine Names in the Holy Qur'an which denote God's loving qualities (such as: 'the Gentle' – 'Al-Latif'; 'the Kind' – 'Al-Raouf'; 'the Generous' – 'Al-Kareem'; 'the Forbearing' – 'Al-Haleem';

---

[21] Khaled Abou El Fadl, *Speaking in God's Name: Islamic Law, Authority and Women* (Oxford: Oneworld, 2001).

[22] Williams, Chapter 4.

'the Absolutely Reliable' – 'Al-Wakil'; 'the Friend' – 'Al-Wali'; 'the Good' –
'Al-Barr'; 'the Forgiving' – 'Al-Ghafur'; 'the Forgiver' – 'Al-Ghaffar'; 'the Granter
and Accepter of Repentance' – 'Al-Tawwab'; and 'the Pardoner' – 'Al-'Afu'), and
in particular by His Name 'the Loving' ('Al-Wadud').[23]

Thus, it is abundantly clear that the Qur'an describes God as loving and
the source of all love. As the great spiritual teacher of Alexandria, Ibn
'Ata' Allah al-Iskandari (d. 1309), taught, understanding God's qualities
brings us closer to knowing God:

> By the existence of His created things,
> He points to the existence of His Names,
> and by the existence of His Names,
> He points to the existence of His Qualities,
> and by the existence of His Qualities,
> He points to the reality of His Essence.[24]

Theological concepts and discourses can only go so far in helping us
approach an understanding of God, and are rather more limited in
helping us feel the presence of God. As the contemporary American
Muslim theologian Sherman Jackson says, 'Theology is ultimately a
negotiated product, the medium through which religious communities
conceptualize and talk about God in the public space, where the only
form of valid knowledge is objective knowledge to which everyone has
ostensibly equal access.' Complementing this form of knowledge, Jackson
says, is 'experiential knowledge'; when it involves persons, it arises out of
relationships. Jackson observes that, in the Qur'an, 'It is God's relationship with Abraham, Moses, Jesus, Pharaoh, the Children of Israel – even
Satan – that informs God's actions toward them, not a fixed list of names
and attributes, even if such a list might apply rightfully to God.'[25]

For Christians and Muslims, it is Jesus and Muhammad, respectively,
to whom we most keenly turn our attention to understand what it means
for a human being to be loved by God and to love God. Unfortunately,
there is a long-standing anti-Islamic polemic that presents what Tim
Winter calls 'needless polarity' in comparisons between the two, with
Muhammad representing justice, and Jesus representing love. Winter

---

[23] Ghazi bin Muhammad, *Love in the Holy Qur'an* (Chicago: Kazi, 2010), p. 15.

[24] Ibn 'Ata'illah, *Kitab al-Hikam*, translated as *The Book of Wisdom* by Victor Danner,
published in one volume with Kwaja Abdullah Ansari's *Intimate Conversations*, trans.
Wheeler M. Thackston (New York: Paulist Press, 1978), p. 108.

[25] Sherman A. Jackson, *Islam and the Problem of Black Suffering* (New York: Oxford
University Press, 2009), pp. 161–3.

argues that Jesus and Muhammad both promote and embody love *and* justice in their missions, depending on how one chooses to interpret the variety of authoritative sources which show their roles at different times. For example, Winter makes the point that Jesus' eschatological role in some readings of the Christian scripture, particularly the fundamentalist denominations, is to serve as a severe dispenser of justice, while Muhammad's is 'to manifest God's forgiveness and mercy' and to represent the principle that 'God's mercy outstrips His wrath'.[26]

It is not certain, but possible, that Williams reflects this polarising frame when he says:

[O]ne area where dialogue between Christians and Muslims will surely be fruitful is in clarifying how far Muslims can in good conscience go in seeing the love of God powerfully at work in circumstances where the world sees only failure or suffering – but also, to anticipate the challenge that some Muslims might make in answer, how far the Christian tradition of accepting suffering on this basis may sometimes lead to a passive attitude to suffering and a failure to try and transform situations in the name of God's justice.[27]

Williams follows this line of inquiry further when he says:

If we were to believe that our failure is a failure or defeat for God, then the temptation will be to seek for any means possible to avoid such an outcome. But that way lies terrorism and religious war and persecution. The idea that any action, however extreme or disruptive or even murderous, is justified if it averts failure or defeat for a particular belief or a particular religious group is not really consistent with the conviction that our failure does not mean God's failure. Indeed, it reveals a fundamental lack of conviction in the eternity and sufficiency of the object of faith.[28]

Williams' extended critique of violence which follows is stated in such a general way that it feels impolite to critique all the problematic implications. A robust response will certainly appear defensive and argumentative. This is an awkward place to be, feeling as though we have been placed in the same spot as we were by Pope Benedict with the accusation that Islam, unlike Christianity, allows the use of violence to support religious goals.

Rowan Williams was appointed Archbishop of Canterbury in the year after the terrorist attacks of 9/11 and continued in this leadership role through the American- and British-led invasions and occupations of

---

[26] Winter, 'Jesus and Muhammad', pp. 31–2.
[27] Williams, Chapter 4.
[28] Ibid.

Afghanistan and Iraq and the subsequent proliferation of violent extremist groups justifying their actions in the name of Islam, such as various al-Qaeda franchises and Boko Haram. London, of course, was attacked on 7 July 2005 by four British Muslims. Is it any wonder, then, that violence is foremost in Williams' mind? This is understandable. What is problematic is the implication that violence is rooted in core Islamic beliefs. Now, perhaps this was not what Williams intended. A traditional Islamic teaching (often attributed to the Prophet Muhammad) is 'Give your friend seventy excuses.' Giving that benefit of the doubt to our friend Williams, we will not dwell on this point, but move to clarify how Islamic teachings define 'success' and give believers the faith to endure suffering.

SUCCESS AND SUFFERING

The Qur'an makes it abundantly clear that worldly success is not necessarily a sign of God's favour. The epitome of human evil in the Qur'an is Pharaoh and 'Pharaoh was mighty on earth' (Q 10:88). Pharaoh oppressed those who believed in God, and no person, only God, could stop him. Those who were patient under his oppression were not losers, but found their true success with God:

> God sets forth as an example of those who have demonstrated faith the wife of Pharaoh when she said, 'My Lord, build me a house in paradise with you and save me from Pharaoh and his doings and save me from the wicked people'.
>
> (Q 66:11)

Where the world sees a 'loser', God does not:

> And their Lord answers their prayers saying, 'I shall never let anyone's work to be lost – whether a male or a female – you are from one another. Those who emigrated or were exiled from their lands and suffered in My cause and fought or were killed – indeed I will efface their sins and admit them to gardens beneath which rivers flow. This is a reward that is with God; and God has with Him the most beautiful reward.'
>
> (Q 3:195)

Sometimes the Qur'an indeed describes the political or military success of the righteous as pleasing to, or brought about by, God. Yet the believers whom God aids are not only Muslims. The Qur'an, for example, characterises the Christian 'Roman' defeat of the Persians as 'God's victory' (Q 30:4). The Qur'an describes both victories and losses as brought about by God (Q 3:123, 3:153). In human history, political power changes hands frequently, and in every situation we must seek the lessons which

God has placed before us: 'If misfortune touches you, it is the case that a similar misfortune has touched other people; thus do we rotate the days among people; thus God knows who believes and he takes witnesses from among you. God does not love those engaged in oppression' (Q 3:140).

The sixth 'pillar of faith' of Islam is to believe in what God has destined (*qadar*), the good and the bad of it, to accept all as part of God's wise command. In his widely taught 'wisdoms' (*ḥikam*), Ibn 'Aṭā' Allāh says:

> To soften for you the suffering of affliction
> He has taught you
> That He is the one who causes trials to come upon you.
> For the One who confronts you with His Decrees of Fate
> Is the same One who has accustomed you to His good choice.[29]

In the words of Habib Ali al-Jifri, believing in *qadar* means having faith 'that the universe is never outside the control of the Lord's mercy, justice and wisdom'.[30] It is this faith that helps Muslims bear every affliction that affects all human beings: death of a child, illness, persecution or poverty. In the words of the fourteenth-century Andalusian spiritual master Ibn 'Abbād of Ronda:

> Long-suffering is one of the stations of certitude and is proportionate to certitude's strength or weakness, increase or diminution. Patience involves restraining the lower self from consenting to voluntary acts and words that are opposed to the Revealed Law and the Mystic Truth, under the sway of one's natural tendencies.[31]

Rowan Williams' comments about accepting suffering are not only related to the issue of violence, but arise out of his long-standing interest in mysticism as well. In his introduction to the Cambridge conference, where he frames his response to *ACW* and emphasises the importance of discussing the different and particular ways in which Islam and Christianity understand God's love, he says that Islam 'does not have anything easily corresponding to the Christian "night of the spirit", the sense of divine absence as maturity in prayer progresses'.[32] Without denying differences

---

[29] Ibn 'Ata'illah, *The Book of Wisdom*, p. 73.

[30] Habib Ali al-Jifri, *The Concept of Faith in Islam*, trans. Khalid Williams (Amman: Royal Aal Al-Bayt Institute for Islamic Thought, 2012). https://rissc.jo/docs/13-faith/120422-HabibAli-ConceptFaith-English-Web.pdf.

[31] Ibn 'Abbād of Ronda, *Letters on the Sūfī Path*, trans. John Renard (New York: Paulist Press, 1986), p. 140.

[32] Rowan Williams, opening address to the conference 'A Common Word and Future Christian–Muslim Engagement' at Emmanuel College, Cambridge, 12 October 2008. http://rowanwilliams.archbishopofcanterbury.org/articles.php/1040/a-common-word-and-future-christian-muslim-engagement. Accessed 5 September 2016.

between Islam and Christianity, yet again the dichotomy proposed must be questioned. In the mystical teachings of Islam, the experience of spiritual 'contraction' (*qabḍ*), an experience of confusion, melancholy and sense of distance from God, is a known station on the path of spiritual growth. The comparative study of Christian and Islamic mystical states and practices would certainly deepen and enrich the discussions generated by *ACW*.

I believe, nevertheless, that the link Williams makes between the inability to tolerate spiritual suffering and the temptation to commit violence is real. A spiritually immature person, unmoored from sound religious teachings and direction, might respond to feelings of spiritual powerlessness with acts of worldly power. It is not surprising, therefore, that within Islam the most common profile of a person who commits terrorist acts is the one who is most alienated from the religious institutions and spiritual teachings of Islam.[33] Christianity and Islam would seem to share a belief in God's wisdom and doing one's best to accept one's unchangeable destiny serenely, while working as agents of God's love and mercy to comfort others who are suffering. Ironically, one of the common polemics against Muslims during the colonial period was that they were too 'fatalistic'[34] in accepting suffering; what they needed was a rational European power to improve their situation. Islam, like Christianity, has tried to find that fine balance between the acceptance of God's inscrutable command and the determination to repair the world that was phrased so beautifully by Reinhold Niebuhr in his 'Serenity Prayer'.[35] Of course, many (such as the Palestinians whose expulsion from their homeland Niebuhr advocated) would point out that the more difficult issue is determining who decides what needs to be changed and what means can be used to effect change. For his part, after his early years as a pacifist, Niebuhr abandoned the Fellowship of Reconciliation and became a 'realist', agreeing with the majority of Christians now, and in the past, that force, including lethal force, can be used for a just cause. Of course, not all Christians agree with Niebuhr's particular political theology;

---

[33] See, for example, the studies of Marc Sageman, including *Leaderless Jihad: Terror Networks in the Twenty-First Century* (Philadelphia: University of Pennsylvania Press, 2008).

[34] Samuel M. Zwemer, *The Moslem Doctrine of God: An Essay on the Character and Attributes of Allah according to the Koran and Orthodox Tradition* (Boston: American Tract Society, 1905), pp. 93–106.

[35] Elisabeth Sifton, *The Serenity Prayer: Faith and Politics in Times of Peace and War* (New York: W. W. Norton, 2003).

nevertheless, most, including Williams, argue that a Christian can – and should – support the use of force, i.e., violence, in some circumstances.

Williams is keen to make a distinction, however, between engaging in violence to protect people's freedoms, and engaging in violence to 'protect transcendent values', saying, 'Transcendent values can be defended through violence only by those who do not fully understand their transcendent character; and if no other value is absolute, no other value can claim the right to unconditional defence by any means and at all costs.'[36] There is much truth in what Williams says, yet one wonders whether it is always possible to distinguish between actions that are aimed at defending people and actions that are aimed at defending a religion.

Christians and Muslims both call upon authorised leaders to defend those who are oppressed; the difficult question is who is authorised to undertake that defence and what are the limits to their authority. Vigilante justice has always been an anathema in Islamic teachings. When the Prophet Muhammad was in Mecca and his followers were tortured and killed in front of him, he used no force to stop this from happening – not because he was weak, but because he had no political authority in the city. It was only after the inhabitants of Yathrib invited Muhammad to become chief of a new political entity, the *umma* of Medina, and these religiously diverse men and women bound themselves to loyalty and mutual defence in the Covenant of Medina, that Muhammad became responsible for their protection. The moral basis for this responsibility was at this time revealed by God in the following Qur'anic passage:

Permission (to fight) is given to those against whom war is waged because they are oppressed; and verily God is All-Powerful to help them – those who have been expelled from their lands without just cause, only saying, 'Our Lord is God'. If God had not allowed one group of people to defend themselves from another, certainly there would have been destroyed monasteries, churches, synagogues and mosques where God's name is extolled greatly. Surely God will help whoever helps Him; verily God is Strong, Eminent.

(Q 22:39–40)

Ensuring the religious freedom of human beings – not just Muslims – is the raison d'être of state power. What the United Nations now calls 'the Responsibility to Protect' is a moral obligation, according to the Qur'an:

Why should you not fight in the way of God when those who are helpless – men, women and children – are saying, 'Our Lord, take us away from this oppressive

---

[36] Williams, Chapter 4.

town and its people and send us someone who will offer protection and send us someone who will offer assistance!'

(Q 4:75)

Sacrificing one's life to protect the weak is, in every culture – secular or religious – the 'greatest sacrifice'. We honour police and soldiers who risk losing their lives, leaving their wives widows, their children orphans, to ensure the safety of others. Even our civil ceremonies of remembrance are imbued with religious language: we keep 'the eternal flame' burning and say the dead soldiers will 'live in our hearts for ever'.

Pacifists would say that it is impossible to keep state violence within moral limits. There is no doubt that many Muslim rulers, in the past and in our time, not only have violated the moral limits on the use of force, but have argued that Islam allows the use of force to promote it over all other religions.

Now, while there certainly are Muslims who commit irrational violence in the 'defence of Islam', using 'any means' and 'at all costs', these are criminals and terrorists, not faithful Muslims. In contrast, the sacred law of Islam limits the means and methods of war. As for the ends of war, the primary aim of the state in classical Islamic thinking was to defend the *people* who wished to live as Muslims. In the age of pre-modern empires, however, when religious and political identities were conflated, both Christian and Islamic states used violence in the defence of religion itself. Enacting laws banning conversion, punishing unorthodox beliefs and behaviours and forbidding criticism of certain theological doctrines – these are just a few of the ways in which pre-modern states used force to defend religion.

Disentangling religious and public interests in the modern period is an ongoing concern. By the late twentieth century, most nations which continued to have Christianity as the official state religion had enacted constitutional means to protect the religious rights of minorities, although there is still work to be done to ensure equal treatment of faith communities. In many cases, religious observances, such as the closure of businesses on Sundays and Christian holidays, are categorised as showing respect for 'cultural heritage' rather than religion. Creative taxonomies, however, cannot conceal the fact that non-Christians are disadvantaged by the fact that they have to seek special accommodations from employers and school administrators if they wish to observe their religious holidays, thus forcing them to make their 'personal' religious beliefs public. Of course, the same disparity exists in most Muslim-majority countries (as well as in Israel). More problematic is the fact that many modern

Muslim states have not yet achieved robust constitutional protections of human rights generally, and the protection of religious freedom and freedom of conscience is particularly lacking in too many Muslim nations today. The persecution of Christians in some Muslim countries, not just by extremists, but in law, is a violation of religious freedom which the Archbishop of Canterbury, and other Christian leaders, have a right – indeed, a responsibility – to address. As a participant in many *ACW* conferences and meetings, I am a witness that this was a regular topic of discussion. As a consequence, support for religious freedom is included in the communiqués and joint statements issued at the close of these meetings. Having our Christian friends remind us of these realities through the *ACW* initiative created a foundation of awareness that led to Muslim leaders speaking out more forcefully about the persecution of Christians,[37] and to subsequent initiatives with an even larger impact. In 2010, the Islamic Society of North America (ISNA), in partnership with Shaikh Abdullah Bin Bayyah, began a series of consultations with Muslim leaders on the rights of religious minorities in Muslim-majority countries. The consultations led ultimately to the 2016 'Marrakesh Declaration' affirming religious freedom and equality of citizens in Muslim-majority countries.[38] To this end, I am convinced that Christian leaders who advocated for the religious freedom of their co-religionists in Muslim-majority countries helped push traditional Muslim scholars to return to the foundational Medinan model of religious freedom and coexistence. This is one of the sweetest fruits of *ACW*.

Terrorism, of course, remains a concern. But terrorism committed in the name of Islam has taken the lives of far more Muslims than people of any other faith. The primary targets of these extremists are other Muslims, and our calls for them to return to the straight path have little impact, because they consider those of us making this call to be traitors to their self-declared Islamic cause. The majority of Muslims are doubly victimised then, first by direct physical attacks by terrorists, and second by having Islam blamed for the violence of the terrorists.

Williams says:

As the world now is, diverse religious traditions very frequently inhabit one territory, one nation, one social unit [...]. In such a setting, we cannot avoid the

---

[37] Ethan Cole, 'Prominent Muslims criticize attacks on Iraqi Christians', *Christian Post*, 16 October 2008. www.christianpost.com/news/prominent-muslims-criticize-attacks-on-iraqi-christians-34859/. Accessed 4 September 2016.

[38] See www.marrakeshdeclaration.org. Accessed 4 September 2016.

pragmatic and secular question of 'common security': what is needed for our convictions to flourish is bound up with what is needed for the convictions of other groups to flourish. We learn that we can best defend ourselves by defending others.[39]

This is certainly true, and it is why one finds Muslims serving in police, military and other security forces in countries where they are minorities, as they do in nations where they are in the majority.

But here we return to the question of how we decide what are the moral limits of defending ourselves. Earlier, we cited Williams' statement that Muslims might criticise Christians for having a 'passive attitude to suffering' and that they fail 'to try and transform situations in the name of God's justice'. This is not a criticism of Christians that I have heard from Muslims. What I do hear is frustration when Christians compartmentalise their religious and political selves, refusing to take responsibility for enforcing moral limits on the coercive means used by their political leaders to defend the commonweal.

Violence was not invented on 11 September 2001. By that time, the people of Iraq had suffered ten years of sanctions which were insisted upon by the United States and Britain in particular. In 1996, journalist Lesley Stahl questioned US Secretary of State Madeleine Albright about the morality of sanctions on Iraq, saying, 'We have heard that a half million children have died. I mean, that's more children than died in Hiroshima. And, you know, is the price worth it?' Albright replied, 'I think this is a very hard choice, but the price – we think the price is worth it.'[40]

Even a nation where Christians and Muslims can live together side by side must be abhorrent to both Christians and Muslims if that nation ensures its security by demeaning the lives of others outside its borders. We do not lose responsibility for the violence committed in our names when our nations have rendered human beings to be tortured outside our lands. This is where the call to 'Love of Neighbour' in *ACW* needs a vigorous, courageous implementation. I propose that it is not religion, rather it is fear, that is the greatest source of irrational violence in our world today. When we are afraid, we forget our ethics; we are willing to do 'anything necessary' to ensure our safety and the safety of those we love.

---

[39] Williams, Chapter 4, p. xxx.
[40] Rahul Mahajan, '"We think the price is worth it": Media uncurious about Iraq policy's effects – there or here', *FAIR*, 1 November 2001. www.fair.org/extra/we-think-the-price-is-worth-it/. Accessed 4 September 2016.

Christians and Muslims, friends together, can do nothing better than to inculcate love for all of humanity – not just love for our co-religionists, and not just love for our fellow citizens or fellow Westerners.

Rowan Williams recognises the urgency of this need, arguing that the just war tradition 'demands internationalism' to prevent states from engaging in war to further their 'private' interests.[41] Many Christian leaders have not refrained from criticising the unjust use of violence by their governments, while others have been enthusiastic supporters of war (showing again that the internal diversity of our traditions makes it very difficult to compare 'Islam' and 'Christianity'). For his part, in a 2003 article entitled 'Weakness and Moral Inconsistency Led Us to War', Rowan Williams called the invasion of Iraq 'genuinely tragic'.[42] Yet before proceeding in the article to suggest the need for a more coherent and consistent international 'ownership' of solutions to this and other conflicts he says, 'Few people have felt that the decisions taken were easy or cheap. Which is why, even for critics of military intervention, just rehearsing the earlier arguments feels futile and distasteful; the weight of the cost lies most heavily on people other than preachers and commentators, – the Armed Forces, the decision-makers, the people of Iraq and the region.' I understand that Williams' point is that it is not fair to put people in charge of the armed forces, then blame them for using violence. But we also cannot designate some of our fellow citizens to engage in these acts of violence, then say that we ourselves are not violent.

In the modern world, Muslims have seen, again and again, that their lives are not valued enough by the dominant (majority-Christian) nations to be protected. The perception that many ordinary Muslims have is that a desire to strengthen Christianity (or Christian heritage) is at the root of political and military decisions that disproportionately negatively impact Muslims. This perception is not irrational, even if it is incorrect. But this is a dangerous dynamic, for it takes us back to medieval power dynamics when Christianity was promoted by some rulers and empires, and Islam was promoted by others, with mutual hostility the norm.

[41] 'Just war revisited – Archbishop's lecture to the Royal Institute for International Affairs', 14 October 2003. http://rowanwilliams.archbishopofcanterbury.org/articles.php/1827/just-war-revisited-archbishops-lecture-to-the-royal-institute-for-international-affairs. Accessed 4 September 2016.

[42] Rowan Williams, 'Weakness and moral inconsistency led us to war', *Times*, 25 March 2003. http://rowanwilliams.archbishopofcanterbury.org/articles.php/655/weaknesses-and-moral-inconsistency-led-us-to-war. Accessed 4 September 2016.

In the 1898 Battle of Omdurman, more than ten thousand Sudanese lay dead on their native soil while British invading forces celebrated with a heartfelt Christian hymn, 'Abide with Me'.[43] No claim was ever made by an English general or monarch that the battle was undertaken for religious reasons. This was not a violent attack on Islam for the sake of Christianity. This was not 'violence to defend transcendent values'. Yet the facts on the ground were that ten thousand Muslims were killed by Christians who comforted themselves after the slaughter with a Christian hymn. And if it had not been a Christian hymn that they had sung, but rather a secular national anthem, would that radically transform our judgement of the rationality of the event?

Human beings are notoriously self-deceptive. How successful are we really at distinguishing our intentions? In the end, does it matter? Or is what really matters the fact that there are dead bodies on the ground? Suicide attacks by Muslim terrorists and drone strikes by American generals end up with pretty much the same result: mostly 'collateral damage' – bits of human flesh – blasted across the land. Rational violence is as deadly as irrational violence, and in some places, it's an easier sell.

CONCLUSION

It is never possible simply by our own efforts to have a truly fresh start in human relationships and societies. Anything new we create is made from what already exists, and what is new cannot be placed outside this world, in a space untouched by history. Only by the grace of God can something truly new come into being: 'His command, when He desires a thing, is to say to it "Be", and it is' (Q 36:82). His grace does not depend on our actions, yet God created us as beings who must act so that we can grow: 'Blessed is He in whose hand is the Kingdom and He has power over all things; Who created death and life, that He might try you which of you is best in works; and He is the All-mighty, the All-forgiving' (Q 67:1–2). It is God's command that a people will not improve unless they make the effort to change themselves: 'God will never change the blessings with which He has graced a people unless they change their inner selves' (Q 8:53). Directing our will towards actions we believe will be pleasing to God, we trust that the Creator can bring about a dramatic change in our habits and patterns of behaviour, and in the world in which

---

[43] Adam Hochschild, *To End All Wars: A Story of Loyalty and Rebellion, 1914–1918* (Boston: Houghton Mifflin Harcourt, 2011), p. 18.

we live. Our instincts, in human relations, are overwhelmingly pessimistic; we feel stuck in our histories and the emotions which arise out of our histories. Believing in God's creative power, we have faith that 'It may be that God will create love between you and those whom you now consider enemies' (Q 60:7). God knows reality, whereas we only have perspectives ('considering' people enemies). God can and does create love where there is hatred.

6

Love of Neighbour in the Face of Religious Trauma

Reuven Firestone

The document known as *A Common Word* is made up of three sections. The first two deal with the dual command to love God and love neighbour. The third features a Qur'an verse (3:64) that has provided the name 'a common word' to the document itself. While the document is devoted especially to Muslim–Christian relations, its authors have actually initiated a conversation between all three major scriptural monotheistic communities by placing the verse in a consummative position, for the invitation that opens the verse is directed to 'the People of the Book'. In fact, one can read the verse as an invitation not simply to a 'common word', as it is usually translated, but to a 'joint conversation' through shared recognition of the unity of God.[1]

The conversation is possible, according to the document, because the three scriptural monotheisms share the dual command to love God and love neighbour. The creators of the document place the dual command at the heart and centre of monotheism, and cite a number of texts from scripture and tradition among the Abrahamic religions that corroborate the divine imperative to love God and to love neighbour. In some, the sequence is 'love God', therefore 'love neighbour'. In others, the two are separate statements that are then joined together in the interpretative traditions.

In what follows I problematise one aspect of this dual command that I believe needs to be considered outside our usual assumptive religious frameworks. 'Problematise' is a word that is used increasingly in intellectual discourse but rarely defined. In this context the term denotes a

---

[1] I will support this translation later. See the conclusion of the present chapter.

reconsideration of basic assumptions embedded in a common notion. It is intended to defamiliarise what is generally assumed or taken for granted. It means to consider certain challenges – or problems, hence the term – embedded within suppositions associated with the notion or phenomenon to be examined.

Love of God is the epicentre of the document. The command to love God is a difficult and complex notion, and a broad range of understandings have historically been proffered. One can understand love of God as a feeling or an action expressed through meditation or prayer, or feeding the hungry and caring for the environment – preserving and protecting God's creation in innumerable ways. Many, or most, or perhaps *any* way to act out one's love of God will not challenge this foundational command at the heart of the document. Our scriptures and traditions are quite clear about the divine expectation of love of God among all God's sentient creatures. That does not apply, however, for the second half of the dual command, love of neighbour.

ACW combines the two commands as if love of neighbour flowed from love of God. That, however, is not obvious. Is love of neighbour a necessary result of loving God? Is this what God commands consistently? What about the many texts from scripture and tradition that express rage and violence against our neighbours, even commanding their destruction? I cite only one example from each of our scriptural traditions, which should suffice to make my point, though I could cite many more.

Deuteronomy 7:1–2: 'When the Lord your God brings you to the land that you are about to enter and possess and He dislodges many nations before you ... you must doom them to destruction: grant them no terms and give them no quarter.'

Qur'an 9:73, repeated in 66:9: 'O Prophet! Strive (*jāhid*) against the unbelievers and the dissenters, and be ruthless with them. Their resting place is Hell, a miserable destination.'

The New Testament is a bit trickier than the Hebrew Bible or the Qur'an, but its relative lack of calls for violence only reflects the environment of its historical emergence. The Hebrew Bible and the Qur'an, although separated from one another in time by more than a thousand years, both emerged as scriptures in equally hectic and largely unruly social-political contexts in which no trans-tribal rule of law was available to prevent communities from attacking one another whenever it appeared that benefit could be derived from it. In such a context, militancy was necessary for survival, hence the repeated divine calls in these foundational texts for forcefulness and even violence directed against enemies of the new religious movements that emerged alongside and in response to them.

The New Testament, on the other hand, emerged in a violent but highly regulated social-political context that was tightly controlled by the Roman Empire. Because Rome insisted on preserving its monopoly on violence, any kind of militancy engaged in by ethnic or religious groups under its rule resulted in a massive and deadly response by the Roman state. In fact, the early Christians observed exactly this result when militant contemporary religious movements were violently crushed. The historian Flavius Josephus lived in the same period and mentions a number of such annihilated movements in his writings.[2] Early Christians also observed their Jewish brethren, who rose up militarily against the empire and were destroyed. In such an environment, calls for physical violence would be futile even in defence, and almost certainly suicidal, hence the lack of divine call to fight physically against the enemies of the new religious movement.

Historical context is paramount. If the New Testament had emerged in a context like that of the emergence of the Hebrew Bible or the Qur'an, one can be certain that it would have espoused a similar level of violence. The New Testament does indeed express deeply violent emotion against the enemies of the community, but it did not call for violent actions, for reasons that will be immediately apparent to a rigorous historian.

Luke 19:27: [Jesus said], 'As for these enemies of mine who did not want me to be king over them – bring them here and slaughter them in my presence!'[3]

One can argue quite effectively that the citations provided from the three scriptural compilations do not require what most would understand today as love of neighbour unless one argues that 'love of neighbour' indicates the 'tough love' of discipline and castigation that so often leads to cruelty and abuse. In fact, however, sometimes – or perhaps often – love of God and obedience to the divine will as expressed in scripture have been understood by religious people to require anger, or militancy or violence against neighbour on behalf of God's cause. Some still argue

---

[2] Flavius Josephus, *The Complete Works of Josephus*, trans. W. Whiston (Grand Rapids, MI: Kregel, 1960), *Antiquities of the Jews*, book XX, chapter 5, § 1 (p. 418); chapter 8, § 6 (p. 422), § 10 (p. 423).

[3] Many more texts could be cited to support the emotional violence that is so common in the New Testament, even if repressed. See, for example, Matthew 10:34–9, 23:15, 34–6, 25:41–5; Luke 12:49–51; John 8:44; Revelation 19. See also Michel Desjardins, *Peace, Violence and the New Testament* (Sheffield: Sheffield Academic Press, 1997).

today, as some religious leaders have argued in the past, that certain acts of human violence against the religious 'Other' are indeed acts of divine love. But inquisitions and other forms of religiously sanctioned abuse are no longer acceptable in a world that we wish to inhabit today.

The *ACW* document cites many texts from the Qur'an and the Bible to affirm the love-of-God principle. It cites very few to affirm the love-of-neighbour principle, and this seems to reflect the relative paucity of such references. I have not counted the ratio between love-of-God texts and love-of-neighbour texts in the three scriptures; to do so would be a difficult task which would, among other things, require the establishment of criteria to determine which of many thousands of verses should fit in each category. But I think it could easily be argued that the scriptural texts expressing resentment, anger and even rage against neighbour outweigh those that convey love.

And who, exactly, is 'neighbour'? It is usually one's comrade, or at least one who can be recognised and who is reasonably well known. What about those who are not known, who are feared perhaps out of ignorance? What about those who are defined, perhaps because of unfamiliarity, as enemies? In the ancient world, people lived almost exclusively among their own kind. Does loving one's neighbour require loving the stranger? There are certainly scriptural texts that require loving the stranger. In fact, the Talmud notes that the Torah cautions us about right behaviour towards the stranger at least thirty-six times – far more often than the command to love God![4] But there are many other texts that rage against the 'Other', the unfamiliar, the feared, the non-believer, the religious competitor, those who refuse to accept the divine word as articulated by God, prophet or religious leader according to a particular revelation. If we wish to affirm the dual-command schema presented in the document, what are we to do with those parts of our tradition that seem to arrive at a very different conclusion from love of God than love of neighbour?

Studies in what is called 'selective attention' and the process of reading have demonstrated what most of us recognise anecdotally from our own experience – that people focus their attention on what resonates with their personal experience and predilections, while relegating what does not ring familiar to the periphery.[5] We tend to focus on that which confirms

---

4 Rabbi Eliezer the Great noted that 'the Torah warns thirty-six times, and some say forty-six times, not to oppress the stranger' (*Babylonian Talmud*, Baba Metzi'a 59b).

5 Tony Lambert, 'Visual orienting, learning and conscious awareness', in Luis Jiménez (ed.), *Attention and Implicit Learning* (Amsterdam: John Benjamins, 2003), pp. 253–76.

our assumptions or feelings. We tend to ignore that which conflicts with our expectations. When we are in a particular frame of mind, certain scriptural words, phrases, images or verses speak to us, while others do not. When we find ourselves profoundly affected by something that changes our frame of mind and we read the same scripture from a very different mood or perspective, we may suddenly become conscious of verses or images that seem to speak to us in a new voice – material that we had not really noticed previously.

'Reading', we understand today, does not apply only to texts written with letters on parchment, paper or screen. Reading is the act of perceiving everything around us. Life is text. We see and read what we are able to in all the texts of life. Our personal histories – psychological, cultural, spiritual and so forth – profoundly affect what we see around us, how we see it and what we conclude therefrom.

Many who read this collection of essays are joined together because they (we) read life somewhat similarly despite our religious differences, and share a certain perspective on both the content and the intent of the *ACW* document. Most in this community affirm the message of *ACW* and find that it resonates deeply with our own spiritual sensibilities. We find it eminently reasonable, and though we derive from different religions, histories, language communities and so forth, we find common ground.

But what about the many other voices in our communities who can and do cite a different set of scriptural and traditional sources to promote a very different position? What about those voices who condemn the religious 'Other' as sinister, dangerous, even evil? We can argue that they are wrong, and we *do* argue that they are wrong. But they also have compelling arguments and they can and do cite scripture in their support. And their arguments resonate with many people who, because of their own personal histories and frames of mind, read a different message in the same sources from which we cite our scriptural proof texts. This is not simply a tactical issue. It is a deeply spiritual issue, because many of those with whom we would vociferously disagree are as thoroughly convinced of the divinely authorised correctness of their position as we are of ours. And they argue against our position with no less persistence and commitment than we do against theirs. What authority do we have for our standpoints?

Not long ago, the authority of religious office was enough to pronounce the truth. Often, religious authority was also adequate to control the discourse regarding it. In the pre-modern world, religious leaders were much more successful than today in controlling the exegetical discourse on such topics as the dual-command formula lying at the core of *ACW*, though even back then movements and counter-movements existed that espoused different perspectives regarding the divine message and the expectations for action derived from it. With the invention of movable type and the printing press, religious authorities have been far less successful at controlling the discourse. With the invention of the Internet, authoritative religious powers have effectively lost control. It is not enough to espouse a view by citing scripture or doctrine in the name of religious authority. Counter-voices deriving from the same scriptures are cited without end to promote contrary views.

In his response to *ACW*, the then–Archbishop of Canterbury Rowan Williams remarked that 'religious violence suggests an underlying religious insecurity'.[6] He speaks about personal spiritual insecurity in the face of the challenge of other religious claims. He further says, 'The more we as people of faith are serious about the truth of our convictions [I think he may mean '*confident* about the truth of our convictions'], the more likely we will be to turn away from violence in the name of faith, to trust that God, the truly real, will remain true, divine and unchanging, whatever the failures and successes of human society and history.' The archbishop is suggesting here that the problem of religion and violence is internal to the individual. If one were more spiritually or perhaps emotionally secure, one would not feel the urge to join violent groups. The archbishop's words are encouraging, and I believe he is correct with regard to this aspect of the problem. But the problem is not only personal, it is also structural. It is part of the psychological make-up of religion. The tendency towards violence vis-à-vis other religions is built into the DNA of religion and is visible from its very birth. I am considering religions here in view of how they actually function in the real world – in history – and I use the model of a living organism as a means to consider religious institutional behaviour. In what follows, allow yourself to think about religion as a dynamic, living organism rather than as a static system of creeds and practices and beliefs.

Rowan Williams writes about spiritual insecurity in the heart of the individual believer. In the birth pangs that accompany the genesis of religion, one finds not a *spiritual* insecurity but a real, *physical* insecurity born of the shock and pain of emergence into a cold and harsh world. No religion is created *ex nihilo*. Religions are born into worlds in which religions already exist. Islam was born into a religious environment in

---

[6] See Chapter 4 in this volume.

which lived Christians, Jews, Zoroastrians and polytheists of various types. Christianity was born into a religious environment in which lived Jews of various schools, followers of mystery cults and pagans of several varieties. And ancient Judaism was born into a religious environment dominated by numerous well-established tribal religions. Established religions always oppose the emergence of new religions or religious movements because new religious groups are perceived as threatening. When new religions succeed in attracting a large enough following, they are inevitably defied by establishment religions. If the emergent religions are perceived as threatening enough, they are attacked verbally. When perceived as existentially threatening, they are attacked physically.

The earliest historical evidence we have for the births of scriptural monotheisms derives from their scriptures themselves, which serve as witnesses to the God-centred truth of their core tenets and spiritual and behavioural expectations. Each of our scriptures records situations in which members of prior religions tested, challenged, provoked and eventually attacked our religious founders and their companions and followers. These accounts are enshrined in our most sacred texts, and they are couched in disappointment, resentment and anger. In each case, the establishment religions failed to prevent the religious newcomer from succeeding, but the cost was great struggle and suffering on the part of those who led and followed the new faith. Meanwhile, decades, centuries and millennia later, the record of events and struggle lives on in the eternal document of scripture, often decontextualised from the *Sitz im Leben* of the events themselves. They then tend to become learned as eternal truths vis-à-vis the religious 'Other', regardless of context. The result is that those born into a religious community grow up tending to be suspicious and antagonistic towards other religions and their adherents.

What I am describing is a phenomenology of religious parturition, a recognition that our religions originated through a kind of birthing experience. Birth is experienced traumatically by the newborn, even in the best of circumstances. The environment outside the womb feels harsh and painful. But when the genesis of religious life occurs in a contentious and competitive environment in which the young spirit is attacked and ridiculed, it reacts with a combination of emotions ranging from fear to sadness, to anger and, eventually, also to rage. Continuing with the organism metaphor, our three scriptural monotheisms share a phenomenology of religious birth. They also share a fear of attack and the anger and bitterness that assault generates in the victim. The three scriptures that we espouse as fundamental witnesses to the truths we believe in also represent organic reactions to the threats and attacks that the earliest founders and believers of our religious communities experienced. When we read them hundreds or thousands of years later, we are not naturally sensitive to the specific contexts of their genesis. Because the narratives appear in scripture, and because we tend to relate to scripture as timeless expressions of the divine will, we have a tendency to understand these incidents as a generalised and eternal message regarding all who do not share our religious convictions.

We read our scripture, of course, from its particularistic perspective in relation to those who opposed the new religion that it represents. But from a truly neutral perspective, the established religions' ardent opposition to a threatening new religion is only natural. Establishment religions are not inherently evil. When they oppose the emergence of new religious movements they are doing what they believe they must. To put it bluntly, each of our religions was once a *newly birthed* religion that became an *established* religion, and each has played both roles in relation to other religions. From the perspective of established religion, newly emerging religion is anathema to the recognised truth of God. But from the perspective of the newly emerging religion, the opposition of established religion threatens the survival of God's newly revealed truth! All three of our religions have played the role of victim and perpetrator.

While our three faiths share a similar birth experience, birth is a very personal moment. It feels distinctive, exclusive. We experience the trauma of our birth experience as unique, but in truth we all share the feelings of distinctiveness in suffering. Any sensitive reading of other scriptures will attest to this truth. We must stop seeing ourselves only as victims and not as aggressors, and we must have more compassion for those ancient communities which, out of conviction for their deep and abiding sense of God's truth, opposed the genesis of our own religions. To put it in a somewhat unconventional terminology, the 'they' are also the 'we'. They are us.

The anxiety we easily observe among our co-religionists towards the religious 'Other' is profoundly influenced by the birth pangs of our religions and the ways in which our religious communities continue to experience them. The *ACW* document does not address this phenomenology, because that is not its purpose. The fact is, however, that *ACW* and other such documents, in all of their good will, tend to obscure some of the basic and abiding problematic issues that we as religious leaders, theologians, scholars and educators must address directly. It is quite possible to argue from each of our scriptures that love of neighbour *does not* necessarily follow from love of God. And we all know that some fellow believers in all our own religious communities to all intents and purposes make this argument and make it publicly. This is a problem that needs to be addressed directly.

What can we do about it? I believe that we must engage actively at a number of levels. First of all, we need to work within our communities at all phases of education, both formal and informal, to promote the legitimacy of the dual command from the particular perspectives of our own traditions. This needs to be done at all levels, from primary religious education to systematic theology, so that it will become an intuitive reading of our sacred scriptures. In order to be effective we need to consider why some of our co-religionists perceive the divine imperative differently. What leads some of our people to read the identical traditions contrarily? Are they motivated by fear or anxiety, anger or resentment? If we gain a better understanding of the dynamic behind their perceptions, we will be better able to address the gap between us. So we need to consider what is possible in order to help our brothers and sisters in religion achieve a sense of personal grounding through which they can arrive at a more compassionate perspective towards the religious 'Other'.

In Jewish religious parlance this is called *tikkun*, meaning 'repair' or 'mending', 'restoration'.[7] *Tikkun* applies to the self and then spreads outward in waves to affect an ever-widening circle. But *tikkun* works in the other direction as well – from the broadest circle inward towards the individual. When we can mend a broken world and make it better for all its inhabitants, we remove the stumbling blocks of inequity, bias and injustice that stimulate the jealousy, resentment, anger and fear leading people to a narrow and confined perspective. But we must begin at home and in our own communities. Jews call this kind of work *tikkun* or *tikkun `olam*, 'mending the world', but similar aspirations exist in our sister traditions as well. We all must engage in our respective religious communities to determine how, through processes authentic to our traditions, we can best help our co-religionists come to common ground on this document.

We also need to work more charitably with those religious communities outside our own spiritual circles, without the ulterior motives of

---

[7] See David Shatz, Chaim Waxman and Nathan Diament (eds.), *Tikkun Olam: Social Responsibility in Jewish Thought and Law* (Oxford: Rowman & Littlefield, 1997); Eliot Dorff, *The Jewish Approach to Repairing the World* (Woodstock, VT: Jewish Lights, 2008).

mission, conversion or domination. We need to demonstrate through example, exactly as those signatories to ACW have done. The ACW website is an excellent resource for inviting conversation within and across religious boundaries. More can be done, both with the website and in other media by us all, and not only by those Muslims who have initiated this level of the conversation.

We all need to reflect more, deliberate more, brainstorm more – within our faith communities and in partnership with other faith communities – as we have done through the publication of this collection. But we need more. We need to move forward. We need to realise and teach the 'dignity of difference', as Rabbi Lord Jonathan Sacks wrote so effectively in his book of that title.[8]

True love of neighbour means affording respect to the religious beliefs of others, including those religious beliefs with which we may vigorously disagree. There will always be many issues of dogma, theology and practice over which we will differ. For believers in distinct religious traditions there is no way around it, and we need not have unreasonable expectations. But there is an essential core between all three traditions about which we already agree. This is suggested by the verse at the heart of the document. What we need now is to transcend our ingrown fear, born of the trauma of religious parturition, so that we can recognise the dignity and love of the religious 'Other'. Such is the invitation of Qur'an 3:64.

يَا أَهْلَ الْكِتَابِ تَعَالَوْا إِلَىٰ كَلِمَةٍ سَوَاءٍ بَيْنَنَا وَبَيْنَكُمْ أَلَّا نَعْبُدَ إِلَّا اللَّهَ وَلَا نُشْرِكَ بِهِ شَيْئًا وَلَا يَتَّخِذَ بَعْضُنَا بَعْضًا أَرْبَابًا مِنْ دُونِ اللَّهَ

As I suggested at the outset of these remarks, I would translate the verse (with a certain poetic licence) as follows:

O People of the Book, come to a common conversation between us and you; Do we not worship none but God, ascribe no partner to Him, nor take others for lords beside God?[9]

---

[8] Jonathan Sacks, *The Dignity of Difference: How to Avoid the Clash of Civilizations* (London: Continuum, 2002).
[9] An interrogative *alif* for ألا would require a slightly different vocalisation but would not be inconsistent with the consonantal texts.

7

An Overview of Christian Responses to
A Common Word

Sarah Snyder

INTRODUCTION

A Common Word Between Us and You (ACW) has in many ways prompted a deeper, transformative dialogue between Muslims and Christians as it calls for greater collaboration based on the core principles of loving God and neighbour. The majority of responses, however, have been Western, academic or institutional voices, and one wonders about the impact among lay communities, and in Asian, African, South American and other contexts.[1]

Dr Johnson Mbillah, general adviser for the Programme for Christian–Muslim Relations in Africa (PROCMURA) in Nairobi, Kenya, writes:

We hope that *ACW* is not merely thinking of Islam and the West, which generally come to mind when people begin to talk about Christian-Muslim relations, but that it recognizes that in practical everyday life, one must look beyond the Euro-Arab axis of the Mediterranean to the largest meetings of Christians and Muslims that take place in Africa and Asia [in order] to make more sense of Christian and Muslim relations.[2]

Similarly, Franz Magnis-Suseno SJ, Jesuit priest and professor of philosophy in Jakarta, Indonesia, comments:

---

[1] Subsequent translations into Albanian, Bosnian, French, Italian, German, Russian, Polish, Indonesian and, partially, Spanish have extended its reach beyond English- and Arabic-speaking audiences.

[2] Johnson A. Mbillah, 'An African reflection on *A Common Word*', in Christian Troll, Helmut Reifeld and Chris Hewer (eds.), *We Have Justice in Common: Christian and Muslim Voices from Asia and Africa* (Berlin: Konrad-Adenauer-Stiftung, 2010), pp. 87–107, at p. 94.

the letter is only a beginning. Most people of the Muslim and Christian world have not been touched by it. In Indonesia, not once have I heard an allusion to this letter. It has not received any attention. But this should not discourage the writers. The letter is a first. It opens a gap in the ideological fortifications that we have built around each other. It will have its effect.[3]

As is well known, *ACW* emphasises the unity of God as well as love of God and neighbour as common ground for engagement between Muslims and Christians in the world today, but is heavily criticised by some[4] for skimming over fundamental differences. As some chapters in this volume argue, it raises as many questions as answers, not least concerning the very nature of God, love and neighbour. Others, however, view this as a welcome challenge – an invitation into deeper theological dialogue without avoiding difficult conversations.

For a Muslim contributor like Aref Nayed, a Libyan Islamic scholar, Ambassador to the United Arab Emirates and a key architect of *ACW*, it is important to note the distinction between theological, social and ethical dialogue:

For people who believe in divine revelation as the ultimate font and ground for righteous living, as Jews, Christians and Muslims do, theology and theological dialogue must be the foundational ground of all other forms of dialogue. Mere ethical/social dialogue is useful, and is very much needed. However, dialogue of that kind happens every day, through purely secular institutions such as the United Nations and its organisations. If religious revelation-based communities are to truly contribute to humanity, their dialogue must be ultimately theologically and spiritually grounded.[5]

Indeed, the broad spectrum of Islamic schools of thought represented by *ACW* was almost unprecedented, offering hope amidst widespread sectarian and interreligious conflict. The world today has changed dramatically since 2007, witnessing challenges from within and beyond the Islamic world that threaten and undermine relations between diverse communities. *ACW* hints at a powerful mode of reconciliation: despite deeply held but different confessions *within* our traditions, let alone between them,

---

3 Franz Magnis-Suseno SJ, 'A *Common Word* and what it could mean', in Troll, Reifeld and Hewer, *We Have Justice in Common*, pp. 25–51, at pp. 26–7.
4 See, for example, 'GodVoter.org responds to "A Common Word" from Muslims', 31 January 2007, which rejects the claim that Christians and Muslims love 'the One God'. www.acommonword.com/godvoter-org-responds-to-a-common-word-from-muslims-2/. Accessed 29 September.
5 Interview with the *Catholic News Service*, 31 October 2007, quoted by Chris Hewer in his 'Briefing on A *Common Word*' at St Ethelburga's Centre in London on 6 December 2007'.

the spirit of dialogue is for God's sake, not our own. With this spirit in mind, Magnis-Suseno points out:

What is so remarkable in this letter [ACW] is that its argumentation is theological. Working together because we are united by common values is already something very important. But this letter, by arguing in a theological way, goes a step further. It offers collaboration for peace in the world *before* God! In this letter Muslims accept Christians as believers before God, something that, I should think, didn't come easily.[6]

Similarly, David Ford, (now Emeritus) Regius Professor of Divinity at the University of Cambridge, affirms:

This common word does not pretend that there are no differences between Muslims and Christians (for example, on the Christian teaching *about* Jesus rather than the teaching *of* Jesus). It takes a vital step forward, and wisely does this by concentrating mainly on each tradition's scriptures, those core texts that are so often misused but which, in my experience, also have the resources for enabling deeper mutual understanding and trust.[7]

Indeed many Christian respondents to *ACW* appreciated the inclusion of Biblical references in the *ACW* document, and saw it as indication of a high regard for, and recognition of, the way in which Christians value their scriptures. The Pontifical Institute of Arab and Islamic Studies in Rome comments:

We are pleased to see that the biblical and Gospel quotations used in this document come from the sources and that explanations given are on occasion based on the original languages: Hebrew, Aramaic and Greek. This is evidence of deep respect and genuine attentiveness to others.[8]

The Baptist World Alliance calls attention to the way in which *ACW* draws

from the Jewish *Shema,* which begins with a declaration of the oneness of God: 'Hear, O Israel, the Lord our God, the Lord is one'. This is made explicit in Mark 12:28–31, while it is implicit in the parallel passages in Matthew and Luke. You [*ACW* authors] therefore urge that the 'common ground' is not just the two

---

[6] Magnis-Suseno, '*A Common Word* and what it could mean', p. 26.

[7] 'A Common Word between Us and You: A response by Professor David Ford, Director of the Cambridge Inter-Faith Programme', 9 October 2007. www.acommonword.com/category/site/christian-responses/.

[8] Staff members of the Pontifical Institute for Arabic and Islamic Studies (PISAI) of Rome, 'Appreciation of an open letter and call from Muslim religious leaders "A Common Word between Us and You"', 25 October 2007. www.acommonword.com/appreciation-of-an-open-letter-and-call-from-muslim-religious-leaders-a-common-word-between-us-and-you/.

greatest commandments, but the confession of the Unity of God in which they are rooted and out of which they arise.[9]

Concern was expressed by some, however, over the selection of Biblical quotations. The World Evangelical Association, for example, writes:

> In your letter, you only quote from Jesus' mouth that which is in accordance with your faith. This is, of course, your good right and whatever you quote from Jesus, we take very seriously. But we deserve the right to follow *everything* that Jesus said [...]. Muhammad was convinced that Jesus taught the same message as he did and that any word of Jesus in the New Testament that disagreed was, therefore, not Jesus' original message but a distortion.[10]

Daniel A. Madigan SJ, Jesuit priest, Associate Professor and Jeanette W. and Otto J. Ruesch Family Professor at Georgetown University, explains that

> the letter does open itself to a reductionist reading – one that Christians might want to examine more closely – when it says in part III, 'Thus the Unity of God, love of Him and love of the neighbour form a common ground upon which Islam and Christianity (and Judaism) are founded.' [...] In fairness to our Muslim colleagues, it should be admitted that many Christians too will propose a short-hand rendition of Jesus' saying about the greatest commandments [...]. The Gospel is not a simple cut-and-paste job on the Torah, with a more pithy selection of commandments.[11]

Madigan's Chapter 10 in the present volume includes a further elaboration on his critique of the reductionist nature of the use of Christian scripture in *ACW*.[12]

ACW and the ensuing conversations show that despite a tendency in religious dialogue towards agreement and consensus, most traditions embrace the reality of particularity, diversity and dispute, and even encourage healthy debate between believers (e.g., Q 29:46). It is, indeed, through deep disagreement that doors can be opened to more profound understanding and appreciation of the 'Other'. Mbillah argues that

[9] Baptist World Alliance, 'To the Muslim religious leaders and scholars who have written or signed *A Common Word between Us and You*', 26 December 2008. www.acommonword.com/category/site/christian-responses/.

[10] World Evangelical Alliance, 'We too want to live in love, peace, freedom and justice', 2 April 2008. www.acommonword.com/category/site/christian-responses/.

[11] Daniel A. Madigan SJ, '*A Common Word between Us and You*: some initial reflections', 18 January 2008. www.acommonword.com/response-from-daniel-madigan-sj-the-vaticans-commission-for-religious-relations-with-muslims/.

[12] See Chapter 10 in this volume.

we do not need to come to an agreement on theological and doctrinal issues to work together to promote peace and mutual respect. Our common humanity, as the World Council of Churches has always upheld, and our recognition that there are good values in Christianity as in Islam, as Vatican II holds, should bind us together to seek peace, even as we exercise mutual respect for our differences.[13]

Rowan Williams, Archbishop of Canterbury when he wrote his response, highlights five areas of strong potential for dialogue arising from *ACW*, including its focus on the love and praise of God, love of neighbour, scriptural integrity, the life of faith and the presence of differences as well as similarities. He recommends three onward steps for Muslim–Christian dialogue: education about one another's tradition, 'opportunities for lived encounters with people of different faiths' and a commitment to dialogue and peace from all participants.[14] Indeed, his tenure as archbishop was marked by tireless work towards facilitating ongoing opportunities for Muslim–Christian engagement, as chair of the Building Bridges Seminar, by hosting numerous interfaith gatherings at Lambeth Palace, and by leading a conference on *ACW* in October 2008, in partnership with the Cambridge Inter-faith Programme and the Royal Aal Al-Bayt Foundation.[15]

Matthew Hassan Kukah, bishop of the Roman Catholic Diocese of Sokoto in Nigeria, responds to *ACW*:

Let me join millions of men and women of goodwill, to congratulate and thank all those who answered the divine directive to reflect, write and append their signatures to what must be seen definitely as the most inspirational window leading to the arena of dialogue among believers across the world in this new century.[16]

Describing its 'lofty ideals', however, he adds a dose of realism from his own Nigerian context:

It is easy for nations in the west with settled democracies and institutions to take so much for granted in discussing some of the issues captured in this initiative. I make this point because the African situation has often been framed in the

---

[13] Mbillah, 'An African reflection on *A Common Word*', p. 106.

[14] See Chapter 4 in this volume.

[15] For details of this event, see 'A Common Word conference with the Archbishop of Canterbury and Cambridge University: communiqué from *A Common Word* conference'. www.acommonword.com/communique-from-a-common-word-conference/. Accessed 29 September 2016.

[16] Matthew Hassan Kukah, '*A Common Word*: thoughts from Nigeria', pp. 108–23, at pp. 108–9.

most condescending and patronising manner with crises and conflicts presented as inevitable outcomes.[17]

In many ways *ACW* challenges widely held perceptions of religion as the cause of, rather than the solution to, violence, with its overwhelming emphasis on love of God and neighbour. Yet it also raises questions about understanding fundamental concepts such as 'love' across the Christian and Islamic traditions. What does it actually mean to love God, and love one's neighbour? How do Christians understand that 'God is love' (1 John 4:8), and how does this compare with Islamic conviction that God is 'the Merciful Lord of Mercy' (al-Raḥmān al-Raḥīm)? What about the challenge of Trinitarian and Unitarian understanding of the one God? There have been challenging debates in response to *ACW*. What follows is an attempt to record some of the diversity of Christian responses fairly and respectfully, not shying away from inevitable controversies, and including, where possible, non-Western voices.

CONCERNING THE NATURE OF GOD

The Qur'anic verse 3:64, 'Come to a common word between us and you', lies at the heart of *ACW*, and has contributed to some of the liveliest theological debate. English translations of the Arabic *ta'ālaw ilā kalimatin sawā'in baynanā wa-baynakum* include:

'come to a common word between us and you'
(*ACW*, Arthur J. Arberry and W. M. Marmaduke Pickthall)

'come to a just word of common consent'
(Mahmoud Ayoub)

'come to common terms as between us and you'
(A. Yusuf Ali)

'let us arrive at a statement that is common to us all'
(M. A. S. Abdel Haleem)

'come now to a formula acceptable to each of us'
(Kenneth Cragg)

'come to a word that is just between us and you'
(M. Taqi-ud Din al-Hilali and
M. Muhsin Khan)

---

[17] Ibid., p. 109.

'come to an equitable word between you and us'

(Majid Fakhry)

'come let us rally around a discourse common to us and you'

(Tarif Khalidi).

Other chapters in this volume, by Asma Afsaruddin (Chapter 9), Clare Amos (Chapter 12) and Pim Valkenberg (Chapter 11), present further and deeper reflections on the use of scripture in Arabic and English. Here, the focus is on various readings of this verse in relationship to understanding God's unity.

Colin Chapman, Anglican priest and formerly lecturer in Islamic Studies at the Near East School of Theology, Beirut, Lebanon, highlights the words that follow this key phrase in *ACW*, and especially the colon that separates them. He says:

It implies a formula by which Jews, Christians and Muslims are invited to agree: *alla na'buda ill-Allah wa la nushrika bihi shai'an wala yattakhidha ba'duna ba'dan arbaban min dun-illah,* 'that we shall worship none but God, and that we shall ascribe no partner unto Him, and that none of us shall take others for lords beside God'.[18]

In its original Qur'anic context, Chapman points out, the invitation 'come to a common word' seems to ask Jews and Christians to accept an Islamic understanding of the oneness of God. By contrast, Muslims (mis)understand the Christian doctrine of Jesus as God to be *shirk*, the highest form of *kufr* (unbelief), because it puts a created being on the same level as the Creator. Can this verse really be understood as an invitation to genuine interfaith dialogue, given these differences in understanding? The ideal would be for all participants to meet in a context of mutual respect for one another's particularities.[19]

Christian Troll SJ, German theologian, Jesuit priest, member of the Commission of the German Bishops' Conference (DBK) for Interreligious Dialogue and Professor Emeritus in the Graduate School of Philosophy and Theology of the College of St George in Frankfurt, states:

It is important for Muslims approaching dialogue with Christians to understand that this trinitarian monotheism is central to Christian belief and worship and is not an aspect of Christianity that can be negotiated away. In this regard there are some slight ambiguities in the Open Letter, moments at which a Christian

---

[18] Colin Chapman, 'An evangelical Christian reflection on the key Qur'anic text in *A Common Word*' (unpublished paper), p. 1.
[19] Ibid.

might feel that it is suggesting that there are no fundamental differences between the theologies of the two faiths, or at least that these differences do not really matter.[20]

Mark Durie, an Anglican priest in Melbourne, Australia, points out:

In its conclusion, the letter brings its readers right back to its central message, calling Christians to accept 'the common essentials of our two religions'. The switch is complete. **References to loving God and one's neighbour are dispensed with,** and the focus is entirely on the doctrine of *Tawhid*,[21] which is proposed as the common ground for 'all future interfaith dialogue' between Muslims and Christians.[22]

Is there a way forward with this discussion? On 16 September 2009, around twenty Muslim and twenty Christian leaders and scholars, together with Hindu and Buddhist observers, gathered in Kuala Lumpur for a 'Common Word Roundtable'. The co-moderator of that session, Dr Amir Farid Isahak, chairman of Interfaith Spiritual Fellowship Malaysia (INSAF), subsequently reflected on the challenges facing Muslims and Christians discussing the oneness of God (*tawhid*):

The God of the Qur'an defines himself as 'one' in many instances, and that he has no associates or partners (in Q 3:64 and many other verses), does not beget nor was begotten (Q 112:3 and at least 12 other verses). He directly rebuts the Christian concept of a triune (three-in-one) God in many verses and rejects the notion that Jesus is his divine son. [...] In the Muslim context, the one, indivisible God of the Qur'an, who has determined that Jesus is neither his partner nor his son, is telling Jews and Christians not to take Jesus (or any of the Prophets (peace be upon them) or anyone else) to be their Lord, God, or his divine partner or son. And if they do, then they have not surrendered to God.[23]

Isahak offers a way forward, however:

Even if we respectfully agree to disagree on our understanding of the oneness of God, we can certainly agree on these two commandments: to love him completely (no matter how differently we perceive him to be) and to love one another (regardless of our faiths).[24]

---

[20] Christian Troll SJ, 'Towards *common ground* between Christians and Muslims?', 22 October 2007. www.acommonword.com/response-from-prof-dr-christian-troll-s-j/.

[21] Translated as 'the oneness of God'.

[22] Mark Durie, 'Notes for Christians on understanding *A Common Word between Us and You*', January 2008. http://acommonword.blogspot.de/2008/02/notes-for-christians-on-understanding.html.

[23] Amir Farid Isahak, 'One God? Same God?', pp. 199–209, at pp. 203, 204.

[24] Ibid., p. 205.

The Evangelical Alliance's response to *ACW* reminds readers that such straightforward conclusions are not always appropriate. The authors of its response encourage further dialogue around differences, emphasising the intricate relationship between a Trinitarian understanding of God and the theological notion of 'love':

> In your opening summary, you commence with what is obviously a 'call to Christians' to become Muslims by worshipping God without ascribing to him a partner. [...] By referring several times to Quranic statements that state God has no partner and associate, you rightly draw attention to the deepest difference between Islam and Christianity. [...] We know that this is a fundamental difference in our understanding the nature of God; one that will require long and sincere talks, and genuine listening to each other if we are to truly understand each other's position and to move beyond historical caricatures. [...] We draw attention to our differences only to show that we have a long way to go if we want to make love the centre of our discussions.[25]

Some Christian responses expressed concern over traditional Islamic interpretations of the Qur'anic verse 3:64. Bukhārī's collection of Hadith, for example, recalls this verse in the Book of Jihad, immediately after the letter sent by Prophet Muhammad to Heraclius, the Byzantine emperor. The letter includes the words 'Now then, I invite you to Islam, embrace Islam and you will be safe (*aslim taslam*)'. In this context, the invitation to the People of the Book is associated with what is in effect a declaration of war against the Byzantines and is understood in terms of jihad.

In his *Sīrat Rasūl Allāh* (Life of the Apostle of God), Ibn Isḥāq (d. 768) includes an account of the visit of sixty Christians from Najrān to the Prophet in Medina, in which he describes their dialogue with the Prophet – in particular about Jesus. He continues: 'So God sent down concerning their [Christian] words and their incoherence, the beginning of the *sūra* of the Family of 'Imrān up to more than eighty verses.'[26] This, then, according to Ibn Isḥāq, is the 'occasion of revelation', the context in which Qur'anic verse 3:64 was revealed to the Prophet. It has been suggested that since the verses immediately before and after it are polemical, the passage as a whole (Q 3:1–80) is an extended polemic against the Christian doctrines of the Trinity and the Incarnation.

It is important to note, however, that *ACW* does not itself comment on traditional interpretations of the verse; if anything, it offers a fresh and

---

[25] World Evangelical Alliance, 'We too want to live in love, peace, freedom and justice'.

[26] Ibn Isḥāq, *Sīrat Rasūl Allāh*, trans. Alfred Guillaume (London: Oxford University Press, 1967), p. 272.

more hospitable understanding of it. Where some respondents view *ACW* as a subtle call for conversion to an Islamic understanding of God, others recognise acknowledgement of a Christian triune understanding of God. Troll comments:

> It is [...] striking that the Open Letter cites a much less polemical approach taken by al-Tabari, an authoritative early commentator on the Qur'an, to the effect that 'Muslims, Christians and Jews should be free to each follow what God commanded them, and not have "to prostrate before kings and the like"'.[27]

Chapman points out:

> *ACW* is going out of its way to offer a fresh interpretation of the Qur'anic invitation to Jews and Christians, but one that is worked out through a new *ijtihad* and based on an authoritative, early source. Far from demanding that Christians accept an Islamic understanding of the oneness of God, it seems to me to accept that Christians are monotheists *of a kind*, and deliberately refrains from criticising or challenging Christians over their beliefs about Jesus. [...] A *Common Word* opens up new possibilities of dialogue because it seems to recognise that Trinitarian Christians believe in the unity of God and are not tri-theists ('the unity of God, love for Him, and love of the neighbour form a common ground upon which Islam and Christianity (and Judaism) are founded'). These are very crucial areas in which we need to remove misunderstandings about each other's beliefs and move forward in mutual understanding.[28]

CONCERNING LOVE OF GOD AND NEIGHBOUR

Many respondents elaborated on *ACW*'s call to love God and neighbour, often focusing on what they perceived to be the difference between Christian and Muslim understanding of this core concept. In doing so, they often refer to Biblical verses that are not included in the *ACW* declaration, especially the writings of St John and St Paul.

Mor Eustathius Matta Roham, archbishop of Jezira and the Euphrates at the Syrian Orthodox Church of Antioch, clarifies:

> When we talk about the love of God in Christianity, we mean God's love for humanity and human[s]' love of God. In the letter [*ACW*], the love of God in Islam is actually closer to the fear of God in Christianity. The concept of God's love for humanity in Christianity has no similarity in Islam as this concept in Christianity refers to the Doctrine of Salvation, which is the core of Christian faith.[29]

---

[27] Troll, 'Towards *common ground* between Christians and Muslims?'
[28] Chapman, 'An evangelical Christian reflection', p. 3.
[29] Mor Eustathius Matta Roham, 'Response from Mor Eustathius Matta Roham, Archbishop of Jezira and the Euphrates, Syrian Orthodox Church of Antioch', 31

Madigan comments:

In his first letter John says, [...] 'We love [...] because God first loved us' (1 John 4:19). Throughout John's work there is a constant outward movement of love: 'As the Father has loved me, so I have loved you' (John 15:9). That is Jesus' 'new commandment' [...]. A command not to love him, or the Father, but rather to dwell in the love he bears us.[30]

Chris Hewer, lecturer in Muslim–Christian relations, explains:

We need to speak about the love of God within a Trinitarian code of discourse. [...]. [A] Christian understanding of the love of God would need to be incarnational. [...] No Christian understanding would be complete without a discussion of the sacrificial, atoning, redemptive love of God as expressed in Christ and our response in faith.[31]

Chapman writes:

In Christian understanding, *love for God and our neighbour* is seen as a response to *God's love for humankind* [...] sacrificial love for our neighbour is our response to God's sacrificial love towards us: 'In this is love, not that we loved God but that he loved us and sent his Son to be the atoning sacrifice for our sins' (1 John 4:10). What motivates us to love God and our neighbour is the conviction that the God of love lives in us through his Holy Spirit: 'God's love has been poured into our hearts through the Holy Spirit that has been given to us' (Romans 5:5); 'if we love one another, God lives in us, and his love is perfected in us' (1 John 4:12). Christians therefore find it impossible to separate love for God and the neighbour from their understanding of God as a God of love.[32]

WHO IS MY NEIGHBOUR?

Theological debate is equally lively around definitions of 'neighbour' and the Arabic translation of this term. Many respondents reinforce the universal Christian nature of 'neighbour' – extending even to one's enemy (Matthew 5:44).

Mbillah insists that *ACW* captures only the barest minimum of Christian understanding about the relationship between love, God and neighbour. Indeed, love of neighbour is only possible because of God's first love for us. He explains:

January 2008. www.acommonword.com/response-from-mor-eustathius-matta-roham-archbishop-of-jezira-and-the-euphrates-syrian-orthodox-church-of-antioch/.

[30] Madigan, '*A Common Word between Us and You*: some initial reflections'.
[31] Hewer, 'Briefing on *A Common Word*'.
[32] Colin Chapman, 'Response to *A Common Word*' (unpublished paper), p. 2.

This love of God, which depicts the vertical relationship between human beings and God, is, in Christian thinking, incomplete without its horizontal aspect which is love of neighbour.[33]

He then points out:

[I]t is clear that the signatories of ACW have come to an understanding that Christians are neighbours with Muslims and that if these neighbours (Christians and Muslims) are not at peace then the world cannot be at peace.[34]

In sub-Saharan Africa Christians and Muslims form the majority of the population, but Mbillah presses further:

[S]hall we therefore understand that the signatories of ACW see Christian and Muslim neighbourliness as a stepping stone for working towards good neighbourliness with all others, or is their understanding of neighbourliness exclusive to that of Christians and Muslims?[35]

Mbillah recalls Jesus' parable of the Good Samaritan in response to a lawyer's asking, 'Who is my neighbour?' after which he concludes:

The Christian understanding of love for neighbour goes beyond love of those with whom you share a religion, a friend or one with whom you agree. [...] [L]ove of neighbour means – love those who may not love you in return.[36]

Samir Khalil Samir SJ, a Jesuit priest and Islamic scholar from Egypt, comments:

It is most interesting to note that the *vocabulary used* [in ACW] is a Christian vocabulary and not a Muslim one. The word 'neighbour' (in the Christian sense of brethren) does not exist in the Koran; it is typical of the New Testament. In fact, the Arabic text does not use the word 'neighbour/brethren' but 'neighbour (*jâr*)', which only has a geographical meaning (like a neighbour who lives next door), compared to the Christian term *qarîb*, which also means 'brethren'.[37]

Durie points to the Hadith from *Ṣaḥīḥ Muslim* regarding the Qur'anic verse 3:64:

In Islam a 'brother' is understood to mean a fellow Muslim, whereas 'neighbour' (*jar*) refers to someone who is geographically close by. [...] The English

---

[33] Mbillah, 'An African reflection on *A Common Word*', p. 91.
[34] Ibid.
[35] Ibid., p. 92.
[36] Ibid.
[37] Samir Khalil Samir SJ, 'The letter of 138 Muslim scholars to the Pope and Christian leaders', 17 October 2007. www.acommonword.com/the-letter-of-138-muslim-scholars-to-the-pope-and-christian-leaders/.

version of *A Common Word* reports the hadith to be 'None of you has faith until you love for your neighbour what you love for yourself.' However what the Arabic actually says – and this is accurately cited in the Arabic version of the *Common Word* – is: 'None of you has faith until you love for your brother – or he said for his neighbour – what he loves for himself.' The English version of the letter obscures the fact that the main focus of the hadith from the Sahih Muslim is upon loving one's brother, i.e. one's brother-in-Islam. The scholars who wrote *A Common Word* used the heading 'Love of the Neighbour in Islam', but what their content takes the reader to is love for one's fellow Muslim.[38]

It is particularly noted that *ACW* does not address Jewish neighbours. A 'Common Word' at Yale accepts this exclusion as a reflection of the specific need to address the relationship between Muslims and Christians:

Nonetheless, because of the historic tendency of both Christians and Muslims to exclude the Jewish community at times, we believe it is important to be proactive in inviting Jewish leaders and scholars to participate in our discussions.[39]

The bishop of London, Richard Chartres, agrees:

[It] is very important that we do not go ahead in a way that marginalises the Jewish community.[40]

A group of Muslim and Christian scholars and activists, mainly from sub-Saharan Africa, South and South-East Asia, met in Cadenabbia, Italy, in October 2009 to study and reflect on *ACW*. In their official response, they assert:

We accept the challenge of ACW to 'Love your neighbour as yourself', which we understand as applying to the obligation to build secure 'neighbourhoods' in the widest sense of that term. This requires us to confront together the challenges which include poverty and illiteracy, environmental degradation and disease, human-rights violations, gender discrimination and ethnic conflict.'[41]

---

[38] Mark Durie, 'More on loving one's (Muslim) neighbour', 25 March 2008. http://acommonword.blogspot.de/2008/03/more-on-loving-ones-muslim-neighbour-in.html.

[39] Yale Center for Faith & Culture, 'A "Common Word" at Yale: frequently asked questions'. http://faith.yale.edu/common-word/common-word-yale-frequently-asked-questions. Accessed 2 November 2016.

[40] Richard Chartres, 'Response from the Bishop of London to the Open Letter from 138 Muslim scholars and addressed to the spiritual leaders of the Christian world', 12 October 2007. www.acommonword.com/response-from-the-bishop-of-london-to-the-open-letter-from-138-muslim-scholars-and-addressed-to-the-spiritual-leaders-of-the-christian-world/.

[41] Participants at Cadenabbia, 'A message from Cadenabbia', in Troll, Reifeld and Hewer (eds.), *We Have Justice in Common*, pp. 15–8, at p. 16.

In other words, we are required to love our neighbour through acts of neighbourliness that recognise and address the sufferings of others. Speaking from Nigeria, Kukah explains:

Obviously, as long as there is inequality in any society, especially when it is based on a perceived classification or identity, we cannot talk of being children of one God, created in his image and likeness and meant to be the objects of his love. So how should we work towards ending injustice and creating a much fairer society that does not discriminate against some sections or members of the population?[42]

He further spells out what a nation might look like that demonstrates love of neighbour through pursuit of the 'Common Good'. Such a nation will:

• Guarantee [...] a safe haven for the weakest in the society.
• Create a platform that ensures access to justice by all.
• Create a system that favours and promotes security of the family.
• Create a culture of tolerance.
• Ensure programmes that promote public welfare.
• Promote peaceful co-existence and harmony.
• Encourage and promote freedom of expression.[43]

He concludes that most of these ideals are captured in the National Constitution of Nigeria, and yet often remain more theory than practice.[44]

THE RELEVANCE OF *ACW* TO TODAY'S CONTEXT

The daily scenes of horrific violence committed in the name of religion place increased urgency on the need for action beyond dialogue in today's world. Religious disagreements between and within religious communities are too often seen by the wider public as the cause of violence, ignoring the overwhelmingly peace-building tendencies of religious commitment. Has *ACW* contributed any lasting impact to alleviating the pain and suffering of millions of communities worldwide? Some of the voices of those closely involved in *ACW* initiatives express despair at the lack of visible signs of hope.

Madigan urges:

[L]et us not be misled into thinking either that Muslim – Christian conflict is the world's greatest conflict, or even that war is the most serious threat to the human future. [...] What of the world's poor who live under crushing burdens of foreign

---

[42] Kukah, '*A Common Word*: thoughts from Nigeria', p. 115.
[43] Ibid., p. 116.
[44] Ibid., pp. 116–17.

debt and corrupt domestic tyranny? What of the devastating effects on the earth of our poor stewardship of its resources? The new stage in Muslim–Christian dialogue represented by *A Common Word* should not become the occasion for a further narrowing of our attention and a greater obsession with ourselves. If we wish to talk of love, we will not be able to ignore the cry of the poor.[45]

Kukah reflects on the situation for many citizens of his own country of Nigeria:

In their daily lives, the people have no shelter, they have no education, they have no adequate food, they remain vulnerable to diseases, they live in squalor, and so on. It is in this ocean of neglect that the viruses of violence reside. [...] [T]he root causes of these crises are often social discontentment by various segments of the society. Religion provides an appropriate tool to which to appeal to mobilise and channel this discontentment, largely because it is easy to identify it as the basis of privilege or disadvantage. [...] Therefore, to address and reverse the issues as to why so-called religious or communal violence persists in Nigeria, it is important to appreciate the aphorism, *a hungry man is an angry man*.[46]

Mbillah points out that

in many parts of Sub-Saharan Africa people still listen to their religious leaders and take them seriously. It is in this light that ACW's call on Christians to inculcate a spirit of good neighbourliness with Muslims based on their respective scriptural injunctions holds value.[47]

There are ample examples of mutual hospitality within Christian and Muslim neighbourhoods, hosted by mosques, churches and others, that build relationships of trust across deeply challenging lines. This requires the dedication of faith and community leaders – men, women and young people – to initiate and model a new form of collegiality, one that does not compromise on deeply held convictions, but nevertheless opens up safe spaces within which different members of the community can gather.[48]

Al-Tayeb Zain Al-Abdin, professor of political science at the University of Khartoum, Sudan, commends the international World Conference of Religions for Peace (WCRP)[49] and the African association Inter-Faith Action for Peace in Africa (IFAPA),[50] founded by the Lutheran World Federation. Both, he says, 'have been active in peace-making, humanitarian

---

[45] Madigan, '*A Common Word between Us and You*: some initial reflections'.
[46] Kukah, '*A Common Word*: thoughts from Nigeria', pp. 117, 118.
[47] Mbillah, 'An African reflection on *A Common Word*', p. 106.
[48] See, for example, the reconciliation work of the *Rose Castle Foundation*, below.
[49] See www.religionsforpeace.org for details of the many ways in which they are engaging local religious communities around the world.
[50] For more information, see www.ifapa-africa.com.

aid, human rights and combating HIV disease'.[51] The role played by religious leaders in combating Ebola in Sierra Leone and Liberia has also been crucial. This shows that African religious communities are more concerned with working together to solve the practical problems of their societies than with indulging themselves in the discussion of theological differences.

ACW was never intended only as an invitation to conversation among religious leaders and scholars; it was to stimulate both dialogue and action at the local level. This requires a challenging move beyond words, demonstrating ability to form relationships of trust across religious divides that have in the past suffered deep hurts and confrontation. Some respondents to *ACW* reflected this call for action. The United Methodist Council of Bishops pointed out, 'In our Wesleyan tradition, we believe that truth must be enacted in our lives.'[52] The group of Muslim and Christian scholars and activists from sub-Saharan Africa and South and South-East Asia meeting in Cadenabbia, Italy (5 October 2009), focused on socio-political-economic issues, including disparities in income levels, institutionalised corruption, unemployment, poor education and the status of women.[53] The Mennonite Church USA

strongly encourage[s] Christians and Muslims around the world to meet, develop friendships, and cooperate in endeavors of mutual concern as we discuss and bear witness to the theological and ethical foundations of our faith and life.[54]

The following are a few examples of dialogue and action among *ACW* respondents with whom this author has had the privilege to engage.

The Rose Castle Foundation provides safe and facilitated spaces in which to overcome misunderstanding and better understand differences within and between religious communities. Participants learn strategies for 'disagreeing well' – recognising that it is possible to work together for the common good of their communities, without having to compromise on deeply held and different ideological convictions. With careful facilitation, they can move from positions of back to back (conflict), to face to face (dialogue), to shoulder to shoulder (common action).

[51] Al-Tayib Zain Al-Abdin, 'A response to *A Common Word* from an African perspective', in Troll, Reifeld and Hewer (eds.), *We Have Justice in Common*, pp. 124–35, at p. 131.

[52] 'United Methodist Council of Bishops' response to "A Common Word between Us and You"', 5 January 2009. www.acommonword.com/category/site/christian-responses/.

[53] Helmut Reifeld, 'Preface', in Troll, Reifeld and Hewer (eds.), *We Have Justice in Common*, pp. 7–10, at p. 8.

[54] James Schrag, 'The response of the Mennonite Church to *A Common Word*', 5 November 2007. www.acommonword.com/the-response-of-the-mennonite-church-to-a-common-word/.

A core programme of Scriptural Reasoning[55] ensures participants' own scriptures are at the heart of conversation, and the source from which to draw relevance to their particular contexts. Residential hospitality plays a critical role, in which members of different religious traditions share meals and leisure time, and observe one another's habits of worship, as the backdrop to more structured and challenging dialogue and learning. Participants return home equipped to build bridges across challenging divisions, having spent time living and working with those they rarely meet in their own contexts. The work is based in an eight hundred–year-old castle near the border of England with Scotland, once built to withstand the enemy and thereby to protect the bishops of Carlisle, but now re-opening its doors to welcome 'strangers'. It is supported by a daily rhythm of Christian and Muslim prayer for peace and reconciliation.[56]

The Cambridge Inter-Faith Programme (CIP) has discovered many ways to open up a safe space in which those who rarely interact in their 'home contexts' are able to live and work together for a short period.[57] At the heart of its early foundation was a friendship between Professor David Ford (Christian), Professor Peter Ochs (Jewish), and Dr Aref Nayed (Muslim), all active participants in *ACW*. Its International Summer School[58] brings together Jewish, Christian and Muslim faith leaders, many from conflict situations where they are unable or unwilling to meet within their own communities. Carefully facilitated sessions allow attentive listening to one another's sufferings (without the need to agree), and time to step into another's shoes for a little while, before getting back into one's own comfortable pair. Misconceptions of the 'Other' are powerfully exposed, and participants are challenged, and changed in the process. Importantly, however, they remain deeply rooted within their own particular traditions and even emerge with deeper appreciation of their religious conviction, through encountering those beyond or outside it.

The conflict impacting Israelis and Palestinians remains one of the most sensitive areas of dialogue and action, complexly weaving together religious, political and economic tensions. In 2012, a group of senior

---

[55] See www.scripturalreasoning.org for further details. This programme is now co-ordinated by the Rose Castle Foundation, but remains central to the work of the Cambridge Interfaith Programme (see later discussion).

[56] For details of the reconciliation work of the Rose Castle Foundation, see www.rosecastle .foundation.

[57] For the project, see www.interfaith.cam.ac.uk.

[58] For details, see www.interfaith.cam.ac.uk/publiceducationprojects/cipsummerschool.

Jewish, Christian and Muslim leaders met in the Jerusalem Chamber of Westminster Abbey in London to discuss their respective scriptures on the future of Jerusalem and the Holy Land. It was a challenging day, led by the Scriptural Reasoning team of the Cambridge Inter-Faith Programme, but was in many ways a remarkable breakthrough, opening safe space for difficult conversation, and addressing misconceptions and misunderstanding between those present. In November 2013, some of the group visited Belfast in Northern Ireland to learn from a different, but in some ways related, conflict. They met with former paramilitaries, and witnessed the depth of suffering in each community. A significant part of this follow-up was the ability to look at one's own context through the eyes of another. Relationships between participants of greatly differing ideologies and traditions were strengthened in the face of a conflict not their own.[59] In Chapter 14 of the present volume, Mustafa Abu Sway reflects further on the complexities of receiving the *ACW* in the Holy Land today.

The Global Covenant of Religions is a new and powerful movement of religious leaders and their communities willing to challenge violence in God's name publicly. Together they are drawing from the depth of their respective traditions to expose narratives that condone or even promote violence. They are working to strengthen cooperation among religious organisations, governments and civil society in order to protect civilians, mediate conflict, educate youth, and love and serve their neighbours.[60]

Another deeply challenging issue in Muslim–Christian engagement concerns the status of converts, or apostasy. Members of both world religions are committed to sharing a deep and fundamental understanding of 'truth', yet in many contexts it is difficult, if not illegal, to 'evangelise' or convert from one tradition to another. Consequently the issue is often overlooked or unrecognised, resulting in challenging conditions for converts, whose citizenship rights, let alone family membership, are severely restricted. The UK Christian Muslim Forum published 'Ethical Guidelines for Christian and Muslim Witness in Britain' on 24 June 2009, the tenth of which boldly states: 'Whilst we may feel hurt when someone

---

[59] For details of this visit, entitled 'Swords into Ploughshares', see www.fodip.org/articles/swords.pdf. Accessed 30 September 2016.

[60] For initial details of this programme, see www.churchillcentral.com/timeline/stories/the-global-covenant-of-religions. Accessed 30 September 2016.

we know and love chooses to leave our faith, we will respect their decision and will not force them to stay or harass them afterwards.'[61]

On 27 January 2016 many of the world's Islamic leaders, with
around fifty non-Muslim observers, issued the 'Marrakesh Declaration'
concerning treatment of minority groups living in Muslim-majority lands.
Christians and Muslims belong to both majority and minority communities across the globe, historically and today, and have a commitment
to protect and respect one another. They were inspired by what might
be viewed as an early example of 'A Common Word' – the Charter of
Medina, in which a blueprint for relations of the newly emergent Muslim
community with others was established. Fourteen hundred years after the
Charter of Medina, the Muslim leaders at Marrakesh signed a declaration
of intent in which they 'AFFIRM HEREBY that such cooperation [among
all religious groups] must be based on a "Common Word", requiring that
such cooperation must go beyond mutual tolerance and respect, to providing full protection for the rights and liberties to all religious groups in
a civilized manner that eschews coercion, bias, and arrogance'.[62]

Since the declaration was issued, conversations and events worldwide, led primarily by Muslim communities, organisations and leaders,
have explored how the declaration could advance protection of religious
freedom. The Network for Religious and Traditional Peacemakers[63] in
collaboration with the Forum for Promoting Peace in Muslim Societies[64]
has already begun awareness raising, and plans country-level and regional
consultations, including one in the United Arab Emirates in January
2017, to identify how best to implement the declaration's key principles.

The archbishop of Cyprus, Chrysostomos II, some of whose community have long lived in a Muslim-majority context, said:

We absolutely agree with the necessity of respect of religious difference and of
course we disapprove every effort of limitation of religious freedom of Muslims
or anyone else who lives in a nation with majority in Christian population. Of

---

[61] www.christianmuslimforum.org/images/Ethical_Guidelines_for_Witnessv10.pdf.
Accessed 30 September 2016.

[62] Marrakesh Declaration, 'Executive summary of the Marrakesh Declaration on the rights
of religious minorities in predominantly Muslim majority communities', 25–27 January
2016. www.marrakeshdeclaration.org/files/Bismilah-2-ENG.pdf. For more details of this
initiative, see www.marrakeshdeclaration.org.

[63] The Network for Religious and Traditional Peacemakers works with Muslim, Christian
and other community activists to improve the sustainability of peace-building in situations of conflict. For details, see www.peacemakersnetwork.org.

[64] For details, see http://peacems.com.

course, the same respect is demanded for Christian minorities in Muslim countries and especially local Churches, which exist in majority Muslim nations.[65]

CONCLUDING REMARKS

The responses that follow remind us that the framework for transformative dialogue must be a spirit of humility that recognises past and current suffering on all sides, and a willingness to accept some responsibility.

The Mennonite Church USA states:

We recognize that even today in too many situations Muslims are threatened by Christians, and in other situations, individual Christians or communities of Christians in Muslim regions experience restrictions and sometimes hostility. Let us repent of such actions toward one another and work together to assure the integrity and freedom for both communities, Christian and Muslim.[66]

Building Bridges, Cambridge, responds to *ACW* as follows:

We would like to make a joint expression of sorrow and sympathy for those who have suffered either as a direct result of recent incidents which have been attributed to extremists or conflicts in the Muslim world, or indirectly due to hatred arising from such incidents and conflicts. We commit ourselves – with God's help – to resist hatred, bitterness, fear and prejudice which would affect or destroy relationships between people of different communities, and acknowledge that to achieve this we all need to be inwardly changed by God's grace. [...] Most important of all, we need to learn to pray in a God-pleasing way. Jesus himself prayed, as he faced crucifixion, 'Not my will but Yours be done'. If we pray humbly with a listening heart, God will show us, Muslims and Christians, how we can work together, laying aside prejudices and misunderstandings – in this way we will discover the most practical ways to do God's will.[67]

The Evangelical–Muslim Dialogue conference in Tripoli, 'Human Nature and the Divine Presence' (3–6 January 2008), with participants from Canada, the Netherlands, the United Kingdom, Lebanon, Libya, Palestine, Syria, Turkey and the United States, endorsed *ACW* and agreed on the following three principles of dialogue:

---

[65] 'Response from His Beatitude Chrisostomos, Archbishop of Cyprus', 10 November 2008. www.acommonword.com/response-from-his-beatitude-chrisostomos-archbishop-of-cyprus/.

[66] Schrag, 'The response of the Mennonite Church to *A Common Word*'.

[67] John Martin and Stuart Anderson, 'Response to *A Common Word* from Building Bridges, Cambridge', 21 December 2007. www.acommonword.com/response-to-a-common-word-from-building-bridges-cambridge/.

1 frank and honest witness to their respective faiths, without compromise;
2 a willingness to be challenged and transformed through conversation; and
3 a readiness to change preconceived notions and reformulate ways of thinking.[68]

At the Cambridge Inter-faith Programme (CIP) we often talk about discovering a *better quality of disagreement*, rather than seeking common ground. *ACW* invited such deep and theological dialogue, resulting in frank and honest engagement around both differences and similarities in our understanding of God, love and neighbour. At times, these meaningful conversations have contributed to changed lives on the ground, particularly among participants, though there is still much work to be done.

The ability to see ourselves through the 'Other's' eyes is a powerful tool of engagement opened up through carefully facilitated dialogues. Just one very practical example, taken from a recent CIP Summer School (2015), was the decision of Israeli women to wear the *burqa* of fellow Muslim dialogue partners on a day trip to Birmingham. They experienced first hand the responses of others as they walked through the busy streets of this multi-cultural city, and understood a little of what it means to wear an outward covering. Relations between these female participants were transformed, in both directions, as a result of this simple gesture of hospitality. It opened space for ongoing dialogue at a deeper level than is possible in a usual interfaith encounter, and generated lasting relationships, and joint action, between their communities after they returned home to more challenging contexts.

In the months and years since *ACW* was written, we have witnessed numerous examples of dialogue and action, the best of which are held face to face, as part of a longer-term commitment to building relationships of trust. This is a heavy task in over-crowded lives, but one worth striving for. The space created by these dialogues, while at times limited, invites communities to practise being in each other's presence, normalising otherwise strained relationships, while also providing mechanisms for peaceful disagreement. Perhaps it is, in fact, the very act of conversation that is ultimately more important than its content? 'A common word *between us and you.*'

[68] 'Joint Muslim–Evangelical Christian endorsement of *A Common Word* in Libya', 3–6 January 2008. www.acommonword.com/joint-muslim-evangelical-christian-endorsement-of-a-common-word-in-libya/.

8

Seeking Humility and Self-Critique

A *Christological Analysis of* A Common Word

Peter Admirand

In this chapter I will advocate for the need of self-critique and humility within interfaith dialogue and will use *A Common Word* as a test and platform in doing so. While ultimately supportive of the document, I also have some concerns, not dissimilar to some of the concerns expressed by other Christian respondents in this book. I hope that my added voice with the others will spur further dialogue, humility and self-critique among Christians and Muslims. In this regard I will examine *ACW* through a Christological lens to gauge whether the positive call of inviting Christians to dialogue was thwarted or hampered by an insufficiently developed and nuanced Christology within that invitation. To clarify, I am by no means suggesting that Muslims must accept Christ according to traditional Christian belief (rendering Jesus as fully God and fully human) for dialogue to occur. Muslims revere Jesus as a prophet while orthodox Christianity claims that Jesus is also God incarnate. Interfaith dialogue thrives (and only exists) on difference and varying interpretations. Therefore, how *ACW* presents Christian views of Jesus is an important issue that should not be overlooked. Where there is difference, there is also space and opportunity to examine and challenge not only the 'Other's' thoughts, but also one's own. Such a focus, I believe, can help strengthen the aims of *ACW* in bringing Muslims and Christians closer together, without undermining unique identities.

I will first flesh out the aims and hopes of authentic interfaith dialogue and then turn to the Gospel parable of the Pharisee and the tax collector as a guide in our reading of humility and self-critique. I will then attempt to follow Christ's call to remove one's own plank first

(Matthew 7:5),[1] and so turn to my Catholic tradition to examine the historical tenor and current state of Catholicism's openness to self-critique and change. Finally, I will seek similar space for humility and self-critique in *ACW* as I argue for the relevance of Christian belief in Christ to be expressed more clearly within the document too.

INTERFAITH DIALOGUE: RISK, HUMILITY, HOPE

I understand interfaith dialogue to be that face-to-face encounter where one's address to another, as well as being addressed by that 'Other', ought to happen in a mutual space of truth-seeking, tolerance and fellowship. As David Tracy writes, 'there is no genuine dialogue without the willingness to risk all one's present self-understanding in the presence of the other'.[2] While there is no single 'right' way to participate in interfaith dialogue, there are plenty of inappropriate and self-defeating contexts, attitudes and aims. Following this understanding, one engages in interfaith dialogue ideally for the following reasons: (1) to hear another's experiences and beliefs in his or her own words to gain (further) comprehension of that person's faith; (2) to come to understand – and possibly sharpen – how others interpret one's own faith position; (3) to gain new, or forgotten, insights that provide challenging, but possibly liberating, avenues of growth within and towards one's own faith tradition; (4) to confront how certain aspects of one's faith may seem culturally specific, fantastic or doubtful when expressed to another and (5) to identify areas of rich agreement and disagreement for ongoing dialogue and partnership.

In dialogue, participants serve as witnesses to their faiths, entering such a dialogue with various identifiable markers, such as Buddhist or Jewish, and testifying to such belonging through their words and actions. However, the ultimate aim of interfaith dialogue is not to convince the 'Other' of one's so-called superior dialogue. Its aims are transformation, purification and clarity – even if such clarity involves murkier notions of truths, paths and salvations – and spurs on more questions than answers.

Interfaith dialogue, then, can be broken down into at least six models. First, at a more general level, there is the dialogue of life, the most pervasive

---

[1] New Testament quotations are from the *NRSV Bible: Catholic Edition* (Winona, MN: St Mary's College Press, 2000). Qur'anic translations are from M. A. S. Abdel Haleem, *The Qur'an: English Translation and Parallel Arabic Text* (Oxford: Oxford University Press, 2010), except where quotations are from *A Common Word*.

[2] David Tracy, *Dialogue with the Other: The Inter-Religious Dialogue* (Leuven: Peeters Press, 1990), p. 72.

and elemental.[3] It is suffused in our daily actions, words and gestures with one another, no matter how pedestrian or humble. Second, interfaith dialogue can also be oriented towards social justice. Those of various religious and non-religious faiths support a certain cause or work together to help the destitute and oppressed. *ACW* is a key text in supporting such aims. Third, interfaith dialogue can also occur formally at a theological or philosophical level where knowledgeable experts or deep practitioners and advocates of particular faiths come together to discuss specific issues in order to tease out possible connections, clarifications, comparisons, rapprochement or differences. This book is deeply enmeshed in this tradition. Fourth, such a dialogue may also occur at the so-called top level, as major, acknowledged representatives or leaders of a faith convene in formal, often institutional, settings.[4] Fifth, we may also consider recent intermonastic meetings and encounters in which those of one faith tradition study, meditate and reflect in the sacred settings and methods of another.[5] Sixth, Raimundo Panikkar highlights intrapersonal dialogue.[6] In this crucial and ongoing dialogue, we work through many of our own insecurities, doubts and strengths, perhaps waiting to test and try some of these ideas in the presence of another, only to return to that inner space for greater reflection and evaluation. For Catherine Cornille, such returning represents 'an act not only of intellectual and spiritual humility, but also of solidarity with the tradition as a whole, and with individuals who might otherwise never be able to taste the fruits of dialogue'.[7] In a sense all types of dialogues are in some way an ongoing dialogue with this one.[8]

---

[3] Jose Mario C. Francisco, 'Migration and new cosmopolitanism in Asian Christianity', in Felix Wilfred (ed.), *The Oxford Handbook of Christianity in Asia* (Oxford: Oxford University Press, 2014), pp. 575–92, at p. 586.

[4] Dalai Lama, *Toward a True Kinship of Faiths: How the World's Religions Can Come Together* (New York: Doubleday, 2010), p. 139.

[5] Donald W. Mitchell and James Wiseman (eds.), *The Gethsemani Encounter: A Dialogue on the Spiritual Life by Buddhist and Christian Monastics* (New York: Continuum, 1999). In the context of Muslim–Christian prayer, see Jane Foulcher, *Reclaiming Humility: Four Studies in the Monastic Tradition* (Collegeville, MN: Liturgical Press, 2015), pp. 294–7. On the interspiritual movement, see for example Adam Bucko and Rory McEntee, *The New Monasticism: An Interspiritual Manifesto for Contemplative Living* (Maryknoll, NY: Orbis, 2015).

[6] Raimundo Panikkar, *The Intrareligious Dialogue* (New York: Paulist Press, 1978), p. 40.

[7] Catherine Cornille, *The Im-Possibility of Interreligious Dialogue* (New York: Herder & Herder, 2008), p. 80.

[8] For a slightly different division of models of dialogue, see Sheryl A. Kujawa-Holbrook, *God beyond Borders: Interreligious Learning among Faith Communities* (Eugene, OR: Pickwick Publications, 2014), pp. 37–40.

Crucial here is a space for the possibility of self-critique (and space to critique the 'Other's' views), and so a certain amount of relativising of one's tradition may be inevitable. If such a space for self-critique is not available, dialogue would seem to be specious and futile, a chimera, ultimately self-serving. Yet, without specific, clear views, dialogue would also seem unfocused and aimless. The search for and commitment to higher truths cannot be avoided or minimised. Such a search is at the root of our reflections and analysis in this book. At the same time, identifying those truths that are 'higher' demands deep listening and reflection.

A PARABLE: THE PHARISEE AND THE TAX COLLECTOR (LUKE 18:9–14)

A well-known Gospel parable tells of two stock characters. There is a great sinner, a tax collector, who apparently is so humble that he cannot even look up towards God while praying at the Temple. Jesus commends him for this. He is meant to contrast with a Pharisee who prays: 'God, I thank you that I am not like other people: thieves, rogues, adulterers, or even like this tax-collector. I fast twice a week; I give a tenth of all my income' (Luke 18:11–13). The tax collector is the expected villain of the piece, but actually is holy, in contrast to the presumably respected Pharisee who is self-righteous. For Jesus' first-century listeners, such a story had surprise and some appeal, as many like a leader's hypocrisies to be revealed. You might ask, though, who (besides the tax collector's close friends and family and the government's coffers) wants a tax collector praised, even if he is praised for his confession rather than for his actions as a tax collector.[9]

There is another difficulty that may arise from this arguably controversial parable, namely, in its unsatisfying use of the language of justification and the downplaying of good works.[10] This tax collector is not Zacchaeus, who later acts on his admitted sinfulness by mending his

---

[9] While recalling this important parable, and in our post-Holocaust reality, we should be more sensitive to the sometimes inordinately harsh critique of Pharisees in the gospels, aware of the close link between Jesus and many Pharisaical beliefs, especially of the *beit Hillel* – house of Hillel – faction and the link between the later rabbinical tradition and the Pharisees. Thus, denigrating Pharisees is often a trope for denigrating the Jews who did not follow Christ.

[10] For a helpful reading on the parable, see Amy-Jill Levine, 'The Pharisee and the tax collector', in *Short Stories by Jesus: The Enigmatic Parables of a Controversial Rabbi* (New York: HarperOne, 2014), pp. 169–95.

ways and restoring what he had defrauded from others (Luke 19:1–10). If, indeed, the Pharisee is not greedy, dishonest or adulterous, the world would still be a better place with the likes of him than with a tax collector who may feel badly about what he does but continues performing it. The lynchpin for our purposes here is Jesus' words 'for everyone who exalts himself will be humbled, and the one who humbles himself will be exalted' (Luke 18:14).

Similarly, for our purposes here, there can be no meaningful interfaith dialogue if participants do not show the necessary humility in engaging openly with the 'Other's' challenges. While James L. Heft is correct to say that self-correction 'is rarely as effective and accurate as the corrections that come from an informed person of another faith',[11] a self-critical stance still demands, among other virtues, humility and empathy.[12] Here we are not referring to such self-critique as mere parroting; referring to a sinful or pilgrim church is not sufficient. One must deeply and painfully admit and believe one's failings, ignorance, and need for others, individually, communally and institutionally.

BALANCING HUMILITY AND DIGNITY

Before we even consider examining or evaluating the 'Other's' beliefs, or even our own religious tradition or communal, ethnic or national history, we must first examine ourselves individually. Am I honest, sincere, humble, or more likely to be self-righteous and certain? More problematically (and difficult to discern), is my humility really a front for my self-righteousness? Here we are at an impasse: to acknowledge ourselves to be other than humble and sincere is to leave ourselves open to claims of inordinate pride and self-righteousness. Humility carries its meaning from the Latin *humus*, 'earth, ground'. It is about being aware, being grounded and accepting the reality of things, especially if it requires confession. Knowing your reality while driving a car will assist a great deal

---

[11] Reuven Firestone, James Heft and Omid Safi, 'Epilogue: the purpose of interreligious dialogue', in James L. Heft, Reuven Firestone and Omid Safi (eds.), *Learned Ignorance: Intellectual Humility among Jews, Christians, and Muslims* (Oxford: Oxford University Press, 2011), pp. 300–11. See also John Bowden, 'Religious pluralism and the heritage of the Enlightenment', in Roger Boase (ed.), *Islam and Global Dialogue: Religious Pluralism and the Pursuit of Peace* (Farnham, Surrey: Ashgate, 2010), pp. 13–20, at p. 16.

[12] On empathy, one should especially consult the writings of the Dalai Lama, particularly *Toward a True Kinship of Faiths*.

in preventing an accident; similarly, we are not in an agonistic battle of words as evinced in the Melian dialogue from Thucydides' *History of the Peloponnesian War*. We are striving not to convince others we are humble, but to be morally and integrally humble. Humility without integrity does no justice to God, self or one another.

Humility, unfortunately, is an often misunderstood virtue – and in some contexts may even be a moral or political hindrance. For theists, humility, at its core, is honest self-assessment, self-critique and self-evaluation, holding up a mirror to the self and one another, illuminated by the Spirit of God. It neither inflates nor deflates one's strengths or weaknesses. The humility I elevate is necessarily scrappy, rugged and obdurate, one that does not whimper or silence itself in the midst of oppression and injustice.[13] As Laura Swan writes of the Christian Desert Mothers, genuine humility 'does not diminish a person's sense of self-worth or dignity'.[14] Humility is not abject silence, impotence and degradation, but it is keen to learn from others and knows one's limitations and mistakes. Such humility is also needed at institutional levels, and especially in regard to one's nation, religion or philosophy. But again, we must start with ourselves.

Do I, then, consider myself sinful? In truth, I sometimes marvel at individuals who regularly go to the Catholic sacrament of penance and I think, 'Do they really see themselves as sinners so consistently?' Deep down, do I not have more in common with the Pharisee in the parable above than with the tax collector? Moreover, am I not distrustful of those who claim to be sinners or who constantly lower themselves? Is this not a sign of either false modesty or unhealthy self-esteem? As Jesus reminded us, who does not enjoy being raised in status or publicly moved to a higher place? While such a deferential or self-deprecating practice may not work on Wall Street or a typical children's playground, there are places in the world where it makes sense to feign humility, as asserting one's perhaps desired place is considered socially inappropriate and may actually backfire, attracting unwanted scrutiny and a lowering of status, even if undeserved. Thus, we may adjust our public self-assessment depending on where we reside, but this is again

---

[13] The next few paragraphs are adapted from my article '"My children have defeated me!" Finding and nurturing theological dissent', *Irish Theological Quarterly*, 77/3 (2012), 286–304.

[14] Laura Swan, *The Forgotten Desert Mothers: Sayings, Lives, and Stories of Early Christian Women* (Mahwah, NJ: Paulist Press, 2001), p. 26.

strategy. How do we take Jesus' advice maturely, spiritually and with integrity? We want to move beyond mere rhetoric or social conformity, not simply going through the motions of self-critique and humility. Furthermore, in light of the ongoing oppression of women, minorities and other marginalised peoples, we must strive in certain contexts to balance any self-critique or humility with proper self-exaltation and praise. Self-critique is not self-laceration. Rabbi Jonathan Sacks, for example, encourages his fellow Jews to be more proud of their accomplishments and strengths and not inordinately focus on past travesties and horrors.[15]

Here, one is also struck by the need to examine how and whether the promotion of a laudable area or attribute in oneself or one's belief may harm or seem to condemn another. For example, as Amy Jill-Levine reminds Christians, the turn to praise Jesus as an enlightened feminist can have the unhealthy correlation of denigrating all his fellow first-century male Jews as misogynist and hopelessly patriarchal.[16] Thus, in any self-evaluation, we are obliged to be fair and honest towards ourselves and one another while aiming to uphold the dignity of all. This is by no means easy and at best may result in one person partly imitating both the Pharisee and the tax collector in the parable, seeking a more healthy middle ground or a type of the Aristotelian mean.

CATHOLIC PARTICIPATION IN INTERFAITH DIALOGUE: LEARNING OR ENLIGHTENING?

In the context of interfaith dialogue, the humility and sincerity advocated here entail feeling a measure of pride and joy towards my own identity as a Christian along with mature recognition of my own failings, hypocrisies and ignorance. Fortunately, in Pope Francis' *Evangelii Gaudium*, and his lived, ongoing dialogue with his friend Rabbi Abraham Skorka, Catholics are being reminded of such self-critique and interreligious learning and friendship in practice. In his 2013 apostolic exhortation, Pope Francis rebukes fundamentalism on all sides, presumably including both Catholics who wield Vatican dogma like cudgels and the radically pluralist liberals open to everyone except those not as open as

---

[15] Jonathan Sacks, *Future Tense: Jews, Judaism, and Israel in the Twenty-First Century* (New York: Schocken, 2009), p. 252.
[16] Amy-Jill Levine, *The Misunderstood Jew: The Church and the Scandal of the Jewish Jesus* (New York: HarperOne, 2007), p. 131.

they.[17] Two phrases from Francis on interreligious dialogue are worth highlighting: 'True openness involves remaining steadfast in one's deepest convictions, clear and joyful in one's own identity, while at the same time being "open to understanding those of the other party" and "knowing that dialogue can enrich each side".'[18] Important here is the balance of being true to oneself and to core convictions (though what is labelled as 'core' can be part of the intra-church dialogue) while seeking to understand other viewpoints and recognising that participants enrich one another through the dialogue. Such themes are further supported in Pope Francis' support for interfaith dialogue that seeks social justice: 'Efforts made in dealing with a specific theme can become a process in which, by mutual listening, both parts can be purified and enriched. These efforts, therefore, can also express love for truth.'[19] While the church traditionally has claimed the territory of 'enricher' and 'purifier', here the potential to be purified (a powerful and cathartic word) and enriched through dialogue with non-Christians has deep resonance. Such listening, often entailing critique, becomes part of that process of purifying.

Another aspect that cannot be overlooked in this process is the lottery of one's birth and family. Thus, I am also aware that my Christian identity was deeply dependent upon my Christian upbringing, and while this does not determine that I am a Christian today, it plays a key role. Such an acknowledgement should avoid triumphalism and theological one-upmanship. For many, luck and circumstance are key factors in the foundation or non-foundation of a particular religious belief.

Acknowledging, moreover, that I have much still to learn about the core, lived, nuanced faith positions of other traditions points to an awareness of the need for deeper interreligious learning and listening – not judging. Note, here I am referring to the overall question of the viability and the salvific nature of a faith and not specific moral issues that entail the dignity, value or appreciation of life. As there is more agreement than disagreement on such core moral issues in the world's faiths, this area of judging is less relevant than one may think. It is my view that the Christian calling to promote life could learn more deeply from the greater ecological awareness traditionally practised in many indigenous faiths, and in many Eastern traditions. Thus, one may think of the Buddhist notions of

[17] Pope Francis, *Evangelii gaudium*, § 250. www.vatican.va/holy_father/francesco/apost_exhortations/documents/papa-francesco_esortazione-ap_20131124_evangelii-gaudium_en.html. Accessed 6 September 2016.
[18] Ibid., § 196.
[19] Ibid., § 250.

inter-being and co-dependent arising, terms that cannot be fully claimed by Christians but which would still be morally fruitful to contemplate and apply in measured doses. Such interfaith learning would also help to recover ecological awareness and responsibility within Christian tradition and doctrine.[20] The point is that traditions have much to learn from each other but core values of love and respect towards all deeply overlap.

Amid such paeans to interfaith love, we are living in an age of critique, and the church is an easy target for such rebuke. One extreme, but still partly true, account highlights the church's patriarchal, rule-bound, hermeticist, self-referencing core, often linked with at best uninspiring records of fair and equal treatment of non-Catholic peoples, especially the indigenous. It also includes immoral partnerships with military agendas with scant compunction about violence. Concrete details of the Church's failures from the Crusades to the Inquisition need not be repeated here.

Incidentally (and as noted previously), the *Yale Response to A Common Word* followed a similar path in calling Christians to acknowledge their sins and repent. Highlighting, moreover, the uninspiring, or more pointed, appalling role of the Catholic Church at all levels during the Shoah, and the recent child abuse scandals, one could almost be shocked that I still refer to myself as Catholic with some pride.[21] And yet, the preceding picture is not fully complete but is challenged by stories of great moral hope and courage, of Christians who truly take up their crosses and follow Jesus to the end, whether visionaries and social justice advocates like St Francis of Assisi (d. 1226) or St Theresa of Calcutta (d. 1997) or many liberation theologians who call for a humble church of the poor and oppressed striving for justice for all, working towards a greater, more inclusive church in deeper partnership with non-Catholics. Perhaps in such a vision one could see a church which comes to love questions more than answers, as many in the Jewish faith have professed in tradition. As John Roth writes in homage to Elie Wiesel (d. 2016), 'Answers are made to be probed, tested, found wanting. They exist to be questioned, to be turned into questions that force us beyond.'[22] What is encouraging is a church willing to say sorry or admit being wrong, whether in the case of

[20] See, for example, Ilia Delio, *The Emergent Christ: Exploring the Meaning of Catholic in an Evolutionary Universe* (Maryknoll, NY: Orbis, 2011).

[21] Peter Admirand, 'The pedophile scandal and its (hoped-for) impact on Catholic intra- and interreligious dialogue', in Peter Admirand (ed.), *Loss and Hope: Global, Interreligious, and Interdisciplinary Perspectives* (London: Bloomsbury, 2014), pp. 123–36.

[22] John K. Roth, 'Wiesel's contribution to a Christian understanding of Judaism', in Steven T. Katz and Alan Rosen (eds.), *Elie Wiesel: Jewish, Literary, and Moral Perspectives* (Bloomington & Indianapolis: Indiana University Press, 2013), pp. 264–76, at p. 271.

Galileo (even if 350 years later)[23] or the flawed, but still heartfelt, apologies embedded in various gestures of John Paul II towards the Jewish people[24] or in the 1998 Vatican document 'We remember: a reflection on the Shoah'.[25] While the church prefers to speak of developing doctrine – rather than change – as evinced in certain shifts evident in Vatican II, especially the church's support of religious freedom, there is some room for critique and change, even if other words are used instead. David Hollenbach thus rightly highlights the development in Catholic doctrine of support for universal dignity and the practice of Catholic participation in defending human rights 'through a sort of back-and-forth movement between Catholic beliefs and lived experience'.[26]

At this point, a Catholic believer might say: all you have shown is your own petty sinfulness and frailty, and you have blanketed all Catholics by the sinfulness of so-called Christians who act contrary to the faith and to the loving example of Christ. You show openness towards other peoples, which could be commendable; but if you still claim to be Roman Catholic that entails that you acknowledge the complete, final truth of Jesus as revealed to his apostles and passed on to church leaders as the bedrock or deposit of faith. While nothing is certain in human beings, there is perfect certainty in the source of Christ, and it is in Christ – and the church Christ founded and guides – that one takes solace and finds certitude. Such a position is the dominant one in the majority of documents from the Magisterium, perhaps most recently exemplified in the 2000 declaration *Dominus Iesus*. Consider these relevant passages: 'As a remedy for this relativistic mentality, which is becoming ever more common, it is necessary above all to reassert the definitive and complete character of the revelation of Jesus Christ.' And elsewhere in the same document:

Therefore, the theory of the limited, incomplete, or imperfect character of the revelation of Jesus Christ, which would be complementary to that found in other

---

[23] Alan Cowell, 'After 350 years, Vatican says Galileo was right: it moves', *New York Times*, 31 October 1992. www.nytimes.com/1992/10/31/world/after-350-years-vatican-says-galileo-was-right-it-moves.html. Accessed 6 September 2016.

[24] See, for example, Peter Admirand, 'Rifts, trust, and openness: Pope John Paul II's legacy in Catholic intra- and interreligious dialogue', *Journal of Ecumenical Studies* 47/4 (2012), 555–75.

[25] See, for example, Catholic Commission for Religious Relations with the Jews, 'We remember: a reflection on the Shoah', 1998. www.vatican.va/roman_curia/pontifical_councils/chrstuni/documents/rc_pc_chrstuni_doc_16031998_shoah_en.html. Accessed 6 September 2016.

[26] David Hollenbach, 'Human dignity in Catholic thought', in Marcus Düwell, Jens Braarvig, Roger Brownsword and Dietmar Mieth (eds.), *The Cambridge Handbook of Human Dignity: Interdisciplinary Perspectives* (Cambridge: Cambridge University Press, 2014), pp. 250–9, at p. 256.

religions, is contrary to the Church's faith. Such a position would claim to be based on the notion that the truth about God cannot be grasped and manifested in its globality and completeness by any historical religion, neither by Christianity nor by Jesus Christ.[27]

In Harvey Egan's powerful reflection in *Sic et Non*, the important collection of essays commenting on *Dominus Iesus*, he focuses on the perceived criticism of Karl Rahner's theology and insights and ends his article with the subtitle 'Singularity – not pluralism', emphasising 'the immense singularity of many of God's mighty deeds: the one order of creation, the one human race, the one history of revelation and salvation, the one incarnation, the one crucifixion and resurrection, the one mediator between God and humanity, the one triune God, and the one God and Father of our Lord Jesus Christ'.[28] He then calls for a genuine preaching of the gospels throughout the world, looking to the early Christians as a guide: '[T]hey never backed down from preaching Jesus Christ as *the* way, the truth, and the light.'[29] The bravado may seem quaint to some and the highlighting of singularity overdone, but the piece also burns with zeal, respect and love of the Gospel. The position and views are lucid, facilitating dialogue. Jumbled, inchoate or fuzzy beliefs make dialogue difficult (though no less fascinating). Ironically, a religious pluralism without elements of an exclusivist faith is more likely to hinder than to promote dialogue among different faiths and views.

One must also be self-critical, though. In any Catholic–Muslim dialogue, the views of Egan are important so long as they are not the only Catholic views presented. Diversity within Catholic views can ultimately be a help and not a hindrance to the dialogue, as such nuance and diversity should encourage self-critique and so deeper analysis and, ideally, openness. Elements of exclusivity and uniqueness are understandable, and perhaps needed for identity. It seems easier, of course, if one presents a uniform, universal and consistent position of agreement, but such a position bears less weight if it does not reflect reality on the ground. Dialogue, evaluation, testing and prayer should always remain active

---

[27] Congregation for the Doctrine of the Faith, *Dominus Iesus*, §§ 5 and 6. www .vatican.va/roman_curia/congregations/cfaith/documents/rc_con_cfaith_doc_ 20000806_dominus-iesus_en.html. Accessed 6 September 2016.

[28] Harvey D. Egan SJ, 'A Rahnerian response', in Stephen L. Pope and Charles Hefling (eds.), *Sic Et Non: Encountering Dominus Iesus* (Maryknoll, NY: Orbis, 2002), pp. 57–67, p. 66.

[29] Ibid.

methods in seeking out and promoting higher truths that uphold the dignity of God and creation. A church official condemning the horrors of rape embodies (and should embody) that universal stamp. Matters become more complicated, and perhaps in this case detrimental to dialogue and discussion, if equal zeal is shown on more cultural and doctrinal issues such as women priests or gay marriage so that they are presented with that same unquestioned sense of uniform, universal and consistent agreement among the faithful.

A COMMON WORD: A CHRISTOLOGICAL READING

Having presented a reflection on humility and self-critique, while attempting an honest examination of my own faith, I finally turn to *ACW*, in which there is much to praise. Who can or should rebuke any document calling Christians and Muslims, let alone others of good faith, to work for unity through the love of God and neighbour? Most refreshing is its inclusion of various passages from the Tanach and the Christian Scriptures. But a deeper exegesis from a Christian context would have been fruitful.

ACW, of course, is understandably built on Qur'anic moral and doctrinal foundations. What happens, then, if a Christian reads *ACW* through a Christological and Trinitarian lens? Is there room in *ACW* for some level of self-critique, and space for Christian interpretations? Without undermining the more important aims of Muslim–Christian partnership and shared moral values within *ACW*, I am highlighting a note of caution, and the need to embrace such aims while ensuring that unique Christian identity and beliefs are not engulfed in the process. For Christian belief is not only important for a healthy Christian open engagement with Muslims; it is the foundation of Christian ethics and law. Christian doctrine (and, for liberation theologians, praxis) is the basis of Christian life-styles and actions in the world. It is not an optional extra. Christians have to be open to critique and challenge, but also should be allowed the space, and be willing, to witness to their beliefs as the foundation of their engagement with others. How *ACW* allows for Christological or Trinitarian beliefs in the sense of allowing the 'Other' to be an 'Other' has been a major question raised by a number of other contributors to this book, among them notably Daniel A. Madigan's rendering of the use of Scripture in the document as reductionist in Chapter 10.[30]

---

[30] See Chapter 10 in this volume.

One main challenge of interfaith dialogue emphasised in this chapter is to hear and face denial and critique of one's beliefs and still actively engage in ongoing conversation. That Muslims revere Jesus as a prophet is noteworthy. Jesus' prophetic witness in the gospels can be embraced by Muslims and Christians (and Jews). At the same time, however, Christian belief in Jesus' divinity ought to be given more adequate attention in *ACW*, as I will argue later. It is understandable that, for the authors and signatories of *ACW*, the Qur'an is clear and unequivocal about who Jesus is, while contending that opposing claims in the New Testament reveal corrupted scriptures (cf. 'but the wrongdoers substituted a different word from the word they were given', Q 2:59; see also 2:75; 5:13). That is to say that *ACW*'s repeated reference to the oneness of God is built upon Qur'anic quotes, some of whose contexts are refuting Christian belief in Christ as the Son of God, and Trinitarian belief. Let me present a range of examples from the Qur'an to highlight this.

In the Qur'an, we read: 'People of the Book, do not go to excess in your religion, and do not say anything about God except the truth: the Messiah, Jesus, son of Mary, was nothing more than a messenger of God. [...] So believe in God and His messengers and do not speak of a "Trinity" – stop [this], that it is better for you – God is only one God [...]' (Q 4:171; see also 5:75, 'only a messenger').

Elsewhere the Qur'anic text states that Jews believed Ezra was a son of God, rendering the Jewish claim equal to the Christian error, and again the Qur'an is clear: 'May God thwart them! [...] But they were commanded to serve only one God: there is no God but Him; He is far above whatever they set up as His partners!' (Q 9:30–1). The Qur'an further asserts: 'Those who say, "God is the Messiah, son of Mary", have defied God. The Messiah himself said, "Children of Israel, worship God, my Lord and your Lord." If anyone associates others with God, God will forbid him from the Garden, and Hell will be his home. No one will help [such] evildoers. Those people who say God is the third of three are defying [the truth]: there is only one God. If they do not stop what they are saying, a painful punishment will afflict those of them who persist' (Q 5:72–3).

Consider, then, that in *ACW* we read the repeated phrase 'There is no god, but God, He alone, He hath no associate';[31] elsewhere, 'He hath no partner',[32] 'He is the living, who dieth not'.[33] In the light of the preceding references, it is difficult not to consider such claims in the context of

[31] *ACW*, p. 64.
[32] Ibid., pp. 60 and 69.
[33] Ibid., p. 76, fn. 13.

Christian belief in Jesus as fully God and fully human. Contra the Qur'an, Christians believe Jesus of Nazareth died on the cross and rose from the dead. On the one hand, critiques of the Biblical phrasings of the Spirit as divine advocate, rendered as misreading or heretical, or of Jesus as merely a human partner or helper (perhaps in an Arian sense), point to the Qur'an's positive affirmation of God's *tawḥīd* (unity). On the other hand, they can also be read as a disparagement of, or warning against, Christian belief in Jesus as God or in Trinitarian formulas. Again, how should Christians read and interpret such passages in the light of self-critique, humility and the challenge of witnessing to Christian identity and belief?

Interestingly, as Tim Winter has noted in Chapter 1 in this volume, the Qur'an praises Christians at various points; but some suggest that these may have been Christians who held no Trinitarian belief and whose Christology was more in line with the Qur'anic understanding of Jesus; otherwise, if one follows the literal quote, hell seems to await them. The Qur'an is ambiguous, at best, on the point of whether Christians are also saved.[34] Today, there are Muslim scholars, such as Mahmoud M. Ayoub, who highlight the following repeated injunction in the Qur'an to argue that it takes precedence over verses deemed restrictive: 'Surely, those who have faith, the Jews, the Christians, and the Sabeans, who ever accepts faith in God and the Last Day and performs good deeds shall have their reward with the Lord' (Q 2:62; 5:69; see also 2:278). Is this view shared by the majority of the authors of *ACW*? It need not be, for ongoing, healthy interfaith dialogue, but clarity on such an important matter within *ACW* would be reassuring to its Christian readers and supporters.

In my analysis, Christians are called fully to support the notion in *ACW* that Christians and Muslims (and Jews) share a love of God and a love of neighbour. At the same time, Christians may be weary of implied statements that seem to show Christian confusion on core Christological beliefs. To assuage such worries, including a statement of clarification in reference to Christian belief in *ACW* could be instructive and fruitful.[35]

---

[34] For helpful, concise overviews, see Daniel Madigan, 'Christian–Muslim Dialogue', in Catherine Cornille (ed.), *The Wiley-Blackwell Companion to Inter-Religious Dialogue* (Oxford: Wiley-Blackwell, 2013), pp. 244–60, at pp. 245–6; Leonard Grob and John K. Roth (eds.), *Encountering the Stranger: A Jewish-Christian-Muslim Trialogue* (Seattle: University of Washington Press, 2012); and Alan L. Berger (ed.), *Trialogue and Terror: Judaism, Christianity, and Islam after 9/11* (Eugene, OR: Cascade Books, 2012).

[35] For instance, a reference to the Catholic profession of faith: 'The Trinity is One. We do not confess three Gods, but one God in three persons, the "consubstantial Trinity"'

We may be able to learn from our Jewish brothers and sisters in this regard as well, and here I turn to some recent texts which can parallel, and serve as points of contact and comparison for, Muslim–Christian dialogue. The study of Jewish–Christian dialogue and relationships has its own complications, problems and failures, but I want to highlight some particularly noteworthy advances in recent years. The 2000 Jewish document *Dabru Emet* (Speak the Truth) or the December 2015 Orthodox Rabbinic Statement on Christianity *To Do the Will of Our Father in Heaven: Toward a Partnership between Jews and Christians*[36] might be a helpful guide in reformulating problematic passages in *ACW* to represent and include Christian understanding of their Christian faith better. For example, in *Dabru Emet*'s first proposition we read, 'Jews and Christians worship the same God.'[37] Differences are outlined in the explanation, but the heading unequivocally shows acceptance despite such difference. *To Do the Will of Our Father in Heaven* states: 'we acknowledge that the emergence of Christianity in human history is neither an accident nor an error, but the willed divine outcome and gift to the nations'.[38] Unfortunately, in *ACW*, we read the confusing phrase 'Muslims recognize Jesus Christ as the Messiah, not in the same way Christians do (but Christians themselves anyway have never all agreed with each other on Jesus Christ's nature)'.[39] While all Christians have never agreed on how to interpret the doctrine philosophically in its application of Greek terminology – rendering the discussion similar to the debate on the nature of the Qur'an in medieval Islam – the word 'all' is unhelpful here, as most Christians have agreed on the doctrinal formulation itself, whether it is deemed to be Chalcedonian or orthodox Christology. It is disappointing that such a phrase has not been more deeply challenged by both Muslims and Christians, and a clearer and fairer statement, as indicated previously, could help allay any confusion.

(§ 253). See also the *Catechism of the Catholic Church*, § 18. www.vatican.va/archive/ccc_css/archive/catechism/p1s2c1p2.htm. Accessed 6 September 2016.

36 http://cjcuc.com/site/2015/12/03/orthodox-rabbinic-statement-on-christianity/. Accessed 6 September 2016.

37 National Jewish Scholars Project, *Dabru Emet*, 15 July 2002. www.jcrelations.net/Dabru_Emet_-_A_Jewish_Statement_on_Christians_and_Christianity.2395.0.html. Accessed 22 September 2016.

38 *To Do the Will of Our Father*, § 3.

39 *A Common Word Between Us and You: 5-Year Anniversary Edition* (Amman: Royal Aal Al-Bayt Institute for Islamic Thought, 2012), p. 71 (throughout this chapter all references to *ACW* are taken from this edition).

The text more problematically asks Christians to 'consider Muslims *not against*, and thus *with them*, in accordance with Jesus Christ's words here'.[40] 'Here' is the reference to Q 4:171, referred to earlier, in which Jesus is called only a servant, Trinitarian belief is criticised and the threat of punishment again looms for those who maintain such beliefs. Sadly, this is more reminiscent of the problematic opening of *Dominus Iesus*, referred to previously, which was similarly alienating for non-Christians, quoting the most exclusivist and alienating passages from the New Testament, especially the phrase 'He who believes and is baptized will be saved; he who does not believe will be condemned' (Mark 16:15–16). This all-or-nothing position need not be the representative, textual strand of Mark's Gospel: how does it dialogue with and take into account, for example, Jesus' words 'for whoever is not against us is for us' (Mark 9:40)? What does it mean to be against Jesus? Must one doctrinally believe in Jesus as the Son of God to be saved, regardless of moral actions and fidelity towards God? This is an old question which *Dominus Iesus* resurfaced, but the stark, polarising manner of its Biblical interpretations left little space for nuance and development, rendered more evident after Vatican II. It is safe to say that no document by Pope Francis would begin in such a manner.

For our purposes, the issue is how one can be self-critical, hear another's critique and still provide space for the 'Other'. Consider, for example, some recent Jewish voices on Christology, grappling with ways to maintain their Jewish belief and so their rejection of Christ as Messiah for Jews but maintaining a space for Christian belief in Christ as the Son of God. Thus, we have Irving Greenberg's notion of Jesus as a failed but not false Messiah,[41] to Rabbi Byron L. Sherwin's suggestion to call Jesus a 'Messiah Son of Joseph', a messiah who prepares the way for the final Messiah, the Messiah Son of David[42] to Steven Leonard Jacobs' suggestion to 'consider the Christ

---

[40] Ibid.

[41] Irving Greenberg, 'Towards an organic model of the relationship', in *For the Sake of Heaven and Earth: The New Encounter between Judaism and Christianity* (Philadelphia, PA: Jewish Publication Society, 2004), pp. 145–61. See also Irving Greenberg et al., 'Discussion 9: on the meaning of pluralism', in Edward Feinstein (ed.), *Jews and Judaism in the Twenty-First Century: Human Responsibility, the Presence of God, and the Future of the Covenant* (Woodstock, VT: Jewish Lights, 2007), pp. 149–61, at p. 152.

[42] Byron L. Sherwin, '"Who do you say that I am?" (Mark 8:29): a new Jewish view of Jesus', in Beatrice Bruteau (ed.), *Jesus through Jewish Eyes: Rabbis and Scholars Engage an Ancient Brother in a New Conversation* (Maryknoll, NY: Orbis, 2003), pp. 31–44, at pp. 40–1.

as a potentially redemptive messiah'. Of Christ's death, Jacobs writes that it 'has not, either at that moment, or up to this moment, redeemed our world, but only opened the door to that possibility. But it was not then, nor is it now, the only possibility'.[43] Lastly, one may also turn to Michael Kogan, who as a Jew prefers to speak of Jesus as 'the one sent by Israel's God to bring gentiles into the covenant'.[44] None of these attempts is ultimately satisfying, but similar additions in the context of Muslim–Christian dialogue would help to make *ACW* and its foundation even more palatable and attractive for Christians.

CONCLUSION: SEEKING FAITHFUL SELF-CRITIQUES

There are two helpful moments in *ACW* when the text acknowledges a believer as a sinner: a reference to the *Fātiḥa* (first *sūra* of the Qur'an) and the phrase 'when we hope to be forgiven for our sins',[45] and the Qur'anic quote 3:31: 'Say (O Muhammad, to mankind): If ye love God, follow me; God will love you and forgive you your sins.'[46] It is a start, but greater clarity about, if not more openness towards, Christian belief regarding Jesus as God Incarnate would have strengthened and not weakened the document. Again, my suggested clarification earlier would allay any doubt or confusion on this end for Christians while staying true and faithful to Islamic belief. No one can deny that *ACW* has drawn Christians and Muslims together, and for this it must be praised. My critiques and notes of caution are meant to encourage an ongoing self-critique and humility – thus potentially enriching fruitful dialogue and partnership. It is meant to challenge both Muslims and Christians: Muslims to see how the document could be rephrased and repositioned to be more appealing and acceptable to Christians, Christians to engage more openly with Muslim theological differences. This would invite a heavy dose of self-critique and humility and a deeper acceptance of the promisingly pluralist passage from the Qur'an (Q 5:48) which closes *ACW*. Despite our differing beliefs, indeed 'let us vie with each other only in

---

[43] Steven Leonard Jacobs, '"Can we talk?": the Jewish Jesus in a dialogue between Jews and Christians', *Shofar*, 3 (2010), 135–48, at p. 146.

[44] Michael S. Kogan, *Opening the Covenant: A Jewish Theology of Christianity* (Oxford: Oxford University Press, 2008), p. 149.

[45] *ACW*, p. 58.

[46] Ibid., p. 60.

righteousness and good works'.[47] We are again reminded of the Pharisee and the tax collector and the challenge to embody the good qualities of both, namely, balancing the awe of God and shame at one's frailty and failures with a healthy self-esteem embodied by ethical deeds towards others.

---

[47] Ibid., p. 73. For commentary on this verse, see for example Mun'im Sirry, '"Compete with one another in good works": exegesis of Qur'an verse 5.48 and contemporary Muslim discourses on religious pluralism', *Islam and Christian–Muslim Relations*, 20/4 (2009), 423–38; Asma Afsaruddin, 'Finding common ground: "mutual knowing", moderation and the fostering of religious pluralism', in James L. Heft, Reuven Firestone and Omid Safi (eds.), *Learned Ignorance: Intellectual Humility among Jews, Christians, and Muslims* (Oxford: Oxford University Press, 2011), pp. 67–86; Th. Emil Homerin, 'The Golden Rule in Islam', in Jacob Neusner and Bruce Chilton (eds.), *The Golden Rule: The Ethics of Responsibility in World Religions* (London: Continuum, 2008), pp. 99–115; David Thomas, 'Islam and the religious other', in David Cheetham, Douglas Pratt and David Thomas (eds.), *Understanding Interreligious Relations* (Oxford: Oxford University Press, 2013), pp. 148–71; and for commentary on the application of such beliefs, see for example Peter Admirand, 'The ethics of displacement and migration in the Abrahamic faiths: enlightening believers and aiding public policy', *Journal of Ethnic and Migration Studies*, 40/4 (2014), 671–87.

PART III

THE SCRIPTURES AND *A COMMON WORD*

9

The Protocol of Interfaith Dialogue
Qur'anic Imperatives in a Globalising World

Asma Afsaruddin

INTRODUCTION

Interfaith dialogue can be both a richly rewarding learning experience and a minefield, as many of us who have experience in this area can attest. Interfaith encounters may often lead to positive interactions but they are also fraught with the possibility of rancorous exchanges and counter-productive consequences. The latter may ensue when dialogue is engaged in for the wrong reasons (for example, to establish the dominance of one community over another) or by inexperienced and ill-informed people. This volume documents different perspectives on what dialogue entails. Most Muslims recognise, however, that their own history and tradition encourage them to engage in honest and respectful dialogue with the People of the Book (primarily Jews and Christians). The latter group are after all recognised as fellow monotheists, with religious beliefs and teachings that are both similar and different. While similar teachings concerning ethical values create common ground, differences in doctrine and beliefs that are important foundations for each tradition (as Daniel A. Madigan in Chapter 10 and others argue in this book) invite sensitive and carefully crafted discussions that should not cause acrimonious polarisation.

Two questions may fruitfully be posed in this context. First, how may we establish a general protocol of respectful and honest interfaith dialogue that is mutually beneficial and illuminating? Second, what sources can be invoked to establish the authoritative nature of dialogue and its guiding principles? For Muslims the answer to both questions lies in the revealed text of the Qur'an. There are a number of verses in Islam's foundational scripture that specifically deal with the mechanics of inter-faith dialogue and counsel respect for the religious sensibilities of all, within Abrahamic communities and beyond. This chapter will discuss the exegeses of three sets of such Qur'anic verses, Q 29:46; Q 6:107–8 and finally Q 3:64, the famous 'common word' verse.[1] This study will conclude with a reflection upon the further implications of these exegeses for fostering better interfaith understanding between Muslims and their dialogue partners in today's globalising world, implications that could not have been evident to our pre-modern predecessors, who inhabited a very different world.

EXEGESES OF QUR'AN 29:46

This verse states:

Do not dispute with the People of the Book save with what is better; except for those who do wrong among them, and say [to them]: 'We believe in that which was revealed to us and revealed to you, and our God and your God is one, and we submit to Him'.

(Q 29:46)[2]

For Muslims, this is the quintessential verse advocating a protocol of respectful dialogue, particularly with adherents of the Abrahamic religions. The earliest extant commentary on this verse is that of Mujāhid ibn Jabr (d. 722) from the Umayyad period. In his brief but significant exegesis, Mujāhid understands the first part of the verse as counselling Muslims 'to speak [of] goodness (*khayran*) when they [the People of the Book] utter what is wrong/evil (*sharran*)'. Here, 'those who do wrong among them' is glossed as those among the People of the Book who speak falsehood concerning God, for instance by ascribing partners to Him, or those who cause harm to the Prophet Muhammad. Mujāhid lists a variant exegesis, emanating from the Kufan Successor[3] Sa'īd ibn Jubayr (d. 714), that this phrase refers to those among the People of the Book

---

[1] See further my earlier study, 'Discerning a Qur'anic mandate for mutually transform-ational dialogue', in Catherine Cornille (ed.), *Criteria of Discernment in Interreligious Dialogue* (Eugene, OR: Cascade, 2009), pp. 101–21.

[2] All translations of the Qur'an are mine, although I have freely consulted existing English translations.

[3] One of the *tābi'ūn*, i.e., from the second generation of Muslims.

who have not signed a treaty with the Muslims and consequently engage in hostilities against them.[4]

The famous exegete Muḥammad ibn Jarīr al-Ṭabarī (d. 923) comments that this verse is specifically directed at Jews and Christians, who are the People of the Book. As for the critical phrase in the verse, 'save with what is better' (*illā bi-llatī hiya aḥsan*), Ṭabarī remarks that it means 'except for what is good or fine speech' (*illā bi-l-jamīl min al-qawl*), which he explains is a reference to 'an invitation to God by means of His verses/signs (*bi-āyātihi*), and drawing attention to His proofs (*ḥujajihi*)'. In his opinion, 'those who do wrong' among the People of the Book are those among them who ascribe partners to God and refuse to submit to Muslim authority.[5]

It is highly revealing of his time that Ṭabarī spends more time explaining who the wrongdoers are among the People of the Book and the consequences they must face than on fully exploring the implications of the phrase 'save with what is better'. Tellingly, he does not seek to amplify further the common ground delineated by the Qur'an when it states in this verse *that Jews and Christians worship and submit to the one and same God as Muslims*. Ṭabarī's brief explanation that 'save with what is better' refers to 'good or fine speech' (*al-jamīl min al-qawl*) appears to be set in the context of attempting to convince the People of the Book of the truth of Islam.[6]

Some of the later post-Ṭabarī exegetes, however, offer more nuanced and less confessional approaches to this verse. For example, the twelfth-century Muʿtazilī exegete Maḥmūd ibn ʿUmar al-Zamakhsharī (d. 1144) glosses *aḥsan* in this verse as 'what is offered of gentleness (*bi-l-līn*) in response to roughness (*al-khushūna*); of equanimity (*bi-l-kaẓm*) to anger; and of forbearance (*bi-l-ānat*) in the face of vehemence or violence (*al-sawra*)'. Here he references Q 41:34 to lend support to his

---

[4] Mujāhid ibn Jabr, *Tafsīr Mujāhid*, ed. Abū Muḥammad al-Asyūṭī (Beirut: Dār al-kutub al-ʿilmiyya, 2005), p. 205.

[5] Muḥammad ibn Jarīr al-Ṭabarī, *Jāmiʿ al-bayān fī taʾwīl al-Qurʾān* (Beirut: Dār al-kutub al-ʿilmiyya, 1997), vol. 10, pp. 149–50.

[6] The eleventh-century exegete al-Wāḥidī (d. 1076) similarly understands 'what is better' as a reference to 'the Qurʾan and invitation to God through His verses/signs and drawing attention to His proofs'. See his *al-Wāsiṭ fī tafsīr al-Qurʾān al-majīd* (Beirut: Dār al-kutub al-ʿilmiyya, 1994), vol. 3, p. 422. The earlier eighth-century exegete Muqātil ibn Sulaymān (d. 767) also glosses the phrase as a reference to the Qurʾan and understands 'those who do wrong' as referring only to 'the wrong-doers from among the Jews' (*ẓalamat al-yahūd*). See his *Tafsīr Muqātil ibn Sulaymān*, ed. ʿAbd Allāh Maḥmūd Shiḥāta (Beirut: Muʾassasat al-taʾrīkh al-ʿarabī, 2002), vol. 3, p. 385.

interpretation. This verse states: 'Repel [evil] with what is better; then the one between whom and you enmity prevails will become like your friend. But none achieves it [this state of affairs] except for those who are patient and of great fortune.' Zamakhsharī notably illustrates the difference between *ḥasana* and *aḥsan* by offering concrete examples of what constitutes 'that which is better' in the face of wrongdoing. An act of goodness (*ḥasana*) in such a situation is to forgive the wrongdoer. To carry out that which is better (*wa-llatī hiya aḥsan*) is to respond with an act of goodness or charity specifically to counter or nullify the original injury and thus to go beyond simple forgiveness. Thus, he counsels, if an adversary 'were to revile you, praise him; if he were to kill your son, then ransom his son from the hands of his enemy; if you were to carry this out, your inveterate enemy would become transformed into a sincere friend full of good will towards you'.[7] Only the people of forbearance and patience (*ahl al-ṣabr*) attain to this and reap goodness (*khayr*) as a result. Through a cross-referential reading of the Qur'an, Zamakhsharī is able to foreground an ethics of forgiveness and reconciliation, which has enormous implications for us today.

He similarly offers a non-confessional understanding of 'those who do wrong among the People of the Book', commenting that they are those who are 'excessively hostile and obstinate, refusing to accept good counsel (*al-nuṣḥ*), and with whom gentleness and compassion (*al-rifq*) are of no avail'.[8] In other words, Zamakhsharī, unlike Ṭabarī, regards these specific members of the People of the Book as being in error not because of their doctrinal beliefs but on account of their abrasive and confrontational behaviour.

It is in the commentary of the Ashʿarī theologian Fakhr al-Dīn al-Rāzī (d. 1210) that we begin to discern the fuller potential of this verse in the context of interfaith dialogue. Rāzī comments that this verse counsels Muslims in general to deal gently with the People of the Book because of the religious tenets they share with Muslims. Jews and Christians, after all, like Muslims, have faith in the one God and believe in the revelation of books, in the sending of messengers and in the final resurrection. Each of these articles of belief is designated a *ḥusn* ('a goodness') by Rāzī. Where the People of the Book are lacking, he continues, is in their

---

[7] Maḥmūd ibn ʿUmar al-Zamakhsharī, *al-Kashshāf ʿan ḥaqāʾiq ghawāmiḍ al-tanzīl wa-ʿuyūn al-aqāwīl fī wujūh al-taʾwīl*, ed. ʿĀdil Aḥmad ʿAbd al-Wujūd and ʿAlī Muḥammad Muʿawwad (Riyadh: Maktabat al-ʿubaykān, 1998), vol. 5, p. 383.

[8] Ibid., vol. 4, p. 553.

failure to acknowledge the mission of the Prophet Muhammad, despite the fact that their scriptures contain references to him.[9] In acknowledgement, however, of the aggregate goodness (*iḥsānihim*) of the People of the Book, Rāzī continues, Muslims should debate with them with what is better/best.[10] Rāzī leaves undefined here the precise nature of 'what is better/best'. But since he next proceeds to say that Muslims should not treat the opinions of Jews and Christians lightly nor ascribe error to their ancestors, then we may assume that 'what is better/best' is a reference to the adoption of conciliatory and respectful modes of interfaith conversations.

In Rāzī's exegesis, therefore, we find on the whole the articulation of a thoughtful, reasoned protocol of dialogue between Muslims and the People of the Book, which stressed commonalities and also acknowledged the differences between them. Although Rāzī does not state this explicitly, his line of reasoning implies that the common ground that may be found between Muslims and the People of the Book on the basis of this verse is broader than the points of contention between them, and it is this common ground which serves as a more fruitful point of departure for interfaith encounters.

In his exegesis of Q 29:46, the fourteenth-century Shāfiʿī exegete Ibn Kathīr (d. 1373) documents the view of the Successor Ibn Zayd (d. 798), who maintained that this verse encouraged Muslims to gain insight (*al-istibṣār*) into the religion of the People of the Book and debate with them with what is better so that there might be greater benefit in it. It is significant that insight and discernment, as connoted by the Arabic word *al-istibṣār* here, are regarded as essential accompaniments to fruitful dialogue by Ibn Zayd. This equation is borne out by another verse (Q 16:125), which exhorts Muslims to 'Invite to the path of your Lord with wisdom and kind counsel'. Rules of interfaith engagement, continues Ibn Kathīr, may further be derived from Q 20:44, in which God counsels Moses and Aaron when they are being dispatched to the Pharaoh 'to say to him words of gentleness so that he may reflect or be fearful [of God]'. According to Ibn Kathīr, gentle, reflective and reasoned speech, which

---

9 This Muslim belief – that the Prophet Muhammad is foretold in the Bible – is predicated, for example, on Q 7:157 and 61:6. Among the passages in the Bible that are understood to be a reference to his coming are Matthew 21:42, Mark 12:11 and John 14:16–17, 15:26, 16:7 and 16:12–14.

10 Fakhr al-Dīn al-Rāzī, *al-Tafsīr al-kabīr* (Beirut: Dār iḥyāʾ al-turāth al-ʿarabī, 1999), vol. 9, pp. 63–4.

leads to critical discernment in the course of such interreligious dialectics, represents 'that which is better', mentioned in Q 29:46.[11]

EXEGESES OF QUR'AN 6:107–8

These verses state:

> Had God willed, they would not be idolaters; but We have not appointed you [the Prophet] a watcher over them, nor are you their guardian. Do not abuse whom they pray to apart from God, or they will abuse [the name of] God in retaliation without knowledge.
>
> (Q 6:107–8)

The early eighth-century exegete Muqātil ibn Sulaymān (d. 767) in his brief exegesis of Q 6:107 states that if God had so willed, He would have prevented the Meccans from being polytheists. But he has not appointed the Prophet their guardian; nor is he their guardian if they refuse to believe in the one God. As for Q 6:108, it informs us that the early Muslims used to curse the idols of the Meccans and God forbade them to do so lest they curse God in their ignorance.[12]

Ṭabarī similarly comments that Q 6:107 affirms that if God had willed, the people of Mecca would not have disbelieved in God and His messenger, but Muhammad was sent only as an emissary and summoner to people and not as an overseer of their actions or as one responsible for their maintenance and welfare. The next verse forbids Muslims to revile the idols of the polytheists, for that would cause them to revile God in their ignorance. According to the early exegete Ismāʿīl ibn ʿAbd al-Raḥmān al-Suddī (d. 745), the occasion of the revelation of this verse was the final illness of Abū Ṭālib, when some of the prominent Qurayshi Meccans pleaded with Abū Ṭālib to make Muhammad, his nephew, repudiate Islam. The Prophet Muhammad refused, famously stating that if they were able to bring down the sun and place it in his hand, he would still not abandon Islam. At that these Qurayshis demanded that the Prophet at least refrain from cursing their gods, or they would curse him and 'the one who commands you'. Then the revelation of this verse occurred.[13] Similar commentaries are given by Zamakhsharī,[14] Rāzī[15] and Ibn Kathīr.[16]

---

[11] Ibn Kathīr, *Tafsīr al-Qurʾān al-ʿaẓīm* (Beirut: Dār al-jīl, 1990), vol. 3, p. 401.
[12] Muqātil, *Tafsīr*, vol. 1, p. 573.
[13] Ṭabarī, *Jāmiʿ*, vol. 5, pp. 304–5.
[14] Zamakhsharī, *Kashshāf*, vol. 2, p. 385.
[15] Rāzī, *Tafsīr*, vol. 5, pp. 108–11.
[16] Ibn Kathīr, *Tafsīr*, vol. 2, p. 156.

The modern, late-nineteenth-century exegete Muḥammad ʿAbduh (d. 1905) reproduces many of the essential points made by his pre-modern predecessors in connection with these two verses. But he goes further than his predecessors in asserting that Q 6:107 makes clear that God, despite being the Guardian and Overseer of humanity, does not force humans to believe in and obey Him. If He were to do so, humans would no longer be humans but become a different species; that is to say, humans by virtue of their humanness have freedom of choice in religious matters. This is therefore doubly true of the Prophet, who was not sent as the guardian of humans. All the prophets through time, continues ʿAbduh, have been 'summoners, not overseers; guides, not tyrants, obligated not to restrict even by an inch the God-given freedom of humans in matters of faith'.[17]

ʿAbduh further asserts that this verse must be understood as containing a general prohibition against reviling anyone's religion and creed. Thus, Muslims may not insult Christians and vice versa, Sunnis may not revile the Shiʾa and vice versa, and so forth. One who reviles other people does so, he says, out of 'love for one's self and culpable ignorance'.[18] ʿAbduh makes a distinction between valid criticism and gratuitous insult intended to give offence. Therefore, one may describe the idols of the polytheists as 'neither causing harm or benefit, nor capable of drawing near and interceding', as occurs in the Qurʾan, which is merely a descriptive account and in itself not offensive and therefore not proscribed. However, he maintains that even if this valid criticism were to cause greater harm, then one should refrain from uttering it.[19]

It is noteworthy that ʿAbduh quotes Q 29:46 in this context. By invoking this verse here, he is clearly implying that the injunction contained in it to debate with the People of the Book with what is better has a broader applicability to all interreligious and intra-religious conversations. Considered together, these two verses – Q 6:108 and 29:46 – create a moral imperative to conduct dialogue with all religious groups with congeniality and without recourse to offensive and harsh language.[20]

---

[17] Rashīd Riḍā and Muḥammad ʿAbduh, *Tafsīr al-Qurʾān al-ḥakīm*, ed. Ibrāhīm Shams al-Dīn (Beirut: Dār al-kutub al-ʿilmiyya, 1999), vol. 7, pp. 548–9.

[18] Ibid., p. 549.

[19] Ibid., pp. 551–2.

[20] Ibid., p. 550.

EXEGESES OF QUR'AN 3:64

Last, but not least, we arrive at the famous 'common word' verse, which states:

Say, O People of the Book, let us come to a common word (*kalima sawā'*) between us and you that we will not worship but the one God nor ascribe any partner to Him or that any of us should take others as lords besides the one God. If they should turn their backs, say: 'Bear witness that we submit to God (*muslimūn*)'.

(Q 3:64)

This verse, which has received a lot of attention lately (as discussed further later), is concerned primarily with Muslim relations with Jews and Christians. Some of our exegetes reflect upon whether this verse deals exclusively with Jews or with Christians, or both together, and what exactly the Arabic word *sawā'* as it occurs in this verse signifies.

In his brief commentary, Muqātil glosses *kalima sawā'* as 'a word of justice, which is sincerity' (*kalimat al-'adl wa-hiya l-ikhlās*) to be agreed upon by Muslims and the People of the Book that they will worship but the one God and not ascribe partners to Him. Muqātil understands this verse to be directed primarily at Christians.[21]

Ṭabarī glosses the term *ahl al-kitāb* in the verse as a reference to both Jews and Christians (*ahl al-Tawrāt wa-l-Injīl*; 'People of the Torah and the Gospel'), who are summoned to 'a just word between us and you'. The 'just word' signifies that 'we should believe in the unicity of God and not worship anyone else; repudiate (*nabra'*) all other beings as objects of worship except Him, and that we should not ascribe any partner to Him'. The locution 'that any of us should take others as lords besides the one God' is understood to mean that one should not obey any human in matters which contravene God's commandments, or exalt another by prostrating before that other as one prostrates before God.[22]

Besides referring to just/justice (*al-'adl*), continues Ṭabarī, the word *sawā'* means 'straight/upright' (*mustawiyan*). The verse commands the Prophet to exhort the People of the Book to arrive at 'a just [word] between us and you'. There were others, such as Abū l-'Āliya, who maintained that the common word was a reference to the statement 'There is no god but God.'[23]

21 Muqātil, *Tafsīr*, vol. 1, p. 281.
22 Ṭabarī, *Tafsīr*, vol. 3, pp. 300, 302.
23 Ibid., pp. 301–2.

Moving on to Zamakhsharī, he similarly points out the different interpretations of *ahl al-kitāb*, variously understood to be a reference to the Christians from Najrān (see later discussion), to the Jews of Medina, or to both communities. 'Common' (*sawāʾ*) refers to what is '[deemed] upright by us and you, regarding which the Qurʾan, the Torah and the Gospel do not differ'. The 'word' or 'statement' (*kalima*) is elaborated upon by the verse itself: 'that we worship none but God and not ascribe partners to Him and that none of us should take others as lords besides the one God'. If the People of the Book disregard this summons, concludes Zamakhsharī, then Muslims are free to assert that they have submitted to God.[24]

In contrast to what has now become the standard commentary on Q 3:64, Rāzī in the late twelfth century offers us a strikingly distinctive reading of this important verse. In summary, he understands this verse to be concerned specifically with the Christians of Najrān – a reference to a powerful historical example in favour of interfaith engagement during the life of the Prophet Muhammad. During this episode, a delegation of sixty Christian men from the town of Najrān travelled to visit the Prophet in Medina in the year 630. The men were received kindly by the Prophet and they are said to have engaged in frank discussion regarding the doctrines and beliefs of their respective religions. At the end of the vigorous discussion in which both sides agreed to disagree on key doctrinal issues, the Christian delegation concluded a pact with the Prophet, according to which they were granted full protection of their churches and their possessions in return for the payment of taxes. They were also allowed to pray in the mosque at Medina over the protests of some.[25]

Q 3:64, according to Rāzī, was revealed after the Prophet had engaged in this vigorous debate with members of the Christian delegation. Apparently, he had overwhelmed them to a certain extent with the fervour of his arguments. Rāzī comments that it is as if God was saying to Muhammad in this verse, 'Give up this manner of speaking and adopt another which the sound intellect and upright disposition recognize as speech founded upon fairness and justice (*al-inṣāf*).' Accordingly, the Prophet abandoned disputation with the Christians of Najrān and instead, as the verse exhorted him, invited them more gently to arrive at

---

[24] Zamakhsharī, *Kashshāf*, vol. 1, p. 567.
[25] Martin Lings, *Muhammad: His Life Based on the Earliest Sources* (Cambridge: Islamic Texts Society, 1995), p. 326.

a common word or statement based upon fairness between them, with no preference shown towards anyone at the expense of another. This common word or statement is, as given in the verse, 'that we worship none but God and do not ascribe partners to Him'.[26]

The conciliatory nature of this verse directed towards the Christians of Najrān (and therefore, by extension, to all Christians) is indicated by the appellation *ahl al-kitāb* for them, according to Rāzī. He further regards this as the best of appellations and the most perfect of titles, for 'it designated them as the people of the Book of God' (*jaʿalahum ahlan li-kitāb Allāh*). Its equivalents are the titles conferred upon those who have memorised the Qur'an, as in the address 'O the bearer of the Book of God' (*yā ḥāmil kitāb Allāh*), and upon the exegete of the Qur'an, 'O commentator upon the Speech of God' (*ya mufassir kalām Allāh*). Such honorifics are intended to express respect for those who are so addressed and to cultivate their good will, and to persuade people to abandon the path of disputation and obstinacy and embark instead on a quest for fairness or justice. 'A common word' is understood by Rāzī to refer to 'a word which embodies fairness or equality between us', and no one is accorded any preference. *Al-sawā'* is specifically 'justice and fairness' (*al-ʿadl wa-l-inṣāf*). Fairness (*al-inṣāf*) furthermore implies equality, says Rāzī, because it implies equal sharing (*niṣf*) between people, and thus entails the avoidance of oppression, which involves getting more than one's equal share, for oneself and others. 'A common word' is ultimately a word that is just, upright and egalitarian.[27]

In their comments on this verse, Ibn Kathīr[28] and 'Abduh[29] essentially replicate much of what is stated by Rāzī and their views need not be repeated here.

CONCLUSION

The Qur'anic verses discussed in this chapter were selected for their relevance to relations between Muslims and non-Muslims. From a

---

[26] Rāzī, *Tafsīr*, vol. 3, p. 251.

[27] Ibid., p. 252.

[28] Ibn Kathīr, *Tafsīr*, vol. 1, p. 351. Ibn Kathīr also lists a different referent for this verse on the authority of Ibn 'Abbās reporting from Abū Sufyān: Khosroes, the king of Persia, to whom Abū Sufyān carried a letter of summons from the Prophet.

[29] Riḍā/'Abduh, *Tafsīr*, vol. 3, pp. 268–71. 'Abduh mentions that this verse occurred in the letter sent by the Prophet to Heraclius, the patriarch of Rome, inviting him to accept Islam (see ibid., p. 270).

contemporary vantage point, most of the pre-modern exegetes allude to the wide-ranging implications of these verses for interfaith dialogue, but a few tended to undermine the irenic potential of these verses. Thus in his commentary on Q 29:46, which many of us may be inclined to privilege as promoting, even mandating, courteous and respectful interfaith encounters, Ṭabarī disappointingly reads into it an unequal relationship between Muslims and the People of the Book and the requirement on the former to instruct the latter in matters of doctrine.

It can be argued that this indictment is somewhat unfair, because Ṭabarī's historical circumstances were not conducive to the kind of open and honest interfaith dialogic conversations that we can imagine today, and which indeed are sometimes possible today. But even in different historical periods in the pre-modern era, other exegetes, Zamakhsharī and Rāzī, for example, would discern in this verse (and in others) a more irenic and universal injunction to cultivate gentler, respectful relations among religious communities. Zamakhsharī's and Rāzī's views are thus more strikingly congenial to our ears. After all, easier physical and intellectual access to other people's cultures and thought has made many of us in the twenty-first century more receptive to different ways of worshipping and of engaging the world, which in turn facilitates interaction with one another on a more egalitarian basis. The constellation of verses examined in this chapter could therefore provide the interpretative stimulus today for the emergence of a genuine pluralism in Muslim ethical and moral thinking vis-à-vis other religions and peoples.

And we see this hermeneutic process already underway to a certain extent in a number of academic and popular forums. A case in point is provided by the recent exegesis of the Qur'anic phrase *kalima sawā'* in the *A Common Word* (*ACW*) statement issued initially by 138 Muslim scholars and clerics addressed to Christians.[30] All the exegetes we surveyed are in agreement that it is primarily a reference to 'a word of justice', which in itself is open to interpretation. Justice is thus variously interpreted as 'sincerity' by Muqātil, as 'upright' and an assertion of the oneness of God by Ṭabarī and Zamakhsharī, and as 'fair' and 'equitable' by Rāzī, Ibn Kathīr and 'Abduh. With interpretative creativity, the signatories to the *ACW* statement may be regarded as having distilled these various significations of justice into the pithy commandment 'Love God and your neighbour'. Such interpretative discernment in the context of dialogue is born of deep

---

[30] The original statement and now a much-expanded list of signatories may be found at www.acommonword.com/. Accessed 12 February 2016.

reflection on the whys and wherefores of interfaith encounters and necessity. In our fractious and fragile post–September 11 world, a common word must of necessity be not just a 'good word' but a 'better word' that establishes commonalities, heals relations and offers the prospect of much more than was previously imaginable in interpersonal and intercommunal relations. 'Repel evil with what is better', entreats the Qur'an; the 'better' in this case, as movingly explained by Zamakhsharī, means going the extra mile, such as by praising your enemy when he reviles you and saving the life of his son when he takes the life of your own. For most humans, such a commandment goes against the grain.

Gentleness and civility in interfaith conversations may lead to genuine 'insight' into and understanding of the 'Other', as Ibn Kathīr suggests by deploying the word *al-istibṣār* in his exegesis of this verse. Similarly, Rāzī emphasises the spiritual solace and refinement one attains when one makes a practice of responding with kindness and charity to those who do us harm, and the transformations one may effect in the wrongdoer by one's forbearance and self-restraint.

Going beyond our pre-modern commentators, 'Abduh states that the verses in Q 6:107–8 contain a firm categorical prohibition against denigrating any religion, and that this prohibition applies to intra-religious discourses as well. Giving vent to gratuitous criticism suggests self-centredness and ignorance of the basic rules of social harmony on the part of the individual, he affirms. But more importantly for us, 'Abduh discerns in these verses God's bestowal of free will on humans to choose to believe or not. Freedom of religion is a God-given right which no one, including prophets, may encroach upon, he says firmly. 'Abduh's counsel is especially relevant in our troubled times, beset by sectarian controversy in many parts of the world. Our survey of both pre-modern and modern exegeses shows that, through a faithful reading of these selected verses from the Qur'an, we are able to retrieve a broad scripture-based protocol for conducting respectful and fruitful interfaith and intra-faith encounters that are particularly appropriate for our time.

10

Our Next Word in Common

Mea Culpa?

Daniel A. Madigan

It was the impending launch of a new online journal that elicited from me what then were entitled 'some initial reflections' on *A Common Word*.[1] A couple of months were scarcely enough time to take the measure of this historic initiative, nor to consider all the issues it raised, but editors are insistent. Perhaps it was the fact that there were relatively few published Roman Catholic responses that seemed to give that early response an authority it could not really claim, and assured it a longer life than it would otherwise merit. Since then many more authoritative and representative Christian voices have had an opportunity to be heard, and the letter's author, discussants and signatories have told us more about their perception of the context from which it emerged. This chapter offers the chance to develop those initial reflections by taking a longer-term view of *ACW*'s approach, and also taking into account more recent comments on the document from Muslims as well as Christians.

ACW is 'bookended' by appeals for peace. It notes that, since together we make up more than half the world's population, there will be no peace in the world unless Muslims and Christians find a way to live at peace with one another. Though Prince Ghazi bin Muhammad in his 'Two Years Summary' of the process noted some small progress towards peace and understanding, he could also identify areas where things had

---

[1] Daniel A. Madigan SJ, '*A Common Word between Us and You*: some initial reflections', *Thinking Faith*, 18 January 2008. www.thinkingfaith.org/fr/articles/20080118_9.htm. Accessed 7 September 2016. Reprinted in *A Common Word Between Us and You: 5-Year Anniversary Edition* (Amman: Royal Aal Al-Bayt Institute for Islamic Thought, 2012), pp. 165–75.

deteriorated.[2] The sense of urgency he expressed initially in 2007 and again in 2009 has surely not been alleviated in the intervening years. More people are likely to agree with *ACW* that 'our common future is at stake. The very survival of the world itself is perhaps at stake'. In a world that is increasingly ready to see our current situation as a winner-takes-all struggle between two incompatible civilisations, *ACW* remains a welcome reminder that there is an alternative: we can still try to envision a common future.

The signatories rightly believed that the resolution of our conflicts lies not merely in political negotiation but in finding a common religious basis that can ground our mutual commitments and give them an authority beyond the calculations of temporary expediency. Both among Christians and among Muslims there has been an ever-stronger tendency to define our differences and conceive of our politics in terms of religion, thus virtually ensuring that they cannot be resolved. Therefore, it is crucial to find, as Prince Ghazi put it, 'a theological platform to bring faithful Muslims and Christians together in a kind of world-wide peace movement'.[3] According to Tim Winter, the concern that eventually gave rise to the document went back several years before its publication to the period immediately following the 11 September attacks in the United States, and to the emergence, or perhaps re-emergence, during and even within the administration of George W. Bush of what seemed to be a conservative Christian vision of religiously justified military and economic hegemony.[4] At the same time, according to another member of the *ACW* core group, Sohail Nakhooda, it was the unfortunate speech

---

[2] HRH Prince Ghazi of Jordan, '"A Common Word between Us and You": two years summary', Oct 2007–Oct 2009'. www.acommonword.com/two-years-summary-oct-2007-oct-2009/. Accessed 7 September 2016.

[3] Ibid.

[4] See Tim Winter's discussion in Chapter 1 in the present volume. As a participant in the group that helped develop the document, Winter offers important insights into the intentions of those involved with the drafting of the letter, and he makes more explicit some of its less direct statements. It seems, for example, that the reference to 'those who nevertheless relish conflict and destruction for their own sake or reckon that ultimately they stand to gain through them' may have had in mind also those who planned to profit from the eventual reconstruction of the infrastructure that would be destroyed in the invasion of Iraq. For a more extensive treatment of the issue, see Winter's 'America as a Jihad state: Middle Eastern perceptions of modern American theopolitics', *Muslim World*, 101/3 (July 2011), 394–411. See also Murad Hofmann, 'Differences between the Muslim and the Christian concept of divine love', Fourteenth General Conference of the Royal Aal al-Bayt Institute for Islamic Thought (Love in the Holy Qur'an), Amman, 2007, pp. 1–2. www.aalalbayt.org/en/respapers.html#rd14. Accessed 7 September 2016.

given by Pope Benedict XVI at Regensburg in September 2006, coming on the heels of the Danish cartoon controversy in the previous year, that impelled the scholars associated with the *Amman Message* to address Christian leaders through *A Common Word*.[5]

Understanding this background helps, perhaps, to explain why *ACW* takes without apology as its key text what could seem like an invitation but which, when read in the context of the polemics of *Sūrat Āl ʿImrān*, is more like an ultimatum (or an invitation, a *daʿwa*, to Islam, as Michael Louis Fitzgerald noted in Chapter 3 in this volume):

> Say thou: 'O People of the Scripture! Come to a common word between us and you: that we shall worship none but God, and that we shall ascribe no partner unto Him, and that none of us shall take others for lords apart from God.' And if they turn away, then say ye: 'Bear witness that we are the ones who have submitted (*muslimūn*).'
>
> (Q 3:64)

ACW, for all its openness and freshness of approach, was not a surrender in the face of the contentiousness, attacks and provocations of those years. According to Prince Ghazi, 'A *Common Word* does not signal that Muslims are prepared to deviate from or concede one iota of any of their convictions in reaching out to Christians – nor, I expect, the opposite. Let us be crystal-clear: *A Common Word* is about equal peace, NOT about capitulation.'[6] Where there are conditions in *ACW*, they are political rather than theological. For example, Christians are assured in part III that Muslims 'are not against them and that Islam is not against them'. Then come the conditions (stipulated in Q 60:8): 'so long as they do not wage war against Muslims on account of their religion, oppress them and drive them out of their homes'. Though the original context of this is said to be Mecca, which oppressed its first Muslim citizens, the verse is given broad contemporary application. Many extremists will use precisely this verse to justify enmity towards Israel and anyone who supports it. George W. Bush's catastrophic military adventures in Iraq and Afghanistan, and the so-called War on Terror are easily interpreted as attacks on Islam. Given the religious rhetoric Bush employed for political advantage, and the outspokenness of many of his Evangelical

---

[5] Sohail Nakhooda, 'The significance of the Amman Message and the Common Word', a lecture given in Amman on 30 December 2008. www.acommonword.com/The-Significance-of-the-Amman-Message-and-the-Common-Word.pdf. Accessed 7 September 2016.

[6] Ghazi bin Muhammad, '*A Common Word between Us and You*: theological motives and expectations', cited by Joseph Lumbard in 'The uncommonality of "A Common Word"', in *ACW: 5-Year Anniversary Edition*, pp. 11–50, at p. 43. Emphasis in the original.

supporters, the wars that he began – and which are far from resolved yet – can easily be portrayed as a return to medieval crusading, and thus they put in jeopardy all Christians, particularly those living in the war zones. Even Western cultural and economic hegemony is sometimes read as aggression and so taken as legitimising a violent response against any members of that culture, as, for example, the indiscriminate killings in Paris in November 2015 bear witness. *ACW*'s reassurance that Islam and Muslims are not opposed to Christians entails a quite major conditional clause imposed by the Qur'an itself. This is surely an important focus for continuing dialogue with the *ACW* group and other Muslims.

There can be little objection to the aim of establishing with *ACW* 'a common faith-based mutual touchstone' to which Muslims and Christians can hold each other, and themselves.[7] An agreed commitment to an ethic of love, with its dual commandment to love God and love the neighbour, is surely a worthy starting point for dealing with our conflictual relationship, even if, as Rowan Williams observed in his response, *ACW*'s treatment of love of the neighbour is quite brief and is a topic that needs to be explored together in more depth.[8] However, this 'equal peace' seems to be predicated upon a theological levelling – Prince Ghazi's term 'a theological platform' perhaps indicates this. Tim Winter put it quite explicitly: '*A Common Word* sought to rise above the insecurities and debating tricks of so much interreligious conversation to remind us in a rather unsettling way that we are variations on a single theme, that of ethical monotheism.'[9] Ethical monotheism is no bad thing, of course, and actually quite an exalted aim. However, it is not the Gospel.

It is surprising to note how often even academic analysis falls back on such pieties, and how glibly each religion can be reduced to a particular variation on the generic theme of religion. *ACW* itself does not quite fall into that trap, since it confines itself to speaking only of the Abrahamic traditions of Christianity and Islam (with Judaism making the occasional, parenthetical appearance). Yet the letter does open itself to a reductionist reading – one that Winter signals and that Christians might want to examine more closely – when it says in part III, 'Thus the Unity of God, love of Him and love of the neighbour form a common ground upon which Islam and Christianity (and Judaism) are founded.' There has been an undeniable affirmation earlier in the paragraph that the obligation to

---

[7] Ghazi, 'Two years summary'.
[8] See Chapter 4 in this volume.
[9] Chapter 1 in this volume.

love God and one's neighbour is a common element in the sacred texts of our traditions. However, there follows a shift to the more questionable claim that the dual commandment of love is the *foundation* of all three traditions. Apart from the fact that the dual commandment is not explicit in the Qur'an and that *ACW* has to go to some lengths to demonstrate that it is implied there, it is far from clear that it can be taken to be the essence of Christianity.

In fairness to Muslim colleagues, it should be admitted that many Christians will also propose a shorthand rendition of Jesus' saying about the greatest commandments as the kernel of his teaching and the foundation of Christianity. But are they right? Is that all there is to the Gospel? What can be the point of the Word's becoming incarnate if it is simply to remind the world of a few important verses from Deuteronomy and Leviticus, verses that some of Jesus' contemporaries among the rabbis would also have recognised as summing up 'the Law and the Prophets'? Indeed, in Luke's Gospel it is not Jesus who makes the statement about the dual commandment, but the lawyer who posed the commandment question in the first place. Jesus merely approves his opinion and advises him to follow that reading of the Torah (Luke 10:25–8). Was Jesus' mission primarily to remind humanity of an obligation already revealed centuries before, and were all the rest of his living, dying and rising therefore only ancillary to this?

We should note that when Jesus gives his answer to the question about the greatest commandment, it is always in the context of controversy. Matthew (22:35) and Luke (10:25) both note that it was a question intended to trap him. The cautious answer to a trick question can hardly be considered the foundation of a religion.[10] The subject at issue was commandments, and surely those two are the greatest. However, is there nothing to the Good News other than commandment and obligation? When the lawyer who poses the commandment question in Mark's Gospel warmly reaffirms Jesus' reply, Jesus says to him, 'You are not far from the Kingdom of God' (Mark 12:34). Not far from it, but not quite there.[11] Commandments are fine as far as they go, but the kingdom goes further than that. The culmination of prophecy (as Christians see it) in John the Baptist (Matthew 11:13) can scarcely be compared to

---

[10] In conversation at the Cambridge conference (2008), Prince Ghazi objected to this affirmation, maintaining that, since Jesus was a prophet, his every word was authoritative and therefore the context of entrapment was irrelevant.

[11] I have been indebted to John Reilly SJ for this keen observation since 1972.

the ushering in of the kingdom: 'Truly I tell you, among those born of women no one has arisen greater than John the Baptist; yet the least in the kingdom of heaven is greater than he' (Matthew 11:11). The Gospel is not a simple cut-and-paste job on the Torah, with a pithier selection of commandments. Before all else it is the proclamation of what God has done for love of humanity. What we are to do flows from what God has done and is made possible by it.

GOD'S LOVE FOR US

When *ACW* speaks of 'the love of God', it means our love *for* God, and that almost always in terms of obligation – as witness the repeated use of 'must' and 'should' in part I. Yet personal experience is enough to make us realise that true love cannot be commanded or conditioned; if it is not freely given and received, it is not really love.

No New Testament writer has devoted more attention to the question of divine love than the one known there as 'the disciple whom Jesus loved' and whom Christian tradition calls John. In his first letter he says, 'This is what love is: not that we have loved God, but that God has loved us' (1 John 4:10). 'We love', John tells us, 'because God first loved us' (1 John 4:19). Throughout John's writings there is a constant outward movement of love: 'As the Father has loved me, so I have loved you' (John 15:9); 'Just as I have loved you, so you also should love one another' (John 13:34). That is Jesus' 'new commandment', given to his disciples just before his death. Not a demand that they love him, or even the Father, but rather a command (if, indeed, that is the right word for it) to dwell in the love he bears us. Dwelling in that love means allowing it to transform us so that we in our turn love others. In this context, Jesus uses the telling image of a vine and its branches. The nutrient sap of the vine enables the branches to produce fruit, yet the fruit is for the benefit neither of the vine nor of the branches – it is for others. All love originates in God and flows ever outward from there, transforming all who will allow themselves to be suffused by it. It does not turn back in on itself, demanding reciprocation, but pours itself out for the beloved – even for the ungrateful.

Both John and the apostle Paul recognise the central importance of the fact that it was not as a result of human perfection nor even in response to human repentance that God's love for us was manifested; rather it was while we were still sinners (1 John 4:10; Romans 5:6). If there is a foundation to Christian faith, this is surely a major pillar of it. The parable of the Pharisee and the tax collector (Luke 18:9–14) dramatises another foundational pillar: of the two men who went to the temple to pray, the one who came away at rights with God was not the virtuous man who had fulfilled all his obligations under the Law and so felt entitled to stand before God and boast, but rather the sinner who knew he had nothing to rely on but God's mercy.

An understanding of the primacy and priority of divine love is not lacking in the Islamic tradition, but it did not find a place in *ACW*, possibly because it confines itself to quoting the Qur'an and the Hadith in order to address the broadest possible Muslim audience. Still, *ACW* might have appealed to the verse Q 5:54, in which it is said that 'God will bring a new people: He will love them, and they will love Him.' In his book *Love in the Holy Qur'an*, Prince Ghazi addresses the question of the priority of God's love for us over our love for God, and he cites part of this verse as proof that love originates with God and not with the creature.[12] Commenting on this verse, Sufi writers have often observed that God's love for human beings precedes their love for God, and if it were not for the fact that God had favoured us by His primordial love, mercy and compassion, humanity could never have loved God and His creatures. In this assertion of the priority of God's love for us over our love for God there lies an important point for our continuing theological dialogue. However, the verse taken as a whole is addressing those who have apostatised, warning them that God will bring a new people in their stead. Furthermore, as Ghazi presents it, the priority of divine love is not quite straightforward; it seems still to be predicated on love for the Prophet:

But no one can love God unless God loves him or her, and God does not love anyone who does not love His Blessed Prophet. Therefore, at the heart of the life of a Muslim resides the love of God and of the Prophet, a love that originates with Him and not with the creature as the Noble Qur'ān states so succinctly in the verse, 'He loves them and they love Him,' a verse that expresses clearly that the love that God has for us precedes our love for Him as cause precedes effect.[13]

Ghazi's book demonstrates how complex the apparently shared notion of the love of God actually is. He analyses the Qur'anic text in impressive detail and effectively demonstrates – though this seems not to have been his intention – how distinct its notion of love is from the New Testament

---

[12] Ghazi bin Muhammad, *Love in the Holy Qur'an* (Chicago: Kazi, 2010), p. xxiii. See also ibid., p. 45.

[13] Ibid., p. xxiii. See also ibid., pp. 109–15.

concept.[14] This meticulous study demonstrates something *ACW* glossed over: that each community needs to explore what love – whether of God, for God or for the neighbour – really means in its own scriptures and traditions. It is not up to either to tell the other that when we speak of the dual commandment of love we all mean the same thing. Nor is either entitled to determine what is fundamental or essential in the other tradition. *ACW* took it for granted that the dual commandment of love was a univocal and common fundamental element in Judaism, Christianity and Islam. Yet Ghazi's very 'thick description' of the Qur'anic concept of love shows how thin is the analysis on which *ACW*'s assertion of commonality rests. It relied more on a desire to find common ground than on an exploration of the complex terrain of each tradition.

From the Christian side, one sees in the so-called Yale Response to *ACW* a similar desire to affirm common ground in the dual commandment without at first looking too closely and critically at how tenable that is.[15] Some of the issues that were raised earlier have been acknowledged on a page of 'frequently asked questions' about the *ACW* process on the Yale website. The response to the question about whether our concepts of love are the same concludes with this observation: 'We clearly have only just begun the conversations and interactions on these crucial matters of love of God and of neighbor – this exchange of letters is only the first step in an ongoing and sustained dialogue.'[16] The authors acknowledged that, when they tried to put their response into Arabic, they discovered much more complexity was involved than they had first thought.

WHO IS MY NEIGHBOUR?

Just as there are reservations about how foundational for Christianity is the commandment to love God, so also one must question how fundamental is the commandment to love one's neighbour. There are two elements in the gospels that relativise it. The first comes from Luke's Gospel where Jesus' questioner, having failed to trap him with the commandment

---

[14] See also Hofmann, 'Differences between the Muslim and the Christian concept of divine love', p. 4, where he lists some of the 'peculiarities' of the Christian approach.

[15] This response – the first substantive engagement with the text of *ACW* – began as a letter from Yale faculty members. It was later developed and signed by three hundred Christian theologians and published in the *New York Times*, 18 November 2007. See Yale Center for Faith & Culture, '"A Common Word" Christian response'. http://faith .yale.edu/common-word/common-word-christian-response. Accessed 7 September 2016.

[16] http://faith.yale.edu/common-word/common-word-yale-frequently-asked-questions.

question, has another try and asks, 'And who is my neighbour?' (Luke 10:29). The parable Jesus tells in response – the Good Samaritan – actually turns the man's question on its head. After having described the extraordinarily generous and compassionate response of this religious outsider to a Jew in need, after two of the victim's own religious leaders had already failed him, Jesus asks, 'Which of these three *proved himself a neighbour* to the man attacked by robbers?' The question is no longer, who is to be included in the category of neighbour, and therefore what are the limits of my obligation to love? It is, rather, how can I show myself a neighbour to others by responding to them in love?

The second and more striking element in the gospels occurs in both Matthew and Luke in slightly different forms. Here is Matthew's version:

> You have heard that it was said, 'You shall love your neighbour and hate your enemy.' But I say to you, love your enemies and pray for those who persecute you, so that you may be children of your Father in heaven. For He makes his sun to rise on the evil as well as the good, and his rain to fall on the righteous and unrighteous alike.
>
> (Matthew 5:43–5)

Luke reports that it was in this context that Jesus said,

> If anyone strikes you on one cheek, offer the other also; and from anyone who takes away your coat do not withhold even your shirt. Give to everyone who begs from you; and if anyone takes away your goods, do not ask for them again. Do to others as you would have them do to you. [...] Love your enemies, do good, and lend, expecting nothing in return. Your reward will be great, and you will be children of the Most High; for he is kind to the ungrateful and the wicked. Be merciful, just as your Father is merciful.
>
> (Luke 6:29–31, 35–6)

For Luke this exaggerated and disinterested generosity is the emulation of divine mercy. In Matthew's Gospel it is even more; it is the emulation of God's very perfection: 'Be perfect, therefore, as your heavenly Father is perfect (*téleios*)' (Matthew 5:48). It almost sounds blasphemous – suggesting that humans are capable of emulating God's perfection. Yet it is not simply an imitation or emulation. It is more of a participation. God is loving and merciful, and as that loving mercy embraces us, it draws us into its own flow and dynamic. We become merciful and loving, not because we are imitating God, but because God's own merciful love is acting in us.

'Perfect' is perhaps not a rich enough word to translate the Greek *téleios*. In John's Gospel, the account of Jesus' passion, from his last supper, begins thus (John 13:1): 'Jesus knew that the hour had come for him to leave this world and go to the Father. Having loved his own who were in the world, he loved them to the end (*eis télos*).' He loved all the way, we might say; completely. And not just to the bitter end as matters wound down, but rather to the goal or high point. On the cross Jesus again uses the idea of *télos*: 'It is accomplished', he says. *Tetélestai* in Greek: the goal (*télos*) has been reached (John 19:30). He had gone all the way in his mission to express in his living – and now that included dying – the love God has for humanity: a love utterly beyond human calculations; a love that is disarmed, that does not play our power games, that seeks no advantage for itself, that bears everything, even enmity and hatred, without striking back. God revealed, that is to say expressed, that self-emptying love in Jesus, even while human beings were still sinners who preferred alienation from God to the peace with God that was our original state.

Especially in the parables, and most notably in some of those peculiar to Luke's Gospel – for example, the Good Samaritan (Luke 10:30–5) and the Prodigal Son (Luke 15:11–32) – Jesus proposes a gracious generosity that upsets any calculus of equitable sharing and ethical reciprocity. It is this revelation of the generosity and graciousness of God that fully deserves the title *evangelion*, good news.

In the Islamic apologetic tradition, it is not unusual to criticise what is seen as the exaggeration of Jesus' new 'law'. Muhammad's Sunna is proposed, then, as the just and therefore virtuous mean between what is taken to be the mediocrity of Moses' Law and the hopelessly idealistic teaching of Jesus.[17] An example can be found in the now-famous medieval encounter between Emperor Manuel II Paleologos and his

---

[17] Appeal is often made in this context to Q 2:143 and its idea that God made the Muslims *ummatan wasaṭan* – a middle or moderate community. In a paper presented in Amman just before *ACW* was written, one of the original signatories, Murad Hofmann, wrote: 'This leads me to a final consideration concerning the psychological impact of promoting a rule – to love one's foe – that is inaccessible to 99.9 % of all people. Admitting this situation Christians might argue that nevertheless we need lofty ideals to strive for, even if they are virtually unattainable. Muslims might reply that it is detrimental for public morality if unattainable rules are promoted which, of course, are constantly violated by everybody in sight, because that (Christian) approach creates a climate of, and promotes, hypocrisy at a massive scale. I share the latter judgment, being afraid that people used to violating basic rules of their professed moral code might become cynical about morality as such. Indeed there is divine wisdom behind the fact that all religious obligations placed on Muslims while not being easy to fulfil are all within reach of the average believer. In this sense, too, Islam by being more simple is more sane.' Hofmann, 'Differences between the Muslim and the Christian concept of divine love', pp. 10–11.

Persian interlocutor, which Pope Benedict referred to in his Regensburg lecture. Even though the text comes from the emperor, the position of his opponent is common enough even today. Citing one after another several elements of the Sermon on the Mount, he comments:

Where can one find such a man of iron, of diamond, as unfeeling as stone, who could bear such things? Where can one find a person who will bear an offence and cherish the one who insults him; one who will do good to someone ill-disposed towards him? Yet by his excess of goodness he invites that type of hostile person to seize upon him as vultures do upon the corpses of the dead.[18]

The emperor rather glibly responds that the law enunciated by Jesus is only barely beyond our human capacity, and can indeed be put into practice with the help afforded by the one who commands it.[19] However, it may be that the Persian is right and has put his finger on a central point: the all-too-common human response to the kind of generosity and forgiveness prescribed in Jesus' Sermon on the Mount is indeed to take advantage of and even to attack the one who offers it. In effect the emperor's Muslim interlocutor has recognised that that kind of goodness renders one so vulnerable that it can lead nowhere but to the cross. What is described in the sermon – and Jesus' final line in Matthew's version brings this out clearly – is not some attainable human perfection but the very perfection of God. The 'commands' of the sermon are not the crushing imposition of a demanding sovereign. They are a call to enter into the perfect generosity of God, to receive it, to allow it to transform us and to live it out in our turn. This will mean allowing ourselves to be taken for granted, taken for fools, taken down. Jesus does not impose from above this code of behaviour; he lives by it and so dies by it. In doing so, Christians believe, he is revealing the very nature of God.

Christians claim to have seen in Jesus a different way of God's exercising sovereignty: a sovereignty of love, which does not stand on its own prerogatives; a vulnerable sovereignty; a sovereignty that pours itself out in love; a sovereign who washes the feet of his subjects; who reigns not from a throne but from a gibbet, not in a citadel but on a bare hill outside the city. This sovereign does not indulge our disobedience or wink at our defiance, but rather bears the brunt of it, endures the cost of it, thus ultimately robbing it of its power.

---

[18] Manuel II Paléologue, *Entretiens avec un musulman, 7ᵉ controverse*, ed. Théodore Khoury (Paris: Editions du Cerf, 1966), p. 151.

[19] Ibid., pp. 159–61.

A DIFFERENT GOD?

As Sarah Snyder shows in Chapter 7, a number of Christian commentators on *ACW* have maintained that the Qur'an is proclaiming a different God from the one known in Jesus Christ, and that therefore *ACW's* call to Christians to affirm along with Muslims belief in the one God is either nonsensical or perhaps disingenuous. Both Muslim and Christian scholars have replied to this charge by noting that, although there are indeed differences about what we affirm of God, there is no doubt that both traditions are intending to speak of the God who alone is God, of the sole Creator of heaven and earth, of the origin and end of all that is.[20] Maintaining different things about the one God does not constitute believing in a 'different god'. Most Christians would not maintain that Jews believe in a 'different god' just because they do not accept Jesus as the Christ or God as Trinity. We recognise that they are trying, as Christians are, to express the truth about the only God there is. In his response to *ACW*, Rowan Williams interpreted its invitation as saying:

> Let us find a way of recognising that on some matters we are speaking enough of a common language for us to be able to pursue both exploratory dialogue and peaceful co-operation with integrity and without compromising fundamental beliefs.[21]

The accusation that another person believes in a 'different god' is not always just a kind of theological purism that sees religions as separate and incommensurable. It often masks an arrogance, which might be expressed 'Our God is better than your god; so we are better than you.' Such an attitude can be found among both Christians and Muslims. For the Christian, at least, there is a fundamental contradiction at work here. The extraordinary richness of divine mercy revealed in Christ rules out any boasting, since the cross reveals not only the truth of the inexhaustibility of God's love, but at the same time the true extent of human rebellion against God and our resistance to God's graciousness. It is a strange kind of Christian who is puffed up with pride over the fact that Jesus taught love of enemies rather than just love of neighbour. To imagine

---

[20] See, for example, Professor Caner Dagli speaking at a conference on 'Evangelicals and "A Common Word"', Evangelical Theological Society, New Orleans, LA, 18 November 2009. He explicitly addresses some Evangelical leaders who wrote on the subject: https://vimeo.com/48606820 from 6' 10". The Yale *A Common Word*: Frequently Asked Questions page also addresses the question: http://faith.yale.edu/common-word/common-word-yale-frequently-asked-questions. Both accessed 8 September 2016.

[21] See Chapter 10 in this volume.

oneself better than another because one has recognised the depth of God's forgiveness in Christ makes no sense at all, since to recognise God's forgiveness must mean at the same time acknowledging the depth of our need for it.

SHARED VALUES OR SHARED FAILURE?

If there are questions about whether the dual commandment of love is sufficiently central and essential to both our traditions that it can form a common basis for dialogue, we might ask what other more fundamental point we could take for our word in common? In the communiqué from the Cambridge conference on *ACW* (October 2008), Archbishop Rowan Williams and Shaykh Ali Gomaa wrote, 'In this conference we are celebrating the shared values of love of God and love of neighbour, the basis of *ACW*, whilst reflecting self-critically on how often we fall short of these standards.'[22] The risk of a dialogue that grows out of *ACW* is that 'celebrating the shared values' can displace the necessary self-criticism and can end up submerging long-standing grievances and present fears (whether real or imagined) under a veneer of polite appreciation. Our 'shared values' are examined like objects in a museum: you may look at them, but please do not touch! Admire the beauty of the object, but do not question whether it actually works. As happened in Cambridge, those submerged critiques can suddenly rise to the surface in a show of mutual recrimination and 'truth-telling' that seems to derail the dialogue. Sometimes this suppressed critique does not boil over, but even in remaining unspoken it poisons the trust between us.

We too often think that the objective of our work together is for each to affirm that the 'Other' is 'OK'. However, just having high ideals and exacting commandments – even though they may be shared – does not make us 'OK'. If we are honest, we recognise that our lives as individuals and as religious traditions are more clearly marked by failure to observe the ideal of love than by success in achieving it. We see others' failures more easily than our own, and we tend to distance ourselves from those failures for which we are not personally and directly culpable. We have a whole range of excuses that we regularly use to absolve ourselves from any blame: that was political, not religious; those people were extremists,

---

[22] Rowan Williams and Ali Gomaa, 'Communiqué from A Common Word conference', University of Cambridge, 15 October 2008. www.acommonword.com/communique-from-a-common-word-conference/. Accessed 4 September 2016.

not real believers; those few bad apples do not reflect the true nature of our community; we are under attack from you in so many ways and this was just self-defence; what they did was not Islam/Christianity; your community is much worse than ours.[23] And so it goes. We are all familiar by now with how the game is played, and there is no denying that there is an element of truth in the excuses we make. However, those excuses we make to one another also represent a refusal to acknowledge our solidarity in sin, which in the end seems to have more power over us than whatever prophetic or divine ideals we might profess to hold in common.

IS THERE ANOTHER WORD WE HAVE IN COMMON?

Having said all this – having recognised the substantial differences in what we believe about love for God and neighbour – where might we find something we have truly in common that can launch and sustain our dialogue? We are agreed that God is merciful and compassionate, yet we sometimes make that affirmation as though we ourselves did not really stand in need of mercy, as though we ourselves had little need of forgiveness, at least in comparison with others. Could it be that the word in common we are seeking is a word of repentance before God and each other? Could we find the honesty and courage to acknowledge to one another that we ourselves have sinned and that we are entangled together in webs of oppression that stretch across centuries – and this not just in our conflicts with one another, but in our common failure to do justice in the world? We are involved together – historically and even today – in unjust economic structures, in exploitative trade of oil and arms and drugs, in the trafficking of persons and the exploitation of labour, in self-interested and coldly calculating alliances, in aggressions and domination that we dress up in the garb of civilisation and religion, in crimes destructive of humanity that we justify by appeal to humanity's Creator. We too

---

[23] A particularly interesting example of this last defence is seen in the publication by Naveed S. Sheikh, *The Body Count: A Quantitative Review of Political Violence across World Civilizations*, published in 2009 by the Royal Aal al-Bayt Institute for Islamic Thought in the same Interfaith Series as ACW. A draft of this study had been made available the previous year to participants in the Cambridge ACW conference. Regardless of any reservations one might have about the figures cited and the attribution of blame, the findings are sobering. The point of the study is well made: in spite of accusations to the contrary, the 'Islamic civilization' has been responsible for only one-eighth of the number of deaths attributable to the 'Christian civilization.' http://rissc.jo/docs/bodycount_final .pdf. Accessed 8 September 2016.

often despise those who are different in race, ethnicity, gender and belief, and we begrudge the world's poor the little they need just to stay alive.

We may not be individually culpable for all or even any of these things, yet that does not mean we do not have a responsibility here and now to act to redress injustice and to restore peace. As an Australian born in the twentieth century, I am not culpable for the physical and cultural violence done against the indigenous peoples of my country. Yet I have benefited from the prosperity and peace that were part of the charmed existence of white Australians of my generation, and so I have a responsibility to act for justice. I may not be personally culpable for the abuse of minors that went on in the Roman Catholic Church and other institutions. Yet I cannot simply absolve myself of responsibility to effect change in the clerical culture, to show sensitivity towards victims and to advocate for them.

This dialogue of repentance will not be easy, for we are well defended not only against each other but also against the kind of moral perspicacity that takes the true measure of our own history of sin. Is it conceivable that the word we should be trying to come to in common is something like this confession which, although it comes from the Roman Catholic liturgy, could equally be voiced by a Muslim without reservation?

I confess to Almighty God, and to you my brothers and sisters, that I have sinned through my own fault (*mea culpa*), in my thoughts, and in my words, in what I have done and in what I have failed to do.

The dialogue that leads us deeper into the reality of our moral failures could take as its motto the words of the Qur'an: 'Perhaps God will create friendship between you and those you consider your enemies. God is powerful, infinitely forgiving, most merciful' (Q 60:7). When together we are able to acknowledge our need for forgiveness – from God and each other – and to recognise our common reliance on nothing else but God's mercy at work in us and through us, then perhaps affection will be able to replace enmity. That will surely be God's doing.

A *Common Word* or a Word of Justice?

Two Qur'anic Approaches to Christian–Muslim Dialogue

Pim Valkenberg

In this contribution to *A Common Word*, I would like to draw attention to a problem that in my opinion has sometimes hindered the *ACW* document from being an effective instrument in Christian–Muslim dialogue. Both among those who promote the document and among those, including some in this volume, who have raised questions about it, the general idea is that the very term 'common word' suggests a common ground between Muslims and Christians. While I agree that such a common ground is probably intended by the Qur'an in *Sūrat Āl ʿImrān*, and that it is certainly intended by many of those who have signed the *ACW* document, I would argue that it is not a necessary final interpretation of the Qur'anic verse in question. So, I want to look first at the historical context of this specific verse, following what Muslims would call *asbāb al-nuzūl*, the 'occasions of the revelations', and the history of its interpretation, *tafsīr*, Qur'anic exegesis. Second, I want to propose an alternative interpretation, and show the hermeneutical consequences of this interpretation, that tries to avoid the idea of a common ground. Third, I will use the situation in the Netherlands as an example that shows why the *ACW* document might not work in certain contexts unless it is interpreted differently. I do not claim that my proposal solves the problem of a defective history of reception of the document. However, I do claim that it might lead to a somewhat different interfaith hermeneutics that would avoid some of the problems involved in the idea of a common ground between Christians and Muslims.

THE ORIGINAL CONTEXT AND MEANING OF
A COMMON WORD

The text of the 'common word' verse in the Qur'an is as follows:

Say: 'People of the Book, let us arrive at a statement that is common to us all: we worship God alone, we ascribe no partner to Him, and none of us takes others beside God as lords.' If they turn away, say: 'Witness our devotion to Him.'[1]

In this verse (Q 3:64), Muhammad is summoned to urge the 'People of the Book' (usually Jews and Christians) to come up with a statement corresponding to some of the central tenets of the Muslim faith: to worship only one God, without ascribing any partners to Him, and to take none as Lord except God. Yet at the same time the verse apparently foresees a situation in which such corresponding statements will not be possible, since the verse continues with 'if they turn away, say: witness that we are those who have surrendered to God.' The last word is ambiguous in the original text, since the word *muslimūn* means 'those who have submitted to God' but could also be interpreted as referring to Muslims as members of an institutionalised religion, even though the word *muslim* as it appears in the Qur'anic text tends to be generic and refers to an attitude rather than to a specific religion. It is clear that this text talks about two parties who may try to agree, but probably will not succeed in doing so, since the earlier verses also mention the possibility that the other party will turn away. While we can identify the one party as *muslimūn*, either in the sense of 'those who adore the one true God' or in the sense of 'adherents of the religion of Islam' – most scholars say that the first possibility is much more likely than the second[2] – the other party is identified as *ahl al-kitāb*, the 'People of the Book' or 'People of Scripture', referring to those who have received a revelation from God and are thus supposed to acknowledge God's message to them.[3] The fact that they possess a scripture seems to give them something in common with the *muslimūn*, but as in almost all texts about the 'People of Scripture' this common point becomes a reason to reproach them for not living according to the divine guidance.

---

[1] Translation from M. A. S. Abdel Haleem, *The Qur'an: English Translation and Parallel Arabic Text* (Oxford: Oxford University Press, 2010), p. 59.

[2] See Carl W. Ernst, *How to Read the Qur'an: A New Guide, with Select Translations* (Chapel Hill: University of North Carolina Press, 2011), pp. 179–80.

[3] See Daniel A. Madigan, 'Book', in Jane D. McAuliffe (ed.), *Encyclopaedia of the Qur'ān* (Leiden: Brill, 2001), vol. I, pp. 242–51, at p. 251.

In the case of the first part of *Sūrat Āl ʿImrān*, which contains an extended discussion of Christological matters, the Muslim tradition has pointed to a particular story as occasion for this revelation. ʿAlī ibn Aḥmad al-Wāḥidī (d. 1075), who has sampled these 'occasions of the revelations' in a book that forms one of the most important hermeneutical instruments of Qurʾanic exegesis, writes that a Christian delegation from Najrān (an area in present-day Saudi Arabia near the border with Yemen) travelled to see Muhammad in Medina, and that Muhammad allowed them to pray in his mosque. After this, Muhammad told them to surrender to God, but they responded, 'We have already surrendered to God!' According to Wāḥidīʿs version of the story, the Prophet Muhammad then said: 'three things prevent you from surrendering to God: claiming that God has a son, worshipping the cross, and eating pork'. After this, they engaged in a long disputation about Jesus. Upon the Christian confession of Jesus as both Son of God and a human being in the womb of Mary, Muhammad asserted that Jesus could not be the Son of God and a human being at the same time. And this event was, according to Wāḥidī, the occasion of the revelation of the first eighty-one verses of *Sūrat Āl ʿImrān*.[4] This context indicates that the debate here is about the identity of the true *muslimūn*. While Muhammad asserts that he is given the true message of submission to God, the Christians claim that they are the possessors of this true faith, yet they are challenged by Muhammad on the matter of Christology.

On the occasion of Qurʾanic verse 3:61, which again addresses Muhammad, saying, 'If anyone disputes this with you now that you have been given this knowledge, say, "Come, let us gather our sons and your sons, our women and your women, ourselves and yourselves, and let us pray earnestly and invoke God's rejection on those of us who are lying,"' the same story is repeated in Wāḥidī, who then narrates that Muhammad was prepared to take his son in law ʿAlī, his daughter Fāṭima and his grandsons Ḥasan and Ḥusayn to this ordeal; the Christians of Najrān, however, were afraid to expose themselves to God's judgement. Muhammad is reported then to have said, 'By Him Who has sent me with the truth, had they agreed to summon Allah's curse on the liar, fire would have rained on the valley [where the delegation of Najrān had camped].'[5] The text in the Qurʾan suggests that if two parties disagree

---

4 Mokrane Guezzou (trans.), *Al-Wāḥidī's Asbāb al-Nuzūl: Great Commentaries on the Holy Qurʾan* (Louisville, KY: Fons Vitae, 2008), p. 44.

5 Ibid., p. 49.

about their faith, they may start a procedure that invokes God's curse or wrath on them who prove to be wrong. Even though the text is not very clear, the Islamic tradition has associated this verse with a specific practice: a *mubāhala,* or ordeal in which both parties solemnly curse one another in the expectation that God will side with the party who is right, while destroying the party who is wrong.[6] The argument made by the tradition in Wāḥidī's collection is that Muhammad was so convinced of his rightfulness that he was willing to take the most important members of his own family to this ordeal. Confronted with such confidence, the Christians of Najrān decided not to enter the contest, proving themselves wrong.

The mention of fire punishing the liars in the tradition evokes the scene involving the Prophet Elijah and the prophets of Baal on Mount Carmel, according to the first book of Kings in the Hebrew Bible. Elijah challenges king Ahab and the prophets of Baal as follows:

Give us two young bulls. Let them choose one, cut it into pieces, and place it on the wood, but start no fire. I shall prepare the other and place it on the wood, but shall start no fire. You shall call on your gods, and I will call on the Lord. The God who answers with fire is God.

(1 Kings 18:23–4)[7]

When God sends his fire to consume Elijah's holocaust, he finds himself justified to kill the prophets of Baal. So just as Elijah stood against the prophets of Baal, and Abel against Cain (Genesis 4:4–5), God's answer to the challenge proves Muhammad the true messenger of God. According to a tradition, Muhammad uses the situation in which the Christians from Najrān are not certain of their case to impose a tax on them.[8] Ostensibly this later tradition is used as a justification of a situation in which Christians recognise Muslims as their superiors by agreeing to pay the *jizya,* or poll tax. In the Qur'anic narrative, they turn away and evade the challenge. This evasion is evoked in the 'common word' verse once again: 'If they turn away, say: witness that we are those who have surrendered to God.'

Now that we have referred to the context of the 'common word' verse, according to the traditional Islamic sources, we will look more closely at

---

[6] See Mahmoud Ayoub, *The Qur'an and Its Interpreters,* Volume II: *The House of 'Imran* (Albany: State University of New York Press, 1992), p. 188.

[7] All the Biblical quotations in the present chapter are from the New American Bible. 'Lord' is the translation of the Hebrew word Adonai that is put in place of YHWH, the proper name of God in the Hebrew Bible.

[8] Guezzou, *Al-Wāḥidī's Asbāb al-Nuzūl,* p. 49.

the contents of this verse: to worship God alone, without ascribing any partners to Him, and to take none beside God as lords. In three different ways, the content of this verse repeats the central notion of *tawḥīd* in Islam: to affirm that God is one and only, that there can be no partners for God and that no one else can be Lord besides God. Relying on the context, it seems that this is the word that Muhammad enjoined upon the Christians of Najrān when they did not dare to enter into the contest. The famous Muslim exegete Abū Jaʿfar Muḥammad ibn Jarīr al-Ṭabarī (d. 923) relates a tradition which says: 'God commanded the Prophet, when the people of Najrān refused the *mubāhala*, to invite them instead to something easier.'[9] This is not a situation that calls for commonality between partners, but it calls for the verbal equivalent of the *jizya* tax: Christians are to recognise that Muhammad has spoken the truth about what it means to be *muslimūn*, those who submit themselves to God. If Christians and Muslims have a word in common here, it is because Christians accept that the Muslims have rightly confessed the true word of God's oneness. Therefore, Muslim exegetes refer to the Muslim proclamation of faith, or *shahāda*, as an explanation of what is meant here.

While the first two parts of this 'common word' are quite straightforward, the third part, about not taking others as lords, is more complicated. Again, Ṭabarī provides the classical explanation here, referring to 'the obedience which they accorded their leaders, and by which they committed acts of rebellion against God'.[10] As often this interpretation is derived from another Qur'anic verse, this time directed at both Jews and Christians: 'They took their rabbis and monks, as well as Christ, son of Mary, as lords instead of God' (Q 9:31). Another tradition, related by Abū ʿAbd Allāh Muḥammad al-Qurṭubī (d. 1273), states that Christians used to bow down before persons of high status, while according to Fakhr al-Dīn al-Rāzī (d. 1209), the verse implies three points on which the Christians have erred: 'They worship someone other than God, that is Christ. They associate others with Him, and that is because they say that God is three: Father, Son and Holy Spirit. They have affirmed three equal and eternal divine personalities.'[11] So, the first point refers to the Incarnation and the second to the Trinity. But the third point refers to holy persons who are said to be perfect spiritual beings,

---

[9] Ayoub, *The Qur'an and Its Interpreters II*, p. 202.
[10] Ibid., p. 203.
[11] Ibid., p. 206.

because 'the effects of divine indwelling (*ḥulūl*) appear in them', and are therefore considered to possess the attributes of lordship. Some Muslim exegetes, such as the traditionalist Ibn Kathīr (d. 1373), go further, stating that Christians worship the cross and other idols.[12] In his interpretation of this verse, twentieth-century political activist Abū l-Aʿlā Mawdūdī (d. 1979) elucidates the point, saying, 'The invitation here is for the two parties to agree on something believed in by one of them, the Muslims, and the soundness of which could hardly be denied by the other party, the Christians.'[13]

If the contents of the 'common word' verse are in fact Muslim positions formulated against Christians, how can we consider them to be a common word of agreement? The context of the refused ordeal implies that Muslims claim to be right and expect Christians to recognise that. But again, how can this call serve as a common ground between Muslims and Christians? Perhaps it is not meant to be the common ground; perhaps the translation of the Arabic word *sawāʾ* in the text of the Qurʾan is simply misleading. This leads us to the second part of this chapter.

A 'COMMON WORD' OR AN 'EQUITABLE WORD'?

The Arabic text of the 'common word' verse opens as follows: *Qul: Yā ahl al-kitāb; taʿālū ilā kalimatin sawāʾin baynanā wa-baynakum.* 'A common word' is the usual translation for the Arabic *kalima sawāʾ*. While the meaning of the *kalima* here is relatively clear, referring to a kind of statement, the word *sawāʾ* is unclear. It is derived from a root *s-w-y*, which means 'to be equal, to be equivalent, to be at the same level'. Hence 'equal' or 'even' is its basic meaning. But what does 'an equal word' or 'an equivalent word' mean? The translation 'a common word' suggests that there is something in common between the two parties, indicating that Christians and Muslims would be looking for common ground. Yet in my opinion, the expression 'equivalent word' may suggest that Christians are invited to come with a statement that is at the same level as the Muslim creed alluded to in this verse. In that case we would have not one common word, but two words from the two traditions that would

---

[12] *Al-Miṣbāḥ al-munīr fī tahdhīb Tafsīr Ibn Kathīr*, abridged and translated by a group of scholars under the supervision of Shaykh Safiur-Rahman al-Mubarakpuri (Riyadh: Darussalam, 2003), vol. 2, p. 181.

[13] Sayyid Abul Aʿlā Mawdūdī, *Towards Understanding the Qurʾān: English Version of Tafhīm al-Qurʾān*, trans. and ed. Zafar Ishaq Ansari (Leicester: Islamic Foundation, 1988), vol. 1, p. 262, fn. 57.

be at the same level. This appears to be a subtle difference, yet it is of significant importance for the hermeneutical consequences of interreligious dialogue between Muslims and Christians, since two equivalent words do not presuppose commonality but proportionality, as I will explain further later.

First, we note that this alternative interpretation is not unknown among Muslim commentators. One of the early commentators, Ṭabarī, mentioned earlier, says that the word *sawā'* means 'just'.[14] The rationalist interpreter Rāzī holds that 'just' means 'reasonable': it is a rational approach that is acceptable to anyone with sound reason.[15] Some of the modern translators suggest a similar meaning; for instance, the translation by Muhammad Muhsin Khan and Muhammad Taqi-ud-Din al-Hilali is 'come to a word that is just between us and you'.[16] Majid Fakhry's translation reads 'Come to an equitable word between you and me.'[17] The translation by M. H. Shakir has it as 'come to an equitable proposition between us and you'.[18] The translation by Maulana Muhammad Ali published by the Ahmadiyya community also reads 'come to an equitable word between us and you'.[19] Finally, the famous translator Muhammad Asad (Leopold Weiss) translates it as follows: 'come unto that tenet which we and you hold in common', but adds a footnote that says: 'Lit. "a word [that is] equitable between us and you".'[20] This possible interpretation is further supported by the fact that several Muslim commentators, such as Ṭabarī and Muḥammad al-Shawkānī (d. 1834), suggest that there is in fact a textual variant of this specific phrase that reads *kalimatu 'adl^{in}*, which means 'a word of justice'.[21] Zeki Saritoprak concludes that this interpretation, which connects the 'word of justice' with dialogue about

---

[14] Ayoub, *The Qur'an and Its Interpreters II*, p. 203.

[15] Ibid., p. 205.

[16] Muhammad Muhsin Khan and Muhammad Taqi ud-Din al-Hilali, *Interpretation of the Meanings of the Noble Qur'ān in the English Language* (Riyadh: Darussalam, 1996), p. 90.

[17] Majid Fakhry, *An Interpretation of the Qur'an* (New York: New York University Press, 2000), p. 62.

[18] M. H. Shakir, *The Qur'an Translated* (Elmhurst, NY: Tahrike Tarsile Qur'an, 2004), p. 51.

[19] Maulana Muhammad Ali, *The Holy Qur'ān: Arabic Text with English Translation and Commentary* (Dublin, OH: Ahmadiyya Anjuman Isha'at Islam Lahore, 2002), p. 155.

[20] Muhammad Asad, *The Message of the Qur'ān Translated and Explained* (Bristol: Book Foundation, 2003), vol. 1, p. 91.

[21] See Zeki Saritoprak, 'How commentators of the Qur'an define "Common Word,"' in John Borelli (ed.), *A Common Word and the Future of Christian–Muslim Relations* (Washington, DC: Prince Alwaleed Bin Talal Center for Muslim–Christian Understanding, 2009), pp. 34–45, at p. 40.

questions of righteousness and justice, might be of particular importance for contemporary Muslim–Christian and Muslim–Jewish dialogue. In a personal correspondence, my friend and mentor David Burrell, who keeps reminding me of the importance of the ACW process, suggested 'appropriate (statement)' and 'apposite (statement)' as alternative translations. Now, we can turn to the hermeneutical consequences of these translations, and how these may influence the ACW initiative.

TWO – OR THREE – HERMENEUTICAL APPROACHES TO DIALOGUE

As I discussed earlier, the idea of 'a common word' between Muslims and Christians is based on a text from the Qur'an, associated with the visit of a Christian delegation from Najrān that ended with the Prophet Muhammad's call to come to 'a common word'. We have seen how this encounter may be characterised as a form of dialogue with polemical elements. In some Muslim sources, the verse is understood as an invitation to embrace Islam. We find such interpretation in the commentaries of Ibn Kathīr or Mawdūdī, an interpretation that posits the word or statement in question clearly on the side of the Muslim tradition. But this interpretation will not further dialogue between Muslims and Christians, and is not in agreement with the declared intention of the authors behind the ACW document.

The second possible interpretation is the most common among present-day Muslims, and is also the interpretation intended by the authors of the ACW document. This hermeneutical stance posits an area of overlap between the two traditions of Islam and Christianity, and is therefore often interpreted as 'a common ground'. This particular interpretation is apt to contribute to dialogue between Muslims and Christians for those who are willing to agree with the supposition that there is a common ground between the two religions involved. While that may be true for many Christians involved in dialogue with Muslims, it is questionable whether this can be said of the majority of mainstream Christians who are not directly involved in the ACW process. In fact, this particular interpretation of the Qur'anic verse as seeking a common ground may hinder them from participating in that process, because they are not willing to admit in advance that there is a common ground between Christianity and Islam. In a different context, I explained how this reluctance to acknowledge a common ground may elucidate the Vatican's hesitancy to react to the document; famously Cardinal Jean-Louis Pierre Tauran (at the time of writing the president of the Pontifical Council for Interreligious Dialogue) suggested that a theological dialogue with Islam would not be possible, as long as Muslims did not admit the possibility of critical approaches to the Qur'an.[22] After six months of silence, the Vatican proposed a Catholic–Muslim Forum based on common ethical principles such as human dignity, the value of human life and freedom of religion.[23] Thus, the Vatican seems to prefer a dialogue on the basis of common ethical values, which can be seen as a form of 'common word' between Catholics and Muslims, which is different from the content suggested by the Muslim authors of the *ACW* declaration: love of God and love of neighbour.

Yet one may argue for a third hermeneutical approach. It is my contention that this approach may give us a better starting point for Christian–Muslim dialogue, since it does not posit a common ground as the basis for dialogue between Muslims and Christians, but suggests that both traditions may find a *kalima sawā'* in their own treasures. Accordingly, one tradition would challenge the other to find an equitable or a just statement. In the case of the 'common word' verse, the interpretation I advocate does not suggest that Christians agree with the Muslim creed (the first hermeneutical approach), nor that they find common ground in loving God and neighbour (the second hermeneutical approach), but that they look for a statement that has a similar function for them as the statement 'we worship God alone, we ascribe no partner to Him, and none of us takes others beside God as lords' has for Muslims. This particular hermeneutical approach would validate any statement by Christians which recognised the oneness of God but at the same time expressed the uniqueness of the Christian faith as an equitable statement. I would propose that the beginning of the Gospel according to John, 'In the beginning was the Word, and the Word was with God, and the Word was God' (John 1:1), may serve as such an equitable statement, as it expresses Christian faith in the Triune God without unnecessarily introducing terminology that would be problematic for Muslims to accept.[24]

---

[22] From an interview with Cardinal Tauran in the French daily *La Croix*, as released by Zenit.org, 19 October 2007. www.acommonword.com/cardinal-praises-muslims-for-eloquent-letter/. Accessed 3 September 2016.

[23] See Pim Valkenberg, 'Moslims & Christenen: Een gemeenschappelijk word?' *Tijdschrift voor Theologie*, 50 (2010), 273–84 (summary p. 285). See also Joseph Lumbard, 'The uncommonality of "A Common Word"', *A Common Word Between Us and You: 5-Year Anniversary Edition* (Amman: Royal Aal Al-Bayt Institute for Islamic Thought, 2012), pp. 11–50, at p. 17.

[24] For reflections on the possible role of Johannine theology in Christian–Muslim dialogue, see Daniel A. Madigan SJ, 'Particularity, universality, and finality: insights from

However, John 3:14, 'God so loved the world that he gave his only Son, so that everyone who believes in him might not perish but might have eternal life', would cause difficulties. I do not suggest that the first statement is somehow better than the second, but that it *functions* better as an equitable statement, following this third hermeneutical approach to the 'common word' Qur'anic verse (Q 3:64).

Proposing this hermeneutical approach, I am also taking my lead from the fifteenth-century cardinal Nicholas of Cusa (d. 1464), who tried to interpret the Qur'an in such a way that it would give glory to God without detracting from Christ.[25] He interprets the Muslim critique implied in the 'common word' verse as encouraging Christians to speak about the Trinity in such a way that it does not imply any family relationship or heavenly association.[26] When talking about the Trinity, Christians should avoid language that can easily be misunderstood, not only by Muslims but also by other Christians. We know that some of the most common terms, such as 'Father' and 'Son' but also 'person', are likely to be misunderstood, and therefore we should be careful not to raise any unnecessary obstacles in dialogue. I do not suggest that we should not employ these words, but rather that we should use them wisely and appropriately; and in my view, that is exactly the meaning of *kalima sawā'* in Q 3:64. Let me quote the contemporary Muslim theologian Joseph Lumbard on this:

[ACW] does not seek to syncretize or to proselytize. Participants in this initiative have even taken pains to emphasize the need for recognizing the fundamental differences between the two traditions. Rather than watering down theological positions in the name of cooperation and thus bringing Christian and Muslim communities together at their margins, it asks both communities to speak from what is central and authoritative to each.[27]

the Gospel of John', in David Marshall (ed.), *Communicating the Word: Revelation, Translation, and Interpretation in Christianity and Islam* (Washington, DC: Georgetown University Press, 2011), pp. 14–25.

[25] See Jasper Hopkins, 'The role of *pia interpretatio* in Nicholas of Cusa's hermeneutical approach to the Koran', in *A Miscellany on Nicholas of Cusa* (Minneapolis: Arthur J. Banning Press, 1994), pp. 39–55. Quoted in Pim Valkenberg, 'Learned ignorance and faithful interpretation of the Qur'an in Nicholas of Cusa (1401–1464)', in James Heft, Reuven Firestone and Omid Safi (eds.), *Learned Ignorance: Intellectual Humility among Jews, Christians, and Muslims* (Oxford: Oxford University Press, 2011), pp. 34–52.

[26] Nicholas of Cusa, *De pace fidei* 9, quoted in Valkenberg, 'Learned ignorance and faithful interpretation', p. 43.

[27] Lumbard, 'The uncommonality of "A Common Word"', p. 22.

This sums up well my proposed third hermeneutical approach: to propose something from the centre of one's own tradition that would serve as an equitable word to the word proposed by the other tradition.

As a final remark, I would like to emphasise once again an alternative reading of the text: 'a word of justice'. This translation may open up new possibilities for a dialogue between Muslims and Christians that centres on matters of peace and justice rather than on dogmatic statements. I know that dialogues on social justice are often more fruitful than theological dialogues, and I can see how these are a form of dialogue that helps those who are in minority situations – whether that be the Muslims in the United States or the Christians in the Middle East – more than verbal exchanges do. So I suggest this as a further elaboration of the possible meanings of the *ACW* verse without embarking on detailed explanation here.

THE *A COMMON WORD* PROCESS IN THE NETHERLANDS

The *ACW* document has not experienced a rich history of reception in the Netherlands, which is presumably the case in most other European countries. If there is anything remarkable about this limited reception in the Netherlands, it is the ambivalence with which the text was received by mainstream Protestants in this country, including those who are engaged in Christian–Muslim dialogue. A good example of this ambiguity is an open letter from a number of Protestant pastors and theologians to the synod of the (united) Protestant Church in the Netherlands, on the occasion of a rumour that this synod would publish a largely positive response to *ACW*.[28] This open letter interprets the *ACW* initiative as presupposing a common ground between Muslims and Christians.

The authors of the open letter developed three kinds of objections to this idea of a common ground between the two religions: a practical, a procedural and a theological objection. Their practical objection is that we should not seek commonality with Islam as long as there is no guaranteed freedom of religion for Christians in Muslim-majority countries. The procedural objection is the absence of Judaism as the third partner in this

---

[28] The text of this open letter and a number of responses have been published by the periodical *Begrip Moslims Christenen* in 2009 as volume 35/4. Before that, the same periodical had published the text of the *ACW* document in a Dutch translation with some responses in volume 33/4-5.

conversation – this objection is related to the specific place of Israel in the official founding documents of the Dutch United Protestant Church, which state that 'the church is called to implement its irrevocable bond with the people of Israel'.[29] Finally, the theological objection is to the presupposition that Muslims and Christians worship the same God. It is true that the theological discussion about whether Christians, Jews and Muslims worship the same God has a long history and a notable presence in the actual theological arena.[30] This discussion will go on for a long time – probably as long as the religions involved exist.[31]

Yet, the Dutch open letter shows that it is the presupposition of the common ground that makes the *ACW* document unacceptable not only for Evangelicals and Israel-oriented Christians, but also for a good number of mainline Protestants. My suggestion is that a different interpretation of the document, as not presuming a common ground but leaving room for an 'equitable word' or a 'word of justice' from the centre of Christian theology, might help in the process of creating greater reception of the document. If Joseph Lumbard's suggestion (above) stands, there is no need to water down the differences between the two religions in order for them to collaborate practically as well as theologically.

---

[29] See *Kerkorde van de Protestantse Kerk in Nederland,* first article, section 7: 'De kerk is geroepen gestalte te geven aan haar onopgeefbare verbondenheid met het volk Israel'. www.protestantsekerk.nl/Lists/PKN-Bibliotheek/Kerkorde-en-Ordinanties-PKN-originele-versie-2004.pdf. Accessed 3 September 2016.

[30] At the annual meeting of the American Academy of Religion in 2012, two books were advertised with almost the same title: Jacob Neusner, Baruch Levine, Bruce Chilton and Vincent Cornell (eds.), *Do Jews, Christians and Muslims Worship the Same God?* (Nashville, TN: Abingdon, 2012), and Miroslav Volf (ed.), *Do We Worship the Same God? Jews, Christians and Muslims in Dialogue* (Grand Rapids, MI: Eerdmans, 2012).

[31] My own contribution to this ongoing discussion is published as 'God(s) of Abraham: sibling rivalry among three faiths', *Christian Century,* 21 June 2016. http://christiancentury.org/article/2016-06/gods-abraham. Accessed 7 September 2016.

The Use of Christian Scripture in *A Common Word*

Clare Amos

As part of my work for the World Council of Churches, where I was until December 2017 Programme Coordinator for Interreligious Dialogue and Cooperation, I helped to run, each summer, a course which brings together young Jews, Christians and Muslims, to study together and, as the course publicity puts it, 'build an interfaith community'. It is held at the Ecumenical Institute at Bossey in Switzerland and lasts for three weeks. One of the elements which I have been responsible for introducing into the course is the practice of 'Scriptural Reasoning'. This is an activity which has become quite widespread in interreligious circles over the last twenty years. In a Scriptural Reasoning session a theme, which can be either practical or more explicitly theological, is chosen. An example of the first could be 'water', of the second 'the understanding of God'. Then scriptural texts are chosen to illustrate the theme. Normally a Scriptural Reasoning group includes Jews, Christians and Muslims, so the scriptural texts would come from the Tanakh (Hebrew Bible), the Christian Bible and the Qur'an. Sometimes not all three Abrahamic faiths are represented, in which case the selection of scriptural texts is more restricted; conversely there has been the desire in recent years to open up the practice of Scriptural Reasoning to members of the Hindu or Buddhist faiths, which then leads to the inclusion of texts from the Vedas, for example. During the session each scriptural text in turn is briefly introduced by a participant from that religious tradition. The texts then provide the launch pad for a discussion of the topic in question.[1]

---

[1] For more information about the practice of Scriptural Reasoning, see the website www .scripturalreasoning.org, which has links with the Cambridge Interfaith Programme

The introduction of this practice of Scriptural Reasoning as part of the Bossey Interreligious Course has been a clear success. I think it is because it enables the participants to engage with each other on topics of mutual concern, in a way that they feel honours and takes seriously their own sacred texts. It holds together the importance of one's own religious particularity and a willingness to be open to the insights of those of other religious traditions. It also, incidentally, prompts a number of other scripture-related discussions, such as the ambivalence about the common ownership of the Hebrew Bible/Old Testament by Jews and Christians, and whether or not texts drawn from the Hadith or prophetic tradition in Islam and rabbinic sources in Judaism should be included within the scriptural texts selected to represent each religious tradition.

The comparison between this practice of Scriptural Reasoning and the development of *A Common Word* has been made by a number of scholars and interreligious practitioners.[2] This is not surprising, as many of those who have been influential in the development and spread of Scriptural Reasoning are also personally linked to the circle around Prince Ghazi bin Muhammad of Jordan, who is recognised as the prime mover in the publication of *ACW*. For example, Dr Aref Ali Nayed, who was influential in the process leading to the publication of *ACW*, published shortly after its appearance an article in which he referred to the document as an example of 'dialogical scriptural reasoning'.[3] To what extent is this comparison justified? How far does the use of scripture in *ACW* reflect the thinking behind the development of Scriptural Reasoning? The starting point for the verbal presentation made in Dublin in December 2013, on which this chapter is based, was a wrestling with the issue of the similarities and differences between the understanding of scripture in Scriptural Reasoning and in *ACW*. However, both in my verbal presentation and in this chapter I have found myself needing to range more widely, touching on a number of concerns. Ultimately, therefore, this chapter seeks to explore key issues relating to the use of Christian scripture in *ACW*.

(CIP). Accessed 18 September 2016. CIP has been instrumental in introducing Scriptural Reasoning within the United Kingdom context as well as worldwide through its international summer schools, academic conferences and public events.

[2] See for example Edward Pentin, 'A scriptural round table of Jews, Muslims and Christians', 5 April 2011. www.terrasanta.net/tsx/articolo.jsp?wi_number=2959&wi_codseq=%20%20%20%20%20%20&language=en. Accessed 18 September 2016.

[3] Aref Ali Nayed, 'The promise of "A Common Word"', October 2007. www.interfaith.cam.ac.uk/resources/acommonword/thepromiseofacommonword. Accessed 18 September 2016.

Although I also touch briefly on the way Muslim scriptural texts are used, that is not my main purpose in this exploration.

It is appropriate to begin by expressing my appreciation for the creative and committed work which went into the publication and distribution of *ACW*. In his response to the document, the former Archbishop of Canterbury, Rowan Williams, rightly referred to a 'helpful generosity of intention'.[4] For several reasons, it is a really significant step in terms of Christian–Muslim relations, as many others have acknowledged. First, it is clearly a Muslim initiative; in many Christian eyes, at least in modern times, it is generally perceived that it is Christians rather than Muslims who have taken the initiative for dialogue between Christianity and Islam. Indeed, Michael Louis Fitzgerald has outlined the many Catholic initiatives we had in the twentieth century up to the time of *ACW*.[5] Second, and more importantly, it takes seriously the need for theological dialogue and reflection as part of a wider interreligious engagement. I have participated in too many interreligious meetings in which it has been blandly stated that 'we are not here for theological dialogue, we only want to dialogue about practical and social concerns, and issues of peace and justice'. When that is said, it is generally a signal that the discussion over the next couple of days is going to end up feeling rather shallow and unsatisfactory. From my perspective as a Christian I cannot, and do not want to, separate the theological from the practical: the one I believe necessarily flows from the other, ethics stems out of doctrine, and the two must not be separated. The pattern of Paul's letters, in which theological and Christological grounding is set out, and then followed by a 'therefore' and some key ethical consequences, is, I believe, a fundamental paradigm. So I genuinely give thanks for the breakthrough offered by *ACW* in its insistence that, though 'the future of the world depends on peace between Muslims and Christians' means that questing together for peace is important, that quest has also to be grounded in the 'foundational principles of both faiths',[6] which are explored in the document.

Third, I appreciate the basic courtesy with which Christian scripture has been treated in the document. We have moved far away from the unhelpful polemics engendered when Muslims sought to engage with Christians on the basis of the so-called Gospel of Barnabas, which most

---

[4] Chapter 4 in this volume.
[5] Chapter 3 in this volume.
[6] *A Common Word* (English version), p. 2. All page references to *A Common Word* are taken from the pdf download available on the *ACW* website: www.acommonword.com/downloads-and-translations/.

mainstream Christian thinkers would discount as a medieval forgery. The Gospel of Barnabas is simply ignored in and absent from *ACW*, which is, I think, the right way forward. The choice of the translation used for Christian scriptural texts is clearly intended to suggest a mark of respect for these scriptures: in the English version of *ACW* it is the New King James Bible, which conveys somehow a sense of the sacredness of the text, even though it also has an archaising feel. The English translation (paraphrase) of the Qur'an which is used in the document, that of Muhammad Marmaduke Pickthall, *The Glorious Qur'an*, has a similar archaic feel. I will return to the question of Bible translations later. One interesting feature to notice in relation to the document is that the language of the key subheadings of the document, *Love of God* and *Love of the Neighbour*, appears as if taken from the primary Christian texts quoted, rather than the Muslim ones. Indeed the concepts *Love of God* and *Love of the Neighbour* on which the document is centred appear much more obviously and overtly in Christian than in Muslim scripture. Seeking to read the document with an objective eye one feels compelled to say that the synthesising of the Qur'anic texts on pages 4–8 of the document under the heading *Love of God in Islam* seems to be somewhat forced and to result from the a priori decision to use the expression in order to match up with its Christian equivalent. Similarly, the section headed *Love of the Neighbour in Islam* on page 11 is expounded by four Muslim texts in which the word 'neighbour' appears only once, and though the word 'love' appears three times, in no case does it have 'neighbour', or indeed a human person, as its direct object.

As for the Christian texts used in the document, the key Biblical passage quoted is the discussion between Jesus and the scribe/Pharisee/lawyer about the greatest commandment in the Law, in the versions appearing in Matthew 22:34–40 and Mark 12:28–31. Both the Marcan and the Matthean versions of this discussion are quoted, either in part or in whole, more than once at different points in *ACW*. Deuteronomy 6:4–5, which is actually referenced in Mark 12:29, is also used, as is Leviticus 19:18, which is referenced in both Mark 12:31 and Matthew 22:39. Biblical references are given to eight texts in Deuteronomy, and one in the Book of Joshua, which command the love of God, and to the Lucan parallel to Mark 12 and Matthew 22; however, with the exception of Joshua 22 none of the texts to which the references allude to is actually quoted.

Rather separately, in a brief final section of the document three New Testament texts are quoted, one each from Matthew (12:30), Mark (9:40) and Luke (9:50), which relate to the issue of those who are 'for' or 'against' us. The 'us' here presumably refers to the Christian community. *ACW* explores briefly how these texts, which are apparently contradictory – with Mark and Luke agreeing with each other against Matthew – can somehow be synthesised. Then in the penultimate paragraph of the document, Matthew 5:9 and 16:26, 'Blessed are the peacemakers' and 'What profit is it to a man if he gains the whole world and loses his soul?' are used, though not really to argue a substantive point.

It is worth noting that, unlike Qur'anic quotations, which are normatively introduced by the phrase 'God says' or 'God says in the Holy Qur'an', none of the Biblical texts is introduced by the phrase 'God says'. Those from the Gospels which are apparent quotations of the words of Christ are introduced by the expression 'Jesus Christ said' or 'Jesus Christ the Messiah said', which parallel the way that Muslim texts from the Hadith are introduced, 'the Prophet Muḥammad said'. From a Christian scriptural perspective that is not intrinsically problematic. Indeed it is worth noting that when Jesus Christ is mentioned in this way, his name is accompanied by the reverential Arabic sign denoting a prophet. Perhaps more questionable, however, is the clear determination of *ACW* not to introduce the Old Testament texts – particularly that from Leviticus which is presented in its Biblical context as the direct words of God – with the expression 'God says'. The words of introduction to the Leviticus text, 'It remains only to be noted that this commandment is also to be found in the Old Testament',[7] seem designed to evade this sensitive issue.

To begin by exploring the texts which focus on the Great Commandment, I was intrigued why two versions of Jesus' discussion were quoted one after another, those from Matthew and Mark. It is, I think, because of the subtle differences in the two versions, which mean that for the purposes of the authors of *ACW*, elements of both texts are needed to support their argument. Although the central focus of both the Matthean and Marcan texts is on loving God and loving the neighbour, it is Matthew alone who ends the discussion with the pronouncement of Jesus, 'On these two commandments hang all the Law and the Prophets' (Matthew 22:40). This sentence is clearly important for the argument of the authors of *ACW*, since it reinforces the centrality of the two commandments at the heart of scripture. It is used for that purpose in the third and concluding section of the document.[8] On the other hand, and perhaps surprisingly,

[7] *ACW*, p. 12.
[8] Ibid., p. 15.

Mark, unlike Matthew, prefaces the first commandment mandating love of God with the opening sentence of the *Shema*, 'Hear, O Israel, the Lord our God the Lord is One', which of course also prefaces this commandment within the Book of Deuteronomy. And this is clearly also important in the minds of the authors, for their premise is that the requirement to love God and neighbour is ultimately founded upon the essential unity of God. From a Christian perspective, however, the willingness to set the text of one Gospel alongside another, and the combining of their separate emphases somehow into one, smack of a harmonising tendency within scripture.

The amount of attention and discussion given on page 9 of the document to the anthropological vocabulary of love within the Biblical text, 'with heart and soul and mind and strength', can feel puzzling to some Christian readers. In the Biblical text, both in the New Testament and in Deuteronomy, the words seem primarily designed simply for emphasis. At this point, however, one needs to read back into the previous Islamic section of the document, where connections are made between the 'complete and utter devotion to God', exemplified by linking it to human intelligence and will as well as feeling and emotion, and the unity of God, exemplified by the explicit belief that God has no partner or associate.[9] It would seem that this argument from the Islamic section has then been carried over into the discussion about Christian texts. Here it feels somewhat forced and constrained by the Muslim parallel: although *ACW* describes the unity of God as 'prefacing' the two commandments and being the ground that 'they arise out of', in Christian eyes there is not quite the same intrinsic connection between these two elements, unity and love.

Perhaps what is equally significant, however, is what is not said or included within *ACW*. In some ways, it might be seen as surprising that the parallel to Matthew 22:34–40 and Mark 12:28–34 found in Luke 10:25–8 is not spelt out in the text in more detail, because its link to the parable of the Good Samaritan which immediately follows offers a powerful practical and narrative example of what is meant by the love of neighbour. However, it also raises rather too sharply the question as to whether, in the eyes of the authors of *ACW*, the neighbour is the one like us or the one not like us. That question has exercised a number of Arab Christians in particular: are they considered as 'neighbours' in the fullest sense by Muslims in Middle Eastern societies? Nor is the scribe's response,

[9] Ibid., pp. 4–8.

Mark 12:31–4, to Jesus' instruction in Mark 12:28–31 included among the Biblical quotations given in full in the document. This is perhaps surprising as the scribe's response begins by picking up on the *Shema* and strenuously asserting that 'God is one', which on the surface at least fits in well with the stress on the unity of God in *ACW*. But, I suspect that the primary reason why not much attention is given to Luke or this second half of Mark is that the words come out of the mouth of the scribe or lawyer rather than out of the mouth of Jesus.

At a conference titled 'Transforming Communities: Christians and Muslims Building a Common Future' in Geneva in November 2010 under the auspices of the World Council of Churches, the Royal Jordanian Aal Al-Bayt Institute and the World Islamic Call Society,[10] in which I was asked to address the issue of education in the Christian tradition, I noticed this and commented that in a number of religious cultures the educational philosophy, and perhaps even the philosophy of revelation, was considerably more didactic than it was in the Christian West. As I commented then – and my comments were deliberately posed as questions rather than assertions – 'Is it characteristic of a Christian understanding that I should rejoice, both spiritually and educationally, in the fact that there are these three different descriptions of the encounter between Jesus and his dialogue partner, and that these include a description of the scribe as his own teacher? Is it also significant that *ACW* should choose to focus on the descriptions given in Matthew and Mark of Jesus instructing the scribe, but omit the Lucan and Marcan portrayals of the scribe coming to discover this for himself through his encounter with Jesus?'[11]

But the most significant scriptural omissions from *ACW* are the parts of the New Testament which do not appear in the document at all, and which are not even referenced. I am thinking especially of the Gospel of John, the first letter of John and the Pauline corpus. In purely numerical terms both are startling omissions. A quick search for the word 'love' in the NRSV on the Oremus Bible browser suggests that the word 'love' appears thirty-nine times in the Gospel of John, over against thirty-six in the three synoptic gospels put together. In the comparatively short first letter of John alone there are thirty instances of the word. The situation as regards Paul's letters is more complicated, because of the dispute among

[10] For further information on the conference and the papers presented, see muslimsandchristians.net. Accessed 18 September 2016.

[11] Clare Amos, 'Education, education and education', 3 November 2010. http:// muslimsandchristians.net/documents/EducationClareAmos.pdf. Accessed 18 September 2016.

Christian scholars as to which of the letters ascribed to Paul were actually written by him, but even taking a super-minimalist position which sees only Romans, Galatians and the two Corinthian epistles as genuinely his, there are sixty instances of the word 'love' in these four letters.

Given the basic premise of *ACW* of the centrality of the love of God and neighbour in Christian faith it is perhaps surprising, therefore, that texts from Paul and John should be excluded in this way. However, this omission is almost certainly due to two interlocking factors. The first is the Christological lens without which Paul and John cannot be read; the second is in both sets of writings the affirmation that our love of God is a response to the fact that God first loved us – an affirmation explicitly made in 1 John 4:19 and implied elsewhere in the writings of John and Paul, which are further commented on in Daniel A. Madigan's chapter.[12] For Christians the phrase 'Love of God' is a subjective genitive before it is an objective genitive. I suspect that both affirmations are ones which the writers of *ACW* would find difficult to acknowledge explicitly in a document which, though ostensibly addressed to a Christian audience, was undoubtedly written with one eye on their Muslim co-religionists. The paucity of Christology in *ACW* – in which effectively Jesus is simply presented as a messenger of God's Law – has been commented on by others. Sarah Snyder's chapter points to some of these Christian responses.[13]

With my focus being on scripture in this chapter, I want, however, to address a relevant issue, namely, that a key hermeneutical principle for the Christian interpretation of the Bible is that it needs to be understood 'incarnationally'. And by that I do not mean, at least primarily, that all texts should be interpreted with a Christological focus, though of course there has been a long and venerable tradition within Christianity that has done precisely that. It is rather that there needs to be an interplay rather than a separation between humanity and divinity, and that this dialogue enriches our understanding both of God and of human beings. Indeed, I would suggest that dialogue and duality are characteristic of an incarnational frame of understanding. For example, that model of teaching to which I referred earlier, in which one is not so much taught didactically as encouraged to discover wisdom for oneself through encounter with another, is an incarnational model of learning. The willingness of most modern Christian Biblical scholars to take seriously the

[12] Chapter 10 in this volume.
[13] Chapter 7 in this volume.

importance of context and process in the development of the Bible, so that we can rejoice over and honour the insights that Mark or Matthew themselves have fed into the gospels which bear their name, is also an example of an incarnational spirit. In my opinion, however, this is an area where the writers of *ACW* would be very nervous to tread. For our present purposes – perhaps most important of all – an incarnational framework refuses to separate out love of God from love of humanity, precisely because we are required to see the face of God in our brother and sister and even our neighbour. It is expressed eloquently at several points in 1 John, in particular, 'Those who do not love a brother or sister whom they have seen, cannot love God whom they have not seen' (1 John 4:20). That is a foundational principle of Christian theology which the authors of *ACW* may find problematic to come to terms with; at least it is not really reflected within the document. Yet it is perhaps the other side of the coin to a Muslim insistence on the unity of God. On page 13, *ACW* states categorically: 'Thus the Unity of God, love of him and love of the neighbour form a common ground upon which Islam and Christianity (and Judaism) are founded.' However, a Christian understanding of divine unity, and indeed what is meant in Mark 12:32 when the scribe states that God is one, is that the love of God and the love of neighbour are not two separate and potentially competitive commandments, but complementary aspects of the one reality.

Perhaps the most obvious point where *ACW*'s use of Christian scripture appears forced to many Christian eyes, partly as a result of the framework in which the document's authors are working, comes on page 15 when three Biblical quotations are drawn on to answer the question as to whether Christianity is necessarily opposed to Muslims. The first quotation, from Matthew 12:30, states that 'he who is not with me is against me'; the following two, from Mark 9:40 and Luke 9:50, state that 'he who is not against us is on our side'. The text of *ACW* then goes on to state, 'According to the Blessed Theophylact's Explanation of the New Testament, these statements are not contradictions because the first statement refers to demons, whereas the second and third statements refer to people who recognised Jesus, but were not Christians.' While acknowledging that the different texts present problems of interpretation, many Christian scholars today would rather speak about the possibility of paradox and the different contexts of the three Gospel writers than call upon the Blessed Theophylact, who actually lived between 1055 and 1108 CE and is therefore hardly an early source to resolve the untidiness of Christian scripture.

There are two other brief, but intriguing, details relating to *ACW*'s understanding and use of Christian scripture. The first is the headings of the subsections 'Love of God as the First and Greatest Commandment in the Bible' and 'Love of the Neighbour in the Bible'. In both instances, in the Arabic version of the document the expression used to translate 'the Bible' is not *al-Kitāb al-muqaddas* but *al-Injīl*, the Muslim expression for the Gospel. Yet both subsections actually draw upon Old Testament as well as New Testament texts, so the *Injīl* does not seem a totally appropriate expression to use in this instance. Perhaps it leaves us with the feeling that the authors of *ACW* are a little uncomfortable with the messiness of the Christian understanding of scripture, which sees the Old Testament as part of Christian scripture and at the same time acknowledges that the Hebrew Bible is the scripture of Judaism.

The second comment is partly a question. As mentioned previously, the English version of *ACW* uses the New King James Version for its Biblical quotations. The archaising feel of this particular Biblical translation somehow fits in with the sense that the document wants to keep incarnation at a distance. In note 15, the document acknowledges its use of the New King James Version. It is surprising to see that in the Arabic and French versions of the document note 15 says (in Arabic and French, respectively), 'Herein all Biblical scripture is taken from the New King James Version.' In other words, it is an exact translation of the English note. So, either the note is wrong, or what we have in *ACW* is a translation into Arabic and French of the New King James Version by the authors of the document.[14] My perception is that it is the latter, so that rather than choosing an accepted and published Arabic or French translation of the Bible for the Biblical quotations, the authors have made their own Biblical translation from an English version of the Bible.[15] It would be an understatement to say that a Christian author of *ACW* would have done things differently, and would have chosen an already published translation for Biblical quotations in the Arabic and French (and other language) versions of the document. The fact that many Muslims and Christians would deal differently with this issue of translation in relation to the Bible seems to be not accidental, but rather rooted in what Andrew Walls calls the 'translation principle', which he considers fundamental to

[14] As checked against the Arabic and French translations of the document at www .acommonword.com. Accessed 6 January 2016.

[15] This of course raises the question as to what language *ACW* was originally written in, but as Tim Winter points out in Chapter 1 of this volume, it was English first rather than Arabic. See Chapter 1 in this volume.

Christianity,[16] and which for Walls is rooted in the Christian doctrine of incarnation.[17]

I began by raising the question of a possible relationship between *ACW* and the practice of Scriptural Reasoning. In the final analysis, there seems to be one fundamental difference between the practice of Scriptural Reasoning and *ACW*'s use of Christian scripture. A principle of Scriptural Reasoning is that the adherents of a faith should be its primary interpreters, even though they then need to share their scriptures with the 'Other', letting the 'Other' read, learning from their insights, and reflecting together in a dialogical conversation. That dialogical sense of exploration of scripture is not quite present in *ACW*. Perhaps for all its value – and I genuinely do believe that there is much of importance within it – my final question about *ACW* would be whether it skates too much over the real differences between our faiths, not least the different understanding of revelation and the nature of scriptural authority; this question reflects Daniel A. Madigan's critique of *ACW* as espousing a reductionist reading of the scripture.

The *ACW* document several times draws on the Qur'an to address the Christian community as 'People of the Scripture'. But the very fact that it does so in such a way perhaps raises the fundamental question which Christians themselves need to reflect on in their dialogue with Islam, as to how similar (or otherwise) Christianity and Islam are in the role that their respective scriptures are called to play within the community of faith. Ironically, perhaps it is the attempt on the part of *ACW* to seek theological similarities that may raise questions in some Christian minds. In this regard, the former archbishop of Canterbury, Dr Rowan Williams, in a lecture given in Birmingham University in 2003 spoke eloquently of the joy of difference:

We have to see how very other our universes are; and only then do we find dialogue a surprise and a joy as we discover where and how we can still talk about what really matters most – holiness, being at peace, and what truly is.[18]

---

[16] 'The translation principle in Christian history', in Andrew F. Walls, *The Missionary Movement in Christian History: Studies in the Transmission of Faith* (Maryknoll, NY: Orbis Books, 2005), pp. 26–42.

[17] 'Incarnation is translation. When God in Christ became man [sic], Divinity was translated into humanity, as though humanity were a receptor language' (from 'The Ephesian moment', in Andrew F. Walls, *The Cross-Cultural Process in Christian History* (Maryknoll, NY: Orbis, 2002), pp. 72–81, at p. 79).

[18] Rowan Williams, 'Christian theology and other faiths', 11 June 2003. http://rowanwilliams.archbishopofcanterbury.org/articles.php/1825/christian-theology-and-other-faiths. Accessed 2 September 2016.

PART IV

THE RECEPTION OF *A COMMON WORD*

13

A *Common Word* as Potentially Reflected in Different Languages

Rusmir Mahmutćehajić

INTRODUCTION

Even a cursory glance through archives and libraries whose origins and dissemination belong to the period of ever-faster multiplication of the written word brings to light any number of texts of general invocation to good or evil will towards others, of approval or denigration, justification or condemnation of individuals as the 'Other' in terms of their belonging or not-belonging. One might define the book as a higher form of written public address that connects an author with readers who are strangers to him or her. The open letter entitled *A Common Word between Us and You* and signed on 13 October 2007 by 138 Muslim intellectuals, was originally and primarily directed towards the Christians of the contemporary world. Its authors were united in their intention of speaking out on matters of importance to humanity as a whole and, in particular, on the hostile and threatening representations held by Christians of Muslims and by Muslims of Christians.

In the letter, the signatories stake a clear claim to speak on behalf of a part of humanity, a part that defines itself through its link to revelation through the prophet known as the Praised. They also make clear that they consider themselves and their letter as primarily addressing another part of humanity, namely, the heirs to the revelations contained in the Torah and the gospels. Finally, they make clear that, in their view, all these sacred traditions carry within themselves principles that offer grounds for mutual respect, solidarity and relations that protect the dignity of the individual from any form of supposedly justified infringement or violation. The word they invoke as common to both sides in this conversation transcends any differences between the sides and is, as a matter of absolute necessity, immanent in every aspect of our shared humanity – of human nature.

Neither of the labels deployed in the letter, of Muslims or of Christians, the 'us' and 'you', respectively, can be considered firmly grounded in a closed or totalising representation based exclusively on instrumental reason (as opposed to transcendentally grounded intellect). These 'identities' are, of course, treated in discussion as though they were clearly bounded conceptual entities, incorporating strict, and at times strictly policed, propositional systems, but such reductive treatment does not actually make them so. They are always more than any given representation of them. How do Muslims view Christians and how do Christians view Muslims? At first glance, this question may not appear a particularly difficult one to answer clearly and unambiguously. Any attempt to do so, however, soon finds itself struggling with modern ideas of the collective as transcending the individual and so has difficulty distinguishing clearly between what is essentially modern in these ascribed identities and what is essentially traditional.

It is important to remember that concepts and ideas have no existence beyond the concrete and living individual. This is in spite of the many ways in which modern scientific concepts and the associated propositional systems are made to appear to exist quite independently of the individual. For such world images, knowledge is presented as an external and self-sufficient entity, increasing independently from generation to generation, so that humanity itself is realised as a dependent variable of the growth of knowledge in history, leaving no room in the teleology for the concrete individual. From this perspective, rightness is simply de-anthropologised knowledge.

In truth, however, a concept exists only as reflected in a concrete self, in a self that bears it. It is always a matter of a representation held by a concrete self. And each self has a right to its representations and needs them if it is to be functional. One may fairly say that there are as many representations as there are selves, or more, indeed. This is not least because each individual consciousness is itself in ceaseless flux, rendering it consciously different from moment to moment. Moreover, no self is surplus to requirements. Each self has its own, inalienable role to play in the revelation of the First and the Last, the reason and purpose of all things. For did not God say to all people, through His prophet, the Praised, 'Truly, I have put my trust in God, my Lord and your Lord; there is no creature that crawls, but He takes it by the forelock. Surely my Lord is on an upright path' (Q 11:56)?

It is worth pointing out that the call to a 'common word' issues from an impossible homogeneity on the part of its signatories and relates to an equally impossible homogeneity on the part of those to whom it is addressed. In reality, the act of reading the call will necessarily refract differently from individual to individual, from language to language, and in each different ethnic, cultural and political community.

In the following text, we will take a closer look at the broader semantic fields associated with the dichotomy thus instituted between the authors of the letter and its potential recipients, as well as ways in which it is reflected in the complicated circumstances of today's world and in particular in the plural society of Bosnia.

'BETWEEN US AND YOU'

All things in existence, including human beings, share an undeniable connection with the Creator. This is their endowment of both reason and purpose. God is neither like unto nor comparable with anything, but is nonetheless present in all things and immeasurably close. Consequently, this connection is always authentic and irreducible. This means that our individual self-representation is both itself absolute and caught up in a continuous process of simultaneously approaching the principle and withdrawing from it. Moreover, nothing we can know as individuals has the power to exclude the knowing self from the relationship of knowing and so render itself independent and separate from the knower.

God is the principle of all existence and so of each individual. Each individual is a type of refocusing of that principle and thus an instance of the first created principle of all of us together. After all, to create one individual human being is the same as to create all of us together (see Q 31:28). Everything comes from God and returns to Him (Q 2:156). He gave existence and guidance to all things (Q 20:50). Each individual's return is unique, as was his or her creation. God says in the Recitation, 'Now you have come to Us, one by one, as We created you upon the first time, and you have left what We conferred on you behind your backs' (Q 6:94). To return to God is to realise our humanity after our original and authentic potential, so as to deserve it. In this process, none stand guarantee for the individual, any more than the individual stands guarantee for others (see Q 6:164). The process of return is an absolute settling of accounts, for every particle of good and every particle of evil the individual has done (Q 99:7–8).

Our created nature is absolutely permeated with reason and purpose, transcending all the worlds, for we alone have been admitted to the knowledge of all the names (Q 2:31). This initiation is for each of us an incision and injection into Being. It is a pre-formation for ascent and return to God by becoming conscious of the relationship between servant and Lord. That relationship is based on free will, as the condition of good faith and so of the proper relation between the individual of faith and God as faithful. Even when violence threatens the pursuit of such a relationship, it remains God's wish 'to be gracious to those that were abased in the land' (Q 28:5). That each individual is related to God in this way is precisely what produces individual responsibility to use our power and strength to protect and liberate those whom such violence prevents from pursuing full and authentic self-realisation for themselves. In the Recitation, God said of this:

> How is it with you, that you do not fight in the way of God and for the men, women and children who, being abased, say: 'Our Lord, bring us forth from this polis whose people are evil doers, and appoint to us a protector from Thee, and appoint to us from Thee a helper'?
>
> (Q 4:75)

Through His prophet, the Praised, God speaks to the faithful of Himself: 'Seek Me amongst the weak, for it is for the sake of the weak that you are well-provisioned and assisted.'[1] That God is on the side of the weak and that He imposes the obligation to seek Him amongst them in the very act of fulfilling our responsibilities towards them are clear from the essential core of the Recitation as a whole.[2] This responsibility is reflected both in the right or claim of the weak and the duty and debt of the powerful, which are laid down by God as the nature of our relationship to Him.

We are only ever able to make out in the signs on the horizon a part of all that exists in the infinite flux of creation. It is nonetheless enough to allow us to draw clear conclusions about ourselves, the world and God, in accordance with the principle 'Who knows him- or herself, knows his

---

[1] Abū 'Īsā Muḥammad ibn 'Īsā al-Tirmidhī, *al-Jāmi' al-kabīr: Sunan al-Tirmidhī* (Beirut: Dār al-gharb al-islāmī, 1998), vol. 3, p. 258.

[2] See also the sacred tradition whereby God is described to be with the sick, the hungry and the thirsty (Muslim, *Ṣaḥīḥ*, trans. 'Abdul Ḥamīd Ṣiddīqī (Riyadh: International Islamic Publishing House, n.d.), vol 4, p. 1363).

or her Lord.'³ So, understanding the world's dependence on the necessary principle entails an understanding of our own personal dependence on that principle, as well as of our relationship with God as dichotomous and resolved only in His unity.

No individual is fully self-identical for two different moments in time. Difference is inherent to being. What we are now is only possible on the basis of some form of recollection of what we have been and some form of assumption as to what we may become. We are torn between so many possibilities, both past and present. We may refer to ourselves as 'I' or 'we' with regard to any number of them, while drawing similar distinctions between a singular and a plural 'you'. Faced with such diversity in identification of self and other and of mediating identities, and even of the self as another, our quest must focus upon that higher and more sublime capacity to return and rise up to God, in line with our innate, maternal principle and in imitation of our best and finest example, whom we shall never overtake, however, because the upright path of return is itself without end, ever open and onward. Our perfect example on this path is, of course, the Praised, sent by God Himself, as the other who reveals what is proper to the self.⁴

Just as we find ourselves relating to the Lord in various ways, we are also linked to and through all things in the world and all people. The obstacles we encounter on our paths of self-discovery, determination and realisation are intimately linked to these various relationships. Wherever we end up and whatever we make of ourselves, however, it is vital to remember that we are not God nor can we ever be Him. Even together with the world, we are nothing in comparison to Him. But God is everything in comparison to us. The Word or *Logos* is a means of bridging this infinite disparity and gap, whether between the world and God or between the individual and God. As soon as the Word enters the world, it enters human discourse and speech and the attempt is made to subordinate it to instrumental, and so instrumentalised, reason, within the logical matrix of de-transcendentalised language.

---

³ This tradition has been accepted as sound in the Muslim intellectual tradition. It is not included in the canonical collections of the Prophet's sayings. It entered the traditional current in a way that was not subject to standard exoteric rules. It is sound on the basis of what it discloses, but is unconfirmed by the chain of transmission. For more, see William C. Chittick, *The Sufi Path of Knowledge: Ibn al-'Arabi's Metaphysics of Imagination* (Albany: State University of New York Press, 1989), pp. 250–2.

⁴ See Q 43:43 and 11:56.

Enclosed within a propositional system, the reduced word is constantly being broken up and made anew in accordance with the laws of analytical reason or logic, securing for those involved in the process an endless youth and a tropism towards the utopian end of history. It is the de-transcendentalised Word that energises the this-worldly teleology within which it has been enclosed, as the old is endlessly replaced by the new, the humble by the high, and mythic utterance, spirit and revelation come to seem unnecessary, discarded as some form of flotsam from the past. Once the Word has been thus reduced to a world from which the Holy Spirit has been exiled, revelation, whether as act, claim or content, ceases to be anything but a word that appears in the thought of an individual, subject to his or her rational control. It becomes a means for the subordination of others and far from a guarantee of their inviolable sanctity.

In the Recitation, God reminds us that He sent down the Word into the heart of His servant by means of the Holy Spirit (Q 16:102), the Spirit of Truth (Q 26:192–4). The uniqueness of the Word, as against the countless multitude of interpretations offered of It over the historical course of time, ensures Its indivisibility from the Holy Spirit, the Spirit of Truth. This Spirit cannot be confined within a propositional system. The reduction of the individual to a measurable quantity or, as is sometimes said in modern times, the death of higher reality, threatens the connection between Word and Spirit. Once severed from Infinite Spirit, the Word necessarily becomes finite, mere word, confined within one of the two available propositional systems, namely, the system of modern theology or the system of modern science.

LANGUAGES

The very title of the letter, *A Common Word*, calls its intended readers to attend to God's command to the prophet known as the Praised that he address the peoples of the book, saying:

People of the book! Come now to a word common between us and you, that we serve none but God, and that we associate not aught with Him, and do not some of us take others as Lords, apart from God. And if they turn their backs, say: 'Bear witness that we are people of peace.'

(Q 3:64)

The people(s) of the book, to whom this revelation was directed through the Prophet, are to be found amongst all linguistic, racial and ethnic communities, in all political orders and civilisations. Regardless of which path they have chosen towards God, they are expected to recognise themselves in this call and to accept the good that transcends all particulars and to discover the meaning of their humanity in the different aspects of their variety, in accordance with the Revelation:

O mankind, We have created you male and female and appointed you races and tribes, that you may know one another. Surely the noblest among you in the sight of God is the most mindful of you. God is all knowing, ever mindful.

(Q 49:13)

The authors of *ACW* recall the circumstances attendant upon our very humanity and the dangers of failing to understand the paradox of belonging, as given shape by the Prophet in the tradition: 'Be patient until you meet your Lord, for no time will come upon you but the time following it will be worse than it.'[5] We must become strangers to the very identities that inform our relations in the world in order to find a home in the self. In the time since that statement was uttered, humankind has raised itself up from a position of prostration before nature to attain a previously unimaginable degree of control and power over it. These changes in our understanding and knowledge of the material world have not brought us closer to God, however, as is evident from the perplexity audible in the voice of the physicist Steven Weinberg as he said, after all his research into and experience of the discovery of physical laws, 'The more the universe seems comprehensible, the more it seems pointless.'[6] In short, the unheralded and unexpected modern increase in our knowledge of the world has only made the chasm between humanity and God seem even more appallingly unbridgeable.

It is possible that *ACW*, as imagined by its authors on the basis of their reading and interpretation of God's own epistles to humanity, may well contribute to bridging that other, ever-growing and ever more threatening chasm between the Muslim 'them' and the Christian 'them'. But we must ask, is this really a chasm between 'Christians' and 'Muslims'? Is it not, rather, one between political powers which invoke these sacred traditions, as representations wielded in a schismo-genetic dance of mutual othering and distancing, even as their very modes of life are themselves increasingly

---

[5] Bukhārī, *Ṣaḥīḥ*, trans. Muhammad Muhsin Khan (Beirut: Dar al-Arabia, 1985), vol. 9, pp. 151–2.

[6] Steven Weinberg, *Dreams of a Final Theory: The Scientist's Search for the Ultimate Laws of Nature* (New York: Vintage Books, 1994), p. 255. For his later views about the question of God and the meaning of the Cosmos, see chapter 11, 'What about God?', ibid.

informed by essentially similar, growing propositional systems, which allow no place for the mystery of relationship to God?

The Divine Word is manifest in creation and its various worlds, which serve as stages on which the Word is presented, whether it be on the horizons of the world or in and through the various languages of humanity. This Word may thus take on countless forms and meanings in this constant process of differentiation, its essence remaining one and the same, in accordance with the revelation 'And We never sent a Messenger before thee except that We revealed to him, saying, "There is no God but I; so serve Me"' (Q 21:25). Indeed, even here, the Word differs within Its own discourse, manifestly differently in each individual. Consequently, messengers or apostles came to bear warning to all nations (Q 10:47), speaking in the language of the nation from amongst whom they were raised up (Q 14:4). This warning was, however differently couched, one and the same perennial message received from God in each and every language that exists or has ever existed. This very multiplicity of human language is one of God's signs (Q 30:22).

There are between six and seven thousand language communities in the world today, each with its own primordial language. These communities are not equal in size. They range from the approximately 900 million speakers of Mandarin Chinese as a first language, who make up close to one-sixth of all the people in the world, to the approximately 300 million native speakers of English and the similar number for Spanish, all the way down to the smallest of communities; more than half the languages in the world are spoken by fewer than 5,000 people each, more than 1,000 languages by fewer than 10 individuals.[7]

Those languages with only a few native speakers are today at risk, given the worldly dominion of quantity and power. The vulnerability of these languages in turn entails a threat to the dignity of those who speak them. That 'word common to us and them', however, entails that the claims and rights of the weak and vulnerable always outweigh the claims and rights of the powerful. Those with great power are irretrievably in the debt of those without any. Surely here, then, faced with such differences in power, we should expect to find a need for greater awareness of the 'common word', whose overriding concern is with our responsibility towards the individual besieged by political violence, cultural racism and arrogant abuse to dishonourable purpose.

[7] See Nicholas Ostler, *Empires of the Word: A Language History of the World* (London: Harper Perennial, 2006), p. 7.

We may therefore find it unacceptably reductive to treat these two calls by God, the first to the People of the Book, the second to everyone, in terms of the modern distinction between 'us' and 'them', as the letter *ACW* seems to, insofar as it entails an exclusion of the transcendental. Both as individuals and as adherents of different linguistic, racial, ethnic, confessional and political communities, even the authors of the letter themselves do not make up a homogeneous unity. Surely, their call is addressed first and foremost to themselves as People of the Book and only then to others. It is their responsibility to themselves that should be being placed in the foreground, followed only then by their responsibility to those closest to and around them and then to the world as a whole. An address to the People of the Book is, of course, normally wrongly considered amongst Muslims a discourse directed primarily towards Jews, Christians and others, and, in principle, as they are seen by Muslims and not in terms of their own self-understanding or as viewed from the perspective of transcendence.

From that perspective, the primary reference of the call to serve no one but God and to associate no person or thing with Him and to take no one for one's Lord but God is the utterer. The only way for the caller to confirm that by which he or she considers him- or herself a person of peace, related to Peace through being at peace, is by responding with all of his or her being as being that. Only from such a position, from a witness that is itself a response to the call, is there any possibility for this call to others to be convincing and effective. Just as the Word is manifest in language, and so in talking and listening, the speaker is always at some type of advantage over the listener, disposes of more power, as it were, and so is in a position of debt and duty towards the listener. For the same reason, the listener has a greater right and claim than the speaker. This right obliges the listener to respond in speech to the speaker, who becomes listener in turn, and so to recognise the conversion of the former speaker's debt and duty into a right and claim. These reversals and responses are continuous and constant and it is only through them that we can achieve ascent towards the higher potentials of our nature.

CORRUPTION

The *ACW* open letter, it must be admitted, came about under circumstances of despair on the part of pretty much everybody observing or involved in the life of that part of humanity which tends to be called Muslim, whether by itself or others. In the globalised world of human affairs as caught up and amplified in cyberspace, political, economic and social disorder in most of what is called the Muslim world and its endemic weakness – in comparison to the West, at least – have provoked fear on the part of the Muslim majority, facing an irrefutable discrepancy between Muslim ideals and the realities of supposedly Muslim states. The response, born of fear, to these intolerable political, economic and cultural conditions has been a hypocritical and moralising sentimentalism, which has opened up room for various forms of individual pathology and associated extremism to appear and develop.

The differences that constitute the world – male and female, race and tribe, language and confession – are not presented or accepted as a gift from God to humanity on its upward path towards realisation of its original and authentic nature as created in most beautiful uprightness. Forms of service to others than God and of the association of myriad values to Him have self-evidently multiplied, as individuals, groups, institutions and political orders have been mistaken in turn for the definitive factors determining human destiny. The practice of humiliating our fellows in order to rule over them more easily is widespread throughout the world, as the gaze of the oppressed is averted by a scapegoating logic that blames others, while hypocritically insisting on one's own righteousness.

A moral and political corruption has surely spread across the face of the earth and its strength is most appalling in precisely those parts from which the signatories of the *ACW* letter come and in whose name they stake a claim to speak. They are surely right to ask what God has to say of such arrogant human projects that represent themselves as ordering the world. First and foremost, such projects reflect the form of consciousness given body by theology and science as strict propositional systems and their consequences make clear that they are processes of corruption and disorder misrepresented as order. As God says in the Recitation, 'When it is said to them: "Do no corruption in the land," they say, "We are the only ones to put things right." Truly, they are the workers of corruption, but they are not aware' (Q 2:10).

It is important to recognise that people do not, as a rule, spread corruption consciously. Rather, they suppose themselves to be acting in their own best interest and according to conscience. In some way or another, they experience the power of reason as offering them an entirely independent faculty of judgement and righteousness of action, so that there is not and cannot be any authority or instance of judgement that transcends them. For this very reason, a question of crucial importance presents itself: what level of awareness of this situation is possible from within the framework of the major modern propositional systems, the theological and the scientific, given that they allow no room for the Word, except as subordinated to the rule of reason and logic, and insofar as the Holy Spirit has become per se incomprehensible, an obsolete mythic discourse of a bygone age when men knew too little of themselves, of the world or indeed of God? This question is important precisely because, in the Recitation, God refers to the spreading of corruption as an act of human hands: 'Corruption has appeared in the land and sea, for what men's own hands have earned, that He may let them taste some part of that which they have done, in order that they may return' (Q 30:41).

Each of us therefore bears a certain individual responsibility for this corruption. Becoming aware of this is to admit that no individual, language, race or nation lacks the capacity for or access to relationships of speaking and listening that promote consciousness of our full humanity, based on acceptance that all things that exist have their claims on the individual, just as each individual realises him- or herself through debt and duty, or rather through a countless multitude of debts to all of creation as the cumulative manifestation of the Creator.[8] Corruption is a consequence of a falling off or shortfall in this mutual response of claim to debt and debt to claim by all that is in existence, as God says in the Recitation: 'Had God not driven back the people, some by means of another, the Earth would have been surely corrupted; but God is bounteous unto all beings' (Q 2:251).

None of us is an undifferentiated monad. We are split internally, disclosing and covering over, from moment to moment, finding and losing our original perfection as human beings. In this we are served by our connections with the world and other people, through hearing and seeing and speaking and showing. Our intellectual nature manifests itself through our awareness of ritual and the path, but it is confirmed by virtue, which is to say by humility, generosity and the attempt to do all things in the fairest possible way. Bearing witness to God as the One, we also testify that there are various ways to Him, as many as there are people. These ways and those who travel them are, however, given direction by the sacred traditions, as open and broad paths with room enough for all who tread them. Accepting and respecting these different paths and ways are a form of coming to know and support order in the world and so of constantly and continuously requiting one another, responding

---

[8] The Prophet known as the Praised tells a man to 'accord each thing its right that has a claim on him' (Bukhārī, *Ṣaḥīḥ*, vol. 3, pp. 107–8).

to speech by listening, to listening with speech, to a debt with a claim, and to a claim with a debt. As God says in the Recitation:

Leave is given to those who fight because they were wronged – surely God is able to help them – who were expelled from their habitations without right, except that they say: 'Our Lord is God.' Had God not driven back the people, some by the means of others, there would have been destroyed cloisters and churches, oratories and mosques, wherein God's Name is much mentioned.

(Q 39:40)

To maintain order on Earth and to prevent its ruination depend on recognising and maintaining the sanctity and inviolability of the different paths towards God and their traditions. If these various paths and traditions are most evidently symbolised by 'cloisters and churches, oratories and mosques', whose purpose in life is 'much mentioning' the divine name, then the very existence of these major symbols of our relationship with God as a guarantee of order presupposes that whatever ways do exist to protect the sanctity and inviolability of the dignity of the individual necessarily entail a certain degree of openness towards God's simultaneous immanence and transcendence. Through them, we may discover and realise the meaning of the signs on the horizons around us and within our own selves, as well as the reason and purpose of being in existence at all.

BOSNIAN PLURALISM

How was the *ACW* open letter received in Bosnia, and could its reception have been any different in this country, whose tragedy marked the end of the twentieth century in Europe? To what extent do the concerns of the letter reflect the tragic experiences of the Bosnian Muslims, subjected as they were during the final decade of the twentieth century to expulsion and murder sufficiently severe to merit formal censure as Europe's final genocide, an astonishing phenomenon in itself, given that the act in question was just one in a series of progressive, but largely forgotten, such episodes in the destiny of this nation?[9] In this country, during four years of that final decade of the second Christian millennium, more than

---

[9] On the fate of the Balkan Muslims, including the Bosnians, in the early twentieth century, see Justin McCarthy, *Death and Exile: The Ethnic Cleansing of Ottoman Muslims, 1821– 1922* (Princeton, NJ: Darwin Press, 1995). For the 1992–5 war against Bosnia, see the award-winning study by Michael A. Sells, *The Bridge Betrayed: Religion and Genocide in Bosnia* (Berkeley: University of California Press, 1998).

150,000 Muslims were killed, more than a further million expelled from their houses and, as an integral part of this process, more than one thousand mosques were destroyed.

Throughout its history over the past millennium, Bosnia has been a European space, but one in which religious pluralism survived in a manner visibly different from that prevailing in any other area on the continent. Even at the beginning of this second Christian millennium, there was an evident dynamic in Bosnia of tension between different Christian Christologies and ecclesiologies. The tradition of Cyril and Methodius was early established, so that one may speak of a general community of Slavic churches through South-Eastern Europe. Indeed, the religious formation of the area of Bosnia can only be understood within this wider framework.

The political and religious aspirations of the various ethnic groups of the region took on three distinct forms in Bosnia: the Eastern Orthodox, associated with Serbian political and ecclesiastical entities; the Roman Catholic, associated with Western religious processes; and the Bosnian *krstjan* autocephaly, which appeared and survived against the background of this Bosnian pluralism. This third component can only be understood in terms of its relations with the other two churches, relations which developed in a dialectic of tensions, including the Great Schism in 1054 and afterwards, and were always embedded in a framework of political power relations that extended across Bosnia's immediate and wider context. Caught between these theological and ecclesiological disputes, the adherents of the Bosnian church no doubt sought in their own language their own path towards answers to the questions of God, prophecy and return.

In their search, the news reached them of witness to the Paraclete, whom Jesus the Christ had announced to his disciples. This news necessarily had a totally other burden for them than for their neighbours of other Christianities.[10] The Bosnian church had made an important contribution to shaping and preserving Bosnian religious, cultural and political particularisms during the Middle Ages.[11] During the fifteenth century, it ceased to exist, however, and from that point on the Eastern Orthodox and Roman Catholic Churches coexisted in the country alongside a

---

[10] See, for instance, Lejla Nakaš, 'The Holy Spirit Paraclete in Bosnian apocryphal texts: an Arebica transcript from the 17th century', *Forum Bosnae*, 56 (2012), 129–48.

[11] On the cultural heritage of the period, see Herta Kuna, *Srednjovjekovna Bosanska Književnost, Forum Bosnae*, 45 (2008), 7–383.

Muslim majority, who were the main heirs of that Bosnian Christianity, at least with regard to language and land, places of cult and customs.

It is, of course, true that the Muslim community, as one element of Bosnian religious pluralism, took on form and shape within the framework of the Ottoman sultanate, while preserving its self-definition as Bosnian. In this way, the Bosnian Muslim community, as heir to the legacy of the Bosnian *krstjani*, developed a form of esoteric identity that provided grounds for a thoroughly Muslim intellectuality, with its associated rituals and forms of virtue. In short, the one developed or grew out of the other, as the people of Bosnia continued to find the fundamental rationale for a specifically Bosnian way of being Muslim in their interpretation of their evangelical heritage. The political framework within which this happened is of secondary importance at best.

The expansion of the Ottoman Empire into South-Eastern and Central Europe did bring the people of Bosnia into a situation very different from their previous one of being squeezed between two universal churches. This new situation has been well described by the Bosnian historian Hazim Šabanović, as follows:

> The Bosnian pasha ruled over an area greater than any Bosnian king. In this territorial expanse, which stretched from Šabac to the sea and from Zvečan to Virovitica, the central region of Bosnia represented a sort of matrix that now took on a greater significance. Indeed, the significance of Bosnia grew even greater, in later days, as it became a frontier and peripheral pashalik of the Ottoman Empire at almost all points. One peculiarity of the Bosnian pashalik was that, during the period in question, it was the only one whose seat and territory were entirely on southern Slavic (Yugoslav) land, while the matrix at its heart was formed by a previously existing southern Slav state. Insofar as the Bosnian eyalet extended over a much greater territory than that of the former kingdom, so the idea of Bosnia itself became much broader.[12]

In whatever ways the idea of Bosnia and its meanings may have changed over more than ten centuries, it is nonetheless possible to draw a number of conclusions about them. First, the idea never ceased to refer to a religiously plural society and territory. Second, regardless of the theological and ecclesiological differences between the various elements of that pluralism, the people of Bosnia all spoke a single language, one moreover used beyond the boundaries of the Bosnian territory itself. Third, it was never possible to consider any parts of Bosnian territory as settled by

---

[12] The quote is my own translation from Hazim Šabanović, *Bosanski Pašaluk: Postanak i Upravna Podjela* (Sarajevo: Svjetlost, 1982), pp. 79–80.

only one religious community. Fourth, there are few European territories, if any, where one can find so holistic and integrated a society as in Bosnia, regardless of the religious differences or the modern ideological constructions built upon them. Fifth, what has divided Bosnian society are processes of the modern construction of nationhood after an image of the nation for which religious differences offer an important mechanism for establishing cultural racism as a compensatory substitute for the nation's own impossible universality.

Modern conceptions of national sovereignty in national states, whose emergence was part of the same European processes whereby the two major propositional systems – the theological and the scientific – were formed, pushed the people of this region to pursue the national goals of liberation from foreign rule and of unification within homogeneous national states. Such liberation was to be pursued in the struggle against the political power of the Ottoman sultan, identified with the Turks, or Muslims more generally, and of the Austro-Hungarian Empire, considered Christian. The culture of national liberation and unification entailed a particular marking out of the 'Turk' and 'Turkish' as the political enemy. Once that enemy had disappeared, remaining Muslims nonetheless continued to be identified with it and so to be represented as theological enemies, albeit in a way that was not fully identical with how the Jews were represented as the theological enemy in European constructs of the 'Other'.[13] The theological hostility (construction as enemy) towards Jews was based on their rejection of Jesus' status as messiah. Muslims, on the other hand, as the essentially political enemy, were simply rejected as having no theological basis for being who they are, at least from the European nationalist perspective. Once they had ceased to count as political enemies, their reduction to merely theological enemies necessarily involved defining them as pseudo-theological enemies, because from this perspective the core of their identity is apostasy.

The various religious elements of Bosnian society are structured into separate organisations, essentially on the principle of a church apparatus. They are related in various ways to holders of political power, both inside and outside the country. Within each, one may distinguish political aspirations, whether in terms of achieving administrative independence or of influencing local political authorities. So, the question of the Word, which should unite the peoples of these various religious apparatuses,

[13] See further in Gil Anidjar, *The Jew, The Arab: A History of the Enemy* (Stanford, CA: Stanford University Press, 2003).

becomes distorted by subjection to political interests, articulated for the most part in terms of modern ideology. Relations between the various elites of these religious organisations are largely determined by their common interests regarding political authority, as well as a common urge to make the boundaries between them as clear as possible, rather than by any commitment to a 'common word'.

Attempting to maintain and reinforce this requirement of independence on the part of their religious organisations, their members tend to represent theological and ecclesiological differences as insoluble and so as hedged about by mutually unintelligible tongues. In this way the confessional separation of people is promoted and maintained, even if public spaces and public goods remain unalterably common. In all this, there is but the muddiest intimation that reasons may indeed be found within the sacred heritage to which each of these religious organisations lays claim for mutual recognition, grounded on fundamental principles and the opening up of a process of listening and talking with one another in order to strengthen their various relationships to God, Whose Word brings together all the elements of existence into a whole.

This ideological radicalisation of the religious traditions under modernity, and their reduction to propositional systems of theology – constructed in the image of the independent and generally opposed propositional system of modern science – reduce and weaken the potential for a convincing interpretation of the political order of social pluralism as necessarily stemming from a religious pluralism grounded in reason. This is an intellectual challenge of the highest order, not least because it implies that all the grounds for making Bosnian society whole already exist within it, but most particularly through the contemporary rediscovery of the potential of traditional intellectuality.

THE TWENTIETH CENTURY AND BEYOND

The territories and nations indissolubly bound to Bosnia by ethnicity, religion and politics entered the twentieth century in part as free states (Serbia and Montenegro) and in part under the alien rule of Austria-Hungary and the Ottoman sultan (Croatia, the Vojvodina, the Sanjak, Kosovo and Macedonia). After the Balkan wars of 1912 to 1913, certain of the European territories of the Ottoman sultan were annexed to Serbia and Montenegro (the Sanjak and Kosovo, for example). After the First World War, the Kingdom of the Serbs, Croats and Slovenes was established. In this new political creation, Bosnia was itself politically erased and divided up administratively, with the intention of destroying any form of political or cultural subjectivity within.

In this way, Bosnian identity – Bosnian-hood, as it were – was almost entirely expunged from political thought. The Orthodox population of Bosnia had associated and formed its national development from the nineteenth century onwards in relation to a generalised Serb-hood, while the Catholic population had done the same with regard to a generalised form of Croat identity. As a result, this pair of religious and ecclesiastical affiliations came to be identified with the two 'progressive' nations, Serb and Croat, which both met and faced off against each other in and through Bosnia. Any aspect of Bosnian society that could not be either disposed of or nationalised was represented as Turkish or Muslim, reduced within the framework of a religious community which, from the perspective of the national viewpoint, had resisted the mandatory nationalisation process, essentially because of its own backwardness and loyalty to the outdated Turkish feudal system.

The Kingdom of Serbs, Croats and Slovenes established after the First World War was later renamed the Kingdom of Yugoslavia. During the Second World War, it took on yet another incarnation as the Federative People's Republic of Yugoslavia, a state in which communists ruled absolutely, primarily in accordance with the principles of Leninist-Stalinist theory and practice. The attitude to Bosnian-hood remained the same, however. Bosnians were not given rights comparable to those accorded to Montenegrins, Croats, Serbs, Slovenians and Macedonians, as that would have entailed conceptualising Bosnia as something other than a purely technical Serbo-Croatian issue, a territory on which the Serb and Croat nations met, while maintaining their distinctness.[14]

The Orthodox population of Bosnia found itself encompassed within a single Serbian Orthodox Church, while the Catholic population found itself within the Roman Catholic Church. The organisational matrices of these churches under their different political systems followed standard European patterns. Yet Muslim religious organisation, given its unique situation in Europe, lacked a comparable model within its own tradition. The community was largely incapable of resisting the various forms of ideological and organisational influence coming from the political system within which it operated. It was pushed in various ways to adopt and advocate an essentialisation of Islam, a type of reification, which acted

---

[14] See, for instance, Vasa Čubrilović, 'Istorijski osnovi Republike Bosne i Hercegovine', *Prilozi Instituta za Istoriju Radničkog Pokreta Sarajevo*, 4 (1968), 23–42.

to separate it from both the tradition and the culture of Bosnian social pluralism. Yet it was precisely on that social pluralism that the community could have grounded its own existence and activities, while resisting subordination to foreign ideological authorities.

During the Second World War, genocide was committed against the Bosnian Muslims, building on the earlier political discrimination against them and representation of them in terms of cultural racism and orientalism.[15] They were considered to have occupied a place to which they had no right under any of the prevailing ideologies. This rendered them impure. As obstacles to fulfilment of the national teleologies, they had to be changed, expelled or killed.

During the process of the dissolution of Yugoslavia, the full force of various political powers came crashing down once more on Bosnian social pluralism, again largely on the Muslims as a non-national obstacle to national teleologies. A need to distinguish clearly between the Serb and Croat nations in Bosnia was assumed and the simple existence of Muslims represented the major obstacle in this process. Once again, narratives surfaced whereby the mere existence of Bosnian Muslims was interpreted as foreign and dangerous. These new expulsions and the associated destruction again reached the level of genocide.

In spite of all these various forms of destruction during the twentieth century and in spite of the denial of any possibility of grounding Bosnian religious pluralism in principle, the country survived the twentieth century and entered the twenty-first as a sovereign state, in which followers of different faiths – Muslim, Serbian Orthodox, Roman Catholic and Jewish – continue to live together. Society here has been traumatised and divided, and it must face up to its need to find a way out of its current condition of impasse towards a sustainable political order that will act as a framework for harmonious religious pluralism.

Relations among the ethnic, religious and political components of Bosnian pluralism survived over the twentieth century largely on the basis of political pragmatism, or through an indifference to difference or in the best cases on the basis of the liberal doctrine of the autonomy of the human self. For the Yugoslav nationalists, the presence of Muslims was a transitional phase to be overcome on their path towards nationalisation within a wider Serb-hood or Croat-hood or both. For the Yugoslav communists, religious and national identities were both transitional

---

[15] See Vladimir Dedijer and Antun Miletić, *Genocid nad Muslimanima 1941–1945: Zbornik Dokumenata i Svjedočenja* (Sarajevo: Svjetlost, 1990).

phases on the path towards the dictatorship of the working class and a classless society, so that both religious and national identities were considered as consequences of lower levels of social development and relations within them.

Insofar as Muslims, under the dominant national archaeologies and teleologies, were incapable of becoming a nation in the full meaning of the term, they by definition lay outside progressive social relations, outside any possibility of national enlightenment under the propositional systems of theology and science. That they were conceived in such negative terms by others brought about various forms of ideological hybridisation amongst the Muslims, including self-orientalisation and a feeling of lesser worth, the imitation of processes seen amongst others, but not fully understood and various forms of fundamentalism, generally embraced in a state of emotionalist and moralising confusion that only served to deepen the mental and intellectual agony of the people.

Bosnia has been established as an independent state, but as one in which the question of its social pluralism remains as yet unresolved. Three simultaneously ethnic and religious labels are supposed to constitute communities as political peoples or nations, the apparatus of state serving largely as the means for maintaining and developing this particularism. Under these circumstances, the way in which religious differences are interpreted is, in principle, much the same as in most European states. There is a tendency to territorialise ethnic and religious distinctions within forms of political sovereignty. This is in conflict with Bosnia's cultural unity and religious pluralism, neither of which can be restricted to just one part of Bosnia's territory, whether in the present or at any point in the country's past.

Concepts of civil equality – that is, the full equality of all citizens throughout the territory of the state – are opposed by the dominant political elites, given their ideological interpretation of Bosnian pluralism as based upon an instrumentalised construct of collective rights, which any such concept of individual citizenship would necessarily undermine. This active conflict between concepts of collective and individual rights is due not least to the fact that both derive from an essentially schizophrenic dichotomy within European political philosophy itself. Reflecting on *ACW* against this background suggests at least three potentially relevant conclusions.

First, the question certainly arises as to the potential for grounding plural society, or at least strengthening it, through the reaffirmation of our awareness of the common source of the various traditions, and to what extent this offers an important source of renewal for Bosnian pluralism.

Second, the hardening of boundaries between religious organisations is often viewed as guaranteeing their autonomy and protecting their respective domains; however, in combination with their conservatism, particularly in exploring and investigating each other's intellectual heritage, it is currently a major obstacle to articulation of the public sphere as one in which individuals of different affiliations and with claims to different paths towards God may develop their shared awareness of their responsibilities to each other in shared political projects.

Third, educational systems at all levels, which have for the most part developed within a framework determined by the Enlightenment, its legacy and the associated attitudes towards religious intellectuality, continue both directly and indirectly to reproduce and sustain the destructive ideological dogmatisms of nationalism, racism and orientalism, particularly with regard to interpretation of Muslim elements of the world system.

CLOSING REMARKS

The letter *A Common Word between Us and You*, whose title is a quote from the Recitation, calls on its recipients, who are envisaged for the most part as Christian, to start looking at Muslims in the terms of their own Scriptures. It is the authors' belief that, by doing so, they will find the same grounds, a certain common ground, as Muslims do in their scriptures.

Even though it is not explicitly stated in the letter, this construction presupposes that the authors for their part accept that the Jewish and Christian Scriptures themselves form part of their own Muslim heritage. Such an assumption is not difficult to justify. In reality, however, it is not merely underrepresented, but actually for the most part explicitly rejected, under current political, cultural and economic conditions in the Muslim world, informed as they are by various and mutually contradictory ideological interpretations of religious intellectuality.

The feeling on the part of the authors that their letter has a major potential to reduce tensions and conflict itself demands a theoretical and practical re-articulation of political thought, and that most particularly amongst Muslims themselves. The call to a 'common word' is especially relevant to its own signatories and those in whose name they speak. It is only once they have themselves become fully conscious of that 'common word' that they can begin to offer any form of convincing witness of their own selves to others, at which point it becomes irrelevant whether those others are Jews, Christians, Buddhists or followers of any other aspect of the world's diversity. Only in this way will those who identify with the Muslim intellectual tradition be able to become convincing participants in a more general conversation aimed at realising our common humanity through a shared search for God amongst the weak.

There have been initiatives to present *ACW* in Bosnia and to promote both awareness and discussion of it. The letter itself has been translated and published by a local Muslim non-governmental organisation, the Centre for Advanced Studies,[16] while the official interfaith body of the main official religious communities, the Interreligious Council, has, in cooperation with such organisations as the Friedrich-Ebert-Stiftung (Friedrich Ebert Foundation), organised activities with theological students from the four major religious communities (Catholic and Orthodox Christian, Muslim, and Jewish) and with the public to present and discuss the letter and the responses to it.[17] Another non-governmental organisation whose membership is drawn from all the ethnic and religious communities in the country, the International Forum Bosnia (IFB), has hosted a number of the leading individuals associated with *ACW* and the response to it as speakers at international conferences on Unity and Plurality in Europe, held every August in Mostar. Thus Professors Miroslav Volf, David Ford and Ali Aref Nayed have all spoken on *ACW* and the Muscat Manifesto at the conference in consecutive years. The IFB also organises conferences in Sarajevo to mark the UN Interfaith Harmony Week in early February every year, at which theologians and religious leaders from the various communities discuss related questions, very much in the spirit of the letter.[18]

Such responses to *ACW* in Bosnia necessarily arise within the structure of reified divisions outlined here. This structure tends to hold the interlocutors apart from each other even as they seemingly engage in dialogue, so that apparent dialogue too often serves to reinforce the structure itself, precisely because it is based upon 'respect' for the different 'nature' of the other. What is lacking is any effective method of deconstructing

---

[16] Details of this translation may be found on the Centre's website, at http://cns.ba/cns-izdanja/zajednicka-rijec-za-nas-i-vas/. Accessed 19 September 2016.

[17] The activities of the Interreligious Council may be explored through their website, www .mrv.ba. Accessed 19 September 2016.

[18] The activities of International Forum Bosnia may be explored on their website, www .forumbosna.org. Accessed 19 September 2016.

the symbolic structures that support mutual distancing and replacing them by a properly ethically based recognition of our common essence. Initiatives like *ACW* can certainly help in this endeavour, but they can equally be abused by those who view dialogue as a tool for managing division.

14

'Love Thy Neighbour'

A Moral Imperative?

Mustafa Abu Sway

The *A Common Word* initiative, though sophisticated and well-founded theologically, aims at attaining practical objectives of peace, and creating a harmonious and respectful *convivencia* between Muslims and Christians, especially, as has been noted a few times in this volume, in the light of such conflict and anxiety in the world today. But it might also help us correct what we teach about the 'Other' religious tradition, by focusing on our need to love God and neighbour.

The *Open Letter to His Holiness* which preceded *A Common Word* was an open, honest but respectful response to Pope Benedict XVI's controversial Regensburg lecture on 13 September 2006. This earlier letter aimed at correcting some factual mistakes that were included in what the pope said about Islam. The lecture, which was not focused on Islam per se, nevertheless reflected two main stereotyped images: that Islam is violent and irrational. It is important to stress, of course, that different faith communities suffer from mutually stereotyped images; this is why interfaith dialogue is crucial, not least to try to deconstruct such views. Unfortunately, the *Open Letter* did not get a satisfactory reaction, and that led a year later to *A Common Word*. The inception and the background for this development are discussed elsewhere in the present volume. Be that as it may, the Regensburg lecture did make Muslims and Christians reflect together. In the light of the ensuing debate, I was invited to write in the Catholic academic journal *Nuntium* on 'situating reason in Islam'.[1] This was a modest response to one of the two stereotyped

---

[1] Mustafa Abu Sway, 'Situare la ragione nell'Islam', trans. B. Scolart, *Nuntium*, 35–6 (2008), (*Fede, Ragione, Ricerca e Dialogo*), 93–7.

images, but there is a major difference between a papal lecture and an academic article; very few people read theological journals compared to the millions who listen to a pope and potentially internalise the wrong message about Islam and Muslims. It is of the utmost importance that religious leaders be careful what they say about the religious 'Other'.

Therefore, in the light of this responsibility, we see *ACW* as the most generous interfaith document initiated by contemporary Muslims, as it engages with the Christian world. It highlights original theological and ethical commonalities, and calls for peace between Muslims and Christians, which would translate into world peace, thanks to the sheer number of their followers, who constitute a majority of world population, as has been pointed out in the opening of the document. It is important to add here that there is no exclusion of other religions in the light of this address to Christians. The document is not meant to belittle other actors who could contribute to world peace. The document, in fact, shows that there is a clear need: for a new practical pact between the major religions, a pact to end all forms of occupation, colonialism and neo-colonialism; to stop supporting and recognising brutal dictators and regimes that discriminate against religious minorities and to end apartheid. There is a need to bridge the economic gap between the North and the South, which means an end to the debt incumbent upon nations of the global South; this was indeed the call of Pope Paul John II at the turn of the millennium, so that people will have enough food, and access to fresh water and sanitation, which are organically related to fighting diseases, and see an end to illiteracy.

ACW in a sense sides with John Paul II's practical emphasis. However, *ACW* does so with an elaboration on the Oneness of God in Islamic theology, and loving the neighbour as praxis. It is one of two very important religious initiatives coming from Amman, Jordan, led by HRH Prince Ghazi bin Muhammad, addressing intra-faith and interfaith relations from an Islamic perspective. Though authored by Prince Ghazi, *ACW* was endorsed by world Muslim leaders and became the global leading interfaith engagement between Muslims and Christians, with responses from the highest Christian authorities of various churches, as has been noted previously.

It is no surprise that notable Western religious and academic institutions responded positively towards *ACW*. The golden rule enjoined by *ACW* was wired in the first place into the book of Deuteronomy, an important Jewish legacy that becomes one of the marks of holiness for Jews, Christians and Muslims. However, the reception of this call in the Holy Land remains a challenging question. One has to ask why it is then that the Abrahamic faiths forgo holiness in exchange for power. Rather than living together in peace, we end up in a seemingly intractable conflict. Why is it that, in the Holy Land in particular, justice and basic human rights are being sacrificed on the altar of nationalism? The inability to administer justice by loving the neighbour is detrimental to a wholesome relationship with God, even if you pay lip service and profess faith in His Oneness.

Just as world peace is dependent on peace between Muslims and Christians in the world, peace in the Holy Land is dependent on Jews, Christians and Muslims loving their neighbours as themselves and finding a way to reflect a godly life together. We view as tragic that in the world today there still exists a power structure that permits persecution, apartheid and the siege of whole communities for no fault of their own. It is a structure that often implicitly rains death indiscriminately on homes, schools and hospitals, using the most sophisticated weapons. At the same time, it is important to note that no injustice should justify the killing of innocents, including suicide bombings or intentional attacks on the elderly, children or religious institutions. ACW calls us to counter such disastrous activities not with violence but with loving our neighbour. The call is yet to be heard.

Am I my brother's keeper? ACW's definitive answer is yes. If one is true to the belief in the Oneness of God, then it follows that one has to be true to respecting life and protecting the original oneness of humanity, where no preference is given to any ethnicity, real or constructed. Our African sisters and brothers are still suffering in most places, regardless of their religion or nationality. The whole South in general is still aching under the weight of the recent colonial past; the North is not devoid of suffering either. ACW calls with unequivocal voice for world peace, beginning with recourse to the 'common word' between Christians and Muslims, who form together the majority of the world population, with the assumption that others will follow.

The Oneness of God, or *tawḥīd*, is the cornerstone of the document and of Islamic theology. The verse 'Nothing is like unto Him' (Q 42:11) indicates that He is unique in His majestic attributes and beautiful names, that we do not ascribe anthropomorphic attributes to Him, that He is not bound by His creation, including time and space, and that we neither associate, nor worship, anyone or anything with Him. As the great medieval Islamic luminary Abū Ḥāmid al-Ghazālī (d. 1111) writes in his *Revival of the Islamic Sciences*, essential to *tawḥīd* is to see everything as coming from God, and to regard God as the real actor in all coexisting universes, including the one in which we live, and the one to which we have no access yet.[2]

The true *tawḥīd* is also unitive. The theological Oneness of God should translate into the oneness of humanity, having the same purpose of life, united by the revelation and spirituality, and having the same road map leading towards God. But humanity is far from being united. Many choose a godless life, and many, despite their claims to religiosity, choose to be unjust towards their fellow human beings, causing them unnecessary suffering. Violence, whether caused by a state, a group or an individual, has become the hallmark of our times. It is as if we are witnessing the manifestation of a tradition in which the Prophet Muhammad prophesied a day, the time of chaos, in which the killers do not know why they kill, and the killed do not know why they are killed.[3] The true *tawḥīd*, however, requires that one should live by the ideals revealed in the Qur'an and manifested in the life of the Prophet. Loving God and being loved by God are among the major principles associated with following the prophetic path:

Say, [O Muhammad], 'If you should love God, then follow me, [so] God will love you and forgive you your sins. And God is Forgiving and Merciful.'

(Q 3:31)

By the same token, to follow the Prophet is to follow his Sunna, the second source of the Islamic worldview, the details of which include the relationship with, and the status of, the neighbour. Neighbours, Muslim or non-Muslim, are entitled to good neighbourly relations. The Prophet warned his followers against harming their neighbours, lest they jeopardise their own position in the hereafter.[4] Another prophetic tradition states:

By God! He is not a [true] believer! By God! He is not a [true] believer! By God! He is not a [true] believer whose neighbour is not safe from his evil behaviour.[5]

---

[2] Abū Ḥāmid al-Ghazālī, *Iḥyā' 'ulūm al-dīn* (Beirut: Dār al-Maʿrifa, n.d.), vol. 1, p. 33.
[3] Muslim, *Ṣaḥīḥ*, 'Fitan wa-ashrāṭ al-sāʿa', 2988 and 5177.
[4] Muslim, *Ṣaḥīḥ*, 'Īmān', 69.
[5] Bukhārī, *Ṣaḥīḥ*, 'Adab', 5670.

'Love thy neighbour' is, therefore, a call for caring, sharing and protection, which means that 'love' would be verified against the record of action of both the 'lover' and the 'beloved'. It is a promise relevant also to political performance. People, regardless of their diverse backgrounds, appreciate justice; they dislike double standards, whether on the local level (no two sets of law), or the international level (international law applied to all without veto in favour of certain countries that function above international law with impunity). The Islamic worldview does invite Muslims to go even beyond tolerance, reaching the level of *birr*, a beautiful treatment usually associated with one's parents:

God does not forbid you from those who do not fight you because of religion and do not expel you from your homes – from being *righteous* toward them and acting justly toward them. Indeed, God loves those who act justly.

(Q 60:8)

Translating *birr* as 'righteousness'[6] reflects one good moral aspect, but falls short of capturing the full extent of what *birr* truly entails. It is *all* the good things. Yet there are conditions without which *birr* of the non-Muslim neighbour is put on hold. These conditions are war against Muslims and forced displacement of the civilians from their dwellings. So the creation of peace and the return of those displaced refugees to their homes are two preconditions for *birr*. Displacement is a signifier to all the injustices that could be reversed, such as land confiscation and residency revocation. While both are crimes under international law, the latter is more akin to ethnic cleansing. It reflects ancient tribal thinking that is not compatible with what is accepted internationally as basic human rights.

The Qur'an addresses humanity, reminding us of our shared family roots, that we belong to the same parents, a single male and a single female. It was a divine plan that from these same parents we became many peoples and tribes, so that we may know one another (*li ta'ārafū*):

O mankind, indeed We have created you from male and female and made you peoples and tribes *that you may know one another*. Indeed, the most noble of you in the sight of God is the most righteous of you. Indeed, God is Knowing and Acquainted.

(Q 49:13)

'*That you may know one another*' does entail a road map for coexistence, the presence and maintenance of which are an indication for

---

[6] See the Saheeh International (Jeddah: Abul-Qasim Publishing House, 1997) *Translation of the Meaning of the Qur'an*.

peace, first within the same society, only to be translated later on into civilisational *convivencia*, where intra-state relations will be based on moral principles rather than interest. Thus, knowing one another should not be reduced to superficial introductions. Knowing one another means working hand in hand against poverty, famine, illiteracy, disease and natural and political calamities, problems that plague mostly the Southern Hemisphere. It means unveiling the humanity of the peoples and individuals we are dealing with, and reclaiming the oneness of the human family, despite serious theological differences that are mostly the work of theologians who continue to create post-revelational constructs, many with horrendous political implications.

In contrast to enmity, I share a personal story. When I was a baby still suckling, my mother breastfed Lamis, the daughter of our Christian neighbours. This was not because her mother lacked milk, but was rather an act of love. Lamis and I are sister and brother according to Islamic law, and that is how I feel. Being raised with such stories is very important in nurturing care and respect for the 'Other'! Acts of love that uphold theological discourse inform the way forward.

Contrary to Samuel Huntington's book *The Clash of Civilizations and the Remaking of World Order*, a title that reflects a thesis that claims future conflicts will erupt around cultural fault lines, Islam advocates a position that civilisations *do not* clash! Civilisations are cumulative, overlap and cross-fertilise each other, and have common characteristics to the degree that we are encouraged to think about human civilisation being one, with unique phases and manifestations, yet without the will to clash. The concept of a unified human civilisation, however, does not deny the possible existence of real power structures that conduct wars against one another. World War I and World War II were fought by many Western countries that allegedly belonged to the same civilisation; nevertheless, they fought against each other. The more recent neo-imperial wars, such as the 2003 invasion of Iraq, form a continuum of where modernity went wrong. Oil, water, land and other resources continue to fuel conflicts. The idea that culture rather than material interests will define future conflicts promises endless wars.

There are responses that can be proposed from a religious perspective. These include adopting the concept of sharing with other communities across borders, as a religious value, even when it runs against national interests. The same can be said about using alternative non-fossil fuel so that we do not destroy the environment that God has created for us, even if we have to act unilaterally. But a war based on cultural differences, especially perceived differences, is a zero-sum game. The Qur'an considers hostility between human beings as a temporary state of affairs that could potentially change for the better:

And not equal are the good deed and the bad. Repel [evil] by that [deed] which is better; and thereupon the one, whom between you and him is enmity, [will become] as though he was a devoted friend.

(Q 41:34)

The Qur'an in fact associates enmity with Satan; only with Satan is enmity perpetual with no room for change. 'Indeed, Satan is an enemy to you; so take him as an enemy' (Q 35:6), says the Qur'an. These two Qur'anic verses are linked to one another. The first one focuses on repelling evil, which is primarily seen as an action incited by Satan, who therefore is the true enemy of every human being. This evil may manifest itself in various forms, including war against the 'Other'. Once we realise the source of evil in the world, we should go after the true cause of it, and allow the intermediate agent, the human being, the chance to change course, repent and fix the damage. Most importantly, once any human conscientiously distances himself or herself from Satan, he or she should be welcomed back as a good brother or sister. This is *convivencia*.

Conflict resolution, therefore, should focus on putting an end to all causes of conflict, including social, economic and political injustices, in order to foster better relations. Perpetual negotiations that keep whole nations suffering under unjust rule for decades are not conducive to 'loving thy neighbour' unless this love means speaking truth to power, and taking practical measures to upset the power structure that perpetuates the conflict. 'Love thy neighbour' is applicable to individuals in as much as they support peaceful coexistence. It is not fair to expect victims to love those who inflict harm on them, or those who provide material or moral support to injustice. 'Love thy neighbour' is not applicable to institutions, states and countries when they function according to their self-interest and do not abide by moral principles and universal values of justice, goodness and human welfare.

In addition, new thinking is required to deconstruct post-revelational theological categories that advance bellicose narratives. Sheikh Abdullah bin Bayyah, one of the most prominent contemporary Muslim scholars, issued a religious ruling categorically prohibiting *jihād al-ṭalab* (instigating war when there is no eminent threat), which prohibits Muslims from initiating war against non-Muslims, but permits self-defence.[7] Equally important are the Christian voices that call for rethinking the theology of 'just war', including Pope Francis.[8] Both of these Muslim and Christian voices have the same moral concerns. I would add that a 'just' war is not possible because of the sheer lethal power used. Even the so-called rubber bullets, once they kill a child, they kill the child's future, the potential to grow, get married and create a family. Nothing is benign in the world of weapons. Countries that export weapons might help create conflicts or sustain them.

To pave the way for *convivencia*, which has manifested itself in various stages of human history, as for example in Andalusia, the Qur'an celebrates ethnic and cultural differences, and the diversity of colours and languages. These natural and cultural differences are pointers into the direction of God:

And of His signs is the creation of the heavens and the earth and the diversity of your languages and your colors. Indeed, in that are signs for those of knowledge.
(Q 30:22)

According to the Qur'anic notion of the *ahl al-kitāb*, the status of the People of the Book ranks higher than that of any other non-Muslim community. These are religious communities that originated in revelation and share the same prophets and messengers as Muslims. This is part of the Islamic creed. All revealed books have the same divine source, except for those parts altered by errors of human transmission. All these books form part of a linear history of revelation where humanity is kept informed about the divine plan for humankind, beginning with Adam and Eve's story in the garden, with the aim of returning to paradise.

The Qur'an systematically builds the case for a cordial relationship between Muslims and the People of the Book. The Qur'an permits doing business with them and sharing meals with them; Muslim men are allowed to marry from amongst them, creating a maternal family that is Jewish or Christian. These, and many other inter-human relationships, foster an inclusive and colourfully rich mosaic (Q 5:5). The Qur'an brings 'Love

---

[7] www.youtube.com/watch?v=JXlhg2fQDiI, 17 July 2014. Accessed 23 September 2016.

[8] 'Time to rethink: Vatican rethinks "just war" theory', *CathNews*, 15 April 2016. http://cathnews.com/archives/cath-news-archive/24910-vatcian-conference-rejects-just-war-theory; 'Pope Francis might jettison idea of a "just war"', *Crux*, 26 May, 2016. https://cruxnow.com/church/2016/05/26/pope-francis-might-jettison-idea-of-a-just-war/. Accessed 23 September 2016.

thy neighbour' closer to home in the case of Christians, by stating that they are closer to Muslims in amicability:

and you will find the nearest of them in affection to the believers those who say, 'We are Christians.' That is because among them are priests and monks and because they are not arrogant.

(Q 5:82)

A number of examples from the early history of Islam demonstrate further this cordial relationship between Muslims and Christians. The Christians of Najrān, a region in the south-west of the Arabian Peninsula, visited the Prophet in Medina and stayed in the mosque. Islamic historical records, including the narration of Ibn Isḥāq in Ibn Hishām's Sīra, show that during their visit this Christian delegation performed their prayers and worshipped at the Prophet's mosque.[9] ʿUmar ibn al-Khattāb, the second Caliph, who absorbed this prophetic ethos, concluded, according to tradition, the most celebrated interfaith agreement with Patriarch Sophronius of Jerusalem, c. 636, guaranteeing Christians protection, freedom of worship and the sanctity of their holy places.[10] When Patriarch Sophronius invited ʿUmar to pray inside the Sepulchre church, ʿUmar declined politely, stating that he feared future generations of Muslims might claim this as a right.[11] These stories continue to inculcate mutual respect, urging us to celebrate diversity, and to promote mutual understanding and respect for the 'Other'.

Today, we are witnessing violence in many parts of the world, including Arab and Muslim lands and countries. Most of the victims are Muslims, but others, including Christian minorities, suffer at the hands of extremists whose worldview fails to recognise either the letter or the spirit of Islam. Exemplary relationships between Muslims and Christians continue to exist in places such as Jordan, a safe haven for refugees from the neighbouring countries where the centuries-old *convivencia* collapsed. At the same time, Islamophobia is rampant in Western countries that have a Christian majority, with some countries passing laws that are uncalled for, such as the prohibition of mosque minarets in Switzerland. If only those who voted 'yes' could see how churches, cathedrals and mosque minarets rub shoulders in many a city in the Arab world. Acts of violence and discrimination done by a minority of Muslims and Christians

---

[9] Ibn Hishām, *al-Sīra al-nabawiyya* (Jeddah: Muʾassasat ʿulūm al-Qurʾān, n.d.), p. 575.

[10] Ibn Wāḍiḥ al-Yaʿqūbī, *Taʾrīkh*, ed. ʿAbd al-Amīr Muhannā (Beirut: al-Aʿlamī, 2010), vol. 2, p. 37.

[11] Ibn Khaldūn, *Taʾrīkh*, ed. Khalīl Shiḥādah (Beirut: Dār al-fikr, 1988), vol. 2, p. 268.

to each other are the antithesis of the religious worldview that calls for love of the neighbour. There is a need to move interfaith dialogue from the ranks of the elite to grassroots movements, to educate the masses from the pulpit about the respect with which one should treat the 'Other'. Interfaith dialogue should vigorously aim at changing the reality that tolerates bigotry and hatred. It should also face the political elements that cash in on xenophobia in order to attain higher office.

Subscribing to the message of *ACW* means choosing a political system that has at its core true love of God, and its implications for neighbours. There is no one Islamic political system that has been revealed. There are, instead, revealed mores and values. Muslims have experimented with, created, accepted and adjusted various forms of governance over more than fourteen centuries. While it is difficult to pinpoint all aspects of Islamic governance, suffice it to say that it has to accommodate and respect its religious minorities.

15

'An Unknown Word'

Reflections on the Reception of A Common Word in Germany

Matthias Böhm

INTRODUCTION

Pope Benedict XVI was the first German to be elected to the papacy for nearly five hundred years. As some have reminded us, *A Common Word* is thought to be a response to his Regensburg lecture in 2006. Though the focus of the lecture was not on Islam, the fact that this German pope gave the Regensburg lecture in Germany with controversial insertions about Islam suggests that there was and maybe still is a wide discussion about this topic in Germany. A wider conversation should be expected in Germany and across the West, as questions concerning Islam and interreligious dialogue between Christians and Muslims have become more pressing since 9/11. Indeed, with the migrant crisis in Europe, engaging with Muslims has become inevitable.

The *ACW* invitation to take part in interreligious dialogue received positive feedback and response in Germany. In 2008, the Eugen Biser Award[1] was conferred on the major contributors of *ACW* in recognition of their extraordinary contribution to Muslim–Christian dialogue and their constant endeavours towards promoting peace among the nations. The award was presented at a ceremony in Munich, Germany, on 22 November 2008 and given to HRH Prince Ghazi bin Muhammad bin Talal, Shaykh Al-Habib Ali Zain Al-Abidin Al-Jifri and Reisu-l-Ulema Dr

---

[1] For further information (in English) about the Eugen Biser Foundation dedicated to promoting interfaith dialogue, see www.eugen-biser-stiftung.de/en/home.html. Accessed 12 October 2016.

Mustafa Cerić.[2] In 2009, there appeared a publication including various responses by the Eugen Biser Foundation entitled *Antwort der Eugen-Biser-Stiftung auf den offenen Brief 'A common word between us and you' von muslimischen Wissenschaftlern und Würdenträgern* (Response of the Eugen Biser Foundation to the open letter 'A Common Word between Us and You' by Muslim scholars and dignitaries).[3] In the first two years after Pope Benedict XVI's lecture in Regensburg, a number of conferences took place and various articles were published[4] to reflect on the effects of this discussion, though not much happened afterwards.[5] It is worth noting, however, that on the ground, in parishes and mosques, *ACW* remains no more than a marginal document. Yet Muslim–Christian dialogue is not lacking in Germany. Today there are numerous initiatives and attempts at developing this dialogue further. Therefore, this chapter aims to reflect on the awareness level of *ACW* in Germany and to discuss the question why *ACW* was and is currently no more than 'an unknown word' in Germany. Before delving into this theme, it is necessary that we first look at some facts, figures and institutions related to the Muslim presence in Germany. It is also important to look at the questions that are the focus of interreligious discussion in Germany today.

[2] '*A Common Word* wins the Eugen Biser Award of 2008.' www.acommonword.com/a-common-word-wins-the-eugen-biser-award-of-2008/. Accessed 11 April 2018.

[3] Eugen Biser and Richard Heinzmann (eds.), *Antwort der Eugen-Biser-Stiftung auf den offenen Brief 'A common word between us and you' von muslimischen Wissenschaftlern und Würdenträgern* (Stuttgart: Kohlhammer, 2009).

[4] Such as Rowan Williams (then Archbishop of Canterbury), 'A Common Word for the Common Good', Chapter 4 in this volume; Internationales Katholisches Missionswerk Missio, Aachen (ed.), 'Ein gemeinsames Wort zwischen uns und euch: Der Dialog zwischen Muslimen und Christen', *KM Forum Weltkirche*, 2 (2008), 32–3; Friedmann Eißler (ed.), *Muslimische Einladung zum Dialog: Dokumentation zum Brief der 138 Gelehrten ('A Common Word')* (Berlin: Evangelische Zentralstelle für Weltanschauungsfragen, 2009); Arbeitsgemeinschaft Christlicher Kirchen in Baden-Württemberg, 'Arbeitshilfe zum Brief der 138 muslimischen Gelehrten: Ein Wort, das uns und euch gemeinsam ist', *Impulse zum Gespräch* 1 (2011), 1–55; Harold Vogelaar, 'Eine interreligiöse Antwort auf das Dokument "Ein gemeinsames Wort zwischen Uns und Euch"', *CIBEDO-Beiträge zum Gespräch zwischen Christen und Muslimen*, 3 (2011), 113–9. See also http://cibedo.de/?s=a+common+word and http://cibedo.de/?s=brief+der+138. Accessed 12 October 2016.

[5] The Eugen Biser Foundation invited Prince Ghazi for a one-day conference in Munich, where he and a Catholic theologian, Tobias Specker SJ, Junior Professor of Catholic Theology in Relation to Islam, spoke on 'Love in the Qur'an and Christianity'. See HRH Prince Ghazi and Dr Tobias Specker, *A Common Word between Us and You* Lectures, Eugen-Biser-Stiftung, Hochschule für Philosophie, Munich (9 November 2013). www.eugen-biser-stiftung.de/themen/dialog-aus-christlichem-ursprung/islam/a-common-word-between-us-and-you.html. Accessed 12 October 2016.

MUSLIMS IN GERMANY

The former federal president of Germany, Christian Wulff, is known for his famous statement in 2010, 'Islam belongs to Germany', a statement which was repeated by Chancellor Angela Merkel in 2015. This pronouncement was and still is widely discussed, not only in political circles but also in general public debates as well as among the Muslim community in Germany. However, the level of awareness of this single sentence is many times higher than that of *ACW* and its content. It is necessary to ask why such a sentence creates much wider discussion than a document such as *ACW* when the letter could, in form and content, provide serious opportunities for debates, especially in interreligious dialogue. The answer to this question has to take several facts into account.

It is important to remember that, in comparison to other European countries such as the United Kingdom, France or Spain, the Muslim presence in Germany has a short history. Until the middle of the twentieth century, evidence of Muslim life in Germany is very rare. Except for some tombs of prisoners of war from the Ottoman Empire and of Ottoman diplomats, and a mosque in Berlin founded by the Ahmadiyya community in 1925, there is nothing except some political and scientific exchanges with a few Muslim countries. This can easily be explained by the fact that Germany, as we know it today, did not yet exist during the classical European colonial period – there were hardly any German colonies. When in the late nineteenth century the German empire acquired some lands as colonies (for example, the territory formerly known as German South-West Africa, Namibia today), none of them had a predominantly Muslim population. There was nothing comparable to the British Empire or the Dutch or French colonies. Until the 1960s there was hardly any significant presence of Islam or of Muslims in Germany.[6]

This situation radically changed in the 1960s. Because of a growing economy in Germany there was an increasing demand for workers, which led the German government to sign a number of agreements with several countries to allow the recruitment of workers, especially for factories and in industrial areas. As a consequence of these recruitments, many so-called guest workers (*Gastarbeiter*) travelled to Germany, among them a huge number of workers from majority-Muslim countries. Contracts were signed with Turkey in 1961, Morocco in 1963 and Tunisia in 1965.

---

[6] See Sekretariat der Deutschen Bischofskonferenz (ed.), *Christen und Muslime in Deutschland*, Arbeitshilfen 172 (Bonn: Sekretariat der Deutschen Bischofskonferenz, 2003), pp. 9–10.

This was the beginning of a dynamic and growing Muslim presence in Germany. At first, the idea was that these guest workers would stay in Germany for a few years to work and earn money, and then leave Germany to return to their countries of origin. But they opted to stay, taking their families to Germany; they now live here as the fourth generation of citizens or residents with an 'immigrant background'.

It was some time before it was realised that these people took to Germany not only their labour, but also their religion. And this religion, Islam, was something new for Germany and there was – and still is – a lack of information about what exactly Islam and being Muslim mean. It was especially the churches that began to realise this. During this time, CIBEDO was founded by the White Fathers in the late 1970s. CIBEDO stands for 'Christlich-Islamische Begegnungs- und Dokumentationsstelle', which could be translated as 'Centre for Christian–Muslim Encounter and Documentation'. The motivation behind this initiative had initially been above all to help the large number of Muslim guest workers who entered Germany in the 1960s and 1970s to gain access to German society and help them to create an infrastructure for their spiritual needs. The great majority of them came originally from Turkey, but a significant number also from Morocco, Tunisia and the then-Yugoslavia. The second motivation was more academic, namely, to collect all kinds of information about Islam and the development of Islam in Germany. In order to cope with the new situation in Germany and the prevailing lack of knowledge of it, the White Fathers began to collect a large amount of material, which today forms a rich store of documentation. For quite a long time the documentation has been only on paper, in hundreds of thematic files which are still maintained and being expanded. Most of the documentation is nowadays in digital form. Apart from the documentation, the White Fathers also built up a library, which is still maintained and consists of about 12,000 books on Islamic studies, Christian–Muslim dialogue and Islam in Germany. Today, this library stands out in Germany as the largest collection of literature on Christian–Muslim dialogue. Nearly twenty years ago, the Catholic Church in Germany realised that all topics concerning Islam and interreligious encounters between Christians and Muslims were – and still are – the focus of increasing interest, not only for Christians but for society as a whole. In 1998, the White Fathers decided to withdraw from running the institution and CIBEDO became a department of the German Bishops'

Conference devoted to dialogue with Muslims and research about Islam in Germany.[7]

There are about four million Muslims living in Germany today, which is about 5 per cent of the German population (80 million in total). Thus the situation has rapidly changed from a nearly non-existent Muslim presence in Germany to an 'Islam in Germany'. In 2008, a survey was carried out that questioned who the Muslims are and what Islam in Germany is or means.[8] The most important findings were as follows. The largest group of Muslims in Germany are those of Turkish origin with 2.5–2.7 million – nearly two-thirds of the Muslim community. Other large groups are from South-Eastern Europe, especially Bosnia (about 13 per cent) and those coming from North Africa (about 7 per cent), especially Morocco and Tunisia. The largest denomination among Muslims in Germany is Sunni with 74 per cent, followed by Alevites with 13 per cent and Shiites with 7 per cent. There are smaller groups such as the Ahmaddiya or Ibadis. About 36 per cent of the Muslims living in Germany consider themselves to be very religious, and 50 per cent religious, especially those of Turkish or North African background.[9] It is interesting to note that this does not indicate a certain way of living their religiosity. Most of these Muslims accept as part of life – more or less – the rules of fasting and the daily prayers. Only a minority take part in the religious events offered by mosques.

There are a number of organisations in Germany that claim to represent Muslims in the country, but only about 10 to 20 per cent of Muslims in Germany actually have membership in one of these organisations or even have any awareness of them. For instance, the German counterpart of the Turkish Diyanet İşleri Başkanlığı (Directorate of Religious Affairs) is DITIB, which is the organisation with the highest awareness level among Turkish Muslims. Other Turkish-majority groups are Milli Görüş and VIKZ (Verband Islamischer Kulturzentren), which are less well known, especially among non-Turkish Muslims. Other organisations based in Moroccan or Bosnian mosques are much smaller and not yet as well structured as the Turkish organisations. Two small, relatively unknown, but important, groups that should be mentioned here are LIB (Liberaler

---

[7] For further information on CIBEDO, see http://cibedo.de/geschichte/. Accessed 11 April 2018.

[8] CIBEDO, 'Muslimisches Leben in Deutschland', *CIBEDO-Beiträge*, 1 (2010), 8–14. http://cibedo.de/wp-content/uploads/2016/01/Muslimisches_Leben_in_Deutschland_Kurzfassung.pdf. Accessed 8 October 2016.

[9] Ibid.

Islamischer Bund) and Muslimisches Forum Deutschland. These were founded in 2015 as groups of liberal Muslims in Germany. Other important umbrella organisations that try to work together and represent all groups of Muslims in Germany include the so-called Islamrat (IR), the Koordinationsrat der Muslime (KRM) and the Zentralrat der Muslime in Deutschland (ZRM).

Representatives of these umbrella organisations claim to represent all Muslims in Germany. The problem about this claim is that they have an awareness level of only 5 to 15 per cent, or 20 per cent with a generous calculation. This suggests that only a minority of Muslims have some knowledge of these organisations. If these organisations are quite unknown, how can their programme or agenda reach the masses? Even if *ACW* is part of their discussions, it may only reach a small number of the Muslims in Germany. Lastly, it is important to note that there is a huge diversity among Muslims in Germany. They are from more than forty nations and differ denominationally, in their ways of living their faith and in their attitudes towards religiosity and practice of faith. Hence it is difficult to speak of 'Islam in Germany' in monolithic terms.[10] Be that as it may, the survey that provided this research did not engage with the question of *ACW*, although the reactions to Regensburg were closely covered in these studies. These findings might give important hints as to why *ACW* is more or less 'an unknown word' in Germany.

AN UNKNOWN WORD

So why is *ACW* an unknown word? An initial answer can be found in the special context of Muslims living in Germany, as discussed earlier. Nearly two-thirds are of Turkish origin. Among the Muslim communities claiming to represent Islam in Germany, the Turkish DITIB is the best known among the Muslim populace. A possible reason why *ACW* is unknown in Germany is that most of the imams in DITIB mosques are sent by Turkish Diyanet to live and work in Germany, usually for about five years. The signatories of *ACW* include two Turkish scholars (Professor Dr Mustafa Çağrıcı, then Mufti of Istanbul, and Professor Dr Ali Özek, Head of the Endowment for Islamic Scientific Studies, Istanbul), who are not official representatives of Diyanet in Ankara.[11] One may assume that

[10] CIBEDO, 'Muslimisches Leben in Deutschland'.
[11] Arbeitsgemeinschaft Christlicher Kirchen in Baden-Württemberg, 'Arbeitshilfe', pp. 29ff. This publication also includes a German translation of *ACW*, the list of signatories and some inputs for working with this document in interreligious dialogue.

the presence of a signature by a representative from the headquarters of Diyanet could raise the awareness level of this letter in Germany. Another interesting fact is that there are more scholars signing the document from Morocco and Algeria, as well as from Bosnia. But groups of Muslims in Germany from these backgrounds, as noted earlier, are not as organised as the Turkish institutions. The question, however, also depends on the extent to which the religious leadership is successful in reaching out to the Muslim masses in Germany. The systems of authority vary.

Another possible reason why ACW is not well known in Germany is related to the German educational system and its institutions. As the OECD (Organisation for Economic Cooperation and Development) has mentioned a few times already, the German educational system is inflexible about allowing young people opportunities for advancement, especially in reaching a higher education.[12] Furthermore, difficulties and problems related to integration, especially in the 1960s and 1970s, are to blame. Since the expectation was that the guest workers would eventually leave the country, there were no attempts, for example, to offer language courses or to raise more cultural awareness on both sides. This necessity was first noticed when the first guest workers' children entered school in Germany. The guest workers worked mainly in industry and were not highly educated, the effects of which are still being felt today. Considering that the content of ACW and especially the Regensburg speech require a certain philosophical and theological awareness also means that this topic may go beyond the questions discussed in mosques or in interreligious dialogue between ordinary Muslims and Christians.

Also, although there is a long and important history of Islamic studies in Germany, Islamic theology has only recently developed in the way in which Christian theology has long been established in German universities. There are now a number of universities in Germany that have offered Islamic theology as a programme of study since 2011 (Tübingen, Münster, Osnabrück, Frankfurt, Giessen and Erlangen-Nürnberg). One

---

[12] Most guest workers in the 1960s and 1970s travelled to Germany as factory workers without professional training, and their children have only rarely had an academic education. See, for example, 'OECD-Sozialbericht: Einkommensungleichheit in Deutschland im Mittelfeld, Vermögensungleichheit hoch', 21 May 2015. www.oecd.org/berlin/presse/oecd-sozialbericht-einkommensungleichheit-in-deutschland-im-mittelfeld-vermoegensungleichheit-hoch.htm. See also 'Keine Schule, keine Lehre, kein Job', Der Spiegel, 15 September 2016. www.spiegel.de/lebenundlernen/schule/oecd-bericht-2016-jugendliche-ohne-schule-ausbildung-beruf-a-1112430.html. Both accessed 12 October 2016.

of the ideas behind these developments is that teachers and imams would be trained in an academic institution in Germany. As these institutions are still quite young, it may take some time until the graduates of these studies make a difference in schools and mosques, or in interreligious dialogue initiatives. Yet it is important to note that for example at the Centre for Islamic Theology in Tübingen, students are familiarised with the text of *ACW*. The fact that the editors of this volume are based at the University of Tübingen is a good start.[13] There is a growing number of young people who are finding deep interest in these questions. Maybe greater engagement would require some years or even generations, but something is on the move that appears to be of great value in increasing the awareness level of *ACW*.[14]

Finally, a third possible answer to why the document is 'an unknown word' may be found if we take a look at interreligious dialogue in Germany in general and examine the topics discussed. I have already mentioned that there were a few conferences held and articles published in the light of *ACW* and Regensburg, but these were short-lived. Islamic theology in German universities only started at this time and therefore there was a lack of Islamic representatives; this topic was not the focus of mosques or parishes. The more academic the questions discussed, the more the debate is limited to an inner circle of experts. The number of people involved in this dialogue of theological exchange is not large, and as Christians or Muslims they know each other because they meet frequently at conferences or other interreligious events. Examples of such meetings include the CIBEDO-Werkstatt[15] and the Theologisches Forum Christentum–Islam.[16] There are also some other initiatives, which have been established especially for students, where Christians and Muslims meet and learn about each other. Examples include summer schools

---

[13] There was also a conference held in Tübingen, part of which focused on the *ACW*. One entire session was dedicated to *ACW*, 'Einführende Lesehilfe in das gemeinsame Wort', at Christlich-Islamisches Symposion: Religion – Kraft des Friedens oder des Unfriedens? (organised by Pädagogische Hochschule Ludwigsburg, Zentrum für Islamische Theologie at Eberhard Karls Universität Tübingen and Mohammed V. University – Agdal, Rabat) held at the University of Tübingen (27 June 2013).

[14] For instance, a PhD dissertation has been completed on *ACW* at Humboldt University in Berlin: Sarah Markiewicz, *World Peace through Christian–Muslim Understanding: The Genesis and Fruits of the Open Letter 'A Common Word between Us and You'* (Göttingen: V&R Unipress, 2016).

[15] For further information, see http://cibedo.de/tagungen/. Accessed 12 October 2016.

[16] For further information, see www.akademie-rs.de/theologisches-forum.html. Accessed 12 October 2016.

organised by the Catholic Academy in Stuttgart for undergraduate and postgraduate students;, an Interfaith Academy organised by Lejla Demiri, which enables Islamic theology students from the University of Tübingen to spend time in Rome learning about Christianity[17] and other initiatives, such as the one in Jerusalem, where Muslim and Christian students from Germany study each other's faith in the Holy Land.[18]

This dialogue, worthy as it is, somehow excludes ordinary Christians or Muslims in parishes or mosques who do not have an academic background. This does not mean that church- or mosque-goers are not interested in dialogue or in the 'Other's' religion. In many parishes, there exist circles for interreligious meetings, often women's circles. And on this level a very important part of interreligious work is done. Here Christians and Muslims invite each other to churches or to mosques, where they may share ideas about religious themes relating to God or Jesus, and the ways in which Islam and Christianity treat these topics. Sometimes they exchange thoughts about religious education, or they may be just cooking together. In other words, they may not be discussing *ACW*, though in most cases they actually live what *ACW* calls for: that is, they learn how to see each other as neighbours. The vision of the future of the initiative outlined by Marianne Farina in Chapter 17 in this volume would be a helpful way of developing contextual theological engagement with the document that relates to academia as well as to grassroots activities.

On the whole, there is still a lack of knowledge about Islam in Germany. However, presentations or speeches about Islam offered by Catholic adult education institutions are very well attended. Topics discussed often relate to basic information about Islam in Germany, focusing on historical questions or Muslim spirituality. There are other important practical questions that need to be addressed in Germany, such as pastoral care in hospitals and prisons, and how to treat Muslim children in Catholic kindergartens or schools. These questions need answers not only by Christians but also by Muslims, and especially by their representatives. It is promising to see that the Centre for Islamic Theology at the University of Tübingen has developed a new MA programme on Practical Islamic Theology with a special focus on pastoral

---

[17] For further information, see 'Vom Klosterleben bis zur Flüchtlingsthematik'. www.uni-tue bingen.de/fakultaeten/zentrum-fuer-islamische-theologie/aktuelles/newsletter/2016/ 12016/veranstaltungen-und-aktivitaeten/vom-klosterleben-bis-zur-fluechtlingsthematik .html. Accessed 12 October 2016.

[18] For further information, see 'Die christlich-islamischen Werkwochen 2014'. www .studienjahr.de/werkwochen.html. Accessed 12 October 2016.

care and social work, the first of its kind in Germany.[19] Indeed, these questions pave the way for a practical implementation of what *ACW* has reminded us of: loving our neighbours, learning to live together in peace and nurturing better understanding. This applies also to questions about violence and terrorism caused by religious fanatics; they have been very much the focus of debates in Germany and elsewhere. But this means that the need to discuss documents such as *ACW* is even more urgent in interreligious circles, especially among the common people.

I have suggested three possible reasons for the lack of awareness of *ACW* in Germany. First, there is not a long history of Muslim presence in Germany. Among Muslims in Germany the largest group is of Turkish origin, yet none of the major signatories of the document is from Diyanet. Second, there are problems related to the German educational system. For a long period it was very hard for young people from workers' families – and most Muslims immigrating to Germany in the 1960s and 1970s were workers – to reach a higher educational level. Islamic theological education in German universities started only in 2011. If *ACW* is treated as part of philosophical, historical and theological education in Germany, it is not surprising that the educational system has not assisted local Muslims to engage with these questions earlier. Third, in theological dialogues *ACW* seems to be but one topic among many others, and there are not very many people involved in this kind of dialogue in Germany who could reach out for a wider awareness of the document among the masses. In parishes and mosques *ACW* has remained mostly a marginal note, but its implications for more practical and pastoral questions are important in trying to foster neighbourly and peaceful relations.

---

[19] For more, see 'Praktische Islamische Theologie für Seelsorge und Soziale Arbeit (Master of Arts)'. www.uni-tuebingen.de/fakultaeten/zentrum-fuer-islamische-theologie/studium/ studiengaenge/praktische-islamische-theologie-fuer-seelsorge-und-soziale-arbeit- ma.html. Accessed 12 October 2016.

16

Taking Inspiration from *A Common Word* for a Musical Dialogue

Amir Dastmalchian

So let our differences not cause hatred and strife between us. Let us vie with each other only in righteousness and good works. Let us respect each other, be fair, just and kind to another and live in sincere peace, harmony and mutual goodwill.

– A Common Word[1]

INTRODUCTION

A Common Word, I suggest, is a call to action and its lengthy theological content a mere preamble. The invitation presented to Christians and Muslims at the end of the document to put aside differences and to respect one another (quoted here) entails the fearless exploration of each other's traditions. With this in mind, I take the opportunity in this chapter to explore the potential for an innovative style of dialogue which challenges preconceived notions of interreligious dialogue. More specifically, I aim to explore the potential for using music in Christian–Muslim engagements given that (1) in some contexts, non-discursive dialogue can be more effective than discursive dialogue, and (2) music is a particularly powerful means of expression. This chapter aims to build a case for Christians and Muslims to engage with each other through the means of music, and aims also to reflect upon some of the dialogues that can be had. The need for this can be seen in the recommendation of Abu-Nimer for the development of

[1] www.acommonword.com/the-acw-document/. Accessed 20 October 2016.

new tools in interreligious dialogue for peace-building and conflict resolution.[2]

THE IMPORTANCE OF ART FOR INTERRELIGIOUS DIALOGUE

Despite the connotations of the word 'dialogue', interreligious dialogue does not have to be discursive (that is, through means of language), nor cognitive (engaging the rational intellect). Indeed, it is better that interreligious dialogue is not, or not only, cognitive and discursive, as attested by a number of authors. Mohammed Abu-Nimer maintains that positive change among interreligious dialogue groups requires not just new information and analysis (change in the head) but also positive emotional experience (change in the heart) and completion of a joint task (change through the hand).[3] Marc Gopin says the idea that we can rely on the use of the word to achieve peace between disputants is 'fundamentally flawed', because when reconciliation occurs, it involves much more than verbal discussion.[4] Gopin suggests that interreligious dialogue should use the widest range of means possible, particularly when considering the many variables in human encounter, such as gender, religion, ethnicity and nationality. Cognitive-discursive dialogue, according to Gopin, favours those who are verbal and aggressive in group encounters and those who are better educated. Conversely, it discriminates against those who favour reconciliation through gesture, symbol, emotion and shared work, and leaves out those who are not part of official negotiating teams.[5]

The importance of alternatives to cognitive-discursive dialogue is beginning to be recognised. For example, W. Alan Smith finds that 'it is far more important to engage in practices of peacemaking, community-building, and transformation at a local level than to simply theorise about peace, the nature of community, and the rationale for societal

---

[2] Mohammed Abu-Nimer, 'Religion and peacebuilding: reflections on current challenges and future prospects', *Journal of Inter-Religious Studies*, 16 (2015), 14–29, at p. 17.

[3] Mohammed Abu-Nimer, 'The miracles of transformation through interfaith dialogue: are you a believer', in David R. Smock (ed.), *Interfaith Dialogue and Peacebuilding* (Washington, DC: United States Institute of Peace Press, 2002), pp. 15–32.

[4] Marc Gopin, 'The use of the word and its limits: a critical evaluation of religious dialogue as peacemaking', in David R. Smock (ed.), *Interfaith Dialogue and Peacebuilding* (Washington, DC: United States Institute of Peace Press, 2002), pp. 33–46, at p. 33.

[5] Ibid., p. 37.

transformation'.[6] Ruth Illman argues that scholarly focus on cognitive-discursive dialogue is an imbalance that results from an incomplete view of religion. Interreligious dialogue, suggests Illman, should engage the emotions as well as the intellect in a bid to seek empathetic recognition of the 'Other'. After all, attitudes which are characteristic of poor relations such as intolerance, distrust and prejudice are seldom the result of rational considerations alone. According to Illman, contemporary forms of religiosity make it all the more important to explore alternative modes of interreligious dialogue with the aim of adopting an altogether more holistic approach to dialogue.[7]

Kenneth Danielson believes that there are reasons to expect cognitive-discursive forms of interreligious dialogue to be less successful than some of the alternatives, where success is measured in terms of observable impact on participants. Danielson explains this expectation through appeal to narrative theory, a theory which builds on Walter R. Fisher's work on narrative and Ernst Bormann's symbolic convergence theory.[8] Narrative theory views humans as storytellers who make sense of their experience through constructing narratives. Forms of interreligious dialogue which make use of the innate and universal human ability to tell and understand stories are therefore likely to be more effective. Conversely, cognitive-discursive forms of interreligious dialogue are only open to those specialised in rational, articulate presentation. The result of this requirement for specialism is that those who are not specialists feel unable to participate in dialogue. Lack of participation leads to lack of impact.

Danielson's analysis follows from consideration of an interreligious dialogue event which was very well received by those involved. The event comprised the screening of a film, which dealt with Jewish themes, to a conservative Christian community. The film screening was followed by a relatively informal question and answer session with one of the Jewish producers of the film. According to Danielson, the event surpassed the expectations of the organisers. One of the important reasons for this

[6] W. Alan Smith, 'Everyone but Rizzo: using the arts to transform communities', *Forum on Public Policy*, 2 (2008), 1–21, at p. 19.

[7] Ruth Illman, *Art and Belief: Artists Engaged in Interreligious Dialogue* (Sheffield: Equinox, 2012).

[8] Kenneth Danielson, 'A narrative approach to interfaith dialogue: explanations and recommendations', in Daniel S. Brown Jr. (ed.), *A Communication Perspective on Interfaith Dialogue: Living within the Abrahamic Traditions* (Lanham, MD: Lexington Books, 2013), pp. 75–90.

success was that the Jewish co-producer, who confessed to not being an authority on Judaism, was not threatening to the mostly Christian audience. Instead, the co-producer was perceived as a person whom the audience felt they could safely confide in without the risk of being corrected.

To complement Danielson's convincing analysis, the affective power of the film which was screened should also be considered as a key factor in the success of the event he discusses. As Smith holds, art can empower marginalised individuals and communities to engage according to their own strengths, rather than in accordance with a form of engagement which may be overly intellectual, if not elitist.[9] Speaking in favour of using art in interreligious dialogue, David Cheetham says, 'There is just a "given-ness" or "abundance" about art and beauty that allows us to simply enjoy our experience of it and share it with others.'[10]

Art would seem to be a good candidate for aiding what Abu-Nimer et al. call 'transformative' dialogue.[11] Transformative dialogue is interreligious dialogue which leaves a permanent impression on participants – much more than, for example, an unremarkable conversation between members of different religious traditions. The event discussed by Danielson would seem to be a good example of transformative dialogue. Elizabeth McLaughlin suggests that another way to achieve transformative dialogue could be through the exchange of religious parables. Like Danielson, McLaughlin realises the importance of a good accessible story – a story which appeals by using familiar people, scenes and objects and which does not threaten with jargon, technicality or anything else. Just as the Christian audience warmed to the Jewish producer through hearing his personal story, so too could one religious group warm to another through hearing their parables.

McLaughlin does not restrict her discussion to written parables but considers also visual and living parables, appealing to examples given in the Bible as well as a contemporary example of a community-made patchwork quilt which was used to send a message of peace as one nation prepared to attack another. For McLaughlin, it is the use of metaphor in parables which disposes them to being good stories and, in turn,

[9] Smith, 'Everyone but Rizzo'.
[10] David Cheetham, 'Exploring the aesthetic "space" for inter-religious encounter', *Exchange*, 39/1 (2010), 71–86, at p. 86.
[11] Mohammed Abu-Nimer, Amal Khoury, and Emily Welty, *Unity in Diversity: Interfaith Dialogue in the Middle East* (Washington, DC: United States Institute of Peace Press, 2007), pp. 15–16.

lends them to transformative dialogue.[12] But, I suggest, if metaphor is a key reason why parables are well suited to interreligious dialogue then it follows that other forms of art could similarly be well suited to interreligious dialogue. After all, art is rich in metaphor and can, therefore, be used to tell interesting stories.

Summarising the discussion so far, it can be said that there is a particular need for interreligious dialogue which engages the emotions as well as the intellect. It is this type of dialogue which has the potential to transform participants beyond mutual distrust, prejudice and ignorance. Various types of art, whether in the form of film, embroidery or something else, can break down barriers and lead to substantive discussions. Art can be especially impressive if it uses metaphor to tell a story.

It should be kept in mind that while metaphor can make expression, whether verbal or non-verbal, more impressive, it can also make expression more exclusive if used in a particular way. If metaphor were to be employed in such a way that only those initiated could understand it then it would give rise to forms of dialogue as specialist as cognitive-discursive interreligious dialogue. For art to have the greatest impact in interreligious dialogue the stories and metaphors involved must, therefore, not be cryptic – although different audiences will, of course, have different preferences for this.

As well as having the potential to transform participants in interreligious dialogue, art fulfils the more basic need of providing information about a religious tradition which cannot be imparted by description alone. Illman notes an inverse relationship between information and prejudice: the more information we have about each other, the less prejudice we feel.[13] One who is familiar with the art of a religious tradition is, perhaps, aware of much more than one who only has a theoretical understanding of the religious tradition. George Pattison explains that art

---

[12] Elizabeth W. McLaughlin, 'The power of living parables for transformative interfaith encounters', in Daniel S. Brown Jr. (ed.), *A Communication Perspective on Interfaith Dialogue: Living within the Abrahamic Traditions* (Lanham, MD: Lexington Books, 2013), pp. 123–38.

[13] Ruth Illman, 'Plurality and peace: inter-religious dialogue in a creative perspective', *International Journal of Public Theology*, 4 (2010), 175–93, at pp. 178–9; 'Curiosity instead of fear: literature as creative inter-religious dialogue', *Journal of Inter-Religious Dialogue*, 1 (2009), 7–14, at p. 9. Illman cites a work by Omid Safi; however, it transpires through personal communication that another reference was intended, namely, Gerrie ter Haar, 'Religion: source of conflict or resource for peace?' in Gerrie ter Haar and James J. Busuttil, *Bridge or Barrier: Religion, Violence and Visions for Peace* (Leiden: Brill, 2005), pp. 3–34, at p. 31.

has a capacity to reveal the fundamental values of a religious tradition as well as something of the style of those traditions.[14] Pattison's assertion is corroborated by the Globethics.net report based on an international conference on interreligious and inter-cultural dialogue held in Nairobi, Kenya. Globethics.net says that creative arts such as music, visual arts and dance can express 'the values attached to a context as well as the values behind the intention of the artist'.[15]

It is hoped that the case for using art in interreligious dialogue is now clear. The remainder of this chapter seeks to work from this theoretical grounding to explore how successful, if not transformative, dialogue might be achieved between Christians and Muslims using music. In the next section, I focus on what Muslims can offer in terms of musical dialogue given that the issue of music is a particularly contentious topic in the Islamic tradition.

MUSIC AND THE ISLAMIC TRADITION

There is no known culture, past or present, in which music is not found.[16] According to Steven Brown et al., 'Music making is the quintessential human cultural activity, and music is an ubiquitous element in all cultures large and small.'[17] Furthermore, a person unfamiliar with a form of music is more likely to be able to understand it than he or she is a foreign language.[18] It follows that music is a prime candidate for being considered an art which lends itself to being shared between different religious traditions. At least one might think so. However, when it comes to the Islamic tradition, the 'shareability' of music is not completely obvious, with many Muslims expressing the view that music is forbidden (*ḥarām*). Such sentiment would seem to undermine the very idea that music can be

---

[14] George Pattison, *Art, Modernity and Faith: Restoring the Image* (London: SCM Press, 1998), p. 155.

[15] Globethics.net, *Globethics.net Principles on Sharing Values across Cultures and Religions'* (Geneva: globethics.net, 2012), p. 17. www.globethics.net/web/ge/texts-series. Accessed 20 December 2012.

[16] Josh McDermott and Marc Hauser, 'The origins of music: innateness, uniqueness, and evolution', *Music Perception*, 23/1 (2005), 29–59, at pp. 29, 30.

[17] Steven Brown, Björn Merker and Nils L. Wallin, 'An introduction to evolutionary musicology', in Nils L. Wallin, Bjrön Merker, and Steven Brown (eds.), *The Origins of Music* (Cambridge, MA: MIT Press, 2001), pp. 3–24, at p. 3.

[18] Bruno Nettl, 'The universal language: universals of music', in *The Study of Ethnomusicology: Thirty-One Issues and Concepts* (Urbana: University of Illinois Press, 2005), p. 49.

used to facilitate dialogue between Muslims and Christians (or, for that matter, Muslims and any other group) – but is this really the case?

To answer the question whether the use of music in dialogue involving Muslims is doomed to failure we can begin by noting Lois Ibsen al Faruqi's hierarchy of forms of 'sound art' in the Muslim world.[19] Faruqi says that some of these forms of sound art are considered to be music by Muslims and some are not. Faruqi says that the hierarchy is 'inexplicit' in Islamic culture 'but nevertheless powerfully implied'.[20] I would add, by way of emphasis, that Faruqi's hierarchy is implied by all groups and trends within the Muslim world. At the top of the hierarchy is the recitation of the Qur'an. The Muslim reverence of the Qur'an as the verbatim transcription of the revealed word of God has the effect that the recitation of its verses becomes the exemplar for all other forms of sound art in the Islamic tradition. The more an expression of sound art resembles the recitation of the Qur'an, the more it has been welcomed and approved in the Muslim world. Conversely, the less an expression of sound art resembles the recitation of the Qur'an the more it has been viewed with scepticism and hostility. Muslims have reserved the term 'music' for these latter forms of sound art (such as the sensuous music of nightclubs) which bear no resemblance to the recitation of the Qur'an. It follows that Muslim hostility towards music is largely a matter of semantics. In Muslim parlance, 'music' refers to reprehensible forms of sound art and it is these which are shunned rather than all forms of sound art. Generally speaking, for Muslims the term 'music' could never be used to refer to anything sacred. As Seyyed Hossein Nasr observes, Muslims would consider it blasphemous to label the recitation of the Qur'an as music, yet its recitation nonetheless exhibits musicality.[21]

A number of characteristics distinguish the musicality of the Qur'an recitation from the musicality of forms of sound art that are not warmly received in the Muslim world. Firstly, the recitation of the Qur'an is never instrumentally accompanied. Secondly, rules pertaining to the correct recitation of the Qur'an (as specified in the science of *tajwīd*)

---

[19] Lois Ibsen al Faruqi, *Islam and Art* (Islamabad: National Hijra Council, 1985); 'Music, musicians and Muslim law', *Asian Music*, 17 (1985), 3–36; 'The Shari'ah on music and musicians', *Al-'Ilm*, 11/9 (1989), 33–53.

[20] Al Faruqi, 'Music, musicians and Muslim law', p. 7.

[21] Seyyed Hossein Nasr, 'Islam and music: the legal and the spiritual dimensions', in Lawrence E. Sullivan (ed.), *Enchanting Powers: Music in the World's Religions* (Cambridge, MA: Harvard University Center for Study of World Religions, 1997), pp. 219–35, at p. 220.

place constraints on rhythm. For example, a double *m* should be recited for two counts and a long vowel followed by a quiescent letter (often occurring upon stopping at the end of a verse) should be recited for either two, four or six counts. Thirdly, the ideal recitation of the Qur'an uses one or more classical Arab melodies (*naghamāt*). The melodies which are most commonly used are varieties of seven melodic modes (*maqāmāt*) called Ṣabā, Nahāwand, 'Ajam, Bayāt, Sīkā, Ḥijāz and Rast.[22]

The regulated rhythm and bounded melodic range of the Qur'an recitation ensure that flamboyance is not one of its hallmarks. However, this is not to say that a recitation of the Qur'an shows no creativity on the part of the reciter. A reciter has a great deal of freedom to recite within the melodic modes just so long as the rules of *tajwīd* and nature of recitation as worship are respected. In other words, the reciter improvises when reciting, choosing through musical intuition how to match the different notes of a melody to the words being recited. Shifts in melody can be particularly impressive to the listener given that different melodies evoke different emotions. Ṣabā, for example, is used when reciting verses about divine punishment, whereas Rast is used to recite verses about divine reward. Changes in register can also be used by a reciter to convey intensity or the sense of different speakers in a dialogue.

Naturally, a brief written description of the Qur'an recitation can do little to convey the sense of what the recitation actually sounds like. However, Kristina Nelson's description of a recitation in Egypt does tell a little of the experience.

Suddenly the power of the phrase seizes the scattered sensibility of the crowd, focusing it, and carrying it forward like a great wave, setting the listeners down gently after one phrase and lifting them up in the rising of the next. The recitation proceeds, the intensity grows. A man hides his face in his hands, another weeps quietly. Some listeners tense themselves as if in pain, while, in the pauses between phrases, other[s] shout appreciative responses to the reciter. Time passes unnoticed.[23]

It should be borne in mind that the private recitation of an individual does not necessarily match the public recitation of an accomplished reciter. While any given individual's recitation will have its merits, a

---

[22] In this order, the first letters of each mode can be usefully read in Arabic as ṣuni'a bi-saḥar, or 'work by morning'. It should not be unmentioned that not all 'Arab melodies' originated in Arabia, as testified by some of the names of the melodies.

[23] Kristina Nelson, *The Art of Reciting the Qur'an* (Cairo: American University in Cairo Press, 2001), p. xiii.

fully artistic recitation will require the skill and experience of an accomplished reciter.

Besides the recitation of the Qur'an, the call to prayer and recitation of liturgy (such as pilgrimage chants) also exhibit a musicality with which Muslims can universally identify. While acknowledging Muslim reservations surrounding the term 'music', it would seem appropriate – in order to adopt more widely recognisable language – to label these three genres of sound art as the sacred music of the Islamic tradition. While one cannot deny that other forms of sound art exist in the Muslim world, I would argue that it makes more sense – at least in the first instance – for Muslims to engage in musical interreligious dialogue by using the recitation of the Qur'an, the call to prayer and recitation of liturgy rather than by using divisive types of sound art. This means not only that Muslims should choose wisely the type of music they present to Christians but also that Christians should not expect anything else from Muslims.

SACRED MUSIC AND INTERRELIGIOUS DIALOGUE

It has been acknowledged that Muslims have reservations regarding music, but a type of music was identified in the previous section that Muslims could present to Christians in order to have a musical engagement. The underlying assumption of the previous section was that whatever music Muslims feel able to present, Christians would be able to reciprocate. One may object that, in dialogue, one party should not be able to dictate the framework of dialogue to the other, and therefore it is wrong to focus on Muslim musical sensitivities. Such an objection fails to recognise that dialogue must be accommodating in order to have the greatest chance of succeeding. Constructing a dialogue framework which inherently excludes groups and individuals can only limit the success of dialogue.

In his discussion of religious fundamentalism (which might better be termed 'religious conservatism'), Peter A. Huff draws attention to the issue of exclusion.

Despite fundamentalism's imposing presence on the religious landscape, interreligious dialogue tends to operate as if it did not exist. Fundamentalists and their concerns are rarely represented in interfaith encounter. If fundamentalism is acknowledged at all, it is branded as the prime threat to international spiritual harmony. In fact, nothing exposes the limits of pluralism better than the phenomenon of fundamentalism.[24]

---

[24] Peter A. Huff, 'The challenge of fundamentalism for interreligious dialogue', *Cross Currents*, 50 (2000). www.crosscurrents.org/Huff.htm. Accessed 5 June 2013.

Huff also says, 'Interreligious dialogue will never fulfil its unique mission until it recognizes the fundamentalisms of the world as valued conversation partners.' I believe we would do well to keep Huff's advice in mind. After all, it is quite conceivable that most Muslims do not follow a conservative approach to music but nonetheless think that it is the approach that they should take ideally.[25]

Keeping Huff's advice in mind means being wary of dialogue initiatives which are avant-garde and which are focused more upon music than upon prayerful reflection on forms of worship which have a musical character. It is my impression that many interreligious music concerts seeking to engage Muslims find examples of sound art from the Muslim world which are controversial and unrepresentative. It is of course natural to select dialogue partners with whom one can identify, but this should not be at the expense of recognising other possible dialogue partners or at the expense of gaining a balanced view of an entire religious tradition.

That music may be different from what was expected – for example, that it may be without instrumentation or dance – is a point that perhaps many well-intentioned interreligious music concert organisers would do well to recognise. Fortunately, with regard to Christian–Muslim dialogue, obvious examples of sacred music exist within the Christian tradition which accord with the sacred music of the Islamic tradition. I refer to Gregorian, Ambrosian and (especially) Mozarabic chants which – to my mind – are manifestly comparable to Islamic chants and allow one to imagine the types of matters Christians and Muslims could fruitfully explore together.

Dialogue between Christians and Muslims that is focused upon sacred music would have, no doubt, two broad aspects. On the one hand there would be the aspect of information, in that participants would become better informed of one another's traditions. On the other hand there would be the personal aspect, in which participants would become acquainted with one another's human stories. Both aspects are required to foster mutual understanding and to break down barriers. So, in terms of information, one would not only come to recognise the sounds of another tradition but would also come, for example, to understand when they are heard. It may be that some sounds are heard on particular occasions and are associated with particular festivals, or it may be that some sounds are a regular part of the soundscape of a religious tradition. Furthermore,

[25] Cf. Jonas Otterbeck and Anders Ackfeldt, 'Music and Islam', *Contemporary Islam*, 6/3 (2012), 227–33, at p. 228.

there is much to be learnt regarding the development of sacred music within a religious tradition which will reveal the relationship of a tradition with beauty. One commonly offered justification for the tradition of the Qur'an recitation, for example, is the instruction of the Prophet Muhammad to beautify the Qur'an with the voice.[26]

In terms of the personal, one of the most apparent things is that sacred music requires the performance of individuals and performance involves overcoming challenges. Such challenges could relate to training, preparation before a performance and dealing with nervousness. Sacred music also requires an audience and this means human stories can be told by performers about the receptions they have received from audiences and from individuals within audiences. Conversely, there are stories to be told by individuals who are not musically trained of the affection they have for hearing sacred music and the meaning it has for them.

With all the conversations, experiences and sharing to be had with musical dialogue one wonders how this form of dialogue could ever be received negatively. Yet online banter by 'intifada' et al. surrounding the Opera and Koran Meet Gregorian concert, held in 2008 in Sydney, Australia, was just that: negative.[27] Although comments made about the event on the online forum MuslimVillage cannot be taken too seriously, because they do not originate from a controlled empirical study, my sense is that the comments may indicate some of the challenges to be faced in encouraging Muslim participation in interreligious dialogue by means of music. Participants in the discussion were concerned that the Qur'an was to be recited in an event where 'music' was to feature – the suggestion being that the sacred should not be defiled by appearing beside the profane, a suggestion that indicates the attitude of some Muslims towards music. One participant of the discussion appeared to be uncomfortable with the Qur'an being recited in any secular venue. There was also (perhaps with a rather exclusivist attitude) concern that it would be an 'insult' to the Qur'an to place it on the same level as opera music and Gregorian chant. Some participants could not express the reason for their discomfort with the event, although one such person recognised that it was a

---

[26] One of the various statements reported of the Prophet regarding beautiful recitation is 'Whosoever does not beautify (*yataghann*) the Qur'an is not from us'. This statement is reported by, among others, Bukhārī in his *Ṣaḥīḥ* ('Tawḥīd') and Majlisī in *Biḥār al-anwār* ('Qirā'at al-Qur'ān bi-l-ṣawt al-ḥasan').

[27] Intifada et al., 'Opera & Koran Meet Gregorian', *MuslimVillage Forums*, 2008. http://muslimvillage.com/forums/topic/46669-opera-koran-meet-gregorian. Accessed 1 December 2013.

chance for non-Muslims to hear the recitation of the Qur'an. The discussion involved sixteen different participants, one of whom decided to attend the event and commented that she was happy she did so. However, this participant also commented that she enjoyed the Sufi whirling performance (*samāʿ*), which could suggest that she was more comfortable with instrumental music in the first place (the *samāʿ* is often instrumentally accompanied and respect for the practice could indicate a more lenient disposition).

The negative banter relating to the Opera and Koran Meet Gregorian concert reminds us of not only the need for musical dialogue to take Huff's advice seriously and to be focused on worship rather than music, but also the need to account for different perspectives. While recognising that the fearless exploration of one another's traditions enjoined by *ACW* may require controversy, it seems to me that avoiding unnecessary controversy is bound to be more beneficial.

CONCLUSION

The argument of this chapter has started from the invitation of *ACW* to Christians and Muslims to put aside differences and to respect one another. My contention is that stronger relations require intelligent and inventive forms of dialogue. The standard form of interreligious dialogue, which is cognitive and discursive, is neither the only way in which Christians and Muslims can engage with each other nor necessarily the most effective type of engagement in all circumstances. Artistic, and especially musical, dialogue initiatives offer an alternative to cognitive-discursive dialogue initiatives and offer the opportunity for the spirit of dialogue to touch the lives of those whom it may otherwise never reach. While Muslims may be suspicious about anything called 'music', there are forms of sound art that are an inextricable part of the Islamic tradition and these would seem to correspond closely to certain forms of sound art in the Christian tradition. The suggestion is then that musical dialogue initiatives could be devised in a way that allows them to have wide appeal among both Christians and Muslims. As Christians and Muslims become better informed of one another's traditions and personal stories, it is hoped that the invitation of *ACW* will become a reality.[28]

[28] This chapter was written on the basis of research conducted during a Foundation for Interreligious and Intercultural Research and Dialogue fellowship programme, in collaboration with the University of Geneva. The fellowship was kindly financed by the Levant Foundation.

PART V

A COMMON WORD AND THE FUTURE

17

A Common Word as Contextual Theology

Marianne Farina

Since its beginning, the *A Common Word* initiative has organised significant dialogues, studies and joint statements about the commandment to *love God and love neighbour* as revealed in Christian and Islamic sacred texts. These sessions have explored various dimensions of this commitment and can serve as a foundation for expanding the dialogues. In this chapter, I offer suggestions for developing a new phase of *ACW* discussions.

At the core of my suggestions is a conviction that Christian–Muslim dialogue and comparative theological study benefit greatly from implementing an inductive process for analysis and reflection. This requires gathering together participants from local communities, social groups and the academy into the discussion of sacred texts. To this end, I believe that a contextual theological model is critical to the future *ACW* deliberations.

To support this claim, I will develop my argument in three parts. First, I will describe contextual theology and show the importance of this approach for contemporary theological engagement. Second, I will identify a model of contextual theology that I consider appropriate for deepening *ACW* dialogues. Finally, I will offer a few suggestions on ways that *ACW* programmes could develop this model for theological study and interreligious dialogue.

WHAT IS CONTEXTUAL THEOLOGY?

Contextual theology recognises that there are three critical sources for theological study: scripture, tradition and context.[1] As Stephen Bevans

[1] Stephen B. Bevans, *Models of Contextual Theology* (Maryknoll, NY: Orbis Books, 2004), p. 4.

notes, a 'contextual approach to theology is in many ways a radical departure from the notion of traditional theology, but at the same time it is very much in continuity with it'.[2] In speaking of *context* as a third source, he describes how this element changes the whole equation by drawing experiences of individuals and their faith communities into the task of theological inquiry.[3] Speaking directly about interpreting sacred texts, Bevans says:

> When we recognize the importance of context for theology, we are also acknowledging the absolute importance of context for the development of both scripture and tradition. The writings of scripture [...] do not simply fall from the sky. They themselves are products of human beings and *their* contexts.[4]

Therefore, when speaking of context, we are claiming that the reception and interpretation of sacred texts happen within socio-cultural realities, past and present. Revelation is an encounter with God's living Word that helps us discover the meaning of our existence in the midst of common concerns and our hopes for the future.

Sacred texts, faith practices and their interpretations have always been mediated through cultures, i.e. contexts. The many books of the 'Bible' with their variety of literary styles reflect 'different times, different concerns, and even different cultures'.[5] In Islam too, for instance, the Qur'anic discipline *asbāb al-nuzūl* (occasions of revelation) maintains a history concerning the event of particular revelations in the Qur'an. These accounts, along with collections of narratives that form a Sunna of the Prophet Muhammad, are representative of a community reading its sacred texts and understanding their meaning. In this way, contextual theology is normative, i.e., 'traditional'. C. S. Song, whose work addresses the need to do Christian theology from the 'womb' of Asia, describes this critical need for grounding our reading of texts in a theological 'home', stating that '[t]here is no such thing as a theology immune from cultural and historical influences. Theology is not culturally and historically neutral. A neutral theology is in fact a homeless theology. It does not belong anywhere'.[6]

---

[2] Ibid.
[3] Ibid., p. 5.
[4] Ibid.
[5] Ibid., p. 7.
[6] C. S. Song, *Tell Us Our Names: Story Theology from an Asian Perspective* (Maryknoll, NY: Orbis Books, 1982), pp. 52–3.

Such realisations press us to consider how, without understanding the context, our interpretations of scripture or theological ideas become esoteric, monolithic or even oppressive to our communities. Whose theology is this if it is detached from, and unresponsive to, local cultural realities? Creating exchanges between the academy and local communities who receive, contemplate and live their faith in various contexts is essential. It is the local theological enterprise that, as Robert Schreiter reminds us, engages 'the energies of more than professional theologians'.[7] He notes that doing theology in the local contexts points to those for whom theology is, in the first instance, intended: 'the community itself, to enhance its own self-understanding'.[8] Schreiter emphasises that this critical engagement requires a dialectic that is responsive to cultural realities (the ethnographic model) while remaining ready to challenge those same social structures in order to 'uncover forces of oppression, struggle, violence, and power' (the liberation model).[9] In this way, reflections on scripture and tradition include the conscious reflexive experiences of believers, and the professional theologian becomes more of a midwife who assists the 'giving birth to a theology that is truly rooted in a culture and moment in history'.[10]

Because of the inductive process of these inquiries, contextual theological approaches challenge inherited conceptions about God and one another in certain cultures and societies. God's word calls us to examine our ways of living and thinking and to respond in each age and context anew, especially in those areas where we might resist change. This being so, contextual theology is a sacred epistemology, wherein 'human experience, current events, and culture are areas of God's activity and sources of theology'.[11] Theological reflection on sacred texts then is more than an objective study of God formulated by experts; it is a transformative enterprise forming communities of faith capable of an authentic life-giving response to God's revelation.

Moreover, Bevans' work builds upon the two basic model dynamics outlined by Schreiter. He describes six theoretical models of contextual theology. His study illustrates the eclectic nature of this approach as it

---

[7] Robert J. Schreiter, *Constructing Local Theologies* (Maryknoll, NY: Orbis Books, 1985), p. 16.
[8] Ibid.
[9] Ibid., p. 15.
[10] Leonardo N. Mercado, *Elements of Filipino Theology* (Tacloban City, Philippines: Divine Word University Publications, 1975), p. 13.
[11] Bevans, *Models of Contextual Theology*, p. 22.

seeks to incorporate contemporary-pluralistic realities. Those engaged in contextual theological process introduce their particular social and historical circumstances into the reflections. Thus there is also the possibility that several models of contextual theology will be operative in the theological method.

In my experiences with diverse cultures in Asia and Africa, theological reflection is always contextual. Our work is typical of what Bevans calls the *praxis model* of contextual theology. Scripture, tradition and realities 'close to the ground' help us to 'see analytically, judge theologically, and act politically, pastorally'.[12] Crises, such as loss of tribal lands, migration to the cities, the struggle to keep local institutions afloat, conflicts among religions and fighting greedy national and transnational projects, and successes, such as growing literacy rates, women's employment, successful farm cooperatives and general health concerns, became critical to reading and reflecting on sacred texts. Our experiences pose questions that emerge from the challenges and concerns of the community. Addressing these questions through social analysis and theological reflection contributes to a dynamic reading and interpreting of scripture. For example, one of the practices we fostered in Bangladesh was to engage in the 'pastoral spiral' process whether we were reading scripture, seeking guidance for community development or addressing problems in the community.

The pastoral spiral, also called 'the pastoral circle', has become a method in Catholic social teachings for putting one's faith into practice. Although this hermeneutical process is often presented as a four-step method, my research and ministry have led me to see it as a schema of seven steps: (1) experience, (2) analysis and theological reflection, (3) new vision, (4) planning, (5) action, (6) evaluation and (7) new reality/experience.

The process brings the local community's experiences into dialogue with social analysis and reflection on sacred texts. The hermeneutical method helps the faithful to come to a deeper understanding of the social concern, as it gives new insights to sacred texts. This is what is known as 'reading the signs of the times'. Often these dialogues will involve experts in social and theological fields of study. Through addressing questions such as What is happening? Why? What does this mean for us both

---

[12] Leonardo Boff, 'What are Third World theologies?', *Concilium*, 199 (*Theologies of the Third World: Convergences and Differences*, ed. Leonardo Boff and Virgil Elizondo) (1988), 3–14, at p. 12.

pastorally and theologically? How should we respond? The community recognises God's call to embrace a 'new vision'. In order to answer this call, the community designs action steps to make the vision a reality. In this part of the process, the community identifies specific groups and their responsibilities for executing these plans. The next part of the process is evaluation. It is a critical component of the whole process. It sets in motion accountability for fulfilling the designated responsibilities and offers an opportunity for the community to reflect on the pastoral planning process itself. This last reflection brings the community to a new moment and so the pastoral spiral is an ongoing process of deliberation. Thus, it can become a dynamic method for the contextual study of sacred texts as communities 'read the signs of the times'.

Each of the seven steps of this process has epistemic qualities. Together they shape a community's faith and praxis. In the process, we recognise that the lives of believers, which include their social commitments, are a critical resource for interpreting scripture. Joined with those from the academy, that is, the professional theologians, communities engage in discernment and prayer to 'hear' God's word. As Schreiter notes:

In the development of local theologies, the professional theologian serves as an important resource, helping the community to clarify its own experience and to relate it to the experience of other communities past and present. Thus the professional has an indispensable [...] role. The theologian cannot create a theology in isolation from the community's experience; but the community has need of a theologian's knowledge to ground its own experience [...]. [T]he theologian helps to create the bonds of mutual accountability between local and world church.[13]

This process can bring a variety of voices into the theological process: those within a tradition, those from other traditions and especially the voices of the marginalised. Thus theology is a living encounter, a new experience of God, a new reading of the past and a new consciousness of reality. This is not a project that simply applies interpretations of sacred texts to contexts but one that recognises the presence of God's revealing word in human experience. Each step of the pastoral spiral is an opportunity for intellectual, spiritual and moral growth, because participants realise God's word is present, calling them to deeper conversion.

Thus, engaging the *praxis model* for the study of any text, for instance the *love commandment* in the gospels and in the Qur'an, has the potential to be a formative exercise that bears fruit beyond the initial dialogues or studies. *ACW* initiatives, which are explored and discussed in the present

[13] Shreiter, *Constructing Local Theologies*, p. 18.

volume, are just that – beginnings. In what follows, I offer an example of how a contextual approach might contribute to future developments in *ACW* studies and dialogue.

A CONTEXTUAL THEOLOGICAL MODEL FOR
A COMMON WORD

Studying the history and reception of *ACW* programmes, I believe that an inductive contextual approach to the study of the 'common word' could augment the interreligious learning of these dialogues. Embracing a contextual model for *ACW* fosters two significant actions. The first is full engagement in four critical dialogues: life, social justice projects, spiritual experiences and theological study. The second is the offer of a forum that goes beyond formal gatherings and academic settings into Christian and Muslim faith communities. Although recent *ACW* dialogues have produced a number of important initiatives, such as community outreach programmes, academic courses and subsequent theological studies, we still need to review these programmes as faith communities and academies in order to address how we see God working with us and through us in these dialogues. To this end, I propose a combination of two models of contextual theology: the *praxis model*, which connects concrete experiences with scriptural reflection and communal discernment, and the *transcendental model*, which is characterised by attentiveness to the 'affective and cognitive operations in the self-transcending subject'.[14]

The *praxis model*, as noted previously, calls for the implementation of the pastoral circle or spiral process and includes various groups in the dialogue. It can contribute to mutual understanding and cooperation among these groups and at the same time to the development of a local theology. In the interreligious context, the beliefs, values and purposes of religious traditions are the lens through which moral discernment occurs. Through these deliberations, communities realise ways to put their faith into just and liberative action, as they become more deeply aware of the integral goodness of all creation.

The *transcendental model* emerges from the dynamic of revelation itself. God calls us into being, and through contemplation of the sacred texts and their interpretation we come to a greater understanding of God, self and others. 'It is knowing as we are known',[15] as Parker Palmer

---

[14] Bevans, *Models of Contextual Theology*, p. 103.
[15] Parker Palmer, *To Know as We Are Known* (New York: Harper One, 1993).

famously avers. The learning we experience is recognition of our capacity for relationship with God.[16] It is a grasping of truth that goes beyond extrinsic information about God or others and reaches into the interior depth of a person's integrity, which Thomas Merton claims is 'celebrating a common identity, a common consciousness',[17] a 'true communion on the deepest level'.[18]

Thus in combining these two models, forming a praxis-transcendental *model*, we begin with a conviction that the reality of the 'love commandment' in our sacred texts is a dynamic encounter flowing from experience. It is a phenomenological and hermeneutical approach to the reading and interpretation of texts. Scriptures are not 'out there', existing somehow independently of our experience.

The encounter with these texts, mediated through local realities, calls us to greater authenticity as religious and cultural subjects. We ask questions about our own perceptions, conscious of the way biases can hinder true insight. We realise that when we speak about knowledge of God, we speak about God's call to remain in relationship with God and others. As persons who are 'attentive, intelligent, reasonable and responsible',[19] we discern God's presence in the various aspects of our study and dialogue. Thus the 'common word' becomes a 'common consciousness', aware of being drawn nearer to God and one another. We learn how to 'obey', that is, to listen deeply to the call to love God and neighbour. As we look to the future of *ACW* exchanges, the praxis-transcendental *model* has much to offer. Attention to contextual realities, and contemplation of the personal and communal transformations taking place in these exchanges, will add new insights to the 'common word' Christians and Muslims share.

ENGAGING THE MODEL: FORUMS FOR CREATING AND SUSTAINING STUDY AND DIALOGUE

Building on the good work done thus far with *ACW*, the final part of this chapter addresses how we might apply the praxis-transcendental method to these exchanges. Included in this proposal are several features

---

[16] Ibid., p. 51.
[17] Thomas Del Prete, *Thomas Merton and the Education of the Whole Person* (Birmingham, AL: Religious Education Press, 1990), p. 143.
[18] Ibid., p. 141.
[19] Bernard Lonergan, *Method in Theology* (Toronto: University of Toronto Press, 1990), p. 290.

of Catholic and Muslim programmes for dialogue and of the Christian–Muslim dialogues that the Church of England's 'Building Bridges' seminars began in 2002 under the aegis of the then-Archbishop of Canterbury, Dr George Carey.

The development of a contextual approach to *ACW* study and dialogue begins with recognising how critical it is for the initiative to move beyond academic or leadership circles. Seminars with a broader representation will help Christians and Muslims 'read the signs of the times', which is essential to interpreting the meaning of the common call or word to *love of God and love of neighbour*. Therefore, a context approach would help *ACW* gatherings (1) to expand the dialogue circles, (2) to begin studies and dialogues with experience and (3) to integrate evaluation into the process so that participants become attentive to ways the dialogues contribute to deeper knowledge of God, self and others. In what follows, I offer some approaches to dialogue and programmes that address each of these three aspects.

In 2015, the Roman Catholic Church celebrated the fiftieth anniversary of the closing of the Second Vatican Council. One of the critical documents written by this council was *Nostra Aetate* ('In our time'). In this declaration, the Catholic Church expressed its desire to dialogue with world religions. The discussions that preceded the declaration's approval by the bishops noted that dialogue with world religions is God's project. The bishops recognised that the Catholic Church has a responsibility to make ecumenical and interreligious dialogue more relevant to a community's experience and efficacious in creating greater understanding and cooperation among different communities.

What is significant for the formulation of this declaration, I contend, was Blessed Pope Paul VI's inaugural encyclical, *Ecclesiam suam* ('His [Christ's] Church').[20] Some of the important features of this document point to the need for a contextual approach to dialogue.

The encyclical was published in the summer of 1964. Addressing all members of the church and people of good will, Paul VI says that the mission of the church is based on three guiding principles: deeper self-knowledge, renewal and dialogue (§§ 9–15). Thus through 'dialogue with

---

[20] Paul VI, *Ecclesiam suam*, 6 August 1964. www.vatican.va/encyclicals/documents. For the text, see http://w2.vatican.va/content/paul-vi/la/encyclicals/documents/hf_p-vi_enc_06081964_ecclesiam.html (Latin) and http://w2.vatican.va/content/paul-vi/en/encyclicals/documents/hf_p-vi_enc_06081964_ecclesiam.html (English). Accessed January 2016.

the modern world' (§ 14), the church will contribute to the building of world peace:

Our aim must be to educate mankind to sentiments and policies which are opposed to violent and deadly conflicts and to foster just, rational, and peaceful relations between States. [...] Our mission is to bring men together in mutual love through the power of that kingdom of justice and peace which Christ inaugurated by His coming into the world.

(§ 16)

Not only was this the first time the word 'dialogue' had been used officially in church documents, but it was the key principle supporting the other two, because each venture into self-knowledge or renewal depended upon a spirit of humility, openness and dialogue. These aspirations resonate well with the essential goals articulated in the *ACW* invitation:

Finding common ground between Muslims and Christians is not simply a matter of polite ecumenical dialogue between selected religious leaders. Christianity and Islam are the largest and second largest religions in the world and in history. Christians and Muslims reportedly make up over a third and over a fifth of humanity respectively. Together they make up more than 55% of the world's population, making the relationship between these two religious communities the most important factor in contributing to meaningful peace around the world. If Muslims and Christians are not at peace, the world cannot be at peace.[21]

A closer review of *Ecclesiam suam* illustrates how the three guiding principles (self-knowledge, renewal, dialogue) identified by Paul VI contribute to a contextual theological approach. In this encyclical, Paul VI describes *deeper-self knowledge* as a critical look at ourselves as church to determine whether we truly bear in our life and work the image of the one who called us into being (§§ 9–10).

This, Paul VI claims, leads to the second principle, of *renewal*. If our witness to the faith and truth of our beliefs is found wanting, then we have the duty as persons and communities to acknowledge our faults and recommit ourselves to reform (§ 11). Next, he notes that *dialogue* is an essential process for reform that aims to 'bring men together in mutual love through the power of that kingdom of justice and peace which Christ inaugurated' (§ 12–16).

Paul VI focuses then on his understanding of dialogue. First, he says that God is the initiator of dialogue because God's word continually speaks to human beings (§ 71). Through dialogue, he says,

---

[21] *A Common Word*. www.acommonword.com/the-acw-document/. Accessed 20 October 2016.

we can remain open to new possibilities for promoting human dignity and freedom as we 'listen not only to what men say, but more especially to what they have in their hearts to say' (§ 87). The dialogues differ according to the particular groups, but each requires intelligible, humble, confident and prudent conversations (§ 81) with others. Dialogue, Paul VI states, 'thrives on friendship, and most especially on service' (§ 87). He notes as well that these friendships are founded on the faith and that these beliefs are a resource for establishing rights and duties as we seek the good of all humankind (§§ 97–8). The insights that God both initiates and sustains dialogue as well as that friendships are important constitute significant aspects of a transcendental approach to dialogue.

In focusing on ways the church, cultures and societies can promote this dialogue, Paul VI identifies four essential interlocutors. Using the idea of concentric circles, he describes the key groups: the largest circle is all humankind, among whom there are those who profess no religion at all; then come members of world religions; next other Christians and finally the internal or intra-faith circle of Catholic communities. The vision of dialogue proposed by Paul VI seeks to promote ongoing interaction within groups and a type of fluidity among them so that participants are cognisant of, committed to and influenced by the various voices within any circle of dialogue and across the other dialogue circles.

The fourth inner circle represented the experience of the Second Vatican Council, which was taking place at the time of Paul VI's writing of this encyclical. In this letter, he emphasises that the 'work' of deeper self-knowledge and renewal needs Catholic-to-Catholic dialogues:

How greatly we desire that this dialogue with Our own children may be conducted with the fullness of faith, with charity, and with dynamic holiness. May it be of frequent occurrence and on an intimate level. May it be open and responsive to all truth, every virtue, every spiritual value that goes to make us the heritage of Christian teaching. We want it to be sincere. We want it to be an inspiration to genuine holiness. We want it to show itself ready to listen to the variety of views which are expressed in the world today. We want it to be the sort of dialogue that will make Catholics virtuous, wise, unfettered, fair-minded and strong.

(§ 113)

Critical to these dialogues is inclusion of grassroots groups, an approach that Paul VI would himself embrace in subsequent studies and writings.

I believe the proposal of the intra-faith circle of dialogue, and Paul VI's connecting this dialogue to the other three circles of dialogue, is the genius of the document. This Catholic–Catholic dialogue brings integrity to the other dialogues. Through them we come to a deeper knowledge about ourselves and identify areas needed for further growth and renewal. This keeps our dialogue with others humble because we realise our need for ongoing conversion. Additionally, openness to learning from members of our faith community who hold different viewpoints reminds us of the eclectic nature of our own tradition. It also helps us cultivate the virtue of hospitality to ideas of religious 'Others' and not to see them as monolithic traditions.

The Catholic Common Ground Initiative, the Salam Institute for Peace and Justice and the Building Bridges seminars correspond in particular ways to Paul VI's three principles and dialogue model. These endeavours contain important elements for integrating a praxis-transcendental approach into *ACW* dialogues and studies. A brief description of each highlights these points.

THE CATHOLIC COMMON GROUND INITIATIVE

Founded in 1996 by Cardinal Bernardin of the Roman Catholic Archdiocese of Chicago, Illinois, USA, the Catholic Common Ground Initiative (CCGI) sought to create a forum that would engage Catholics in dialogue with other Catholics about theological, ecclesial and social concerns.[22] Over the last twenty years, topics have included the changing roles of women, human sexuality, health care reform and immigration. Through lectures, conferences and programmes in Catholic parishes, schools and organisations, the initiative promotes a type of dialogue that honours various perspectives on these topics in order to recognise the deeper values represented by varying points of view. The CCGI seeks to reduce polarities and divisiveness within the Catholic communion. The roundtable discussions begin with the community's experience of a particular concern, which leads to further analysis and reflection. The goal is to promote mutual understanding between Catholics who differ on church and social concerns. Focused on honest sharing and dialogue, the CCGI often becomes the model and a means for greater self-knowledge and cultivating fruitful exchanges with groups outside the Catholic communion, that is, the wider circles of dialogue in Paul VI's model.

---

[22] *Catholic Common Ground Initiative.* www.catholiccommonground.org. Accessed January 2016.

SALAM INSTITUTE FOR PEACE AND JUSTICE

Another important example of intra-faith dialogue is the Salam Institute for Peace and Justice (SIPJ).[23] The SIPJ was founded a decade ago by Dr Mohammed Abu-Nimer. It unites academicians and practitioners in intra- and interreligious dialogue and conflict resolution training based on models developed from the Islamic tradition. The SIPJ lists six major areas of operation: research and evaluation, peace-building intervention and training, interreligious and intra-religious dialogue, development and relief, resources and publication and education and curricular development. Each of these efforts is integral to showing how, as one of its leaders stated, 'Together, Muslim and non-Muslim peace-builders can work toward building the capacity of local initiatives to ensure that basic human rights are upheld throughout the world.'[24] Critical to the success of these operations is the introspection and evaluation process they focus on: 'internal dialogue among Muslims on themes of community, non-violence, democracy and peacebuilding',[25] which become formative in the developments promoting interfaith dialogue and actions between Muslims and non-Muslims communities, and the 'ongoing work of identifying and evaluating the condition and development of madrassahs in the Islamic world'.[26]

THE BUILDING BRIDGES SEMINAR

These seminars were begun in January 2002 by George Carey, the then-Archbishop of Canterbury, and continued under the direction of Rowan Williams, who was Archbishop of Canterbury from 2002 until 2012.[27] They have been chaired by Daniel A. Madigan since 2012. The annual seminars have brought together international Christian and Muslim scholars for intensive three-day study and discussion. The explorations focus on a particular subject and on the Christian and Islamic sacred texts that offer insights into the topic under discussion. The seminar opens with public lectures, usually on the first evening, and then continues with

[23] www.salaminstitute.org. Accessed January 2016.
[24] Salam Institute for Peace and Justice, 'Message from the founder'. http://salaminstitute .org/new/?page_id=333. Accessed January 2016.
[25] Salam Institute for Peace and Justice, 'Our approach and services'. http://salaminstitute .org/new/?page_id=449. Accessed January 2016.
[26] Ibid.
[27] https://berkleycenter.georgetown.edu/projects/the-building-bridges-seminar.   Accessed January 2016.

private sessions on the following days. The subjects discussed in these seminars range from sacred texts, prophecy, theological anthropology, secularism, modernity, the role of religion in society, justice, human rights and the common good to the dialogue between religion and science.

What is striking about these sessions is the way the discussions offer a variety of perspectives both within each tradition and across the two traditions. Each topic is systematically examined, and the exploration brings forward different and sometimes conflicting interpretations of the texts and traditions. Central to these meetings, as Archbishop Rowan Williams has noted, is the way participants 'watch each other engaging' with their sacred texts. In this way, we enter into dialogues that are 'fundamentally oriented toward getting to know one another's hearts'.[28] Also, recent seminars have included pastoral dimensions of the topic investigated, introducing a creative inductive process into the deliberations. For example, the 2012 seminar 'Death, Resurrection, and Human Destiny'[29] not only discussed the Christian and Islamic teachings about death and resurrection but also included discussions about funeral rites in each tradition. An earlier seminar on prayer (2011) had also provided a unique approach by including personal perspectives on prayer in addition to scholarly presentations on the topic.

Elements from these examples – the Catholic Common Ground Initiative, the Salam Institute for Peace and Justice and the Building Bridges seminar – are important in developing a praxis-transcendental *model* for theological study and dialogue. The CCGI points to the importance of an intra-faith dimension to dialogue. We see similar approaches in Islam with the *Amman Message* initiative.[30] Muslim scholars and leaders convinced that '[t]here exists more in common between the various schools of Islamic jurisprudence than there is difference between them'[31] have initiated a project for collaborative study. Chapters in this volume explore the history and development of this study. In fact, the *ACW* project has become one of its most important fruits.

As noted in Paul VI's recommendation, this inner dialogue can have a positive effect on addressing divisions within communities and foster

---

[28] Rowan Williams, 'Preface', in David Marshall and Lucinda Mosher (eds.), *Death, Resurrection, and Human Destiny: Christian and Muslim Perspectives* (Washington, DC: Georgetown University Press, 2014), pp. xxi–xxiv, at p. xxii.

[29] Ibid.

[30] 'The three points of the Amman Message V.1'. http://ammanmessage.com/the-three-points-of-the-amman-message-v-1/. Accessed 15 August 2016.

[31] Ibid.

proper attitudes for interreligious and civic dialogues. The Salam Institute promotes this inner dialogue, making it a strong evaluative dimension to various exchanges and programmes for Islamic education and social action. The CCGI and the SIPJ offer forums in which sacred texts and their interpretations emerge from and fold back into intra-communal reflections. The dialogue with others is enhanced by a reflexivity that asks, 'Who are we becoming through these engagements?'

In the Building Bridges seminar two critical aspects come to light. The first is the systematic study on a given topic and the care with which various perspectives are offered from within each tradition. Thus participants can develop an appreciation for the richness of sacred teachings and the diversity of scholarly perspectives not only in their own tradition but in another's as well. The second important element drawn from these seminars is the way they connect academic study with pastoral and personal dimensions. Though the seminars do not seek to develop outreach programmes, the proceedings, which include the papers, in-depth discussions, personal experiences and comprehensive summaries of the sessions, have the potential to become resources for local dialogues, course studies or pastoral ministry planning.

CONCLUDING REMARKS

As noted earlier, some *ACW* initiatives have also served as a resource for future study and dialogue. Of note here is the *ACW* conference that took place in 2009 at Georgetown University. At the conclusion Dr Ibrahim Kalin proposed a number of action steps for follow-up by participants and their communities.[32] These commitments are documented in a formal statement but the results of the proposals are largely unknown. There is documentation in the *ACW* five-year anniversary book concerning these programmes and others. What I am recommending is an inductive, inclusive and evaluative process for the study of, and dialogue about, 'our common word' that, like God's word itself, is ongoing.

Interestingly, the 2009 Georgetown conference's subtitle was 'A Global Agenda For Change', a title that captures well a future for *ACW* ventures, if based on a praxis-transcendental contextual approach. As explored in the preceding examples, *ACW* benefits from expanding the dialogue circles and introducing the pastoral spiral process into textual studies.

---

[32] For major *ACW* events, see www. acommonword.com/a-common-word-between-us-and-you-a-global-agenda-for-change-2/. Accessed January 2016.

Critical in this process is to begin with the community's experience and integrate evaluative features that can help participants become attentive to ways these dialogues contribute to deeper knowledge of God, self and others. Such a review might also include opportunities for reflection after the meetings, so that participants take responsibility for fulfilling the commitments ratified in documents or proposals.

The first step is to invite different voices from within our traditions to explore the meaning of the sacred common commandment of love of God and neighbour. Rather than balkanise the process, the approach seeks to include all voices, especially those marginalised within our own communities. Though the *A Common Word between Us and You* letter receives many new endorsements, we might want to ask, 'Who is missing from these discussions and how can we draw these groups into *ACW* deliberations?' When asking these questions we need to look within our own traditions as well as across other faith traditions. In fact, this was a process that the drafters of *ACW* began before they issued the 2007 invitation letter to Christians. These scholars and leaders had met the year before to find common ground among Muslim communities, which led to the inception of the *Amman Message*, whose link to *ACW* is meticulously analysed by Jonathan Kearney in Chapter 2 in the present volume. It is from these efforts that the interreligious initiative emerges. What we lack in the *ACW* platform is an ongoing forum for intra-faith and interfaith reflection by Christians and Muslims involved in these dialogues.

The second step is to engage the pastoral spiral process in both the intra- and interreligious dialogue about our sacred texts. This inductive process reminds us that our sacred texts are living texts. God speaks to us now through our concrete realities. We, as faith communities, respond to God's commandment of love in ways that promote human flourishing and the common good.

ACW discussions about our common commitment to love God and neighbour could become an important foundation for projects fostering social justice, because they are informed by studies and dialogues about our sacred texts that have found a home in the shared context realities of our communities. *ACW*'s recent development of the World Interfaith Harmony Week programme is a good example of the potential inherent both in local-to-global outreach projects and in local-community-to-academic-study-and-reflection. Perhaps we could require that each of these projects, as well as future *ACW* seminars, use the pastoral spiral in the development, study and evaluation of their programmes.

Included in this suggestion is a third aspect – the formative dimension of the praxis-transcendental model. Through the sharing of experiences, analysis, reflection, creative vision, concrete action and most importantly evaluation we can come to realise how studies about sacred texts and projects inspired by sacred texts contribute to knowledge of God, self and others. Reflecting on how we have followed through in the commitments made during these gatherings and projects is also an important aspect of this evaluation. Evaluation processes keep *ACW* as a dynamic enterprise rather than an archived initiative. Whether we are engaged in dialogues of life, spiritual experience, social action or theological study, taking time to evaluate our encounters tutors us in a deep listening to the movements of the Spirit in persons and communities. These deliberative processes could embolden us to engage in difficult dialogues, finding ways to discuss seemingly intractable problems and concerns.

Thus, I believe that a praxis-transcendental contextual approach can foster new developments in comparative studies and dialogue. Through this model we become contemplative-hermeneutic partners responsive to diverse and complex realities. Successful interreligious encounters will be measured by the way we continually deepen our dialogues through these experiences. In this way, we together bear a 'common word of and presence to' God's continual loving and just action in the world.

18

A *Common Word* and Abū Ḥāmid al-Ghazālī's Love of God

Yazid Said

INTRODUCTORY REMARKS

The chapters in this book reflect two aspects that characterise the engagement with the *A Common Word* initiative. Both of these aspects are important. First, we see a clear warning from Christian scholars against a reductionist understanding of common speech in Islam and Christianity, clearly spelled out in Rowan Williams' official response to *ACW*, and particularly well articulated in Chapter 10 by Daniel A. Madigan. This aspect suggests that even when we acknowledge our convergence on love of God and neighbour, this convergence does not mean that love of God and neighbour is a neutral foundation upon which we have added extra doctrinal teachings. Instead, our understanding, even discovery, of the need for love of God and the type of human life that that relationship produces are rooted in our doctrines. There is no escape from acknowledging the importance of our doctrinal differences. By not taking a reductionist view of *ACW*, we make a clear attempt to see here some kind of depth and integrity in each voice where the engagement expresses seriousness of conviction on both sides. When dialogue recognises this level of seriousness, it comes out of depths, not shallow politeness. Often those involved in 'comparative religious studies' miss the purpose of comparing when they assume that we are saying the same thing but in different ways. They do not point to the different foundational questions that each tradition produces with regard to creation and human nature. *ACW* may not have aimed to relate to these differences in the first place, but it has allowed this conversation to happen. This book argues that these doctrinal differences do not frustrate the possibility of *theological* dialogue between Muslims and Christians. Indeed, in Chapter 3 Michael Louis Fitzgerald provides a helpful account of the varieties of dialogue that have taken place throughout the last fifty years, especially in Catholic circles. Discovering more about these differences makes us closer to one another, not further away.

The second important aspect of the engagement with *ACW* clearly spelled out here is the recognition of common goals and common marks of faith as we seek the good of our world. Talk about love of God and neighbour could become a matter of stale and pious cliché; therefore, a number of contributors in this volume have focused on the importance of what *ACW* has called for in terms of common action for the common good in the light of world affairs today, and have even seen this as the main purpose of the initiative. Thus, Tim Winter in Chapter 1 reflects on how poignantly relevant *ACW* is to where Christians and Muslims stand in the world today, arguing that the conception of *ACW* was a reaction to the worrying conflicts of our world. Most discussions on world affairs tend to focus on the Middle East, over which so many storm clouds are hovering, and where Western policies in the region have so much to answer for. Mustafa Abu Sway in Chapter 14 refers to the many symbols of fear and despair in the Holy Land today. This is not a volume for rehearsed arguments about Middle Eastern politics. It is enough to point out that many see the current state of affairs in that region either as one community, the Muslim, turning its back on another community – the Christian, the Yazidi – or as one Muslim community, the Sunni, turning its back on another Sunni community or on the variety of Shi'ite traditions, or the Shi'ite community turning its back on the Sunnis, despairing of anything that looks like a common good and a shared future.

The Middle East is not the only context for despair, however; the many disturbing signs of discrimination against Muslims and rising anti-Semitism in the West are signs of despair too.[1] We have a particularly strong reminder of the Bosnian context in Chapter 13 in this book – the West in some quarters choosing the 'works of darkness', to use the words of the collect for the first Sunday in Advent in *The Book of Common*

---

[1] Martha Nussbaum's *The New Religious Intolerance* (Cambridge, MA: Belknap Press of Harvard University Press, 2012) expands on various developments in Europe and North America that express fear of Muslims. Since the publication of this book, a number of other developments have taken place across the West that show how fear of Muslims can pass into the realms of the irrational.

Prayer.[2] In fact, whether in the USA today, or in Europe or in the Middle East, no one seems to have a clue where justice and sanity are to be found.[3] Therefore, being called to action based on the principle of love in these varied contexts is no empty call for a pious cliché. Loving God and loving neighbour is not where we are. So, how do we learn to put love where there is no love, informed by our respective traditions? What are the practical implications of this act? What does it teach us about our two faiths? Daniel A. Madigan notes that

an understanding of the primacy and priority of divine love is not lacking in the Islamic tradition, but it did not find a place in *ACW,* possibly because it confines itself to quoting the Qur'an and the Hadith in order to address the broadest possible Muslim audience.[4]

In this concluding chapter, my intention is to remedy the lack of some of those reflections on divine love and loving God by having recourse to premodern forebears, with special reference to the one I call my medieval Muslim friend, Imām Abū Ḥāmid al-Ghazālī (d. 1111), while recalling at the same time the works of St Augustine of Hippo (d. 430) as a dialogue partner with Ghazālī, mainly towards the end of the chapter. The chapter will explore how their reflections enrich our current debate and our engagement in the future as well. It is fitting to relate to Ghazālī as someone who is widely considered to have been the normative teacher of pre-modern Islam. As such, scholars have often compared Ghazālī with Western thinkers such as René Descartes (d. 1650), Immanuel Kant (d. 1804) and Meister Eckhart (d. 1328).[5] Others have shown an interest in comparing Augustine with Ghazālī.[6] Focusing on the meaning of love

---

[2] *The Book of Common Prayer* is the traditional service book of the Church of England and is central to its faith. It was first compiled in the sixteenth century by Thomas Cranmer and was later modified in 1662. It remains at the heart of the Church of England's worship today.

[3] The recent publication by John Milbank and Adrian Pabst, *The Politics of Virtue: Post-Liberalism and the Human Future* (London: Rowman and Littlefield, 2016), presents a compelling analysis of the collapse of contemporary political polarities in the West and of the need to know where we want to see our values anchored if we wish to pursue the common good.

[4] See Chapter 10 in this volume.

[5] Tamara Albertini, 'Crisis and certainty of knowledge in al-Ghazali (1058–111) and Descartes (1596–1650)', *Philosophy East and West*, 55/1 (2005), 1–14; Amin Abdullah, *Kant and al-Ghazali: The Idea of the Universality of Ethical Norms* (Frankfurt: Landeck, 2000); Joseph Politella, 'al-Ghazali and Meister Eckhart: two giants of the Spirit', *Muslim World*, 54/3 (1964), 180–94.

[6] James Achilles Highland, *Alchemy: The Transformation of the Soul in the Conversion Narratives of Augustine and Ghazzali (Saint Augustine, Muhammad Ghazali)*, PhD

among these different figures will show that exploring our doctrinal differences will lead us supremely to an understanding of humility before God as we listen to one another. Indeed, we could say that the future of Muslim–Christian engagement hangs on our ability to inhabit this exercise of humility, which Christ crowns first in the Beatitudes (Matthew 5:3).

THE CONTROVERSY OF LOVING GOD

Augustine, as is well known – quoting an even older authority, Cicero – wondered what made a society of human beings different from a pile of stones. This is his main question in the *City of God*.[7] He argues that a political community is one where people have a shared love; in that shared love the society finds its deepest kind of coherence. And here is one point where Ghazālī becomes a relevant and an interesting conversation partner to Augustine, where he says: *al-mar'u ma'a man aḥabba*, 'a man will be with those whom he loves'.[8] This appears in the 'Book of Love, Longing, Intimacy and Contentment', as Eric Ormsby translated it, which is the thirty-sixth chapter of Ghazālī's magnum opus, *Iḥyā' 'ulūm al-dīn*, 'The revival of the religious sciences'.

Ghazālī's 'Book of Love' proves to be relevant for discussion about Muslim–Christian dialogue, not just a dissertation on how to be 'nice' to God. As to doctrinal reflections, it has long been recognised that Ghazālī's many gifts did not include what a modern audience would regard as the popular touch: he combines in one book different strands of knowledge which he inherited; and as to loving God, what appears from the text is that the question is a matter of life and death. He goes through the discussion with acute psychological acumen, while thinking rationally through the theological questions that are most fundamental for him, showing perhaps why doctrine and theology do matter.

The book's relevance lies partly in the fact that Ghazālī is reacting essentially to those who argue that 'love has no meaning apart from persistent obedience to God the Exalted and that genuine love is inconceivable

---

dissertation (Southern Illinois University at Carbondale, 1999). See also Mohamed El-Moctar El-Shinqiti, 'A painful quest for God: The preconversion moment of Augustine and al-Ghazali', *Birey ve Toplum*, 2/3 (2012), 67–84.

7 Augustine, *City of God*, 2:21 and 19:21, in Philip Schaff (ed.), *A Select Library of the Nicene and Post-Nicene Fathers of the Christian Church* (Grand Rapids, MI: Eerdmans, 1979), vol. 2.

8 Abū Ḥāmid al-Ghazālī, *Iḥyā' 'ulūm al-dīn*, ed. Muḥammad 'Abd al-Malik al-Zughbī (Cairo: Dār al-manār, n.d.), vol. 4, p. 427.

except between the same genus and species'.[9] He will respond to this claim and explain further that love of God has to be real, not just figurative. As will be explained further later, this was also a Christian debate and Ghazālī here is presenting a form of honest dialogue with those he disagrees with. Ghazālī does not quite identify an individual or group that he opposes. But Ormsby helpfully summarises some of the positions Ghazālī disagreed with in the introduction to his translation – positions that originate in the different Islamic theological and legal schools, *kalām* and *fiqh*, of the time. First, Ormsby mentions the younger contemporary of Ghazālī, the Muʿtazilite Abū l-Qāsim al-Zamakhsharī (d. 1144), who, commenting on Q 3:31, says that 'man's love of God has only one meaning and that is "obedience", striving for his approval and in not doing whatever necessarily brings His wrath and punishment'.[10] This, however, was not only a Muʿtazilite position. The earlier Shāfiʿite jurist Ibn Surayj (d. 918) also argued that love could only be understood as obedience to God.[11] A hundred years after Ghazālī, Fakhr al-Dīn al-Rāzī (d. 1209), a fellow Shāfiʿite and Ashʿarite theologian, would clarify further that Ghazālī was objecting to a view common among the theologians, the *mutakallimūn*, of the time, namely, that love of God means obedience to God.[12]

While Ghazālī explains his disagreement with his forebears and some of his contemporaries, he refers to Q 5:54, 'He loves them and they love Him', which, as Madigan notes, *ACW* does not strive to engage with in depth.[13] *ACW* reminded us that God in the Qur'an is described as 'loving', *al-Wadūd* (Q 11:90, 85:14). But the main concern arising among these early Muslim scholars is how a loving God can still maintain the important gulf between God and humanity. Certainly God loves

---

[9] Ghazālī, *Iḥyāʾ*, vol. 4, p. 425. The translation is that of Eric Ormsby, *Al-Ghazālī: Love, Longing, Intimacy and Contentment: Kitāb al-maḥabba waʾl-shawq waʾl-uns waʾl-riḍā: Book XXXVI of The Revival of the Religious Sciences, Iḥyāʾ ʿulūm al-dīn* (Cambridge: Islamic Texts Society, 2011), p. 2. All subsequent translations are those of Eric Ormsby.

[10] Cited in Ormsby, *Al-Ghazālī: Love, Longing, Intimacy and Contentment*, p. xi; Abū l-Qāsim Maḥmūd al-Zamakhsharī, *al-Kashshāf ʿan ḥaqāʾiq al-tanzīl wa-ʿuyūn al-aqāwīl* (Cairo: Maṭbaʿat Muṣṭafā al-Bābī al-Ḥalabī, 1972), vol. 1, p. 424.

[11] Cited in Ormsby, *Al-Ghazālī: Love, Longing, Intimacy and Contentment*, p. xiv; and in Ignaz Goldziher, 'Die Gottesliebe in der islamischen Theologie', *Der Islam*, 9 (1919), 144–58, at p. 158.

[12] Fakhr al-Dīn al-Rāzī, *al-Tafsīr al-kabīr* (Cairo: al-Maṭbaʿa al-bahiyya al-miṣriyya, 1938), vol. 8, p. 18.

[13] See Chapter 10 in this volume.

his creatures, some of Ghazālī's opponents might suggest, but how can there be a *relationship* of love between the Almighty – the unchangeable, omnipotent Lord of heaven and earth – on the one hand, and human beings, on the other hand? Is a *mutual* relationship of love possible in this instance? And this is indeed a serious question: not only is it a question about God's freedom, but it also raises the issue of how to understand one's behaviour in a proper framework, not as a mere theory. This is an example of why our different theological understandings of these questions are not merely theoretical, but are about how we live. Understanding love as obedience has been one practical solution in some Muslim circles. Loving God is a matter of keeping within the rules. For Zamakhsharī and others, indulging in an imaginative intimacy with God was a dangerous Sufi practice.[14]

The discussion, however, was not simply between Sufis and non-Sufis. Another controversy embroiled the Sufis themselves in difficult discussion and disagreements about the appropriateness of the use of the word *ʿishq*, implying passionate and even erotic love, in describing the love of God. In his book, Ghazālī refers to an episode with a certain Ghulām al-Khalīl (d. 888), an earlier Sufi, who put Abū l-Ḥusayn al-Nūrī (d. 907) and some seventy-five other like-minded Sufis on trial for using *ʿishq* to express their love of God.[15] In other words, not all Sufis agreed on the use of this term either. Ghazālī would have been exposed to all these debates, and the discussion could go on at length if we were to examine a number of his revered sources, such as Abū l-Qāsim al-Qushayrī (d. 1074) and his father-in-law, Abū ʿAlī al-Daqqāq (d. 1015), who also did not favour the use of the term *ʿishq*.[16]

More interestingly, in reaction to all these arguments, Ghazālī remains circumspect, preferring mostly to use the Qur'anic term, *maḥabba*, as an expression of the love of God. Obedience, *ṭāʿa*, remains part of the vocabulary of Ghazālī. Like many of his scholarly colleagues before and after him, Ghazālī stresses a certain expected etiquette in expressing love and worship of God;[17] perhaps mature faith after all does put emotions into a secondary place. But, when all of this is said and done, that is not all for Ghazālī. Despite his measured approach, he still argues for the suitability of using the word *ʿishq*, intimate passionate love, to describe this

---

[14] Ormsby, *Al-Ghazālī: Love, Longing, Intimacy and Contentment*, p. xii.
[15] Ibid., p. 136.
[16] Alexander D. Knysh, *Al-Qushayri's Epistle on Sufism* (Reading: Garnet, 2007), p. 328.
[17] Ghazālī, *Iḥyā'*, vol. 4, p. 475.

intercourse between creator and creatures.[18] He argues that Sufi saints are not wrong in accepting the truth of this passion.

It is important at this stage to remember that Ghazālī was also well read in the philosophical tradition of Greek antiquity as it was made available through Arabic sources. These sources produced texts in Arabic on love, notably Avicenna (d. 1037), who has an epistle titled *Risāla fī l-'ishq* ('The epistle on love'),[19] and Aḥmad ibn Muḥammad al-Miskawayh (d. 1030), whose work *Tahdhīb al-akhlāq* ('The refinement of character traits') has a section ranking different kinds of affection.[20] While for some Sufis *'ishq* denotes immoderation, for Miskawayh it is an 'excess' which culminates in love of God.[21] Ghazālī seems to follow Miskawayh more closely on this.[22]

Scholars have varied in their assessment of these sources and their significance for Ghazālī. Richard Walzer delineates the sources of this philosophical language of love, tracing them back to Aristotle's *Nicomachean Ethics*, which became available in Arabic via the commentary of the Neoplatonist Porphyry.[23] Walzer also refers to the revival of Plato's *eros* by Neoplatonic and Christian authors of late antiquity, such as Plotinus, Gregory of Nyssa, Proclus and Pseudo-Dionysius the Areopagite. All of this, Walzer believes, had its influence on Arabic thought. Other scholars may argue against this kind of delineation of sources, as such arguments might suggest at first glance that Islam was an arid Semitic tradition whose own vocabulary only allowed it to develop notions of law and obedience, so that it had to learn the language of love from other sources.[24] A few points can be made in response to this concern.

First, as has been pointed out earlier, the debate was not just a Muslim one. It reminds us of the kind of austere Protestant reactions exemplified by

---

[18] Ibid., pp. 465–71.

[19] Emil Fackenheim (trans.), 'A treatise on love by Ibn Sina', *Mediaeval Studies*, 7 (1945), 208–28.

[20] Constantine K. Zurayk (trans.), *The Refinement of Character: A Translation from the Arabic of Aḥmad ibn Muḥammad Miskawayh's Tahdhīb al-Akhlāq* (Beirut: American University of Beirut Press, 1968), pp. 123–35.

[21] Ibid., p. 133.

[22] On the influence of Miskawayh, see W. Montgomery Watt, *Islamic Philosophy and Theology* (Edinburgh: Edinburgh University Press, 1985), p. 71.

[23] Richard Walzer, *Greek into Arabic: Essays on Islamic Philosophy* (Oxford: Oxford University Press, 1962), p. 241.

[24] Binyamin Abrahamov chronicled the teachings on love in the works of Ghazālī and 'Abd al-Raḥmān al-Dabbāgh (d. 1296) in his *Divine Love in Islamic Mysticism: The Teachings of al-Ghazâlî and al-Dabbâgh* (London: RoutledgeCurzon, 2003); he argues for a Greek, Jewish and Christian influence on Islamic notions of love.

the writings of the Swedish Lutheran theologian Anders Nygren. Nygren argues that Augustine synthesised Greek *eros* with Christian *agape*, and that Thomas Aquinas (d. 1274) developed it further.[25] For Nygren, however, Martin Luther (d. 1546) recovered a truer understanding of *agape*. Nygren seems to suggest what the earlier Islamic *mutakallimūn* were saying, namely, that among certain Christian theologians *eros* corrupts *agape*. And like the Islamic discursive theologians, Nygren is saying that you cannot love God in such mystical fashion, questioning even the suitability of using *agape* to describe human love for God, as that would be tantamount to some kind of possessive human love that relates to God as one relates to human lovers. He interprets Paul's texts to suggest that love of God can only be about good faith in him.[26]

Indeed, the debate has a medieval precedent, which Pope Benedict alluded to in his now-famous 'Regensburg lecture'. The pope contrasted the Thomist masterful synthesis of philosophical argument and biblical faith with the Franciscan John Duns Scotus' (d. 1308) emphasis on the utter transcendence of God, presenting a critique of this medieval Franciscan tradition. Indeed, the pope argued that Scotus comes close to Ibn Ḥazm (d. 1064) in the Islamic tradition in his emphasis on transcendence, which would make it impossible to have a personal relationship with God. To use the pope's words: 'God does not become more transcendent if we push him further away.'[27]

Also, the accusations concerning certain Sufi practices are reminiscent of reactions to some dramatic emotional ways of expressing love to God in the history of Christian saints. Francis of Assisi (d. 1226) gave himself to weeping and mourning in long vigils of prayer; he was accused by some of his contemporaries of madness and psychological trauma.[28] St John of the Cross (d. 1591) conscientiously followed the stricter ancient Carmelite rule by his own choice; some of the other Carmelite friars avoided him because they considered him too fanatical in his love of God.[29]

---

[25] Anders Nygren, *Agape and Eros*, trans. Philip S. Watson (London: SPCK, 1954), p. 183.

[26] Ibid., p. 128.

[27] For the text of Pope Benedict XVI's lecture, 'Faith, reason and the university: memories and reflections', see http://w2.vatican.va/content/benedict-xvi/en/speeches/2006/september/documents/hf_ben-xvi_spe_20060912_university-regensburg.html. Accessed 25 November 2016.

[28] Michael Robson, *St Francis of Assisi: The Legend and the Life* (London: Geoffrey Chapman, 1997), pp. 25–6.

[29] Richard Hardy, *The Life of St. John of the Cross: Search for Nothing* (London: Darton, Longman and Todd, 1982), p. 23.

Second, it is difficult to deny that Islam developed in the same Greek intellectual framework as Christianity. The question is how to relate to this heritage. The engagement with the Greek heritage should be seen in positive terms. A number of scholars have produced significant work on the originality of this engagement with notions of love in Sufi texts.[30] The fact that affirming love of God was heavily utilised in Islam's mystical register cannot be denied either; in fact, Rāzī sides with Ghazālī in the discussion,[31] showing perhaps that Ghazālī's texts made their impact very quickly. The use of philosophical language, therefore, should not be seen as a negation of the Qur'anic emphasis on love, but, as with Christian doctrine, the resort to philosophical language was an important tool in universalising the tradition itself.

Third, the fact that Ghazālī incorporated philosophical ideas does not mean that he was passively copying such ideas. Despite some of the informed views of some contemporary scholars of Ghazālī who like to emphasise his debt to Avicenna,[32] Ghazālī remains mainly an ethicist and a jurist, not a philosopher, as they like to suggest. His purpose was to exhort people into faith, not simply to explain philosophical theory. If we were to sum up Ghazālī's argument, we could say that he frames the discussion on love and obedience within a particular contemplative epistemology that puts the meaning of law and of knowledge within the perspective of what Ghazālī calls the 'heart'. He synthesises scriptural texts with texts from Islam's formative period and adds them to some logical argumentation – what he calls *shawāhid ʿaqliyya* – but always speaking, as it were, from the perspective of the heart's love of God. Indeed, Ghazālī calls the heart the sixth sense after the five main senses of creatures.[33] Therefore, Ormsby suggests, 'Love and knowledge

---

[30] Louis Massignon, *The Passion of al-Hallaj: Mystic and Martyr of Islam*, trans. Herbert Mason (Princeton, NJ: Princeton University Press, 1982); Hellmut Ritter, *The Ocean of the Soul*, trans. John O'Kane (Leiden: Brill, 2013); Annemarie Schimmel, *Mystical Dimensions of Islam* (Chapel Hill: University of North Carolina Press, 1975); William C. Chittick, *The Sufi Path of Love: The Spiritual Teachings of Rumi* (Albany: State University of New York Press, 1983); Carl W. Ernst, 'The stages of love in early Persian Sufism, from Rabi'a to Ruzbihan', in Leonard Lewisohn (ed.), *Classical Persian Sufism: From Its Origins to Rumi* (London: Khaniqahi Nimatullahi, 1993), pp. 435–55.

[31] Rāzī, *Tafsīr*, vol. 8, p. 18.

[32] Frank Griffel, *Ghazali's Philosophical Theology* (Oxford: Oxford University Press, 2009); Jules Janssens, 'Al-Ghazzālī's *Tahāfut*: is it really a rejection of Ibn Sīnā's philosophy?', *Journal of Islamic Studies*, 12/1 (2001), 1–17; Alexander Treiger, *Inspired Knowledge in Islamic Thought: Al-Ghazālī's Theory of Mystical Cognition and Its Avicennian Foundation* (London: Routledge, 2012).

[33] Ghazālī, *Iḥyāʾ*, vol. 4, p. 429.

are intertwined throughout his discourse.'[34] So a basic discussion of the nature of divine law for Ghazālī and of divine revelation should prompt a better-resourced debate on his understanding of love.

GHAZĀLĪ'S LOVE OF GOD

Rāzī might help us to reveal further the distinctiveness of Ghazālī's understanding of love when he explains that, for the theologians who oppose the notion of love for God, 'love belongs to the genus of the will, *irāda*, which, however, stands in no nexus with transient events and favours'.[35] In other words, 'will' among these Islamic debaters has a very abstract meaning; it does not come with feelings, being more akin to Nygren's austere Protestantism. Ghazālī turns the tables upon such claims in his statement 'Love is an expression for the natural inclination to what is pleasurable' (*al-ḥubb 'ibarat^un 'an mayl al-ṭab' ilā l-shay' al-mulidhdh*).[36] Such is the nature of human beings, Ghazālī argues. In other words, his discussion does not begin with an elaboration of the meaning of faith and purity, but with an acknowledgement that our love for God is the result of simply finding pleasure in God, a point already expressed by Miskawayh.[37]

Ghazālī suggests that those who deny such love for God are those who have not come to terms with their theomorphic nature, but are trapped in their animal side, as they cannot see with the sixth sense, the sense of the heart, but only with their five senses. Despite earlier opposition to this kind of language, we find that even the later Ḥanbalite theologian Ibn Taymiyya (d. 1328), who is normally thought of as more rigorous in his orthodoxy, does not deny the claim that our response to God involves some kind of choosing, not only because of God's acts of kindness, but primarily for God's own sake.[38] Ghazālī says: 'no inventory could encompass them [blessings]'.[39] In other words, it is impossible to count all of God's blessings. Therefore, for Ghazālī, the idea of 'will' that 'stands in no nexus with transient effects and events', to go back to Rāzī's words, is a fanciful assumption. We *will* something because we have *shawq* for

---

[34] Ormsby, *Al-Ghazālī: Love, Longing, Intimacy and Contentment*, p. xxiv.
[35] Rāzī, *Tafsīr*, vol. 8, p. 18.
[36] Ghazālī, *Iḥyā'*, vol. 4, p. 429.
[37] See Zurayk, *The Refinement of Character*, pp. 133–5.
[38] Joseph Norman Bell, *Love Theory in Later Hanbalite Islam* (Albany: State University of New York Press, 1979), pp. 70, 73.
[39] Ghazālī, *Iḥyā'*, vol. 4, p. 436.

something; we have the inclination and the desire for it. Ghazālī even jus-
tifies his claim by pointing to the foundational human self-love. He says,
there is no doubt that human beings love themselves. And this self-love
includes the love of prolonging one's life and avoiding death. There is an
interest involved in loving one's self. Even loving your neighbour is an
injunction based on loving one's self.[40]

Though Ghazālī builds up higher manifestations of love that include
love of things for their own sake, he reminds us that in normal conditions
we love others only when there is some benefit in it for us, which includes
people showing kindness to us; we are drawn to their kindness towards
us. The discussion then moves on to the register of beauty; as Ormsby
aptly points out, for Ghazālī 'beauty is one thing which we are capable
of loving for itself'.[41] The argument of course is Platonic. Beauty is an
expression of Truth and a stimulus for creativity.[42] As Truth does not
lie in the self, beauty is still connected to some kind of self-love for it
is drawing away the self to become creative and better fulfilled. Why
does one desire such Truth and beauty? Ghazālī adds: 'human beings are
never perfect' (*kull makhlūq lā yakhlū 'an naqṣ*).[43] One needs God for
perfection. One could say that, like Augustine, Ghazālī is fully aware of
'our limited, embodied condition'[44] as created human beings. Perfection
belongs to God alone. So, if one has true interest in one's good, one needs
to seek the perfection that God alone can give, which reminds us of
Daniel A. Madigan's argument in his chapter about 'seeking the perfection of the Father'. The Augustinian Christian, as opposed to the austere
Protestant like Nygren, might agree with Ghazālī that to have a will in
the abstract, which is pure, could suggest that you have no need for God;
Augustine says, 'Our love for God in this world is a desire, only fulfilled
in the hereafter'.[45] To say that you love God with passion is an acknowledgement of your need for and dependence on God. God is the only one
worthy of true love.

This takes us back to the opening prologue of the 'Book of Love'. In
it we find an implicit connection to Ghazālī's epistemology when he says,
'God has purified the hearts of the saints and purified their inmost beings,

---

[40] Ormsby, *Al-Ghazālī: Love, Longing, Intimacy and Contentment*, p. 13.
[41] Ibid., p. xxvii.
[42] Richard Hunter, *Plato's Symposium* (Oxford: Oxford University Press, 2004), p. 91.
[43] Ghazālī, *Iḥyā'*, vol. 4, p. 441.
[44] Rowan Williams, *On Augustine* (London: Bloomsbury, 2016), p. vii.
[45] Augustine, *On Christian Doctrine*, 1:38, in Philip Schaff (ed.), *A Select Library of the Nicene and Post-Nicene Fathers of the Christian Church*, vol. 2.

revealed to them the splendours of his face until they burned in the fire of His love'; but he adds that God has also 'concealed from them the essence of His majesty so that they wandered astray in the desert of His glory and His might'. The saints at some point give up in despair, until they suddenly hear from what Ghazālī calls the 'pavilion of beauty' a voice saying, 'Patience! o you who despair of gaining the truth because of your ignorance and your haste!'[46] There is a sort of tension here: the saints are called to purify their souls, and the law is part of the mechanism of that purifying technique. However, they do so not simply as a legalistic affair, but as part of their devotion to and love of God. It is making one's life an offering to God, which is not an easy process and does not involve a clear manifestation of God. God reveals and hides at the same time, keeping the two actions in tension. The response of human beings is to receive what is given and to be patient – patient in learning.

As I mentioned in another context,[47] Ghazālī presents a positive as well as a realistic approach to the purpose and meaning of being human – positive in as much as God 'has adorned the aspect of man by granting him good stature and proportion' (*bi-ḥusni taqwīmihi wa-taqdīrihi*),[48] realistic in as much as God safeguards man from increase and decline in his aspect and measurements.[49] This means that the goal of an equilibrium that connects the finite human reality with the object that fulfils human flourishing is something that is *progressively* achieved. It is not achieved through a simplistic obedience to divine commands. Rather, one's will is guided towards those acts that make the person grow towards divine character traits.[50] Attaining such wisdom is not an easy affair.[51] Therefore, the assumption is that human existence is inescapably temporal. Human beings are at their best when they are learning beings, those who seek *'ilm*, knowledge.

Similarly, in the 'Book of Love', Ghazālī again argues that human transformation is in loving *and* learning; but he would also warn that despite the beauty of knowledge it remains nothing compared to God's

---

[46] Ormsby, *Al-Ghazālī: Love, Longing, Intimacy and Contentment*, p. 1.

[47] Yazid Said, *Ghazālī's Politics in Context* (Abingdon: Routledge, 2013), pp. 68–73.

[48] Ghazālī, *Iḥyā'*, vol. 3, p. 71; translation by Tim Winter, *Al-Ghazālī: On Disciplining the Soul: Kitāb Riyāḍat al-nafs & on Breaking the Two Desires: Kitāb Kasr al-shahwatayn, Books XXII and XXIII of The Revival of the Religious Sciences, Iḥyā' 'ulūm al-dīn* (Cambridge: Islamic Texts Society, 1995), p. 3.

[49] Ibid.

[50] Abū Ḥāmid al-Ghazālī, *al-Maqṣad al-asnā fī sharḥ ma'ānī asmā' Allāh al-ḥusnā* (Beirut: Dār al-mashriq, 1971), p. 43.

[51] Ibid., p. 11.

knowledge.[52] There is an acknowledgement of the contingency of human learning; in another context Ghazālī would be relaxed about variegated authority, in the same way that he is happy to adhere to all schools of law and warns against fanatical attachment to any of them.[53] Combine all of this with the presence in the 'Book of Love' of a carefully modulated element of voluntarism within the scheme (knowing and loving God cannot be understood without grasping that interest and affect are always at work in knowing subjects), and one might suggest that this makes for a trajectory of Ghazālī's ideas that might in the first instance and in contemporary discussions find affinity with those who stress the contingency of knowledge to matters of perspective. However, this would be a mistaken conclusion. For Ghazālī's interests at the end are in knowing and loving God. And in his 'book of love', as in other parts of his works, he is very keen to stress the total otherness of God in a manner that was common to medieval theological minds; as the Church Fathers argued, all that we know about God is what God can never be.[54] So the contingency of our knowing does not negate the otherness of the known subject, in this case, God. God's total otherness at the same time remains the same, unchangeable. Our purpose is to grow into that knowledge; hence, there remains in his work an element of flexibility towards the different Islamic theological schools of his time. Similarly, though he brands Christians and Jews unbelievers, he adds that they may still have access to heaven.[55]

MUSLIM–CHRISTIAN DIALOGUE IN THE LIGHT OF GHAZĀLĪ'S LOVE OF GOD

In his recent publication titled *On Augustine*, Rowan Williams offers some reflection on the same language of 'measure, proportion and order'

---

[52] Ghazālī, *Iḥyā'*, vol. 4, p. 439.

[53] Ibid., vol. 3, p. 110.

[54] Vladimir Lossky, *The Mystical Theology of the Eastern Church* (Cambridge: James Clarke, 1991), pp. 23–43.

[55] Sherman Jackson, *On The Boundaries of Theological Tolerance in Islam* (Oxford: Oxford University Press, 2002), pp. 92, 126. On p. 92 of Jackson's translation, Ghazālī first suggests that Christians and Jews are only unbelievers as far as the second part of the *Shahāda*, i.e., the prophethood of Muhammad. Does this mean that they are believers in the first part of the *Shahāda*, that is, 'there is no god but God'? It is difficult to tell; for Ghazālī adds on that same page that Jews and Christians are included among the 'associationists', those who associate others with God. Therefore, it is not clear, either, to what extent Ghazālī, along with other medieval Muslim luminaries, accepted that Christians in fact believed in the same God. It is a question that needs further study. The

we encounter in Ghazālī; but in the writings of Augustine, the discussion is focused on understanding the coherence of creation. 'This orderliness [of creation]', we are told, 'is the essence of what we call beauty';[56] like Ghazālī, Augustine draws on familiar Platonic themes;[57] like Ghazālī, he would stress both God's freedom and unknowable nature and His being the source of harmony and beauty.[58] It is clear that one can find common ground in the classical writings of Augustine and Ghazālī, especially in their understanding of the inbuilt human orientation to love the good in God from whom all comes as gift. But, in the 'Book of Love', Ghazālī has a small section in which he criticises Christian doctrine. This will mark a moment of separation between the two. This debate strikes at the heart of Muslim–Christian dialogue and encounter.

As I mentioned at the beginning, it might easily be suggested that there is no need to treat doctrinal differences; for some, they are unnecessary complications. But this would be the wrong reaction. After all, Ghazālī himself, as we have seen, had been in a lengthy dialogue with his own Muslim peers about the meaning and purpose of love. The questions he raised in disagreement with other Muslim scholars are, on the one hand, theological, concerned about God's freedom, and, on the other, they show how a true understanding of love of God affects human behaviour too; in other words, the theological discussion is not simply confined to theory. Similarly, it is important to engage with Muslim–Christian doctrinal disagreements, not simply in order to understand 'ideas' – these disagreements have implications with regard to the moral character of human beings, how Christians and Muslims behave in the light of their understanding of God.

Ghazālī presents his criticism of Christian doctrine as part of his discussion on 'closeness' to God; attaining closeness to God is one of the marks of our love of God. To quote the passage fully, he says:

This is a place (closeness to God) at which one must rein in his pen for on this subject people have diverged, some flawed individuals tending towards open anthropomorphism and others inclining towards gross exaggeration, overstepping the boundary of mere affinity into full-scale union; these latter profess

---

medieval discussions are not as clear as *ACW* when it comes to whether Muslims and Christians believe in the same God.

[56] Williams, *On Augustine*, p. 62.

[57] Ibid., p. 64.

[58] Ibid. For more on Ghazālī's theodicy, see Eric Linn Ormsby, *Theodicy in Islamic Thought: The Dispute over Al-Ghazali's Best of All Possible Worlds* (Princeton, NJ: Princeton University Press, 1984).

ḥulūl to such an extent that one of them could say, 'I am God'. The Christians err concerning Jesus (upon him be peace) when they claim that he is God. Still others say 'humanity (*nāsūt*) has donned divinity (*lāhūt*)' or again, 'Humanity has become one with Him'. Nevertheless, to whom it has been made abundantly clear that anthropomorphism and the drawing of resemblances to God are absurd, along with union (*ittiḥād*) and *ḥulūl*.[59]

Ghazālī is referring here to the different Christian debates on who Jesus is, discussions with which he was obviously familiar. From a historical point of view, we are reminded by Peter Admirand[60] that the early Christological debates pertained more to the way Greek philosophical language was used in expressing who Jesus is. Historians have argued that the use of Greek philosophical language at the time was not optional. Christians had to bring Christian doctrine in line with the current theories. However, Christians were not divided about Jesus' being a unique source of God's self-communication, grace and love; they debated the manner in which that was expressed philosophically. As one earlier scholar put it, 'it shows a strange lack of historical imagination when we talk slightingly about how Christians quarrelled over words, forgetting what these words represented and how they stood for the established conclusions of philosophy as then understood'.[61]

Indeed, Ghazālī, one could say, is still speaking in his own philosophical way too: all that you can speak about is the notion of *qurb*, closeness to God. He suggested in another context that the function of religious language and attributes is analogical; they are words used of God by some sort of analogy (*majāz*), but without implying that there is analogy between man and God either. For him the Divine and the human are connected through the character traits of God, hence the Prophet's call to acquire such character traits: *takhallaqū bi akhlāq Allāh*.[62] It is an attempt to become, metaphorically, similar to God. This does not signify any spatial nearness, but expresses nearness in qualities, a righteous state, which the Sufis call *fanā'*, 'passing away', extinction in God. All you come to see is God, and you cease to see even yourself in that state. This, you might remember, has a Platonic basis in the understanding of the perfectibility of the human being: Man ascends to God through spiritual

---

[59] Ghazālī, *Iḥyā'*, vol. 4, p. 406; Ormsby, *Al-Ghazālī: Love, Longing, Intimacy and Contentment*, pp. 39–40.
[60] Chapter 8 in this volume.
[61] De Lacy O'Leary, *Arabic Thought and Its Place in History* (New York: Dover, 2003), pp. 26–7.
[62] Ghazālī, *Iḥyā'*, vol. 3, p. 82.

discipline,[63] though it is not clear that Plato spoke of 'immersion' in God. Jesus, in this stage of perfection, Ghazālī implies, was deified mistakenly by the Christians.

Interestingly, Augustine, like Ghazālī, calls for a purification of the soul as a means of attaining closeness to God, a kind of journey or voyage to the native land; like Ghazālī, too, he adds, 'for it is not by *change of place* that we can come nearer to Him who is in every place, but by the cultivation of pure desires and virtuous habits'.[64] Where does this leave us? The answer, I believe, is to attempt to explore what motivates each side in their argument. Despite the fact that both Ghazālī and Augustine believe that we are 'desiring beings' – we have *shawq*, which becomes itself when we long for God[65] – for Ghazālī, the worthwhileness of God that we long for cannot be compared to the worthwhileness of human beings. He discusses this under the terms of affinity and similarity, *munāsaba wa-mushākala*. 'What is similar to a thing', he says, 'draws that thing to itself.' But when it comes to the love of God, it is necessary on account of a 'hidden affinity explicable neither as resemblance of form, nor as similarity in outward shape'.[66]

The question then is how does the relationship of passionate love, *'ishq*, manifest itself? Perhaps Ghazālī is alluding here to his own epistemology of taste, *dhawq*, God's gift of light poured into his heart,[67] with no suggestion that the mode of divine action, in this case 'loving', is further explained as it is in Christian Trinitarian theology. For Ghazālī, the epistemology of taste, if you like, is the basis of true knowledge of God's secrets, which he says is only available to those who tread the mystic path and stumble upon such secrets when they have fulfilled the prerequisites of the Way, *shart al-sulūk*. The only exercise of real freedom in an ontological manner for Ghazālī is love that is based on the experience of taste.[68]

For Augustine, on the other hand, 'it is love that *draws* us back to our proper place, that pulls us back to stability and harmony'.[69] That cannot be done through mere speech or information received. God's beauty and

[63] Robert Wisnovsky, *Avicenna's Metaphysics in Context* (London: Duckworth, 2003), p. 97.
[64] Augustine, *On Christian Doctrine*, 1:10.
[65] Ibid., 1:38.
[66] Ghazālī, *Iḥyā'*, vol. 4, p. 442.
[67] Abū Ḥāmid al-Ghazālī, *al-Munqidh min al-ḍalāl*, ed. Samī Daghīm (Beirut: Dār al-fikr al-lubnānī, 1993), pp. 79–84.
[68] Ghazālī, *Iḥyā'*, vol. 4, p. 429.
[69] Williams, *On Augustine*, p. 65. (my emphasis).

worthwhileness for Augustine lie in the fact that the Word became flesh and the Word was God.[70] As Rowan Williams puts it, 'to know God, we must follow the course of the incarnate Word, not look for timeless penetration of the mind'.[71] Why? For Augustine, at the end of the purifying process of the soul we not only come to realise the mystery of the infinite God, but we also come to see an empty hole in ourselves: 'the human being cannot contain and master the divine, but neither can it contain and master itself'.[72] This means that there cannot be final clarity about ourselves for Augustine if we rely simply on Ghazālī's introspection – his methodology of taste. What God has to reveal in drawing us to Himself in Christ is nothing less than God Himself; otherwise, the mode of acting is not meritorious.

At the same time, Augustine agrees that acknowledging the divine in the human is no easy affair. In the *Confessions*, he describes his state before conversion, and how 'your Wisdom, through whom you created all things, might become for us the milk adapted to our infancy. Not yet was I humble enough to grasp the humble Jesus as my God'.[73] In that same passage, he shares his famous conviction that while Neoplatonic philosophy can teach us about the eternal Reason at the heart of things on its own, acknowledging the Incarnation requires a particular kind of humility and caritas. In the words of Rowan Williams:

Christian belief, in other words, was for him not first and foremost the acceptance of certain statements as true, but a sort of moral turning inside-out. Instead of climbing up to Heaven to find the eternal Word, you have to grasp that the eternal Word has come down from Heaven to find you. And this happens when you see yourself not as a boldly questing intellectual mystic, but as a sick person in desperate need of healing, someone whose reality cannot be completed by their own work and attainments but only by a relationship offered completely from outside.[74]

There is no denial of Jesus' humanity here; on the contrary, Jesus' humanity is the necessary motive of his beauty as love in action. But, we might be too big and clumsy to enter into the small space of God's speech to us in the history of Christ and we might need to strip away the layers that have made it difficult for us to enter. Our inability to strip away

---

[70] Augustine, *Confessions*, trans. R. S. Pine-Coffin (Harmondsworth: Penguin Books, 1961), Book IV: xii; Augustine, *On Christian Doctrine*, 1:10.

[71] Williams, *On Augustine*, p. 70.

[72] Ibid., p. 21.

[73] Augustine, *Confessions*, 7:18.

[74] Williams, *On Augustine*, p. 132.

these layers means that when the Truth in Jesus appears, our habitual response is to reject it; hence, he dies because we reject him, and that is the sin that brings him to death. Yet if discovering and learning make us most truly alive, as both Augustine and Ghazālī suggested earlier, and if it is true that this is what happens when people fall in love as an analogy (loving and knowing are connected), then perhaps one could suggest that for the Christian, the life, death and Resurrection of Jesus had such a surprising newness in first-century Palestine that people were amazed at it and started falling in love with God, and learning new things about God, not simply because of his edifying thoughts and wisdom (he mostly made people think and questioned them rather than gave them straightforward answers), but because he showed a God-sized Resurrection in the midst of death and suffering. Conquering death, he was to be present at all times with them, the sign of God's own eternal presence especially in the darkest corners and moments of life.

For Augustine, therefore, Christians did not deify Jesus. They came to acknowledge him as the free gift of God's love and grace, whereby God shows how different and free he is from Neoplatonic determinism, to the extent that he is able to share our life without ceasing to be God. God 'transcends His transcendence'.[75] Acknowledging that gift as God requires humility. Ghazālī would agree with Augustine about the need to strip ourselves from all the rust and layers of our bad habits caused by worldly sins of forgetfulness, thereby arguing for his own version of humility; but he remains steadfast in his Islamic confession of Christ as the perfect lover of God, who acquires the character traits of God, but who cannot be the unique source of God's self-communication, grace and love; man, for Ghazālī, can, after all, achieve the clarity he needs by means of divinely inspired introspection, aided, one could add, by following the path (*Sunna*) of Jesus as the lover of God.

CONCLUSION

Our medieval forebears, then, are more than just a museum piece. They pose some central questions about the purpose of law and how to put one's self in perspective in relationship to God and others and how to engage in deeper dialogue. Perhaps one could say that for Ghazālī the world exists so that we can grow into the likeness of God. Augustine

---

[75] Rowan Williams, *The Wound of Knowledge* (London: Darton, Longman and Todd, 1999), p. 52.

may in fact agree, but will argue that, given the realities of our historical existence, where there are levels of submission to God there is bound to be a tension between the community which lives by God's gift and the unstable social orders around. One needs still a church body, grounded in the gift of God himself, in which we can grow more fully in the likeness of God. Dealing with Ghazālī's refusal of Christian doctrine in this discussion may clarify both the Muslim's view of freedom and obedience and the Christian's reserve about full human transparency in this world and the need to belong to a community as a sacramental presence in the world that allows for true human transparency.

However, this dialogue between Ghazālī and Augustine has also shown that if there is a common word in all of this discourse, I think it has to be in reference to 'humility', not simply converging on love of God and neighbour as an abstract neutral 'idea'. Humility is the much-needed common word for our world today. The Middle East, Europe and America do not need political or religious leaders who are puffed up, unable to see the love of God in others; neither do we need leaders who are simply 'liberal' in a rather abstract sense of the word. Instead we need the sort of figures who feed on the humility of our pre-modern forebears and show concern and action for the important issues of the hour as a result of their love of God. This requires self-criticism on the part of all, which partly means that no one ought to assume what the 'other' says or believes without opening up in conversation to the other.

Christians and Muslims have in their different ways across history and today shown self-righteousness; therefore, we cannot do without Daniel A. Madigan's call for a *mea culpa*.[76] The fruits of this common word may be twofold: first, we need to listen in other traditions to that poverty of spirit that Christ crowned in the Beatitudes; second, we should not so much seek the *triumph* of our respective 'theories', whether Muslim or Christian, as look for a mode of cooperation and care for others in action. This inevitably will reflect our varied understandings of the freedom of God – for the Christian, this freedom is made visible in Jesus in action, not 'theory'.

---

[76] See Chapter 10 in this volume.

Epilogue

This volume aims to continue the 'exegetic and discursive process' begun by the open letter '*A Common Word between Us and You*' (promulgated on 13 October 2007), through 'close reading and study of the text, context and reception' of that document. Therefore, its sections comprise articles relating to the inception of *ACW* that go beyond mere recapitulation of events which provoked the penning of *ACW*, followed by overviews of responses, and close examination of the use of scripture in *ACW*. Some helpful reflections are added from several specific contrasting contexts, particularly Germany and Bosnia, ending with recommendations for new stages in *ACW*-inspired discussion.

There are strong contributions here with solid scholarship undergirding them all, which we hope can provide a helpful resource to scholars, students and lay people of the various Christian and Muslim communities. The chapters we believe flow nicely from one to the other, as authors refer to each other's essays, producing a volume that is more of a conversation than merely a parade of papers. The title of Part I, Inception of *A Common Word*, may seem to be repeating older literature on *ACW*. However, it provides new insights with a significant contribution from Jonathan Kearney's connection between *ACW* and the earlier *Amman Message* in Chapter 2. The main body of the volume interrogates in a fresh way the very assumptions underlying both the *ACW* and some of the better-known responses to it.

The volume, nonetheless, does not exhaust all areas of reception and discussions about the *ACW* initiative and its implications for the world today. Its main aim is to show a way of genuine conversation between Christians and Muslims without losing our care for one another for the good of the world. There is no escape from recognising deep differences. Accepting these differences is the basis on which we proceed in loving one another. As already pointed out in the volume, it is often suggested that Muslims and Christians have managed to co-exist in many places and times in the past and that this can still happen, if we can just forget about 'theological differences'. However, as Tim Winter mentions in Chapter 1, this assumed co-existence was often achieved at the price of political inferiority and social deprivation of both sides. Such conditions were wedded to a theological worldview of either Islam or Christianity, often referred to as 'supersessionism', the assumption that the latest religion replaces the older one, leaving little value for that which precedes. As Winter adds, these conditions of superiority/inferiority no longer fit in the contemporary world. What is the alternative? Only honest theological integrity will pave the way for Muslims, Christians and others to belong together as they argue intelligently in the various contexts of the world today.

There are two areas that need further answers beyond this volume: first, the extent to which *ACW* was received in Muslim-majority countries, for instance, in Turkey,[1] Asia and the Middle East, beyond the Jerusalem contribution made here. Michael Louis Fitzgerald raises this question in Chapter 3. The volume does not provide full answers to it. The second area that will need further reflection is the realm of politics. Can Muslims and Christians own up in the public sphere to where their deepest convictions come from, convictions that are not simply a matter of choice, but values to which they are drawn? This is a challenge for both the current Middle East today and Europe and North America. What are the theological questions that allow for social and political love of neighbour? We hope that the volume will provide the impetus for taking this discourse forward through further research and discussion.

---

[1] For a recent analysis of *ACW* by a Turkish scholar, see Betül Avcı, '"Aramızdaki ortak kelime": Müslüman-Hıristiyan ilişkilerinde güncel bir söz', *Yalova Sosyal Bilimler Dergisi / Yalova Journal of Social Sciences*, 7/12 (2016), 237–54.

Bibliography

Abdel Haleem, M. A. S., *The Qur'an: English Translation and Parallel Arabic Text* (Oxford: Oxford University Press, 2010).

The Qur'an: A New Translation (Oxford: Oxford University Press, 2005).

Abd el-Kader, *Lettre aux Français*, trans. René Khawam (Paris: Phébus, 1977).

Abdullah, Amin, *Kant and al-Ghazali: The Idea of the Universality of Ethical Norms* (Frankfurt: Landeck, 2000).

Abou El Fadl, Khaled, *Speaking in God's Name: Islamic Law, Authority and Women* (Oxford: Oneworld, 2001).

Abrahamov, Binyamin, *Divine Love in Islamic Mysticism: The Teachings of al-Ghazâlî and al-Dabbâgh* (London: RoutledgeCurzon, 2003).

Abu-Nimer, Mohammed, 'The miracles of transformation through interfaith dialogue: are you a believer', in David R. Smock (ed.), *Interfaith Dialogue and Peacebuilding* (Washington, DC: United States Institute of Peace Press, 2002), pp. 15–32.

'Religion and peacebuilding: reflections on current challenges and future prospects', *Journal of Inter-Religious Studies*, 16 (2015), 14–29.

Abu-Nimer, Mohammed, Amal Khoury and Emily Welty, *Unity in Diversity: Interfaith Dialogue in the Middle East* (Washington, DC: United States Institute of Peace Press, 2007).

Abu Sway, Mustafa, 'Situare la ragione nell'Islam', trans. B. Scolart, *Nuntium*, 35–6 (*Fede, Ragione, Ricerca e Dialogo*) (2008), 93–7.

'A Common Word Between Us and You'. www.acommonword.com.

'A common word between us and you', *Islamochristiana*, 33 (2007), 241–61 (English) and 262–80 (Arabic).

A Common Word Between Us and You: 5-Year Anniversary Edition (Amman: Royal Aal Al-Bayt Institute for Islamic Thought, 2012).

Acton, John Edward Emerich, *Lectures on Modern History* (London: Macmillan, 1906).

Admirand, Peter, 'The ethics of displacement and migration in the Abrahamic faiths: enlightening believers and aiding public policy', *Journal of Ethnic and Migration Studies*, 40/4 (2014), 671–87.

311

'"My children have defeated me!" Finding and nurturing theological dissent', *Irish Theological Quarterly*, 77/3 (2012), 286–304.

'The pedophile scandal and its (hoped-for) impact on Catholic intra- and interreligious dialogue', in Peter Admirand (ed.), *Loss and Hope: Global, Interreligious, and Interdisciplinary Perspectives* (London: Bloomsbury, 2014), pp. 123–36.

'Rifts, trust, and openness: Pope John Paul II's legacy in Catholic intra- and interreligious dialogue', *Journal of Ecumenical Studies*, 47/4 (2012), 555–75.

Afsaruddin, Asma, 'Discerning a Qur'anic mandate for mutually transformational dialogue', in Catherine Cornille (ed.), *Criteria of Discernment in Interreligious Dialogue* (Eugene, OR: Cascade, 2009), pp. 101–21.

'Finding common ground: "mutual knowing", moderation and the fostering of religious pluralism', in James L. Heft, Reuven Firestone and Omid Safi (eds.), *Learned Ignorance: Intellectual Humility among Jews, Christians, and Muslims* (Oxford: Oxford University Press, 2011), pp. 67–86.

Ajami, Fouad, *The Vanished Imam: Musa al-Sadr and the Shia of Lebanon* (Ithaca, NY: Cornell University Press, 1986).

Albayrak, Şule Akbulut, *Hıristiyan Fundamentalizmi* (Istanbul: Etkileşim, 2007).

Albertini, Tamara, 'Crisis and certainty of knowledge in al-Ghazali (1058–1111) and Descartes (1596–1650)', *Philosophy East and West*, 55/1 (2005), 1–14.

Alexy II, 'Response to the Open Letter of 138 Muslim theologians', in *A Common Word Between Us and You: 5-Year Anniversary Edition* (Amman: Royal Aal Al-Bayt Institute for Islamic Thought, 2012), pp. 181–6.

Ali, Maulana Muhammad, *The Holy Qur'ān: Arabic Text with English Translation and Commentary* (Dublin, OH: Ahmadiyya Anjuman Isha'at Islam Lahore, 2002).

Al-Rasheed, Madawi, *A History of Saudi Arabia* (Cambridge: Cambridge University Press, 2002).

Amos, Clare, 'Education, Education and Education', 3 November 2010. http://muslimsandchristians.net/documents/EducationClareAmos.pdf.

Anidjar, Gil, *The Jew, the Arab: A History of the Enemy* (Stanford, CA: Stanford University Press, 2003).

Anselm of Canterbury, *Proslogion, proemium*, in J. P. Migne (ed.), *Patrologia Latina* (Paris, 1841–55), vol. 153.

Arbeitsgemeinschaft Christlicher Kirchen in Baden-Württemberg, 'Arbeitshilfe zum Brief der 138 muslimischen Gelehrten: Ein Wort, das uns und euch gemeinsam ist', *Impulse zum Gespräch*, 1 (2011), 1–55.

Asad, Muhammad, *The Message of the Qur'ān Translated and Explained* (Bristol: Book Foundation, 2003).

Ṣaḥīḥ al-Bukhârî: The Early Years of Islam (Gibraltar: Dar al-Andalus, 1981).

Augustine, *City of God*, in Philip Schaff (ed.), *A Select Library of the Nicene and Post-Nicene Fathers of the Christian Church* (Grand Rapids, MI: Eerdmans, 1979), vol. 2, pp. 1–511.

Confessions, trans. R. S. Pine-Coffin (Harmondsworth: Penguin Books, 1961).

On Christian Doctrine, 1:38, in Philip Schaff (ed.), *A Select Library of the Nicene and Post-Nicene Fathers of the Christian Church* (Grand Rapids, MI: Eerdmans, 1979), vol. 2, pp. 519–597.

Avcı, Betül, '"Aramızdaki ortak kelime": Müslüman-Hıristiyan ilişkilerinde güncel bir söz', *Yalova Sosyal Bilimler Dergisi/Yalova Journal of Social Sciences*, 7/12 (2016), 237–54.

Ayoub, Mahmoud, *The Qur'an and Its Interpreters*. Volume II: *The House of 'Imran* (Albany, NY: State University of New York Press, 1992).

Bar-Asher, Meir M., 'Nusayris', in Josef M. Meri (ed.), *Medieval Islamic Civilization: An Encyclopedia* (Abingdon: Routledge, 2006), vol. 2, p. 570.

Barth, Karl, *Church Dogmatics* I/2 (Edinburgh: T&T Clark, 1956).
Church Dogmatics II/1 (Edinburgh: T&T Clark, 1957).

Bell, Joseph Norman, *Love Theory in Later Hanbalite Islam* (Albany, NY: State University of New York Press, 1979).

Berger, Alan L. (ed.), *Trialogue and Terror: Judaism, Christianity, and Islam after 9/11* (Eugene, OR: Cascade Books, 2012).

Bevans, Stephen B., *Models of Contextual Theology* (Maryknoll, NY: Orbis Books, 2004).

Biser, Eugen and Richard Heinzmann (eds.), *Antwort der Eugen-Biser-Stiftung auf den offenen Brief 'A common word between us and you' von muslimischen Wissenschaftlern und Würdenträgern* (Stuttgart: Kohlhammer, 2009).

Blaker, Kimberly, *The Fundamentals of Extremism: The Christian Right in America* (New Boston, MI: New Boston Books, 2003).

Boff, Leonardo, 'What are Third World theologies?', *Concilium*, 199 (*Theologies of the Third World: Convergences and Differences*, ed. Leonardo Boff and Virgil Elizondo) (1988), 3–14.

Bordet, Thierry, *The Significance of Borders: Why Representative Government and the Rule of Law Require Nation States* (Leiden: Brill, 2012).

Borrmans, Maurice, 'The Roman Catholic Church and the letter of the 138 Muslim religious leaders', *Current Dialogue*, 54 (July 2013), 54–8.

Bowden, John, 'Religious pluralism and the heritage of the enlightenment', in Roger Boase (ed.), *Islam and Global Dialogue: Religious Pluralism and the Pursuit of Peace* (Farnham, Surrey: Ashgate, 2010), pp. 13–20.

Brown, Steven, Björn Merker and Nils L. Wallin, 'An introduction to evolutionary musicology', in Nils L. Wallin, Bjrön Merker and Steven Brown (eds.), *The Origins of Music* (Cambridge, MA & London: MIT Press, 2001), pp. 3–24.

Bsteh, Andreas, *Geschichte eines Dialoges: Dialoginitiativen St. Gabriel an der Jahrtausendwende* (Mödling: Verlag St Gabriel, 2013).

Bucko, Adam and Rory McEntee, *The New Monasticism: An Interspiritual Manifesto for Contemplative Living* (Maryknoll, NY: Orbis, 2015).

Bukhārī, Muḥammad ibn Ismāʿīl al-, *al-Jāmiʿ al-ṣaḥīḥ*, in *Mawsūʿat al-ḥadīth al-sharīf*, CD-ROM (Thesaurus Islamicus Foundation, 2002).
Ṣaḥīḥ, trans. Muhammad Muhsin Khan (Beirut: Dar al-Arabia, 1985).

Catechism of the Catholic Church. www.vatican.va/archive/ccc_css/archive/catechism/p1s2c1p2.htm.

Catholic Commission for Religious Relations with the Jews, 'We remember: a reflection on the Shoah', 1998. www.vatican.va/roman_curia/pontifical_councils/chrstuni/documents/rc_pc_chrstuni_doc_16031998_shoah_en.html.

Cesari, Jocelyn, *When Islam and Democracy Meet: Muslims in Europe and the United States* (Basingstoke: Palgrave Macmillan, 2004).

Chapman, Colin, 'An evangelical Christian reflection on the key Qur'anic text in *A Common Word*' (unpublished paper).

'Response to *A Common Word*' (unpublished paper).

Chartres, Richard, 'Response from the Bishop of London to the Open Letter from 138 Muslim scholars and addressed to the spiritual leaders of the Christian world', 12 October 2007. www.acommonword.com/response-from-the-bishop-of-london-to-the-open-letter-from-138-muslim-scholars-and-addressed-to-the-spiritual-leaders-of-the-christian-world/.

Cheetham, David, 'Exploring the aesthetic "space" for inter-religious encounter', *Exchange*, 39/1 (2010), 71–86.

Chittick, William C., *The Sufi Path of Knowledge: Ibn al-'Arabi's Metaphysics of Imagination* (Albany, NY: State University of New York Press, 1989).

The Sufi Path of Love: The Spiritual Teachings of Rumi (Albany, NY: State University of New York Press, 1983).

Chrisostomos, 'Response from His Beatitude Chrisostomos, Archbishop of Cyprus', 10 November 2008. www.acommonword.com/response-from-his-beatitude-chrisostomos-archbishop-of-cyprus/.

CIBEDO, 'Muslimisches Leben in Deutschland', *CIBEDO-Beiträge*, 1 (2010), 8–14.

Cole, Ethan, 'Prominent Muslims criticize attacks on Iraqi Christians', *Christian Post*, 16 October 2008. www.christianpost.com/news/prominent-muslims-criticize-attacks-on-iraqi-christians-34859/.

Congregation for the Doctrine of the Faith, *Dominus Iesus*. www.vatican.va/roman_curia/congregations/cfaith/documents/rc_con_cfaith_doc_20000806_dominus-iesus_en.html.

Congregation for the Evangelization of Peoples and Pontifical Council for Inter-religious Dialogue, 'Dialogue and proclamation: reflections and orientations on interreligious dialogue and the proclamation of the Gospel of Jesus Christ', Vatican City, 19 May 1991. www.vatican.va/roman_curia/pontifical_councils/interelg/documents/rc_pc_interelg_doc_19051991_dialogue-and-proclamatio_en.html.

Cornille, Catherine, *The Im-Possibility of Interreligious Dialogue* (New York: Herder & Herder, 2008).

Cowell, Alan, 'After 350 years, Vatican says Galileo was right: it moves', *New York Times*, 31 October 1992. www.nytimes.com/1992/10/31/world/after-350-years-vatican-says-galileo-was-right-it-moves.html.

Čubrilović, Vasa, 'Istorijski osnovi Republike Bosne i Hercegovine', *Prilozi Instituta za Istoriju Radničkog Pokreta Sarajevo*, 4 (1968), 23–42.

Cucarella, Diego R. Sarrió, *Muslim-Christian Polemics across the Mediterranean: The Splendid Replies of Shihāb al-Dīn al-Qarāfī (d. 684/1285)* (Leiden: Brill, 2015).

Cuffel, Alexandra, 'From practice to polemic: shared saints and festivals as "women's religion" in the medieval Mediterranean', *Bulletin of the School of Oriental and African Studies, University of London*, 68/3 (2005), 401–19.

Dalai Lama, *Toward a True Kinship of Faiths: How the World's Religions Can Come Together* (New York: Doubleday, 2010).

Danielson, Kenneth, 'A narrative approach to interfaith dialogue: explanations & recommendations', in Daniel S. Brown Jr. (ed.), *A Communication Perspective on Interfaith Dialogue: Living within the Abrahamic Traditions* (Lanham, MD & Plymouth, UK: Lexington Books, 2013), pp. 75–90.

Dedijer, Vladimir and Antun Miletić, *Genocid nad Muslimanima 1941–1945: Zbornik Dokumenata i Svjedočenja* (Sarajevo: Svjetlost, 1990).

Delio, Ilia, *The Emergent Christ: Exploring the Meaning of Catholic in an Evolutionary Universe* (Maryknoll, NY: Orbis, 2011).

Del Prete, Thomas, *Thomas Merton and the Education of the Whole Person* (Birmingham, AL: Religious Education Press, 1990).

Demiri, Lejla (ed.), *A Common Word: Text and Reflections: A Resource for Parishes and Mosques* (Cambridge: Muslim Academic Trust, 2011).

Desjardins, Michel, *Peace, Violence and the New Testament* (Sheffield: Sheffield Academic Press, 1997).

Domke, David, *God Willing? Political Fundamentalism in the White House, the 'War on Terror' and the Echoing Press* (London: Pluto Press, 2004).

Dorff, Eliot, *The Jewish Approach to Repairing the World* (Woodstock, VT: Jewish Lights, 2008).

Doughty, Steve, 'Archbishop calls for financiers to set "just and reasonable" interest rates', *Daily Mail*, 15 October 2008.

Dressler, Markus, 'Alevis', in G. Krämer et al. (eds.), *Encyclopedia of Islam III* (Leiden: Brill, 2009), vol. 1, pp. 93–121.

Durie, Mark, 'More on loving one's (Muslim) neighbour', 25 March 2008. http://acommonword.blogspot.de/2008/03/more-on-loving-ones-muslim-neighbour-in.html.

'Notes for Christians on understanding *A Common Word Between Us and You*', January 2008. http://acommonword.blogspot.de/2008/02/notes-for-christians-on-understanding.html.

Dutch United Protestant Church, *Kerkorde van de Protestantse Kerk in Nederland*. www.protestantsekerk.nl/Lists/PKN-Bibliotheek/Kerkorde-en-Ordinanties-PKN-originele-versie-2004.pdf.

Eagleton, Terry, 'Roots of Terror', *The Guardian*, 6 September 2003.

Egan, Harvey D. SJ, 'A Rahnerian response', in Stephen L. Pope and Charles Hefling (eds.), *Sic Et Non: Encountering Dominus Iesus* (Maryknoll: Orbis, 2002), pp. 57–67.

Eißler, Friedmann (ed.), *Muslimische Einladung zum Dialog: Dokumentation zum Brief der 138 Gelehrten ('A Common Word')* (Berlin: Evangelische Zentralstelle für Weltanschauungsfragen, 2009).

El-Shinqiti, Mohamed El-Moctar, 'A painful quest for God: the preconversion moment of Augustine and al-Ghazali', *Birey ve Toplum*, 2/3 (2012), 67–84.

Ernst, Carl W., *How to Read the Qur'an: A New Guide, with Select Translations* (Chapel Hill, NC: University of North Carolina Press, 2011).

'The stages of love in early Persian Sufism, from Rabi'a to Ruzbihan', in Leonard Lewisohn (ed.), *Classical Persian Sufism: From Its Origins to Rumi* (London & New York: Khaniqahi Nimatullahi Publications, 1993), pp. 435–55.

Fackenheim, Emil (trans.), 'A treatise on love by Ibn Sina', *Mediaeval Studies*, 7 (1945), 208–28.

Fakhry, Majid, *An Interpretation of the Qur'an* (New York: New York University Press, 2000).

Al Faruqi, Lois Ibsen, 'Music, musicians and Muslim law', *Asian Music*, 17 (1985), 3–36.

Islam and Art (Islamabad: National Hijra Council, 1985).

'The Shari'ah on music and musicians', *Al-'Ilm*, 11/9 (1989), 33–53.

Fessio, Joseph SJ, 'On Pope Benedict XVI's address at the University of Regensburg', *The Wanderer*, 28 September 2006.

Firestone, Reuven, James Heft and Omid Safi, 'Epilogue: the purpose of interreligious dialogue', in James L. Heft, Reuven Firestone and Omid Safi (eds.), *Learned Ignorance: Intellectual Humility among Jews, Christians, and Muslims* (Oxford: Oxford University Press, 2011), pp. 300–11.

Fitzgerald, Michael L., 'The Secretariat for Non-Christians is ten years old', *Islamochristiana*, 1 (1975), 87–95.

Ford, David, 'A Common Word Between Us and You: A response by Professor David Ford, Director of the Cambridge Inter-Faith Programme', 9 October 2007. www.acommonword.com/category/site/christian-responses/.

Foulcher, Jane, *Reclaiming Humility: Four Studies in the Monastic Tradition* (Collegeville, MN: Liturgical Press, 2015).

Fowden, Garth, 'Gibbon on Islam', *English Historical Review*, 131/549 (April 2016), 261–92.

Francisco, Jose Mario C., 'Migration and new cosmopolitanism in Asian Christianity', in Felix Wilfred (ed.), *The Oxford Handbook of Christianity in Asia* (Oxford: Oxford University Press, 2014), pp. 575–92.

Friedman, Aron, *The Nuṣayrī-'Alawīs: An Introduction to the Religion, History and Identity of the Leading Minority in Syria* (Leiden: Brill, 2010).

Gaudeul, Jean-Marie, *Encounters and Clashes: Islam and Christianity in History, Volume I: A Survey* (Rome: Pontificio Istituto di Studi Arabi e d'Islamistica, 2000).

Gauhar, Altaf, *The Challenge of Islam* (London: Islamic Council of Europe, 1978).

Ghazālī, Abū Ḥāmid al-, *al-Maqṣad al-asnā fī sharḥ ma'ānī asmā' Allāh al-ḥusnā* (Beirut: Dār al-mashriq, 1971).

al-Munqidh min al-ḍalāl, ed. Samī' Daghīm (Beirut: Dār al-fikr al-lubnānī, 1993).

Iḥyā' 'ulūm al-dīn, ed. Muḥammad 'Abd al-Malik al-Zughbī (Cairo: Dār al-manār, n.d.).

Iḥyā' 'ulūm al-dīn (Beirut: Dār al-ma'rifa, n.d.).

Ghazi bin Muhammad, '"A Common Word Between Us and You": two years summary', Oct 2007–Oct 2009'. www.acommonword.com/two-years-summary-oct-2007-oct-2009/.

Love in the Holy Qur'an (Chicago: Kazi Publications, 2010).

(ed.), *True Islam and the Islamic Consensus on the Amman Message* (Amman: Royal Aal Al-Bayt Institute for Islamic Thought, 2006).

Gioia, Francesco (ed.), *Interreligious Dialogue: The Official Teaching of the Catholic Church from the Second Vatican Council to John Paul II (1963–2005)* (Boston: Pauline Books & Media, 2006).

Globethics.net, *Globethics.net Principles on Sharing Values across Cultures and Religions* (Geneva: globethics.net, 2012).

GodVoter.org, 'GodVoter.org responds to "A Common Word" from Muslims', 31 January 2007. www.acommonword.com/godvoter-org-responds-to-a-common-word-from-muslims-2/.

Goldziher, Ignaz, 'Die Gottesliebe in der islamischen Theologie', *Der Islam*, 9 (1919), 144–58.

Gopin, Marc, 'The use of the word and its limits: a critical evaluation of religious dialogue as peacemaking', in David R. Smock (ed.), *Interfaith Dialogue and Peacebuilding* (Washington, DC: United States Institute of Peace Press, 2002), pp. 33–46.

Gourevitch, Philip, *Standard Operating Procedure: A War Story* (London: Picador, 2008).

Greenberg, Irving, *For the Sake of Heaven and Earth: The New Encounter between Judaism and Christianity* (Philadelphia, PA: Jewish Publication Society, 2004).

Greenberg, Irving et al., 'Discussion 9: on the meaning of pluralism', in Edward Feinstein (ed.), *Jews and Judaism in the Twenty-First Century: Human Responsibility, the Presence of God, and the Future of the Covenant* (Woodstock, VT: Jewish Lights, 2007).

GRIC, *The Challenge of the Scriptures, the Bible and the Qur'an* (Maryknoll, NY: Orbis Books, 1989).

'État et religion', *Islamochristiana*, 12 (1986), 49–72.

Foi et justice. Un défi pour le christianisme et pour l'islam (Paris: Centurion, 1993).

Péché et responsabilité éthique dans le monde contemporain (Paris: Bayard, 2000).

Griffel, Frank, *Ghazali's Philosophical Theology* (Oxford: Oxford University Press, 2009).

Grob, Leonard and John K. Roth (eds.), *Encountering the Stranger: A Jewish-Christian-Muslim Trialogue* (Seattle, WA: University of Washington Press, 2012).

Gualini, Muhammad Silvio, *Muslims and Christians Divided under the Same God?* (Bloomington, IN: Author House, 2011).

Guezzou, Mokrane (trans.), *Al-Wāḥidī's Asbāb al-Nuzūl: Great Commentaries on the Holy Qur'an* (Louisville, KY: Fons Vitae, 2008).

Haar, Gerrie ter, 'Religion: source of conflict or resource for peace?', in Gerrie ter Haar and James J. Busuttil, *Bridge or Barrier: Religion, Violence and Visions for Peace* (Leiden: Brill, 2005), pp. 3–34.

Hardy, Richard, *The Life of St. John of the Cross: Search for Nothing* (London: Darton, Longman and Todd, 1982).

Hedges, Chris, *American Fascists: The Christian Right and the War on America* (London: Jonathan Cape, 2007).

War is a Force that Gives Us Meaning (New York: Anchor Books, 2002).

Herlihy, John, *Holy Qur'an: An Intimate Portrait* (Miami, FL: Ansar Books, 2014).

Hewer, Chris, 'Briefing on A Common Word', St Ethelburga's Centre in London, 6 December 2007.

Heydarpoor, Mahnaz, *Love in Christianity and Islam: A Contribution to Religious Ethics* (London: New City, 2002).

Highland, James Achilles, *Alchemy: The Transformation of the Soul in the Conversion Narratives of Augustine and Ghazzali (Saint Augustine, Muhammad Ghazali)*, PhD dissertation (Southern Illinois University, 1999).

Hochschild, Adam, *To End All Wars: A Story of Loyalty and Rebellion, 1914–1918* (Boston and New York: Houghton Mifflin Harcourt, 2011).

Hofmann, Murad, 'Differences between the Muslim and the Christian concept of divine love', The Fourteenth General Conference of the Royal Aal al-Bayt Institute for Islamic Thought (Love in the Holy Qur'an), Amman, 2007, pp. 1–2. www.aalalbayt.org/en/respapers.html#rd14.

Hollenbach, David, 'Human dignity in Catholic thought', in Marcus Düwell, Jens Braarvig, Roger Brownsword and Dietmar Mieth (eds.), *The Cambridge Handbook of Human Dignity: Interdisciplinary Perspectives* (Cambridge: Cambridge University Press, 2014), pp. 250–9.

Homerin, Th. Emil, 'The Golden Rule in Islam', in Jacob Neusner and Bruce Chilton (eds.), *The Golden Rule: The Ethics of Responsibility in World Religions* (London: Continuum, 2008), pp. 99–115.

Hopkins, Jasper, 'The role of *pia interpretatio* in Nicholas of Cusa's hermeneutical approach to the Koran', in *A Miscellany on Nicholas of Cusa* (Minneapolis: Arthur J. Banning Press, 1994), pp. 39–55.

Huff, Peter A., 'The challenge of fundamentalism for interreligious dialogue', *Cross Currents*, 50 (2000), 94.

Hunter, Richard, *Plato's Symposium* (Oxford: Oxford University Press, 2004).

Ibn ʿAbbād of Ronda, *Letters on the Sūfī Path*, trans. John Renard (New York: Paulist Press, 1986).

Ibn ʿAtaʾillah, *The Book of Wisdom (Kitab al-Hikam)*, trans. Victor Danner, published with Kwaja Abdullah Ansari, *Intimate Conversations*, trans. Wheeler M. Thackston (New York: Paulist Press, 1978).

Ibn Hishām, *al-Sīra al-nabawiyya* (Jeddah: Muʾassasat ʿulūm al-Qurʾān, n.d.).

Ibn Isḥāq, *Sīrat Rasūl Allāh*, trans. Alfred Guillaume (London: Oxford University Press, 1967).

Ibn Kathīr, *al-Miṣbāh al-munīr fī tahdhīb Tafsīr Ibn Kathīr*, abridged and translated by a group of scholars under the supervision of Shaykh Safiur-Rahman al-Mubarakpuri (Riyadh: Darussalam, 2003).

Ibn Kathīr, *Tafsīr al-Qurʿān al-ʿaẓīm* (Beirut: Dār al-jīl, 1990).

Ibn Khaldun, *Taʾrīkh*, ed. Khalīl Shihādah (Beirut: Dār al-fikr, 1988).

  The Muqaddimah: An Introduction to History, trans. Franz Rosenthal, abridged and ed. N. J. Dawood (Princeton, NJ: Princeton University Press, 1967).

Ibn Taymiyya, Taqi al-Din, *Réponse raisonnable aux chrétiens*, ed. and trans. Laurent Basanese (Damascus and Beirut: Institut Français du Proche-Orient, 2012).

Illman, Ruth, *Art and Belief: Artists Engaged in Interreligious Dialogue* (Sheffield: Equinox Publishing, 2012).

  'Curiosity instead of fear: literature as creative inter-religious dialogue', *Journal of Inter-Religious Dialogue*, 1 (2009), 7–14.

  'Plurality and peace: inter-religious dialogue in a creative perspective', *International Journal of Public Theology*, 4 (2010), 175–93.

Internationales Katholisches Missionswerk Missio, Aachen (ed.), 'Ein gemeinsames Wort zwischen uns und euch: Der Dialog zwischen Muslimen und Christen', *KM Forum Weltkirche*, 2 (2008), 32–3.

Intifada et al., 'Opera & Koran Meet Gregorian', *Muslim Village Forums*, 2008. http://muslimvillage.com/forums/topic/46669-opera-koran-meet-gregorian.

Isahak, Amir Farid, 'One God? Same God?', in Christian Troll, Helmut Reifeld and Chris Hewer (eds.), *We Have Justice in Common: Christian and Muslim Voices from Asia and Africa* (Berlin: Konrad-Adenauer-Stiftung, 2010), pp. 199–209.

Jackson, Sherman A., *Islam and the Problem of Black Suffering* (New York: Oxford University Press, 2009).

　　On The Boundaries of Theological Tolerance in Islam (Oxford: Oxford University Press, 2002).

Jacobs, Steven Leonard, '"Can we talk?": the Jewish Jesus in a dialogue between Jews and Christians', *Shofar*, 3 (2010), 135–48.

Jan, Abid, *Afghanistan: The Genesis of the Final Crusade* (Lahore: Pragmatic Publishers, 2006).

Janssens, Jules, 'Al-Ghazzālī's *Tahāfut*: is it really a rejection of Ibn Sīnā's philosophy?', *Journal of Islamic Studies*, 12/1 (2001), 1–17.

Jean Damascène, *Écrits sur l'Islam: présentation, commentaires et traduction par Raymond Le Coz* (Paris: Éditions du Cerf, 1992).

Jifri, Habib Ali al-, *The Concept of Faith in Islam*, trans. Khalid Williams (Amman: Royal Aal Al-Bayt Institute for Islamic Thought, 2012).

'Joint Muslim–Evangelical Christian endorsement of *A Common Word* in Libya', 3–6 January 2008. www.acommonword.com/joint-muslim-evangelical-christian-endorsement-of-a-common-word-in-libya/.

Josephus, Flavius, *The Complete Works of Josephus*, trans. W. Whiston (Grand Rapids, MI: Kregel Publications, 1960).

Kāmil, Majdī, *al-Masīḥiyya al-Ṣihyūniyya, al-taṭarruf al-Islāmī, wa-l-sīnāriyū l-kārithī* (Damascus and Cairo: Dar al-kitāb al-ʿarabī, 2007).

Khan, Muhammad Muhsin and Muhammad Taqi ud-Din al-Hilali, *Interpretation of the Meanings of the Noble Qur'ān in the English Language* (Riyadh: Darussalam, 1996).

Knysh, Alexander D., *Al-Qushayri's Epistle on Sufism* (Reading: Garnet Publishing, 2007).

Kogan, Michael S., *Opening the Covenant: A Jewish Theology of Christianity* (Oxford: Oxford University Press, 2008).

Krokus, Christian S., 'Louis Massignon's influence on the teaching of Vatican II on Muslims and Islam', *Islam and Christian-Muslim Relations*, 23 (2012), 329–45.

Kujawa-Holbrook, Sheryl A., *God Beyond Borders: Interreligious Learning among Faith Communities* (Eugene, OR: Pickwick Publications, 2014).

Kukah, Matthew Hassan, '*A Common Word*: thoughts from Nigeria', in Christian Troll, Helmut Reifeld and Chris Hewer (eds.), *We Have Justice in Common: Christian and Muslim Voices from Asia and Africa* (Berlin: Konrad-Adenauer-Stiftung, 2010), pp. 108–23.

Kuna, Herta, *Srednjovjekovna Bosanska Književnost*, *Forum Bosnae*, 45 (2008), 7–383.

Küng, Hans, 'Serious errors of both fact and judgement: an interview with Hans Küng', *The Times*, 16 September 2006.

Lagouranis, Tony, *Fear Up Harsh: An Army Interrogator's Dark Journey through Iraq* (New York: NAL Caliber, 2007).

Lambert, Tony, 'Visual orienting, learning and conscious awareness', in Luis Jiménez (ed.), *Attention and Implicit Learning* (Amsterdam: John Benjamins, 2003).

Levi Della Vida, Giorgio, 'Khāridjites', in E. van Donzel et al. (eds.), *Encyclopedia of Islam II* (Leiden: Brill, 1997), vol. 4, pp. 1074–7.

Levine, Amy-Jill, *The Misunderstood Jew: The Church and the Scandal of the Jewish Jesus* (New York: HarperOne, 2007).

    Short Stories by Jesus: The Enigmatic Parables of a Controversial Rabbi (New York: HarperOne, 2014).

Lewis, Donald M., *The Origins of Christian Zionism* (Cambridge: Cambridge University Press, 2014).

Lings, Martin, *Muhammad: His Life Based on the Earliest Sources* (Cambridge: Islamic Texts Society, 1995).

Linn, Jan G., *What's Wrong with the Christian Right* (Boca Raton, FL: BrownWalker Press, 2004).

Lonergan, Bernard, *Method in Theology* (Toronto: University of Toronto Press, 1990).

Lossky, Vladimir, *The Mystical Theology of the Eastern Church* (Cambridge: James Clarke & Co., 1991).

Lumbard, Joseph, 'The uncommonality of "A Common Word"', in *A Common Word Between Us and You: 5-Year Anniversary Edition* (Amman: Royal Aal Al-Bayt Institute for Islamic Thought, 2012), pp. 11–50.

Lynerd, Benjamin, *Republican Theology: The Civil Religion of American Evangelicals* (New York: Oxford University Press, 2014).

Madigan, Daniel A. SJ, 'Book', in Jane D. McAuliffe (ed.), *Encyclopaedia of the Qur'ān* (Leiden: Brill, 2001), vol. I, pp. 242–51.

    'Christian-Muslim dialogue', in Catherine Cornille (ed.), *The Wiley-Blackwell Companion to Inter-Religious Dialogue* (Oxford: Wiley-Blackwell, 2013), pp. 244–60.

    'A Common Word Between Us and You: some initial reflections', *Thinking Faith*, 18 January 2008 [Reprinted in *A Common Word Between Us and You: 5-Year Anniversary Edition* (Amman: Royal Aal Al-Bayt Institute for Islamic Thought, 2012), pp. 165–75].

    'Particularity, universality, and finality: insights from the Gospel of John', in David Marshall (ed.), *Communicating the Word: Revelation, Translation, and Interpretation in Christianity and Islam* (Washington, DC: Georgetown University Press, 2011), pp. 14–25.

Magnis-Suseno, Franz SJ, 'A Common Word and what it could mean', in Christian Troll, Helmut Reifeld and Chris Hewer (eds.), *We Have Justice in Common: Christian and Muslim Voices from Asia and Africa* (Berlin: Konrad-Adenauer-Stiftung, 2010), pp. 25–51.

Mahajan, Rahul, '"We think the price is worth it": Media uncurious about Iraq policy's effects – there or here', *FAIR*, 1 November 2001. www.fair.org/extra/we-think-the-price-is-worth-it/.

Mahmutćehajić, Rusmir, *On Love: In the Muslim Tradition* (Ashland, OH: Fordham University Press, 2007).

Manuel II Paléologue, *Entretiens avec un musulman, 7ᵉ controverse*, ed. Théodore Khoury (Paris: Editions du Cerf, 1966).

Markiewicz, Sarah, *World Peace through Christian–Muslim Understanding: The Genesis and Fruits of the Open Letter 'A Common Word Between Us and You'* (Göttingen: V&R Unipress, 2016).

'Marrakesh Declaration', 25–7 January 2016. www.marrakeshdeclaration.org.

Martin, John and Stuart Anderson, 'Response to *A Common Word* from Building Bridges, Cambridge', 21 December 2007. www.acommonword.com/response-to-a-common-word-from-building-bridges-cambridge/.

Massignon, Louis, *The Passion of al-Hallaj: Mystic and Martyr of Islam*, trans. Herbert Mason (Princeton, NJ: Princeton University Press, 1982).

Mattson, Ingrid, 'Of fences and neighbors: an Islamic perspective on interfaith engagement for peace', October 2013. http://ingridmattson.org/article/of-fences-and-neighbors/.

The Story of the Qur'an: Its History and Place in Muslim Life, 2nd edition (Malden, MA: Wiley-Blackwell, 2013).

Mawdūdī, Sayyid Abul A'lā, *Towards Understanding the Qur'ān: English Version of Tafhīm al-Qur'ān*, trans. and ed. Zafar Ishaq Ansari (Leicester: The Islamic Foundation, 1988).

Mbillah, Johnson A., 'An African reflection on *A Common Word*', in Christian Troll, Helmut Reifeld and Chris Hewer (eds.), *We Have Justice in Common: Christian and Muslim Voices from Asia and Africa* (Berlin: Konrad-Adenauer-Stiftung, 2010), pp. 87–107.

McCarthy, Justin, *Death and Exile: The Ethnic Cleansing of Ottoman Muslims, 1821–1922* (Princeton, NJ: Darwin Press, 1995).

McDermott, Josh and Marc Hauser, 'The origins of music: innateness, uniqueness, and evolution', *Music Perception*, 23/1 (2005), 29–59.

McLaughlin, Elizabeth W., 'The power of living parables for transformative interfaith encounters', in Daniel S. Brown Jr. (ed.), *A Communication Perspective on Interfaith Dialogue: Living within the Abrahamic Traditions* (Lanham, MD & Plymouth, UK: Lexington Books, 2013), pp. 123–38.

Mercado, Leonardo N., *Elements of Filipino Theology* (Tacloban City, Philippines: Divine Word University Publications, 1975).

Milbank, John and Adrian Pabst, *The Politics of Virtue: Post-Liberalism and the Human Future* (London: Rowman and Littlefield, 2016).

Mitchell, Donald W. and James Wiseman (eds.), *The Gethsemani Encounter: A Dialogue on the Spiritual Life by Buddhist and Christian Monastics* (New York: Continuum, 1999).

Mor Eustathius Matta Roham, 'Response from Mor Eustathius Matta Roham, Archbishop of Jezira and the Euphrates, Syrian Orthodox Church of Antioch', 31 January 2008. www.acommonword.com/response-from-mor-eustathius-matta-roham-archbishop-of-jezira-and-the-euphrates-syrian-orthodox-church-of-antioch/.

Mujāhid ibn Jabr, *Tafsīr Mujāhid*, ed. Abū Muḥammad al-Asyūṭī (Beirut: Dār al-kutub al-'ilmiyya, 2005).

Muqātil ibn Sulaymān, *Tafsīr Muqātil ibn Sulaymān*, ed. ʿAbd Allāh Maḥmūd Shiḥāta (Beirut: Muʾassasat al-taʾrīkh al-ʿarabī, 2002).

Murata, Sachiko and William C. Chittick, *The Vision of Islam* (London: I. B. Tauris, 2006).

Murqus, Samīr, *al-Imbarāṭūriyya al-Amrīkiyya: thulāthiyyat al-tharwa, al-dīn, al-quwwa, min al-ḥarb al-ahliyya ilā mā baʿda 11 Sabtambar* (Cairo: Maktabat al-shurūq al-dawliyya, 2003).

Muslim, ibn al-Ḥajjāj al-Qushayrī, *al-Jāmiʿ al-ṣaḥīḥ*, in *Mawsūʿat al-ḥadīth al-sharīf*, CD-ROM, (Thesaurus Islamicus Foundation, 2002).

Ṣaḥīḥ, trans. ʿAbdul Ḥamīd Ṣiddīqī (Riyadh: International Islamic Publishing House, n.d.).

Nakaš, Lejla, 'The Holy Spirit Paraclete in Bosnian apocryphal texts: an Arebica transcript from the 17th century', *Forum Bosnae*, 56 (2012), 129–48.

Nakhooda, Sohail, 'The significance of the Amman Message and the Common Word', Amman, 30 December 2008. www.acommonword.com/The-Significance-of-the-Amman-Message-and-the-Common-Word.pdf.

Nasr, Seyyed Hossein, 'Islam and music: the legal and the spiritual dimensions', in Lawrence E. Sullivan (ed.), *Enchanting Powers: Music in the World's Religions* (Cambridge, MA: Harvard University Center for Study of World Religions, 1997), pp. 219–35.

Islamic Art and Spirituality (Ipswich: Golgonooza, 1986).

National Jewish Scholars Project, *Dabru Emet*, 15 July 2002. www.jcrelations.net/Dabru_Emet_-_A_Jewish_Statement_on_Christians_and_Christianity.2395.0.html.

Nayed, Aref Ali, 'The promise of "A Common Word"', October 2007. www.interfaith.cam.ac.uk/resources/acommonword/thepromiseofacommonword.

Nelson, Kristina, *The Art of Reciting the Qurʾan* (Cairo: American University in Cairo Press, 2001).

Nettl, Bruno, *The Study of Ethnomusicology: Thirty-One Issues and Concepts* (Urbana & Chicago, IL: University of Illinois Press, 2005).

Neusner, Jacob, Baruch Levine, Bruce Chilton and Vincent Cornell (eds.), *Do Jews, Christians and Muslims Worship the Same God* (Nashville, TN: Abingdon, 2012).

NRSV Bible: Catholic Edition (Winona, MN: St Mary's College Press, 2000).

Nussbaum, Martha, *The New Religious Intolerance* (Cambridge, MA: Belknap Press of Harvard University Press, 2012).

Nygren, Anders, *Agape and Eros*, trans. Philip S. Watson (London: SPCK, 1954).

O'Leary, De Lacy, *Arabic Thought and Its Place in History* (New York: Dover Publications, 2003).

Oliveti, Vincenzo, *Terror's Source: The Ideology of Wahhabi-Salafism and Its Consequences* (Birmingham: Amadeus, 2001).

'Open letter to Pope Benedict XVI'. http://theislamicmonthly.com/open-letter-to-pope-benedict-xvi/.

'Open letter to Pope Benedict XVI', *Islamochristiana*, 32 (2006), 273–97 (in Arabic and English).

Ormsby, Eric Linn, *Al-Ghazālī: Love, Longing, Intimacy and Contentment: Kitāb al-maḥabba wa'l-shawq wa'l-uns wa'l-riḍā: Book XXXVI of The Revival of the Religious Sciences, Iḥyā' 'ulūm al-dīn* (Cambridge: Islamic Texts Society, 2011).

Theodicy in Islamic Thought: The Dispute Over Al-Ghazali's Best of all Possible Worlds (Princeton, NJ: Princeton University Press, 1984).

'Orthodox Rabbinic Statement on Christianity', *To Do the Will of Our Father in Heaven: Toward a Partnership between Jews and Christians*, 3 December 2015. http://cjcuc.com/site/2015/12/03/orthodox-rabbinic-statement-on-christianity/.

Ostler, Nicholas, *Empires of the Word: A Language History of the World* (London: Harper Perennial, 2006).

Otterbeck, Jonas and Anders Ackfeldt, 'Music and Islam', *Contemporary Islam*, 6/3 (2012), 227–33.

Palmer, Parker, *To Know as We are Known* (New York: Harper One, 1993).

Panikkar, Raimundo, *The Intrareligious Dialogue* (New York: Paulist Press, 1978).

Participants at Cadenabbia, 'A message from Cadenabbia', in Christian Troll, Helmut Reifeld and Chris Hewer (eds.), *We Have Justice in Common: Christian and Muslim Voices from Asia and Africa* (Berlin: Konrad-Adenauer-Stiftung, 2010), pp. 15–8.

Pattison, George, *Art, Modernity and Faith: Restoring the Image* (London: SCM Press, 1998).

Pentin, Edward, 'A scriptural round table of Jews, Muslims and Christians', 5 April 2011. www.terrasanta.net/tsx/articolo.jsp?wi_number=2959&wi_codseq=%20%20%20%20%20%20&language=en.

Philips, Kevin, *American Theocracy: The Peril and Politics of Radical Religion, Oil, and Borrowed Money in the 21st Century* (London: Penguin, 2006).

Politella, Joseph, 'al-Ghazali and Meister Eckhart: two giants of the spirit', *The Muslim World*, 54/3 (1964), 180–94.

Pope Benedict XVI, 'Address of His Holiness Benedict XVI to participants in the seminar organized by the "Catholic–Muslim Forum"', 6 November 2008. www.vatican.va/holy_father/benedict_xvi/speeches/2008/november/documents/hf_ben-xvi_spe_20081106_cath-islamic-leaders_en.html.

'Faith, reason and the university: memories and reflections', 12 September 2006. https://w2.vatican.va/content/benedict-xvi/en/speeches/2006/september/documents/hf_ben-xvi_spe_20060912_university-regensburg.html.

Pope Francis, *Evangelii gaudium*. www.vatican.va/holy_father/francesco/apost_exhortations/documents/papa-francesco_esortazione-ap_20131124_evangelii-gaudium_en.html.

Pope Paul VI, *Ecclesiam suam*, 6 August 1964. www.vatican.va/encyclicals/documents. For the text, see http://w2.vatican.va/content/paul-vi/la/encyclicals/documents/hf_p-vi_enc_06081964_ecclesiam.html (Latin) and http://w2.vatican.va/content/paul-vi/en/encyclicals/documents/hf_p-vi_enc_06081964_ecclesiam.html (English).

Putman, Hans, *L'Église et l'islam sous Timothée I (780–823): étude sur l'église nestorienne au temps des premiers 'Abbasides: avec nouvelle édition et traduction du Dialogue entre Timothée et al-Mahdi* (Beirut: Dar el-Machreq, 1975).

Raja, Masood Ashraf, *The Religious Right and the Talibanization of America* (Basingstoke: Macmillan, 2016).

Rāzī, Fakhr al-Dīn al-, *al-Tafsīr al-kabīr* (Beirut: Dār iḥyā' al-turāth al-ʿarabī, 1999). *al-Tafsīr al-kabīr* (Cairo: al-Maṭbaʿa al-bahiyya al-miṣriyya, 1938).

Reifeld, Helmut, 'Preface', in Christian Troll, Helmut Reifeld and Chris Hewer (eds.), *We Have Justice in Common: Christian and Muslim Voices from Asia and Africa* (Berlin: Konrad-Adenauer-Stiftung, 2010), pp. 7–10.

Riḍā, Rashīd and Muḥammad ʿAbduh, *Tafsīr al-Qurʾān al-ḥakīm*, ed. Ibrāhīm Shams al-Dīn (Beirut: Dār al-kutub al-ʿilmiyya, 1999).

Ritter, Hellmut, *The Ocean of the Soul*, trans. John O'Kane (Leiden: Brill, 2013).

Robson, Michael, *St Francis of Assisi: The Legend and the Life* (London: Geoffrey Chapman, 1997).

Roth, John K., 'Wiesel's contribution to a Christian understanding of Judaism', in Steven T. Katz and Alan Rosen (eds.), *Elie Wiesel: Jewish, Literary, and Moral Perspectives* (Bloomington & Indianapolis, IN: Indiana University Press, 2013), pp. 264–76.

Runnymede Trust, 'Islamophobia: a challenge for us all', 1997. www.runnymedetrust.org/uploads/publications/pdfs/islamophobia.pdf.

Šabanović, Hazim, *Bosanski Pašaluk: Postanak i Upravna Podjela* (Sarajevo: Svjetlost, 1982).

Sacks, Jonathan, *The Home We Build Together: Recreating Society* (London: Continuum, 2007).
   Future Tense: Jews, Judaism, and Israel in the Twenty-First Century (New York: Schocken, 2009).
   The Dignity of Difference: How to Avoid the Clash of Civilizations (London: Continuum, 2002).

Safran, Janina M., 'Identity and differentiation in ninth-century Al-Andalus', *Speculum*, 76/3 (2001), 573–98.

Sageman, Marc, *Leaderless Jihad: Terror Networks in the Twenty-First Century* (Philadelphia, PA: University of Pennsylvania Press, 2008).

Saheeh International, *Translation of the Meaning of the Qur'an* (Jeddah: Abul-Qasim Publishing House, 1997).

Said, Yazeed, *Ghazālī's Politics in Context* (Abingdon: Routledge, 2013).

Samir, Khalil Samir SJ, 'The letter of 138 Muslim scholars to the Pope and Christian leaders', 17 October 2007. www.acommonword.com/the-letter-of-138-muslim-scholars-to-the-pope-and-christian-leaders/.

Saritoprak, Zeki, 'How commentators of the Qur'an define "Common Word"', in John Borelli (ed.), *A Common Word and the Future of Christian-Muslim Relations* (Washington, DC: Prince Alwaleed Bin Talal Center for Muslim-Christian Understanding, 2009), pp. 34–45.

Scahill, Jeremy, *Blackwater: The Rise of the World's Most Powerful Mercenary Army* (London: Serpent's Tail, 2007).

Schimmel, Annemarie, *Mystical Dimensions of Islam* (Chapel Hill, NC: University of North Carolina Press, 1975).

Schleifer, S. Abdallah (ed.), *The Muslim 500: The World's 500 Most Influential Muslims, 2013/2014* (Amman: Royal Islamic Strategic Studies Centre, 2013).
   (ed.), *The Muslim 500: The World's 500 Most Influential Muslims, 2014–2015* (Amman: Royal Islamic Strategic Studies Centre, 2014).

Schrag, James, 'The response of the Mennonite Church to A Common Word', 5 November 2007. www.acommonword.com/the-response-of-the-mennonite-church-to-a-common-word/.

Schreiter, Robert J., *Constructing Local Theologies* (Maryknoll, NY: Orbis Books, 1985).

Secretariat for Non-Christians, 'The attitude of the Church towards the followers of other religions: reflections and orientations on dialogue and mission', 1984. www.pcinterreligious.org/uploads/pdfs/Dialogue_and_Mission_ENG.pdf.

Sekretariat der Deutschen Bischofskonferenz (ed.), *Christen und Muslime in Deutschland*, Arbeitshilfen 172 (Bonn: Sekretariat der Deutschen Bischofskonferenz, 2003), pp. 9–10.

Seldon, Anthony, *Blair* (London: Free Press, 2004).

'Tony Blair was driven by God and George W. Bush', in the *Daily Mirror* (London), 6 July 2016.

Sells, Michael A., *The Bridge Betrayed: Religion and Genocide in Bosnia* (Berkeley, CA: University of California Press, 1998).

Shadid, Anthony, 'Remarks by Pope prompt Muslim outrage, protests', *Washington Post*, 16 September 2006. www.washingtonpost.com/wp-dyn/content/article/2006/09/15/AR2006091500800.html.

Shakir, M. H., *The Qur'an Translated* (Elmhurst, NY: Tahrike Tarsile Qur'an, 2004).

Shatz, David, Chaim Waxman and Nathan Diament (eds.), *Tikkun Olam: Social Responsibility in Jewish Thought and Law* (Oxford: Rowman & Littlefield, 1997).

Sheikh, Naveed S., *The Body Count: A Quantitative Review of Political Violence across World Civilizations* (Amman: Royal Aal al-Bayt Institute for Islamic Thought, 2009).

Sherwin, Byron L., '"Who do you say that I am?" (Mark 8:29): a new Jewish view of Jesus', in Beatrice Bruteau (ed.), *Jesus through Jewish Eyes: Rabbis and Scholars Engage an Ancient Brother in a New Conversation* (Maryknoll, NY: Orbis, 2003), pp. 31–44.

Sifton, Elisabeth, *The Serenity Prayer: Faith and Politics in Times of Peace and War* (New York: W. W. Norton, 2003).

Sirry, Mun'im, '"Compete with one another in good works": exegesis of Qur'an verse 5.48 and contemporary Muslim discourses on religious pluralism', *Islam and Christian–Muslim Relations*, 20/4 (2009), 423–38.

Smith, W. Alan, 'Everyone but Rizzo: using the arts to transform communities', *Forum on Public Policy*, 2 (2008), 1–21.

Song, C. S., *Tell Us Our Names: Story Theology from an Asian Perspective* (Maryknoll, NY: Orbis Books, 1982).

Staff members of the Pontifical Institute for Arabic and Islamic Studies (PISAI) of Rome, 'Appreciation of an open letter and call from Muslim religious leaders "A Common Word Between Us and You"', 25 October 2007. www.acommonword.com/appreciation-of-an-open-letter-and-call-from-muslim-religious-leaders-a-common-word-between-us-and-you/.

Swan, Laura, *The Forgotten Desert Mothers: Sayings, Lives, and Stories of Early Christian Women* (Mahwah, NJ: Paulist Press, 2001).

Ṭabarī, Muḥammad ibn Jarīr al-, *Jāmiʿ al-bayān fī taʾwīl al-Qurʾān* (Beirut: Dār al-kutub al-ʿilmiyya, 1997).

Tauran, Cardinal, 'Interview', *La Croix*, as released by Zenit.org, 19 October 2007. www.acommonword.com/cardinal-praises-muslims-for-eloquent-letter/.

The Amman Message (Amman: Royal Aal Al-Bayt Institute for Islamic Thought, 2008). http://ammanmessage.com.

The Book of Common Prayer and Administration of the Sacraments and other Rites and Ceremonies of the Church According to the Use of the Church of England together with the Psalter or Psalms of David (Oxford: Oxford University Press, 1928).

Thomas, David, 'Islam and the religious other', in David Cheetham, Douglas Pratt and David Thomas (eds.), *Understanding Interreligious Relations* (Oxford: Oxford University Press, 2013), pp. 148–71.

Tirmidhī, Abū ʿĪsā Muḥammad ibn ʿĪsā al-, *al-Jāmiʿ al-kabīr: Sunan al-Tirmidhī*, (Beirut: Dār al-gharb al-islāmī, 1998).

Tracy, David, *Dialogue with the Other: The Inter-Religious Dialogue* (Leuven: Peeters Press, 1990).

Treiger, Alexander, *Inspired Knowledge in Islamic Thought: Al-Ghazālī's Theory of Mystical Cognition and Its Avicennian Foundation* (London & New York: Routledge, 2012).

Troll, Christian SJ, 'Towards *common ground* between Christians and Muslims?', 22 October 2007. www.acommonword.com/response-from-prof-dr-christian-troll-s-j/.

United Methodist Council of Bishops, 'United Methodist Council of Bishops' response to "A Common Word Between Us and You"', 5 January 2009. www.acommonword.com/category/site/christian-responses/.

Valkenberg, Pim, 'God(s) of Abraham: sibling rivalry among three faiths', *The Christian Century*, 21 June 2016. http://christiancentury.org/article/2016-06/gods-abraham.

'Learned ignorance and faithful interpretation of the Qur'an in Nicholas of Cusa (1401–1464)', in James Heft, Reuven Firestone and Omid Safi (eds.), *Learned Ignorance: Intellectual Humility among Jews, Christians, and Muslims* (Oxford & New York: Oxford University Press, 2011), pp. 34–52.

'Moslims & Christenen: Een gemeenschappelijk woord?', *Tijdschrift voor Theologie*, 50/3 (2010), 273–85.

Vallely, Paul, 'The fifth crusade: George Bush and the Christianisation of the war in Iraq', *Borderlands: A Journal of Theology and Education*, 4 (Summer 2005), 7–11.

Vogelaar, Harold, 'Eine interreligiöse Antwort auf das Dokument "Ein gemeinsames Wort zwischen Uns und Euch"', *CIBEDO-Beiträge zum Gespräch zwischen Christen und Muslimen*, 3 (2011), 113–19.

Volf, Miroslav, *Allah: A Christian Response* (New York: HarperOne, 2011).

(ed.), *Do We Worship the Same God? Jews, Christians and Muslims in Dialogue* (Grand Rapids, MI: Eerdmans, 2012).

Volf, Miroslav, Ghazi bin Muhammad and Melissa Yarrington (eds.), *A Common Word: Muslims and Christians on Loving God and Neighbor* (Grand Rapids: Eerdmans, 2010).

Wāḥidī al-, *al-Wāsiṭ fi tafsīr al-Qur'ān al-majīd* (Beirut: Dār al-kutub al-ʿilmiyya, 1994).

Walls, Andrew F., *The Missionary Movement in Christian History: Studies in the Transmission of Faith* (Maryknoll, NY: Orbis Books, 2005).

The Cross-Cultural Process in Christian History (Maryknoll, NY: Orbis, 2002).

Walzer, Richard, *Greek into Arabic: Essays on Islamic Philosophy* (Oxford: Oxford University Press, 1962).

Watt, W. Montgomery, *Islamic Philosophy and Theology* (Edinburgh: Edinburgh University Press, 1985).

Weinberg, Steven, *Dreams of a Final Theory: The Scientist's Search for the Ultimate Laws of Nature* (New York: Vintage Books, 1994).

Williams, Rowan, *On Augustine* (London: Bloomsbury, 2016).

'A Common Word and Future Christian–Muslim Engagement', 12 October 2008. http://rowanwilliams.archbishopofcanterbury.org/articles.php/1040/a-common-word-and-future-christian-muslim-engagement.

'Christian Theology and Other Faiths', 11 June 2003. http://rowanwilliams.archbishopofcanterbury.org/articles.php/1825/christian-theology-and-other-faiths.

'Just war revisited – Archbishop's lecture to the Royal Institute for International Affairs', 14 October 2003. http://rowanwilliams.archbishopofcanterbury.org/articles.php/1827/just-war-revisited-archbishops-lecture-to-the-royal-institute-for-international-affairs.

'Preface', in David Marshall and Lucinda Mosher (eds.), *Death, Resurrection, and Human Destiny: Christian and Muslim Perspectives* (Washington, DC: Georgetown University Press, 2014), pp. xxi–xxiv.

'Weakness and moral inconsistency led us to war', *The Times*, 25 March 2003. http://rowanwilliams.archbishopofcanterbury.org/articles.php/655/weaknesses-and-moral-inconsistency-led-us-to-war.

The Wound of Knowledge (London: Darton, Longman and Todd, 1999).

Williams, Rowan and Ali Gomaa, 'Communiqué from A Common Word Conference', University of Cambridge, 15 October 2008. www.acommonword.com/communique-from-a-common-word-conference/.

Williams, Rowan and Larry Elliott (eds.), *Crisis and Recovery: Ethics, Economics and Justice* (New York: Palgrave Macmillan, 2010).

Winter, Tim, *Al-Ghazālī: On Disciplining the Soul: Kitāb Riyāḍat al-nafs & on Breaking the Two Desires: Kitāb Kasr al-shahwatayn, Books XXII and XXIII of The Revival of the Religious Sciences, Iḥyā' ʿulūm al-dīn* (Cambridge: Islamic Texts Society, 1995).

'America as a Jihad state: Middle Eastern perceptions of modern American theopolitics', *The Muslim World*, 101/3 (July 2011), 394–411.

'Jesus and Muhammad: new convergences', *The Muslim World*, 99/1 (2009), 21–38.

Wisnovsky, Robert, *Avicenna's Metaphysics in Context* (London: Duckworth, 2003).

World Evangelical Alliance, 'We too want to live in love, peace, freedom and justice', 2 April 2008. www.acommonword.com/category/site/christian-responses/.

Worthington, Andy, *The Guantanamo Files: The Stories of the 774 Detainees in America's Illegal Prison* (London: Pluto, 2007).

Wüstenberg, Ralf K., *Islam ist Hingabe: Eine Entdeckungsreise in das Innere einer Religion* (Gütersloh: Gütersloher Verlagshaus, 2016).

'The Yale response', *New York Times*, 18 November 2007.

Yale Center for Faith & Culture, '"A Common Word" Christian response'. http://faith.yale.edu/common-word/common-word-christian-response.

'A "Common Word" at Yale: frequently asked questions'. http://faith.yale.edu/common-word/common-word-yale-frequently-asked-questions.

Yamani, Mai, *The Cradle of Islam: The Hijaz and the Quest for an Arabian Identity* (London: I. B. Tauris, 2004).

Yapp, Malcolm, 'Islam and Islamism', *Middle Eastern Studies*, 40 (2004), pp. 161–82.

Yaʿqūbī, Ibn Wāḍiḥ al-, *Taʾrīkh*, ed. ʿAbd al-Amīr Muhannā (Beirut: al-Aʿlamī, 2010).

Zain Al-Abdin, Al-Tayib, 'A response to *A Common Word* from an African perspective', in Christian Troll, Helmut Reifeld and Chris Hewer (eds.), *We Have Justice in Common: Christian and Muslim Voices from Asia and Africa* (Berlin: Konrad-Adenauer-Stiftung, 2010), pp. 124–35.

Zamakhsharī, Maḥmūd ibn ʿUmar al-, *al-Kashshāf ʿan ḥaqāʾiq ghawāmiḍ al-tanzīl wa-ʿuyūn al-aqāwīl fī wujūh al-taʾwīl*, ed. ʿĀdil Aḥmad ʿAbd al-Wujūd and ʿAlī Muḥammad Muʿawwad (Riyadh: Maktabat al-ʿubaykān, 1998).

al-Kashshāf ʿan ḥaqāʾiq al-tanzīl wa-ʿuyūn al-aqāwīl (Cairo: Maṭbaʿat Muṣṭafā al-Bābī al-Ḥalabī, 1972).

Zurayk, Constantine K. (trans.), *The Refinement of Character: A Translation from the Arabic of Aḥmad ibn Muḥammad Miskawayh's Tahdhīb al-Akhlāq* (Beirut: American University of Beirut Press, 1968).

Zwemer, Samuel M., *The Moslem Doctrine of God: An Essay on the Character and Attributes of Allah according to the Koran and Orthodox Tradition* (Boston, New York & Chicago: American Tract Society, 1905).

Index